New Orleans For Dummies, 2nd Edition

S0-BSQ-216

French Quarter and Central Business District: Top Attractions

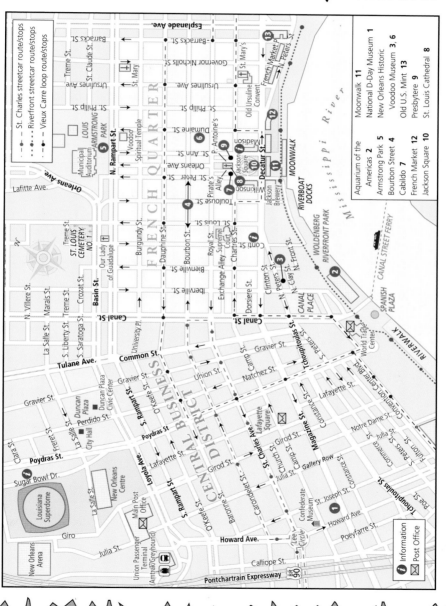

Map legend:
- St. Charles streetcar route/stops
- Riverfront streetcar route/stops
- Vieux Carre loop route/stops

Attractions:
- Aquarium of the Americas **2**
- Armstrong Park **5**
- Bourbon Street **4**
- Cabildo **7**
- French Market **12**
- Jackson Square **10**
- Moonwalk **11**
- National D-Day Museum **1**
- New Orleans Historic Voodoo Museum **3, 6**
- Old U.S. Mint **13**
- Presbytere **9**
- St. Louis Cathedral **8**

- Information
- Post Office

For Dummies: Bestselling Book Series for Beginners

Glossary of New Orleans Terms

Although New Orleanians do speak English, you may need a translator when trying to understand a few terms and phrases. These terms should help you talk your way around New Orleans.

- **Andouille** (*ahn-DOO-we*): A spicy, heavily smoked sausage made from pork.
- **Barbecued shrimp:** Shrimp served in a spicy butter sauce.
- **Beignet** (*ben-YAY*): Pieces of dough, fried fresh and covered in powdered sugar.
- **Café au lait:** Literally, coffee with milk. Usually used to refer to a distinctly flavorful coffee made with chicory. Served with beignets at Café du Monde in the French Quarter.
- **Carnival:** A celebration beginning January 6 ("the twelfth night" after Christmas) and ending Mardi Gras day.
- **Crawfish:** A tiny, lobsterlike creature plentiful in the waters around New Orleans and eaten in every conceivable way.
- **Dirty rice:** Rice cooked with chicken livers and gizzards, onions, chopped celery, green bell pepper, cayenne, black-and-white peppers, and chicken stock.
- **Doubloon:** Metal coins thrown by Mardi Gras krewes during a parade.
- **Dressed:** "Served with the works" — as when ordering a sandwich.
- **Étouffée** (*ay-too-FAY*): A spicy shrimp and crawfish stew served over rice. It means "smothered" in French.
- **Fat Tuesday:** Otherwise known as Mardi Gras, the last day before Ash Wednesday, which is the first day of Lent.
- **Filé** (*fee-LAY*): A thickener made of ground sassafras leaves. Filé is frequently used to thicken gumbo.
- **Grillades** (*gree-YADS*): Thin slices of beef or veal smothered in a tomato-and-beef-flavored gravy. Often served with grits.
- **Gumbo:** A thick, spicy soup, always served with rice. Seafood and chicken-and-sausage gumbo are common varieties.
- **Jambalaya** (*jum-ba-LIE-ya*): The traditional Cajun rice dish that typically includes sausage, chicken, shrimp, ham, and onions.
- **King cake:** An oval, sugared pastry decorated with purple, green, and gold sugar (Mardi Gras colors). The cake contains a small doll representing the baby Jesus. By longstanding custom, whoever gets the baby in his or her piece of cake is obligated to buy the next one.
- **Krewe:** The traditional word for a Carnival organization, a club or group that parades during Carnival season.
- **Lagniappe** (*LAN-yap*): Any small gift or token — even a scrap of food or a free drink. Also, a bonus (loosely translated, lagniappe is "a little extra;" something pleasantly unexpected).
- **Mardi Gras:** French for "Fat Tuesday." Technically, if you say "Mardi Gras Day," you're really saying "Fat Tuesday Day."
- **Muffuletta** (*muff-ah-LET-ah* or *muff-ah-LOT-ah*): Round Italian bread filled with an assortment of Italian cold cuts, cheese, and olive salad. (See Chapter 15.)
- **Oysters Rockefeller:** Baked oysters on the half shell with a sauce of greens and anise liqueur. Antoine's is the home of this succulent dish.
- **Po' boys:** Sandwiches (similar to subs), served on French bread with a variety of fillings. (See Chapter 15.)
- **Pralines** (*PRAW-leens*): A very sweet confection made of brown sugar and pecans; they come in "original" and creamy styles.
- **Remoulade** (*reh-myoo-LAHD*): A thick spicy sauce made in a variety of ways (expect mustard and/or horseradish) and used over seafood or salad.
- **Roux** (*roo*): Simply put, flour cooked in some sort of fat (in Creole and Cajun cooking, usually some kind of vegetable oil). A base for gumbos and sauces.
- **Second line:** A group of people that follows a parade, dancing to the music. Also a musical term that specifies a particular shuffling tempo popularized in much of New Orleans's music.
- **Shrimp Creole:** Shrimp in a tomato sauce that's seasoned with what's known around town as *the trinity:* onions, garlic, and green bell pepper.
- **Tasso:** Smoked, spicy Cajun ham.

Copyright © 2003 Wiley Publishing, Inc.
All rights reserved.
Item 5454-9.
For more information about Wiley Publishing, call 1-800-762-2974.

For Dummies: Bestselling Book Series for Beginners

FOR DUMMIES®

The fun and easy way™ to travel!

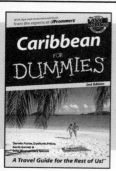
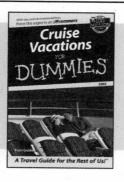

New Orleans

FOR

DUMMIES®

2ND EDITION

by Kevin Forest Moreau

Wiley Publishing, Inc.

New Orleans For Dummies®, 2nd Edition

Published by
Wiley Publishing, Inc.
909 Third Avenue
New York, NY 10022
www.wiley.com

About the Author

Kevin Forest Moreau is a longtime freelance writer and editor. He has recently moved from New Orleans, his hometown of 34 years, to Atlanta, where the gumbo isn't as good.

Dedication

This book is dedicated to my godson, young Simon Greydon Barrows; may you grow up to make your parents proud. Also, to the memory of William Walley Sr., Stephanie Scholl, and Norm Mejia — I wish I'd had the chance to say goodbye to each of you.

Author's Acknowledgments

The author would first and foremost like to thank Mark Walton, for his attention to the minutiae of phone numbers, addresses, and Web sites; Lisa Torrance, for answering any and all questions with patience and good humor; and Michael Kelly, for making this book — and therefore me — look much better than I could have hoped. Extra-special thanks should also go to Pableaux Johnson, for his invaluable restaurant advice, and David Lee Simmons, for his very helpful feedback. Thanks also to Maura York and Jason McCann, who were somehow left out of the previous edition. Special thanks to Jeremy Reed, for being so accommodating, and to Sue Ostermann, Nathan Lenz, Florrie Burch, Elisabeth Bergman, and the rest of the Citysearch Atlanta staff for their patience and understanding as deadlines loomed large. And grateful thanks to the following, in no particular order, for factual and emotional support during both the revision of this book and the move to my new home: Joni Jackson, for her patience and support; Whitney McCray; Sherrie, Laura, Donna, and all Group members past and present; Ann Patteson; Marsharee Chastain; Jennifer Lee; Michael Longshore; and my Wednesday-night trivia teammates at the Local. Thanks most especially to Jason Hippler, Keith Dupree, Fred Barrows, and Tedd Walley for maintaining my links to my cherished Louisiana boyhood, enriched immeasurably by my friendships with each of you.

Publisher's Acknowledgments

We're proud of this book; please send us your comments through our Dummies online registration form located at www.dummies.com/register/.

Some of the people who helped bring this book to market include the following:

Editorial

Editors: Michael Kelly, Tim Gallan

Copy Editor: Robert Annis

Cartographer: Roberta Stockwell

Editorial Manager: Christine Meloy Beck

Editorial Assistant: Melissa Bennett

Senior Photo Editor: Richard Fox

Assistant Photo Editor: Michael Ross

Front Cover Photo: © Bob Krist/ Getty Images

Back Cover Photo: © Mark Segal/ Getty Images

Cartoons: Rich Tennant, www.the5thwave.com

Production

Project Coordinator: Ryan Steffen

Layout and Graphics: Amanda Carter, Julie Trippetti

Proofreaders: Laura Albert, Susan Moritz, Angel Perez, Carl Pierce, TECHBOOKS Production Services

Indexer: TECHBOOKS Production Services

Publishing and Editorial for Consumer Dummies

Diane Graves Steele, Vice President and Publisher, Consumer Dummies

Joyce Pepple, Acquisitions Director, Consumer Dummies

Kristin A. Cocks, Product Development Director, Consumer Dummies

Michael Spring, Vice President and Publisher, Travel

Brice Gosnell, Publishing Director, Travel

Suzanne Jannetta, Editorial Director, Travel

Publishing for Technology Dummies

Andy Cummings, Vice President and Publisher, Dummies Technology/General User

Composition Services

Gerry Fahey, Vice President of Production Services

Debbie Stailey, Director of Composition Services

Contents at a Glance

Maps at a Glance

Table of Contents

Introduction

. . . .

You may think you know all about New Orleans. Which is fine. Many locals feel the same way.

To certain moneyed types, New Orleans is an elegant lady in formal dress, a woman of tradition. She dines at Antoine's and Arnaud's, she attends the opera and the ballet, and she enjoys the classic jazz of Pete Fountain. And each year, she attends the lavish ball of one of the old-line Mardi Gras *krewes* — those organizations full of powerful businessmen who look upon the title King of Carnival as their birthright.

To others, she's a loose party girl, a wild child with a pair of Mardi Gras beads around her neck and a flower in her hair, dancing barefoot to the sweaty rhythms of a second-line parade in the streets of the Faubourg Tremé. She's a pixie, a character straight out of a Tennessee Williams play, with no other aim in life but to "let the good times roll."

To others still, she's a voodoo priestess, an earthy Creole girl who loves to cook, a spectral muse, or a writer with the unfinished Great Southern Novel tucked under her arm.

And the thing is, they're all right. New Orleans is all of these things, and more. She's a study in contradictions, a devout Catholic with a reverence for tradition *and* a whirling dervish who loves to feed her guests excessive meals, regale them with tales of history and adventure, and seduce them with a mélange of street sounds and exotic rhythms.

Still think you know everything about her?

Well, relax. I've known New Orleans my whole life. I've watched as she's beguiled thousands of visitors with her charms, enticing some of them to leave their past lives behind and take up residence in a new and exciting city. And I know that, despite her somewhat unflattering nickname (The Big Easy), her mishmash of African and European cultures, her unique way of speaking, her rich and colorful past, and her hurly-burly geography can be anything but easy to pigeonhole. I also know, as you will too, that accepting that essential fact — that you can never *really* know New Orleans — is the first step toward understanding her.

About This Book

New Orleans For Dummies is a reference book, not an exhaustive, voluminous guide that requires hours of reading. While the information is laid out in the logical order of a step-by-step manual, you don't need to read the book in order from front to back; nor are you expected to remember everything you read — you can just look up and revisit the information as you need it. Each section and chapter is as self-contained as possible so that you can concentrate on what's important to you (and skip the rest).

New Orleans For Dummies is (hopefully) helpful, authoritative, and interesting without getting mired in unnecessary details. You can find everything from when to visit and where to stay, to how to find the best spots to eat, shop, and *laissez le bon temps roulet* (let the good times roll). To find the information you want, just scan the table of contents or the index at the back of the book.

Remember that travel information can change at any time — especially prices. I therefore suggest that you write or call ahead for confirmation when making your travel plans. The authors, editors, and publisher cannot be held responsible for the experiences of readers while traveling. Your safety is important to us, however, so we encourage you to stay alert and be aware of your surroundings. Keep a close eye on cameras, purses, and wallets, all favorite targets of thieves and pickpockets.

Conventions Used in This Book

To fulfill its function as an informative and easy-to-use reference guide, *New Orleans For Dummies* employs a few conventions designed to convey critical information in a simple, straightforward manner.

In this book, I include lists of hotels, restaurants, and attractions. As I describe each, I often include abbreviations for the following commonly accepted credit cards:

AE	American Express
CB	Carte Blanche
DC	Diners Club
DISC	Discover
MC	MasterCard
V	Visa

I divide hotels into two categories: my personal favorites and those that don't quite make my preferred list but still get my hearty seal of approval. Don't be shy about considering these "runners-up" hotels if you're unable to get a room at one of my favorites — remember, your preferences may differ from mine. The amenities and services that the runners-up offer make these accommodations good choices to consider as you determine where to rest your head at night.

I also include some general pricing information to help you as you decide where to unpack your bags or dine on the local cuisine. I use a system of dollar signs to show a range of costs for one night in a hotel or a meal at a restaurant (including entree, drinks, and tip). Check out the following table to decipher the dollar signs:

Cost	Hotel	Restaurant
$	under $75	under $15
$$	$75–$125	$15–$25
$$$	$125–$175	$25–$35
$$$$	$175–$250	$35–$45
$$$$$	over $250	over $45

Foolish Assumptions

As I wrote this book, I made some of the following assumptions about you and what your needs may be as a traveler:

- You may be an inexperienced traveler looking for guidance on whether to take a trip to New Orleans and how to plan for it.

- You may be an experienced traveler who hasn't had much time to explore New Orleans and wants expert advice when you finally do get a chance to enjoy what the city has to offer.

- You're not looking for a book that provides all the information available about New Orleans or that lists every hotel, restaurant, or attraction available to you. Instead, you're looking for a book that focuses on the best places to give you that uniquely New Orleans experience.

If you fit any of these criteria, then *New Orleans For Dummies* gives you the information you're looking for!

How This Book Is Organized

I've designed and organized *New Orleans For Dummies* to serve as two books in one. It's a trip-planning guide to help you figure out (and accomplish) what you need to do to book an interesting vacation that doesn't break the bank. And it's a savvy reference book, boiling off the excessive minutiae of other, more conventional travel guides, leaving you with the essential information you need to enjoy New Orleans, without getting fleeced or disappointed — and without looking like an obvious tourist.

Part I: Getting Started

The chapters in this part introduce you to New Orleans and cover what you need to consider when planning your trip. You get an insider's view of the city's many charms and form a pretty good idea of what you can expect to see and do when you arrive. This part covers when you should visit, factoring in the weather as well as a list of my favorite events. I give you some tips on how to make a realistic budget, while pointing out certain financial pitfalls and ways to cut costs; I also discuss the relative merits of traveling with traveler's checks, credit cards, ATM cards, and, of course, cash. I finish up this part by discussing various resources, attractions, and tips for travelers with special considerations, including families, seniors, gays and lesbians, and disabled visitors.

Part II: Ironing Out the Details

In this part, you get your hands dirty with the details of planning your trip. These chapters cover the pros and cons of booking your trip through a travel agent or a package tour, how to get the best airfare, and the advantages of driving and train travel. I also help you get an idea of the lodging choices available, giving you a brief description of the various areas of the city so that you can choose the best neighborhood for your interests and needs. I show you some ways to get a good rate on your hotel room, explain what you can expect to get for your money, and discuss a number of online hotel-booking sites. Then I give you a list of the city's best hotels, with to-the-point reviews and price information. Finally, I tie up some loose ends regarding car rental, restaurant reservations, event tickets, traveler's checks, and even packing.

Part III: Settling into New Orleans

This part helps you get the lay of the land after you arrive. I take you from the airport to your hotel, describing each of the city's neighborhoods and providing a list of places where you can find tourist information if you need it. I run down the pros and cons of the different ways to get around the city, whether by auto, public transportation, taxi, or your own two feet. And I discuss the places in New Orleans where you can get access to your cash, as well as what to do if you lose your wallet.

Part IV: Dining in New Orleans

Now you get to the, er, meat and potatoes of your trip. Eating is one of New Orleans's great pastimes, and this part gets you up to speed on the local dining scene, including which places are hot and which are largely targeted to tourists. I also give you the skinny on dress codes, before diving into reviews of the best restaurants in the city. And I follow that up with a chapter on places to go for signature local food (including oysters, beignets, po' boys, and muffulettas), snacks, and other lighter (and not so light) bites.

Part V: Exploring New Orleans

This part tells you what you need to know to enjoy the many sights of New Orleans, starting with a visitor's guide to Mardi Gras and a top-of-the-tops list of the city's main attractions. I give you the facts on guided tours to help you decide whether they're right for you (or if you'd rather take your chances exploring on your own). I clue you in on where to shop with a look at big-name stores *and* out-of-the-way specialty shops and galleries. Finally, I provide you with some optional itineraries to help you see the city's best sights, even if you have only one, two, or three days in town. And I follow that up with a list of day trips, in case you want to visit Cajun Country, explore some historic plantations, or lose yourself in one of the area's great natural preserves.

Part VI: Living It Up After the Sun Goes Down: New Orleans Nightlife

If you retire to your hotel room after the sun goes down, you miss out on at least half of what New Orleans is all about. History and food are nice and all, but what's a vacation without some music, dancing, and drinking? This part starts with a rundown of the city's best music spots and then goes on to the best bars and clubs for people-watching, dancing the night away, or finding great beer selections — you know, the important stuff. I also give you the scoop on the city's theater and performing arts scenes, in case you want to temper your drinking and dancing with a play or a night at the opera.

Part VII: The Part of Tens

These chapters present bits of handy information in bite-sized chunks. I take this opportunity to outline some quintessentially decadent New Orleans experiences and run down a list of ten places that look like your usual tourist traps, but actually have something to offer.

You'll also find two other elements near the back of this book. I include an *Appendix* — your Quick Concierge — with lots of handy information you may need when traveling in New Orleans, such as phone numbers and addresses of emergency personnel or area hospitals and pharmacies, contact information for baby-sitters, lists of local newspapers, and more. Check out this appendix when searching for answers to lots of little questions that may come up as you travel.

I also include a bunch of *worksheets* to make your travel planning easier — among other things, you can determine your travel budget, create a wish list of things to do while in town, and draw up specific itineraries. You can find these worksheets easily because they're printed on yellow paper.

Icons Used in This Book

In the margins of this book, you'll find a number of helpful little icons designed to draw your attention to particularly useful bits of information.

Find out useful advice on things to do and ways to schedule your time when you see the Tip icon.

Watch for the Heads Up icon to identify annoying or potentially dangerous situations such as tourist traps, unsafe neighborhoods, budgetary rip-offs, and other things to beware.

Look to the Kid Friendly icon for attractions, hotels, restaurants, and activities that are particularly hospitable to children or people traveling with kids.

Keep an eye out for the Bargain Alert icon as you seek out money-saving tips and/or great deals.

Locations marked by this icon provide perfect opportunities to soak up the city's laid-back, laissez-faire atmosphere.

Where to Go from Here

Because this book is broken up into easily digestible parts and chapters, turn right to the section that interests you. If you already know when you're going to New Orleans and where you're staying, for example, you can skip to Part III (though you may want to make a pit stop at Chapters 3 and 9). If you've been to New Orleans before and know your way around, you can jump straight to Parts V and VI to look for attractions, sights, and clubs that may be new to you. It's up to you; use the table of contents or the index, zero in on what you're looking for, and just take it from there.

Good hunting. Keep your hands and feet inside the vehicle at all times, and don't forget to *laissez le bon temps roulet!*

Part I
Getting Started

The 5th Wave   By Rich Tennant

"I think we should arrange to be there for Cayenne pepper-Garlic-Andouille sausage week, and then shoot over to the Breathmint-Antacid Festival."

In this part . . .

So you want to visit New Orleans, eh? Well, dust off your passport. You won't actually need it, of course, but because New Orleans is easily the most European city in the United States, it'll help you get in the proper frame of mind for your visit.

This part of the book helps you take the first baby steps toward planning your vacation. First, this part gives you the quick insider's lowdown on the Crescent City. Then it helps you decide what time of year you should visit. It also helps you create a workable budget, points out some money-saving tips about cutting costs and avoiding hidden expenses, and lists some invaluable resources for travelers with specific needs — whether you're bringing a large family, need a wheelchair-accessible hotel, are searching for a gay-friendly spot, or just want to take advantage of senior-citizen discounts. After you line up all these ducks in a row, you can dig in and get your hands dirty with the nitty-gritty of trip planning.

Chapter 1

Discovering the Best of New Orleans

- -

- -

Somewhere in the verdant bayous of Southern Louisiana, nestled among the swamps, lies a magical, mythical city. Peopled by voracious Cajun men and exotic Creole priestesses, its streets are home to a constant, 24-hour party that begins in the streets of its storied French Quarter and ends in the sweaty confines of smoky jazz clubs. The festive hoards spend their days dancing in spontaneous public parades and dining on sinfully elegant seven-course meals. And somewhere close to all of this sits the city of New Orleans.

Allow me to explain. If your vision of New Orleans comes from movies, books, or television, chances are your perception is like the city I just described — a fantasy world of non-stop parades and hedonism. Or perhaps you have heard, seen, and read so much about this place that you don't know what to believe. Well, you can put that all behind you. I'll set the record straight.

Feasting on the Great Gumbo Pot

The cardinal sin of writing about New Orleans is to use the dreaded gumbo analogy. Gumbo is a staple food of New Orleans, a rich stew with ingredients usually including shrimp, chicken, sausage (particularly alligator sausage), crabmeat, and oysters — basically, whatever is at hand. The city of New Orleans is a similar creature — a mix of French and Spanish cultures, with touches of African, Caribbean, and even a bit o' the Irish thrown in for good measure. So, making the gumbo analogy is easy and appropriate, much to the consternation of readers and editors rolling their eyes at the common device.

However you describe it, this mish-mash of cultures serves as New Orleans's single most defining characteristic. From the blend of French and Spanish architecture of the French Quarter, to the mix of African rhythms that propels the city's music, to the savory aromas of Cajun and Creole cuisine, New Orleans is a child of its divergent influences. In this sense, it's truly America's most European city, with a feel unlike any other. Having passed through French, Spanish, and American hands during the tumultuous early decades of this country's history, New Orleans absorbed many more diverse influences than its sister cities. You can trace everything unique about the city back to its mongrel nature, and its status as a premier entry point into the New World.

Living the History Lesson

New Orleans has enjoyed a front-row seat to the drama of American history, from the Louisiana Purchase to the Battle of New Orleans. And not all that history is limited to the 18th and 19th centuries. During World War II, New Orleans built the massive troop ships that allowed the Allied Forces to storm the beaches of Normandy on D-Day and turn the tide of that epic conflict.

These days, the city trades off of its rich historic background in ways you may expect. The **Cabildo,** where the Louisiana Purchase was turned over to the United States in 1803, is now an entertaining museum focusing on life in early Louisiana. On the site of the Battle of New Orleans stands **Chalmette Battlefield,** which celebrates that historic battle and houses a cemetery filled with Civil War soldiers. And the **National D-Day Museum,** which commemorates that watershed WWII event with a number of captivating exhibits, also highlights New Orleans's integral part in that struggle.

If New Orleans only played host to a number of impressive museums and historical sites, it would still be a must-see stop for history buffs because of the way in which the city interweaves history and everyday life. In the French Quarter and the Garden District, for example, preservationists have retained much of the city's landmark buildings, which now serve as real homes for real people. And not just the structures are preserved; the buildings retain a sense of poetry and myth as well. Enjoy a drink at **Lafitte's Blacksmith Shop,** the **Old Absinthe House,** or even **Napoleon House,** and you can't help but give in to the lingering shadows of historical figures that once sat there.

Savoring the Music

From the drumming rituals of congregated slaves in **Congo Square,** which loosed African and European rhythms into the city streets, to the piano players hired to entertain customers in the parlors of **Storyville's** once-legalized bordellos, no city boasts a stronger link to its musical past than New Orleans. The syncopated shuffles that thundered out of those slave gatherings propelled stirring spirituals, work songs, and the blues, as well as the animated ruckus of marching brass bands. And this diversity of music sowed the seeds of jazz, rhythm and blues, and rock and roll.

However, you can still find these musical styles in their primal splendor, in the streets where they first came together. Modern day **brass bands** exist in New Orleans as nowhere else on earth, lending their raucous voices to colorful "second-line" street parades (so-called to refer to those revelers that followed marching bands in street parades), mournful and exuberant jazz funerals, and the elaborate rituals of **Mardi Gras Indians.** And modern-day brass bands such as **ReBirth** or the **Dirty Dozen** celebrate their musical roots, while spicing them up with spirited funk and even elements of hip-hop, on the stages of such down-and-dirty hangouts as **Donna's** and the **Funky Butt.**

No musical discussion of New Orleans would be complete without mentioning jazz, brass's contradictory cousin, which combines intellectual experimentation with the emotional abandon of screeching trumpet and clarinet solos. Jazz is alive and well in the city most commonly referred to as its birthplace, in the hands of such venerated musicians as the **Marsalis** clan. Trumpeter Wynton Marsalis and saxophonist Branford Marsalis may be more popular, but even they bow to the decades of wisdom and experience personified in their father, Ellis Marsalis, the closest thing New Orleans has to a jazz figurehead. Other young lions such as Terence Blanchard and Nicholas Payton continue to push the music in exciting new directions all over the world, as well as at local clubs such as **Snug Harbor** and **Sweet Lorraine's.**

Of course, New Orleans claims parental bragging rights on other music fronts, most notably rhythm and blues and its progeny, rock and roll. Locals, such as **Fats Domino, Professor Longhair, Dr. John,** the **Neville Brothers,** and the **Meters,** have thrown their funky contributions into the R&B pot, which continues to bubble its way to a slow boil in such hallowed halls as **Tipitina's** and the **Maple Leaf.** And though you can find their origins farther to the west, the joyous strains of **Cajun** and **zydeco** music both exert strong influence in New Orleans, as well, notably at the Maple Leaf or the world's most musical bowling alley and celebrity haunt, **Mid-City Lanes Rock 'n' Bowl.**

Sampling the Movable Feast

If New Orleanians take one thing even more seriously than their music, it would have to be their food. In fact, when it comes to food, the people of New Orleans are a bit spoiled, and with good reason. Food and music are the hedonistic pleasures of New Orleans.

The twin touchstones of local cooking are **Cajun** and **Creole** cuisine. The roots of Cajun food lie in the households of Louisiana's bayou country, where residents threw all available ingredients into the pot — an economic move that brought us such standards as gumbo, jambalaya, and red beans and rice. Creole cooking, meanwhile, traces its family tree back to the kitchens of New Orleans's Creole population (most often defined by a mix of French, Spanish, and/or African lineage). The Creoles mixed and matched elements of various cuisines, coming up with a homegrown style that emphasizes heavy sauces, complex tastes, and a reliance on seafood, soul food, and spices.

You find elements of both styles of cooking on practically every menu in town, from the classic Monday-night staple red beans and rice to more sophisticated offerings such as Trout Almandine. You'll also find a lot more, because local chefs take the tradition of mixing and matching to heart (and to new extremes). And as with music, New Orleans cuisine is open to interpretation and re-interpretation, especially in the hands of celebrity chef **Emeril Lagasse,** whose ubiquitous mug (thanks to his Food Network shows) and exuberant catch phrases ("Bam!" and "Kick it up a notch!") have become the new face and voice of New Orleans dining. At his restaurants **Emeril's, Nola,** and **Delmonico,** you can feel Emeril's influence in the ultra-modern trappings of what he calls "New New Orleans Cuisine," which takes Cajun and Creole cooking to new stylistic extremes without skimping on substance or taste.

If Emeril is king of New Orleans cuisine, the **Brennans** are its royal family of food. This dining dynasty's stamp is on many of the city's best restaurants, including the namesake **Brennan's** and **Bacco.** Other members of the court include Frank Brigtsen of **Brigtsen's,** Susan Spicer of **Bayona,** and even television celebrity Paul Prudhomme and his **K-Paul's Louisiana Kitchen.** And no tour of the local culinary topography is complete without a mention of such eating embassies as **Commander's Palace, Arnaud's, Antoine's,** or **Bella Luna,** to name just a very few.

Of course, fine dining isn't the only game in town. If the haughty environs of Antoine's represent one end of New Orleans's dining spectrum, its colorful neighborhood joints present the perfect counterpoint. No visit to New Orleans can be complete without a greasy, roast beef po' boy sandwich of the kind found at **Elizabeth's** or the **Central Grocery,** a plateful of shucked oysters from **Acme Oyster House,** practically any seafood dish from **Uglesich's** (the very definition of a seafood dive), or a hamburger from **Port of Call** or **Clover Grill.** (Not to mention the quintessential New Orleans experience, a breakfast of beignets — a tasty fried dough concoction — at **Café du Monde.**)

Doing the Mardi Gras Mambo

As the revered Professor Longhair (a famous New Orleans pianist often referred to as one of the fathers of rhythm and blues) once sang, "If you go to New Orleans, you ought to go see the Mardi Gras." Truer words were never spoken, or sung, whether you're a hard-partying fraternity boy looking for an alternative to spring break in Florida or a modern-day history or sociology buff. While Mardi Gras is often billed, and not without cause, as the biggest free party on the North American continent, it's also both a major religious holiday and a study in cultural anthropology.

The big day itself (Shrove Tuesday, or literally, Fat Tuesday — the last day before Lent) is notable for being the culmination of **Carnival** season, capping a frenzied two-week window of accelerated hedonistic excess before the self-imposed sacrifices of Lent. The idea is that good Catholics (or bad Catholics, if you prefer) cram as much acceptably naughty behavior (in the form of street-side revelry) as they can into that fortnight before the 40-day Lenten season of fasting and repentance. Of course, such significance is lost on all but a handful of locals, because most of the celebrants come only for the party trappings.

Don't feel guilty if you just come for the party, however. For one thing, Mardi Gras has certainly grown into a pop-cultural event all its own. And for another thing, it's filled with a number of fascinating aspects that reward close inspection, from the parades themselves to the pageantry and spectacle of the organizations (or *krewes*) that throw them. An invitation to a krewe's ball is a rare highlight of any local's social season. The parade of the **Rex** krewe (the ultimate Mardi Gras moment) bristles with the pomp and circumstance of hallowed tradition, while the early morning **Zulu** parade is an exhilarating display in its own right. The **Mardi Gras Indians** are the flip side to the exclusive ranks of such krewes as Rex and Endymion. The "Indians" are African-American men who don elaborate, Native American-style costumes in tribute to those who helped in the struggle against slavery. Of course, for a glimpse of elaborate costumes and culture, you needn't look any further than the French Quarter and the raucous festivities of **Gay Mardi Gras.**

Appreciating a City for Lovers

With all that history, music, food, and revelry in the air, New Orleans is one of the most atmospheric cities in the world. And that atmosphere is conducive to nothing so much as romance. From the lush scenery of the **Garden District** to the rolling expanse of water and parkway at the **Moonwalk,** New Orleans is a city built by, and for, lovers. Romance trots lazily through the French Quarter in a **mule-drawn carriage,** floats on the mists of the Mississippi River on a **riverboat cruise,** and lingers in the air (and the food) of idyllic restaurants such as **Bella Luna, Court of Two Sisters,** and **Bistro at Maison de Ville.**

New Orleans's unique atmosphere has inspired the talents of many an artist — from painters to poets — who've made their own contributions to the city's cultural tapestry. That includes writers as diverse as **William Faulkner** and **Tennessee Williams,** who were seduced by the city's charms and penned some of their influential works while under its influence. The list also includes best-selling vampire novelist and Goth icon **Anne Rice,** who fills her books with so many local landmarks they can practically double as travel guides.

The city has much to entice lovers of art and culture, as well. Museum fans in particular will likely suffer from sensory overload as they partake not only of the city's many historical attractions but also such fascinating destinations as the **New Orleans Historic Voodoo Museum,** the **New Orleans Pharmacy Museum,** and of course the **New Orleans Museum of Art.** But art lovers aren't limited to that which they can admire from a distance; **Magazine, Royal,** and **Julia streets** house countless art galleries and antique shops.

Drinking in the French Quarter

No New Orleans travel guide worth its Cajun seasonings can afford to ignore the French Quarter, most often presented to the world as the face of New Orleans. Though far and away the city's most popular area, I want to make clear that New Orleans offers much more than just the Quarter. Though a relatively small slice of the city, geographically speaking — 6 blocks by 13 blocks — the Quarter, for better or worse, acts as the beating heart of New Orleans. In fact, just as the rest of the city grew outward from this original settlement, so does life in New Orleans radiate outward from this focal point.

Its mix of classic and modern ultimately gives the French Quarter its charm. You'll find attractions such as the **Cabildo** and **Jackson Square.** You'll find scores of **antiques shops** and **historic homes,** as well as quaint little touches such as **mule-drawn carriage rides** and **Preservation Hall.** On the other hand, you'll also find the **Aquarium of the Americas,** the tranquility of the **Moonwalk,** and a host of great bars and nightclubs, from the dark environs of the **Dungeon** to the festive atmosphere of **Fritzel's European Jazz Pub,** the evocative ambiance of **Lafitte's Blacksmith Shop,** and the great music of **Donna's.** Not to mention some of the best restaurants anywhere, from **Antoine's** to **Nola,** and the one-of-a-kind experience of **Café du Monde.**

You'll also find **Bourbon Street.** Dotted with loud music hangouts (most of them of the watered-down, tourist-trap variety), dance clubs, and strip joints, the entire boulevard serves as one long salute to the pursuit of unrestrained pleasure. Bourbon Street provides a nightly run-through of the debauchery of Mardi Gras, where tourists wander around reveling in the novelty of being able to drink alcohol on the street, while street performers and con artists (sometimes one and the same) vie for the tourists' attention and money. The street is certainly a feast for the senses, which, despite the lowest-common-denominator appeal, can be oddly exhilarating.

Chapter 2

Deciding When to Go

● ●

In This Chapter

▶ Exploring the pros and cons of the different seasons

▶ Knowing what'll be happening when you arrive

▶ Attending some noteworthy festivals outside of New Orleans

● ●

Although New Orleans will still be New Orleans whenever you decide to visit, the timing of your trip can be a crucial consideration. If you don't like hot weather, you won't want to spend too much time here during the summer months, when the humidity sticks to you like cotton candy. And if you don't like crowds (especially rowdy, drunken ones), the charms of Mardi Gras or Jazz Fest may be lost on you.

If you're planning your trip around a specific event — attending a professional convention or joining the Mardi Gras celebration, for example — you don't really have much say as to when you visit. If you have a little leeway, however, look at what's happening, both event- and weather-wise, before you make your decision. If you're a music buff, for example, three major music festivals (Jazz Fest, the French Quarter Festival, and the International Arts Festival) take place between April and June that merit your attention.

In this chapter, I show you what New Orleans offers at different times of the year, and also run down a list of major festivals and events.

Figuring Out the Secret of the Seasons

New Orleans really has only three seasons: Hot, Cold, and In Between. Except for late spring and early summer (when temperatures are just uniformly hot), the seasons tend to run together. That's because this port city, a natural drop-off point for various cultures, also seems to be a way station for just about every weather pattern visiting the North American continent. A butterfly beating its wings in Kansas City seems to affect the weather in New Orleans.

As a result, bundling up under layers of clothing in the morning and then stripping down to a tank top and shorts by mid-afternoon is not uncommon. Unless you're coming in the dog days of summer, prepare for a little of everything.

The upcoming sections present each season's advantages and disadvantages. For a summary of average monthly temperatures, see Table 2-1.

Table 2-1		Average Monthly Temperatures for Metropolitan New Orleans											
	Jan	Feb	Mar	Apr	May	June	July	Aug	Sep	Oct	Nov	Dec
High °F	61	64	72	79	84	89	91	90	87	79	71	64
Low °F	42	44	52	58	66	71	74	73	70	60	51	46
High °C	16	18	22	26	29	32	33	32	31	26	22	18
Low °C	6	7	11	14	19	22	23	23	21	16	11	8

Spring

Spring is a popular vacation time for many travelers, and New Orleans has more than its share of reasons to visit.

- ✔ The weather is perfect for visiting plantation homes or Audubon Park.
- ✔ Break out your shorts: Average highs are in the 70s and 80s.
- ✔ Jazz Fest, held the last weekend of April and the first weekend of May, turns the city into one giant musical Mecca.
- ✔ Other events, including the rapidly growing French Quarter Festival, make this a "festive" time to visit.

However, visiting in spring does have a few disadvantages:

- ✔ The mercury can climb into the 90s with frightful speed.
- ✔ At the same time, average lows can dip into the 60s and even the 50s. Bring a light sweater or jacket, just in case.
- ✔ In New Orleans, April showers often bring . . . May showers, so bring an umbrella, and be prepared to use it.

Summer

Summertime, and the living is easy, as school is out and shorts and sandals become the standard mode of dress. Here are some valid reasons for visiting New Orleans during the summer:

- ✔ Tourism in New Orleans generally lags in the summer, so it's a great time to beat the crowds and snag a bargain or two in the process.

- ✔ This season brings pleasant breezes and plenty of sunshine, which contributes to lots of colorful vegetation.

But keep in mind the following hard facts:

- ✔ It's *hot*. Average highs are in the 80s and 90s, with temperatures often soaring into the 100s. You may want to limit your sightseeing to cooler hours in the early morning and evening; the afternoons can be unbearable. Drink plenty of fluids, seek shade and air-conditioned buildings, and don't skimp on the sunscreen.

- ✔ It's not just hot, it's humid. In New Orleans, humidity can often be as high as 100 percent, resulting in an atmosphere you can practically drink through a straw. With all that moisture in the air, rain can — and will — fall at the drop of a hat. Keep that umbrella handy, especially if you venture out in the afternoon.

- ✔ School's out; teen foot traffic makes for crowded shopping destinations, and attendance at museums, parks, and other kid-friendly attractions rises as well.

Fall

In my opinion, fall is a beautiful time of year no matter where you are. Here are some autumn bonuses for the New Orleans scene:

- ✔ Fall means a respite from the grisly heat of July and August, making for cool breezes.

- ✔ Those breezes also carry romantic properties that shouldn't be discounted. A lazy evening watching the sun sink on the river is a beautiful experience.

- ✔ Fall also means Halloween, which offers a basketful of revelry options in a city known for playing dress-up. (See "Getting the Lowdown on New Orleans's Main Events" later in this chapter.)

Some things to look out for, however, include the following:

✔ October and November are the driest months of the year (which isn't necessarily a guarantee against sudden downpours).

✔ It's the tail end (and the most active part) of hurricane season, which begins June 1 and ends in November. Most storms come knocking between August and November, so don't discount the possibility of a sudden and abrupt change of location should a big storm hit.

Winter

To some, winter conjures visions of snowflakes (not to mention slick roads and ice storms), but not in the Crescent City. However, here are some reasons why New Orleans offers its own version of a veritable winter wonderland:

✔ Compared with much of the country, New Orleans gets away easy. The weather is often mild to middling cold, and you'll never get snowed in. Plan to bring a lightweight coat or jacket.

✔ The first three weeks of December are traditionally slow for tourism, making it much easier to find a good room at a good rate.

✔ Because it's slow, crowds aren't a big problem in the early part of December, so you won't be waiting in line quite as much as you would during other times.

✔ After December, New Orleans has a lot going on. New Year's Eve in the French Quarter is not to be missed. The Sugar Bowl is played every January 1st. And then there's Mardi Gras. Depending on the year, Carnival can fall almost anywhere in February or early March (more on this shortly).

✔ New Orleans is loaded with romantic atmosphere, making it the perfect spot for a Valentine's Day getaway.

Winter does have its downsides, however. Consider the following:

✔ Although winter here is a cakewalk compared to, say, winter in Chicago, cold weather can catch you unawares if you don't plan (and pack) for the possibility. Occasional cold snaps bring the temperature down to freezing and below.

✔ You may want to make room for a larger coat, as well. The wind-chill factor, which can knock another 10 or 20 degrees off the thermometer, exacerbates the cold weather. (You'll still likely experience topsy-turvy weather patterns, so don't forget to pack some lighter wear.)

✔ After December, New Orleans has a lot going on. If you don't like large crowds and snarled traffic, you'd do better to avoid New Year's and Carnival.

Getting the Lowdown on New Orleans's Main Events

New Orleans truly deserves its reputation as a party capital. No matter what time of year you visit, you'll likely find an excuse to *laissez le bon temps roulet* (let the good times roll). Calendars of local festivals and celebrations never hurt for entries.

If you're coming to New Orleans for a specific event, especially Mardi Gras or Jazz Fest, you need to do a bit more advance planning than you would otherwise. I cannot stress this point enough: Make reservations for these two events (as well as for the Sugar Bowl and the French Quarter Festival) as early as possible. As their dates draw closer, hotel rooms become scarcer than honest politicians (especially honest Louisiana politicians). I recommend that you begin calling between 10 to 12 months ahead of time.

Don't assume you're off the hook if you come for a smaller event such as, say, the Rayne Frog Festival (don't ask; I get to it at the end of this chapter). Even during the less popular (and populous) festivals and events, finding a place to stay can become a Herculean exercise if you wait too long. As the Boy Scouts say, be prepared. Plan ahead.

The following sections present the city's best festivals and events, listed under the months in which they occur. For more detailed information, visit the Times-Picayune and Gambit Weekly Web sites (www.nola.com and www.bestofneworleans.com, respectively), the local Citysearch site (www.neworleans.citysearch.com), or Inside New Orleans (www.insideneworleans.com). An absolutely indispensable resource for information on local and state-level festivals is **Huli's Calendar of Louisiana Festivals and Events.** You can find this publication, which provides dates and background information for a staggering number of festivals, at bookstores and newsstands throughout the city; call ☎ **504-488-5993** for a copy or for specific information.

January

The **Nokia Sugar Bowl Football Classic** (☎ **504-525-8573;** www.nokia sugarbowl.com) takes place on January 1st. The crowds begin pouring into the city around late December, however. This is a great time to visit if you're a football fanatic and can afford to spend lots of money. Because this is a popular event, getting tickets can be pretty difficult, especially during those years when the Sugar Bowl hosts the national college football championship. If you're interested in attending, check a ticket service such as **Ticketmaster** (www.ticketmaster.com).

Carnival (☎ 800-672-6124 or 504-566-5011) runs from January 6 to Mardi Gras day, but really only the last two weeks leading up to Mardi Gras see a huge increase in tourism. You'll be lucky to find a vacant hotel room within 100 miles of the city if you don't make your reservations well ahead of time. Call for specific dates.

Mardi Gras (☎ 800-672-6124 or 504-566-5011; www.mardigrasday.com) can be as early as February 3 or as late as March 9, but it always falls on the Tuesday 46 days before Easter. On this day and most of the two weeks preceding it, life in New Orleans is hectic, to put it mildly. (See Chapter 16 for more information on Mardi Gras.)

February

The **Black Heritage Festival** (☎ 504-827-0112) is usually held in late February or early March. This two-day celebration features craft exhibits, soul food (such as jambalaya, fried chicken, and gumbo), and live music. You'll find festivities along the Riverwalk, in Audubon Park, and at the various Louisiana State Museum buildings.

March

On **St. Patrick's Day** (March 17), celebrations and parades overtake the city. The Downtown Irish Club sponsors a parade the Friday before St. Patrick's Day. Call ☎ 504-525-5169 for more information.

St. Joseph's Day falls on March 19. The city's Italians celebrate, often in conjunction with the Irish St. Patrick's Day, with parades and sumptuous food offerings. Call ☎ 800-672-6124 for more information.

Held over a four-day period in March, the **Tennessee Williams New Orleans Literary Festival** (☎ 504-581-1144; www.tennesseewilliams.net) celebrates the life of this famous playwright with performances, lectures, and walking tours. Noted Williams fan Alec Baldwin is a regular.

April

The **French Quarter Festival** (☎ 800-673-5725 or 504-522-5730; www.frenchquarterfestivals.org) is held on the second weekend in April (unless it conflicts with Easter), and serves as the unofficial start of the city's prime festival season, because it leads directly into the Jazz Fest. Hailed as the state's largest free music festival (and the world's largest jazz brunch), it gets bigger and more popular every year, offering plenty of free entertainment (unlike Jazz Fest, which is by ticket only), with an emphasis on local and regional music and food. As with Mardi Gras and Jazz Fest, check on room availability well in advance.

Known as Jazz Fest, the **New Orleans Jazz & Heritage Festival** (☎ 504-522-4786; www.nojazzfest.com) is held during the last weekend in April (Friday through Sunday) and the first weekend in May (Thursday through Sunday). A diverse lineup of hundreds of musicians (from big-ticket names on down, representing just about every genre under the sun) perform on various stages at the New Orleans Fair Grounds, and many more turn up after hours in the city's music clubs and concert halls as venues capitalize on the eager, music-hungry traffic. The city's crowded, prices are higher, and hotel and restaurant reservations are hard to come by — so plan ahead. Many attendees begin making reservations for the following year's festival even before the current one ends.

May

Celebrated over the last weekend in May, the **Greek Festival** (☎ 504-282-0259; www.greekfestnola.com) features Greek food, crafts, music, and dancing.

June

The **International Arts Festival** (formerly Reggae Riddums) (☎ 888-767-1317 or 504-367-1313; http://internationalartsfestival.com) is another popular music festival, this one with a decidedly Caribbean feel. The festival focuses on calypso, reggae, and regional food, and takes place during the second weekend in June.

July

The popular **Essence Festival** (☎ 800-725-5652 or 504-523-5652; www.essence.com) is both a music festival and a series of seminars on topics of importance to the African-American community, held during the Fourth of July weekend. More than 40,000 people come together for a weekend of seminars, as well as great national and local music. The festival has featured appearances by Gladys Knight, Patti LaBelle, Lauryn Hill, The Isley Brothers, Kenny G, Maya Angelou, Clarence Carter, and Irma Thomas, among many others.

August–September

The weekend before Labor Day marks the arrival of **Southern Decadence** (☎ 800-876-1484 or 504-522-8047; www.southerndecadence.net), which promises just that — decadence, and lots of it. Thousands of gays and lesbians converge upon the city during this festival. They assemble on Sunday in the 1200 block of Royal Street and then head off on a secret parade route known only to the grand marshal. Expect drag queens galore and lots of drinking. The celebration is wild and, like Mardi Gras, not all of the street celebrations are appropriate for young children.

September also marks the start of football season, which means another year of gridiron action for the New Orleans Saints (☎ 504-733-0255; www.neworleanssaints.com). Just after achieving the first play-off season victory in the team's existence at the end of the 2000 season, Saints owner Tom Benson started grumbling about moving the franchise if he didn't get a brand-new stadium from the city and state. At press time, though, a new home looks to be far off, and the Saints should be playing in the Superdome (albeit likely a renovated one) for the foreseeable future.

October

The Louisiana Jazz Federation sponsors **Louisiana Jazz Awareness Month** (☎ 504-834-3632) in October, which features nightly concerts, lectures, and special radio programs.

The **Gumbo Festival** (☎ 504-436-4712) offers attendees every type of gumbo you can imagine — and lots that you can't. The festival also features games, carnival rides, jazz, blues, and Cajun music to help put you in the mood for food — and work off what you eat. The festival is generally held during the second weekend in October.

Halloween is also a pretty big deal in New Orleans. Children can attend the **Boo-at-the-Zoo** (held on and around Halloween; ☎ 504-866-4872) and a yearly program at the **Louisiana Children's Museum** (☎ 504-523-1357; www.lcm.org). Meanwhile, events such as the **French Market Pumpkin Carving and Decorating Contest** (☎ 504-522-2621), and the **Moonlight Witches Run** offer more adult-oriented fun.

And speaking of adult-oriented, the annual **M.O.M.'s Ball,** thrown by a debauched group known as the Krewe of Mystic Orphans and Misfits, is one of the season's hottest hot-ticket events, a legendarily decadent bash. It's an invitation-only event, so you won't find any ticket information, but keep an eye out for it if you're in town and feeling so inclined.

October is also the start of basketball season, which means that by the time you read this, the **New Orleans Hornets** should be settled into their new home at the **New Orleans Arena,** marking the city's second attempt to supplement the Saints with a b-ball franchise (the Utah Jazz originally hailed from here before being wooed away decades ago). Check www.nba.com/hornets or call the Hornets organization (☎ 800-HORNETS) for more information.

November

Thanksgiving weekend brings one of the major social events of the year — the annual **Bayou Classic** (☎ 225-771-3170), a college football rivalry between a pair of Louisiana institutions: Grambling University and Southern University. Make your reservations early if you plan to attend, though, because approximately 75,000 people turn out for the game.

The **Celebration in the Oaks** (☎ 504-483-9415) runs from late November to early January. During this festival, sections of City Park are draped with lights and lighted figures in holiday themes. You can visit the park on walking tours, driving tours, and carriage tours.

December

You won't see Dick Clark there, but the **Jackson Square New Year's** celebration is beginning to resemble New York's — right down to the lighted ball dropping from the top of Jackson Brewery. The city also puts on a very nice fireworks display along the Mississippi River. Count on revelers packing to the gills the major thoroughfares of the French Quarter.

Wanna Go for a Ride? Some Outlying Festivals

Not everything worth doing in Louisiana happens inside the corporate limits of New Orleans. This section gives you a short, but sweet, list of some noteworthy festivals that take place just a brief drive from the city.

Festival International de Louisiane (☎ 337-232-8086; www.festival international.com) is a mammoth celebration of the cultural heritage of Southern Louisiana (primarily a mix of French, Hispanic, and African-Caribbean cultures). It generally takes place during the last weekend of April in downtown Lafayette, about a two-hour drive from New Orleans.

Lafayette also plays host to **Festivals Acadiens** (☎ 337-233-7060), a celebration of Cajun culture held during the third weekend of September. Cajun food and music are the main attractions, with workshops and other activities sprinkled about.

The **Original Southwest Louisiana Zydeco Music Festival** (☎ 337-942-2392; www.zydeco.org) plays every Labor Day weekend in Plaisance (roughly a three-hour drive north of New Orleans), and celebrates the unique joys of *zydeco,* the popular accordion-driven music of the Creoles of Southern Louisiana. Aside from the event itself, an all-day fair is held on Saturday with music, food, and crafts. The celebration extends to the surrounding areas of Lafayette, Opelousas, and Lake Charles.

I'd be remiss if I didn't at least mention the **Rayne Frog Festival,** held every September in Cajun Country, about a two-hour drive from New Orleans in an area west of Lafayette. Cajuns can turn just about anything into an excuse for a festival, as evidenced by this event's frog races and frog-jumping contests. (Didn't bring a frog? Don't worry; you can rent one. Seriously.) On the culinary side, you can also participate in a lively frog-eating contest. For dates and full details, contact the **Rayne Chamber of Commerce** (☎ **337-334-2332;** www.rayne.org).

Chapter 3

Planning Your Budget

*I*n a city with as many temptations as New Orleans, traveling without a budget is the surest way to court financial disaster. With all of the historical attractions, French Quarter souvenir shops, and great restaurants and bars, you won't need to set foot inside the local casino to break your bank. In fact, you can easily max out your credit card simply by sampling all of the city's different culinary delights.

If you're as math-phobic as I am, the very prospect of drawing up a budget probably induces a case of the sweats. If mentioning this fact seems like an odd way to win your confidence, bear with me. I've had a lifetime of experience in exercising both willpower and fiscal common sense in the face of this city's temptations. I know how to stretch a New Orleans travel dollar.

Adding Up the Costs of Your Trip

The best way to get a handle on your budget is to walk yourself through your trip, starting with transportation to your nearest airport (or, if you're driving, how much gas you expect to use per day). For the sake of argument, say you're flying. First, add up the costs for your transportation to the airport, your flight (see Chapter 5 for tips on saving money here), and your ride to your hotel. Next, add the hotel rate per day, meals (be sure to note if your hotel includes breakfast in its room rate), transportation costs, admission to museums and other attractions, and any entertainment expenses you may accrue.

Table 3-1 offers some average costs for you to get started. And the worksheets included in this book (printed on yellow paper near the back of the book) can also help you plan out your trip budget.

Table 3-1	What Things Cost in New Orleans
Expense	**Cost**
Taxi from the airport to the Central Business District or French Quarter	$24
Bus from airport to downtown	$1.50
St. Charles streetcar ride for one (one-way)	$1.25
Riverfront streetcar ride for one (one-way)	$1.50
Bus ride for one (one-way)	$1.25
Average taxi ride for one in the Quarter (add $1 for each extra passenger)	$5
Inexpensive ($) hotel room for two	under $75
Low–moderate ($$) hotel room for two	$75–$125
High–moderate ($$$) hotel room for two	$125–$175
Expensive ($$$$) hotel room for two	$175–$250
Very expensive ($$$$$) hotel room for two	over $250
Moderately priced breakfast for two	$12–$16
Moderately priced lunch for two	$20–$30
Moderately priced dinner for two	$30–$50
Non-alcoholic drink	$1–$1.50
Bottle of beer	$1.50–$4
Cocktail	$3.50–$8
Cup of coffee	50¢–$1.50
Admission to New Orleans Museum of Art	$6
Theater ticket at Le Petit Theatre	$18–$26

The costs of some things, such as hotels, are relatively inflexible. Along with airfare or other transportation costs, lodging makes up the largest part of your expenditures. Other factors, such as transportation in the city, are relatively cheap. The incredible number of restaurants and nightlife choices in New Orleans are as different in cost as they are in variety, and it's entirely up to you whether you opt for a dress-up or dress-down option.

Of course, budgeting your vacation isn't so difficult when you look at it in the abstract, jotting down prices on a piece of paper in the comfort of your own home. Keeping track of your costs after you arrive, however, is another matter altogether. Remember that the key element in budget is "budge," so allow yourself some flexibility — start by tacking a good 10 percent or even 20 percent onto the final budget tally. At the same time, keep in mind that you can easily go from bending your budget to breaking your bank entirely.

Lodging: Your biggest expense

Lodging represents the least elastic part of your budget — after all, you've got to stay somewhere. In this book, I share information about rack rates and how to save money in this area (see Chapter 7), but hotels will still comprise a significant portion of your expenses. You can find inexpensive rooms, though they're usually far from the center of town or they don't offer much in the way of amenities. (Some guesthouses, for example, wanting to emulate that European feel, offer rooms that share a common bathroom for a cheaper rate, or a backpacker room that more closely resembles your closet at home.) If you want to stay relatively close to the French Quarter or the Central Business District, you'll more than likely spend a minimum of $90 to $100 a night. See Chapter 8 for some hotel recommendations and price ranges.

Transportation: How to get around

Getting around the most popular parts of the city is a relative bargain. Many hotels and attractions lie in the French Quarter or Central Business District within a scant few miles of one another. If the sight you want to see is farther than you want to walk — or if you're visiting on a really hot day — a taxi ride won't break the bank. Unless traffic is heavy, the average trip in or around the Quarter should be no more than $5.

For public transportation, hop on one of the city's buses or streetcars. Fares are $1.25 each time you get on (transfers cost an additional 25 cents), but a **VisiTour** pass, good for unlimited bus and streetcar rides, costs only $5 for one day and $12 for three days. Check with your hotel's concierge, or check with the **Regional Transit Authority** (☎ **504-248-3900;** www.regionaltransit.org) for information. Many hotels also offer free shuttles to and from the French Quarter or Central Business District. For more information on getting around the city, see Chapter 11.

Dining: How to save, when to splurge

Dining options in New Orleans range from very inexpensive to astronomical. Almost all options are tantalizing (in different ways, of course); you don't necessarily have to spend a lot of money for a great meal.

If you really want to eat cheap, you can get coffee and beignets for breakfast at Café du Monde for about $2.50, a $5 po' boy for lunch at any one of a hundred places, and dinner for under $15 at a place such as Café Maspero in the Quarter.

However, if you feel like you can't come to New Orleans without having breakfast at Brennan's, dinner at Antoine's, or a great evening at one of the fancier restaurants listed in Chapter 14, make sure to put a little money aside and make reservations in advance.

Sightseeing: See it all without going broke

Attractions are a somewhat more flexible part of your expenses. Your budget for entrance fees and admissions depends, of course, on what you want to see. And if you're traveling with your whole family, you can expect to shell out more for attractions than if you're backpacking with a buddy. Refer to the attraction listings in Chapters 17 and 18 and make a list of your "must sees," and then figure out your costs from the ticket prices given there.

Shopping: Savvy souvenirs

The amount of money you need for shopping makes up another variable part of your budget. After all, you don't have to buy anything at all if that's your style, though self-restraint can be something of an alien concept in New Orleans. Even a scrupulous penny-counter can succumb to shopping fever when wandering the French Market or some of the souvenir shops in the French Quarter. As an international port city, New Orleans offers as many choices as you can imagine. And if you're an antiques buff, forget about it. You may want to leave your checks and credit cards at the hotel before going anywhere near Magazine Street.

If you're just looking for some souvenirs to take home as proof of your trip, you can find whole colonies of shops selling postcards, posters, sunglasses, and T-shirts in the French Quarter. Being tourist shops, however, they aren't exactly cheap. If you really want to save on souvenirs, ask someone to take your picture on Bourbon Street. Voilà! You now have an instant memento of your trip (assuming the person doesn't run away with your camera). See Chapter 20 for the lowdown on shopping in New Orleans.

Nightlife: Live it up for less

Your entertainment dollars will likely stretch farther in New Orleans than in a place such as New York, where a pair of tickets to the theater can require a second mortgage. Most of the nightlife in New Orleans is

relatively inexpensive — but again, your personal preferences determine
the final tally. You'll obviously spend more if you go to the opera than if
you head to the Maple Leaf or the House of Blues for some local music.
Turn to Chapters 23 and 24 for nightlife listings, and Chapter 25 for the
performing arts scene.

Keeping a Lid on Hidden Expenses

No matter how diligently you plan, an item-by-item budget can take you
only so far, because last-minute temptations (especially in New Orleans)
will test your willpower. More importantly, any number of "invisible"
expenditures and nasty surprises can spell disaster if you're traveling
on a seat-of-the-pants budget with very little wiggle room. This section
reminds you of a few below-the-radar expenses to keep in mind.

Hotel taxes and service charges

When figuring the price of your room, don't forget that the hotel tacks
some additional fees onto the base rate. Hotel taxes add a whopping
11.75 percent to your bill. Also, if you have more than two people in a
room, many places charge you upward of $10 apiece for the extra
people. On top of *that,* many hotels levy an "occupancy charge," which
is basically an excuse to squeeze an additional dollar or two out of
your wallet. When you make reservations, make sure you know
whether the price that the hotel quotes you includes taxes and other
such charges. The same goes for package deals.

Also, watch out for the ever-popular "service charges" that appear at
the bottom of many bills. Whenever you order tickets, make reservations, or ask a passing stranger for the correct time, someone seems to
levy a charge for the service rendered. You really can't do anything
about it, in most cases; these charges simply allow some businesses,
such as ticket agents, to make most of their profit. Still, keeping an eye
on such charges when conducting a transaction is a good idea, and
accounting for such built-in charges when planning your budget will
save you some aggravation come bill-paying time.

Hotel amenities

Hotel telephones and minibars are a constant source of nasty mis-
understanding between hotels and guests. Many hotels in the moderate to expensive range offer free local calling from their rooms — but
don't count on it. At those that don't, you can end up paying a couple
of bucks for each call you make, and many hotels don't volunteer this
information when you make a reservation or check in. Minibars in
rooms can also present a potential rude surprise. Just because it's

stocked, doesn't mean it's free: A bottle of water, for example, can run you around $3; a bottle of beer, $5 — to say nothing of goodies such as peanuts or gummy bears, which can set you back $7–$10.

Tipping

Tipping may not seem like a hidden expense, because you must deal with it in everyday life. On vacation, however, those tips for bellhops, hotel maids, waiters, and cabbies can add up.

The golden rule of tipping for most services — including restaurants and taxis — is to add 15 to 20 percent to your bill (before taxes). If you're with a large group, make sure that the bill doesn't already include the tip, because restaurants may add a 15 to 20 percent gratuity for parties of six or more. If you're just drinking at a bar, tipping 10 to 15 percent is typical. You should give bellhops $1 or $2 per bag, maids $1 per day, coat-check people $1 per garment, and automobile valets $1.

Skimping in this area is your call. No one can force you to tip every bartender and cab driver you meet, especially because you may never see them again. However, I recommend making an exception for your hotel maid — especially if you consider clean sheets and well-stocked toiletries more than just luxuries.

Traveler's Checks, Credit Cards, ATMs, or Cash?

How do you pay for that elaborate Mardi Gras costume? Today's travelers have several options from cold cash to virtual money — virtual, that is, until the bill arrives. This section helps you decide which form of currency is right for you.

Traveler's checks: Should I leave home without them?

Traveler's checks make a convenient alternative to carrying large bundles of cash around, and they free you from the hassle of finding an establishment that will accept an out-of-town check, because businesses worldwide recognize and accept them. You can also easily replace traveler's checks if they are lost or stolen.

These days, however, the demand for traveler's checks has lessened, because most cities have 24-hour ATMs linked to a national network. People still widely use them, however, so the choice is yours. Some people find them more convenient than carrying a wad of cash or keeping track of a pile of ATM receipts. Of course, if you run out, you'll have to take time from your trip to go to a bank or other office to get more.

If you feel you need the security of traveler's checks and don't mind the hassle of showing identification every time you want to cash one, you can get them at almost any bank. **American Express** offers checks in denominations of $10, $20, $50, $100, $500, and $1,000. You'll pay a service charge ranging from 1 to 4 percent, though AAA members can obtain checks without a fee at most AAA offices. You can also get American Express traveler's checks over the phone by calling ☎ **800-221-7282;** American Express gold and platinum cardholders who call this number are exempt from the fee.

Citibank offers **Citibank Visa** traveler's checks at Citibank locations across the country and at several other banks. To find the Citibank closest to you, call ☎ **800-645-6556.** The service charge ranges between 1 and 2.5 percent; checks come in denominations of $20, $50, $100, $500, and $1,000. For information on non-Citibank **Visa** traveler's checks, call ☎ **800-227-6811. MasterCard** also offers traveler's checks. Call ☎ **800-223-9920** for a location near you.

Give me some credit

While a credit card can be an invaluable aid when traveling, it can also be a double-edged sword. First the good; credit cards are a safe way to carry money, and they provide a convenient record of all your purchases and expenses in the form of your monthly bill. Also, should the need arise, you can get a cash advance from your credit card at any bank or ATM. (See "The 411 on ATMs" later in this chapter for more information on ATMs.)

Now the bad; you'll end up paying interest on your purchases and expenses — unless you promptly pay off your complete balance. Also, if you get a cash advance from your card, you'll start paying interest the moment you receive the cash, and if you're using an airline credit card, you won't receive frequent-flyer miles on the advance.

Nonetheless, if you want to use your card to get cash, the procedure is fairly simple. At most banks, you don't even need to go to a teller; you can get a cash advance at the ATM if you know your PIN (personal identification number). Make sure you know your credit card PIN before you leave home, especially if you don't use it at home. If you forget your PIN, you can call the phone number on the back of your credit card. If you've set up some pre-arranged way of identifying yourself (such as using your mother's maiden name as a secret password), most banks will give you your PIN over the phone. Otherwise, getting a new one through the mail will probably take five to seven days, so make sure to check this before you leave.

My best advice is obvious — know your limits. Make informed decisions about how often you use your charge card, and only charge what you can reasonably afford. If you're perfectly willing to go into credit-card debt for the rest of the year to pay off your one week of debauchery, go right ahead — but know the consequences going in. As for cash advances, they're expensive — and you begin paying interest immediately — so avoid them except as a last resort.

The 411 on ATMs

ATMs are a quick and convenient source of cash when you're on vacation. As in any major city, you can find them all over New Orleans: inside hotel lobbies, bars, shopping centers, restaurants, supermarkets, daiquiri shops — you name it. You won't have any trouble finding a machine to spit cash in your face, but you may have trouble keeping track of how many times you visit the magic money machine. At the risk of stating the obvious, record each ATM transaction, before you forget about it.

Obviously, if you have the money in your bank account, ATMs are an extremely convenient way to manage your cash while on vacation. Your ATM card allows you to avoid dealing with the hassle of buying traveler's checks or carrying large amounts of cash. The increasingly popular debit card is even better, because it allows you to pay for your purchase right away without the nuisance of credit card interest fees.

Although ATMs are pretty darned convenient, that convenience likely comes at a price. Depending on the bank whose ATM you use, you may get charged both ways: Some institutions charge you a fee for using another bank's ATM, on top of what the other bank charges you for using their machine.

Cirrus (☎ **800-424-7787** or 800-4-CIRRUS; www.mastercard.com/ cardholderservices/atm/) and **Plus** (☎ **800-843-7587;** www.visa. com/atms) are the two most popular networks; check the back of your ATM card to determine your bank's network. Call the corresponding 800 number, or check the Web site, to find out specific locations of ATMs in New Orleans. Both networks are pretty ubiquitous, so you should have little trouble locating a cash machine that you can use. Note, however, that ATMs often place limits on the frequency of use and the amount of cash you can withdraw. In addition, your own bank may impose a fee ranging from 50¢ to $3 every time you use an ATM in a different city.

Cash and carry

No matter how much money you carry in traveler's checks, you should always have some cash handy. After all, you can't ask a vending machine or parking meter if it takes traveler's checks, and most taxi drivers insist on cash as well. As a general rule, you should keep only as much on your person as you'll need for a day or two of shopping, attractions, and travel.

If you're paying cash for your lodgings, don't carry the money around with you — keep it somewhere safe. Put it in your hotel room (safely tucked away where you can find it, maybe in a secret luggage compartment) or, if it makes you feel better and your hotel has one, in the hotel safe.

Tips for Cutting Costs

So you want to save a few dollars, but not skimp on your vacation fun? No problem. Here are cost-saving tips that you can use for any vacation, as well as some specific to the Crescent City.

- **Go in the off-season.** If you can handle the hot weather, you can get some great deals from June through August — but remember that when I say hot, I mean hot. The first three weeks of December is also a good time for getting a deal.

- **Travel on "off" days of the week.** If you can travel on a Tuesday, Wednesday, or Thursday, you may find cheaper flights to your destination. When you inquire about airfares, ask if you can obtain a cheaper rate by flying on a different day.

- **Reserve your flight well in advance (or at the very last minute).** Take advantage of advance purchase excursion (APEX) fares, or watch the last-minute *e-fares* online for bargains. (See Chapter 5 for a discussion of online strategies.)

- **Try a package tour.** For many destinations, one call to a travel agent or packager can net you airfare, hotel reservations, ground transportation, and even some sightseeing — all for a lot less than if you put the trip together yourself. (See the section on package tours in Chapter 5 for specific suggestions of companies to call.)

- **Always ask for discount rates.** Membership in AAA, frequent flyer plans, trade unions, AARP, or other groups may qualify you for savings on car rentals, plane tickets, hotel rooms, and even meals. Ask about everything and you may be pleasantly surprised.

✔ **Reserve a room with a kitchen.** Doing your own cooking and dishes may not be your idea of a vacation, but you'll save a lot of money by not eating in restaurants three times a day. Even if you only make breakfast and pack an occasional bag lunch, you'll save in the long run. Plus you'll never get a heart-attack-inducing shock from a hefty room service bill.

✔ **Ask whether your kids can stay in your room with you.** A room with two double beds usually doesn't cost any more than one with a queen-size bed, and many hotels won't charge the additional-person rate if the additional person is pint-sized and related to you. Even if the hotel does charge you an additional $10 or $15 for a rollaway bed, you'll still save hundreds by not taking two rooms.

✔ **Get out of the Quarter.** Really. To many people, the French Quarter *is* New Orleans, and they want to stay where they think all the action happens. Although you'll certainly see lots of action in the Quarter, New Orleans offers much more for you to see and experience. More to the point, hotels outside the French Quarter tend to charge less than those within the Quarter. So if you don't mind the slightly longer trip to most of the attractions, book yourself into a hotel in the Faubourg Marigny, Uptown, or along the Esplanade Ridge. See Chapters 6, 7, and 8 for more information.

✔ **Pack light.** That way, you can carry your own bags (you won't have to tip yourself) and take a bus rather than a cab from the airport.

✔ **Try expensive restaurants at lunch instead of dinner.** At most top restaurants, lunch tabs are usually a fraction of dinner bills, and the menu often boasts many of the same specialties.

✔ **Study up on public transit.** What can be more romantic than traveling around New Orleans on the streetcar? Not much — and a ride only costs $1.25. The bus, while somewhat less romantic, still costs less than relying solely on taxis. See Chapter 11 for more information.

✔ **Walk a lot.** You'll save money, get some exercise, and see the city the way it was meant to be seen — from the ground and at a slower pace. Be sure to pack a good pair of walking shoes — the last thing you need on vacation is sore feet. (*Note:* Don't overdo the walking if you're in town during a really hot spell.)

✔ **Skip the souvenirs.** Your photographs and memories are the best mementos of your trip, so skip the tourist shops if you're worried about money. After all, you don't really *need* those riverboat salt-and-pepper shakers, do you?

Chapter 4

Planning Ahead for Special Travel Needs

. . . .

In This Chapter

▶ Taking the kids along

▶ Going in your golden years

▶ Rising above disabilities

▶ Finding gay-friendly activities

. . . .

*I*f your familiarity with New Orleans comes courtesy of television or movies, you may get the idea that the city is little more than a year-round bacchanal. While you will find plenty of opportunities to party like it's 2099, the city offers much more than that. In fact, New Orleans is nothing if not a "one size fits all" vacation spot.

Making Your Trip a Family Affair

Although most people associate New Orleans with hard-core debauch-ery, the city is also a popular family destination. The farther away you get from Bourbon Street and the strip clubs in the French Quarter, obviously, the more family-friendly the city gets. But you don't have to leave the Quarter to find a wealth of kid-centric attractions and activi-ties. New Orleans's unique history and its status as a nexus of different cultures provide for a number of fascinating landmarks, museums, and similar sights that entertain and interest both children and adults.

In Chapters 17 and 18 (and throughout the book), I highlight the attrac-tions that your kids should find of interest with the Kid Friendly icon. To get you started, however, kids are sure to enjoy the following places and activities:

✔ Audubon Zoo

✔ Audubon Aquarium of the Americas

✔ Jazzland Amusement Park

✔ City Park

✔ Louisiana Children's Museum

✔ A ride across the river on the Canal Street Ferry

✔ Mimes, jugglers, musicians, and other street performers in the French Quarter, particularly at Jackson Square

You can also call **ACCENT on Children's Arrangements, Inc.** (☎ **504-524-1227;** www.accentoca.com), a company that specializes in tours for children, especially for those whose parents are attending a convention.

You know as well as I do that just because something touts itself as fun for kids doesn't necessarily make it so. Pointing your kids toward a museum that's "good for them" won't work, and often results in eye rolling or the ubiquitous "Dad, you're a dork." I'm not ignorant of this reality, as many travel guides seem to be; in Chapters 17 and 18, I point out which attractions may be more age-appropriate for smaller fries than for jaded teens (and vice-versa). I won't tell you not to bring your kids to a specific attraction; after all, you know your children better than I do. But the guidance should help you plan a daily itinerary that the whole family can enjoy.

Locating kid-friendly accommodations

Because New Orleans is a large tourist destination, you won't have any trouble finding a place to stay that accepts children. Of course, exceptions always exist. You won't likely find many cozy bed-and-breakfast establishments that accommodate children, for instance. But the major hotels? No problem.

Of course, after you find a hotel that accepts children, your work has just begun. Children are notoriously hard to please, and woe betide the weary parent who doesn't take this into account when selecting a place to stay. Sure, most kids are just happy to be away from home, and in close proximity to a rooftop swimming pool. But in case that isn't enough, many (if not most) hotels offer kid-friendly amenities, such as pay-per-view movies or in-house video rental, video games, and even goodies such as chocolate chip cookies upon check-in. You'd also do well to check ahead for nearby restaurants with children's menus (that goes for the in-house restaurant as well). Chapter 8 identifies places I think your kid may like.

Keeping the kids entertained

No matter how much planning you do, kids are still prone to fits of boredom and crankiness. Be sure to take along some toys or activities to help them through the rough patches. Depending on their age or tastes, pack coloring books, comics, books, or a portable radio or CD player to keep them occupied.

Be sure to keep your kids' endurance level in mind when planning your itinerary. Long walking tours can tire kids out faster than adults, and long waits can make them restless. This is where a portable radio or CD player can come in handy. Also, stagger events to keep them enjoyable for kids. A day of pounding the pavement may sap your child's enthusiasm for the next day's trip to that aquarium or zoo exhibit she's been dying to see. You also probably don't need me to tell you that a child's energy level fluctuates wildly, and your little munchkin could catch his second or third wind just as you're ready to collapse for the day. Try to keep an eye on such factors as sugar intake and other stimulants to avoid a serious case of child lag in the middle of a long afternoon.

Relying on baby-sitting services

If you want a night out on your own without the kids, some hotels provide baby-sitting services; check with your hotel's concierge or with the reservations clerk, or check the listings in Chapter 8. If your hotel doesn't provide such a service, you can contact an agency that will watch your children while you wine and dine at Galatoire's. Employees of these agencies will sit with your kids, take them on organized outings, or create a personalized itinerary:

- ✔ **ACCENT on Children's Arrangements, Inc.** (☎ 504-524-1227; www.accentoca.com); licensed, bonded, insured

- ✔ **Dependable Family Care** (☎ 504-486-4001); licensed, bonded, insured; 24 hours

Making the Most of Your Golden Years: Tips for Seniors

People over the age of 60 are traveling more than ever before. And why not? Being a senior citizen entitles you to some terrific travel bargains on car rentals, hotels, and even airfare.

Joining senior organizations

If you're not already a member, do yourself a favor and join the American Association of Retired Persons, known as **AARP** (☎ 800-424-3410 or 202-434-AARP; www.aarp.org). As a member, you're entitled to discounts on car rentals and hotels.

Similar to AARP, **Mature Outlook** (☎ 800-336-6330) offers discounts on car rentals and hotel stays at many Holiday Inns, Howard Johnsons, and Best Westerns. Your $19.95 annual membership fee also gets you a bi-monthly magazine and $200 in Sears coupons. Any Sears customer over 18 can join, but the organization (and the magazine) focuses primarily on people over 50.

Ask about discounts when you book your flight because most of the major domestic airlines (including American, United, Continental, US Airways, and TWA) offer lower fares for senior travelers. In most cities, people over the age of 60 get reduced admission at theaters, museums, and other attractions, and they can often get discount fares on public transportation as well. Carrying identification with proof of age pays off in all these situations.

Reading up on senior travel publications

The Mature Traveler, a monthly newsletter on senior citizen travel is a valuable resource. A subscription costs $30 a year. For a free sample issue, send a postcard with your name and address to GEM Publishing Group, Box 2224 Beaumont St., Suite D, Sacramento, CA 95815 (e-mail: maturetrav@aol.com). GEM also publishes *The Book of Deals,* which gives you the skinny on more than 1,000 senior discounts on airlines, lodging, tours, and attractions around the country. The book is available for $9.95 by calling ☎ 800-460-6676. Grand Circle Travel (☎ 800-221-2610; www.gct.com) offers a helpful publication called *101 Tips for the Mature Traveler.*

Plotting your New Orleans strategy

Enjoying your stay in New Orleans will depend in large part on how you plan for such variables as the distance between your hotel and the attractions you want to see, as well as how you deal with the city's crazy weather. The following sections should help you make lodging and sightseeing decisions based on your own personal needs.

Lodging

Depending on your health, the location of your hotel may be a more important consideration than it is for other travelers. If you plan to do a lot of sightseeing by foot, try to find a hotel that's central to a number of accessible attractions. If you plan to spend most of your time in the French Quarter, you're in good shape; almost everything in this relatively small but eventful area is within walking distance. If walking the Quarter's 13 blocks seems prohibitive for you or a companion, catching a cab is a wise, inexpensive alternative.

Booking with senior-friendly travel agents

Literally hundreds of travel agencies specialize in vacations for seniors (including Grand Circle Travel; see "Reading up on senior travel publications" elsewhere in this section). Watch out, though, because many are of the tour-bus variety, with free trips thrown in for those who organize groups of 20 or more. If you prefer more independent travel, consult a regular travel agent. **SAGA International Holidays** (☎ 800-343-0273) offers inclusive tours and cruises for those 50 and older.

If staying outside the Quarter, make sure your hotel is convenient to public transportation, and in a safe neighborhood. I recommend the **Pontchartrain Hotel,** the **Maison St. Charles Quality Inn,** or the **St. Charles Guest House** (see the listings in Chapter 8) for safety and/or convenience to public transportation. The first two hotels are on St. Charles Avenue, where the streetcar travels. You'll have to cab it to the St. Charles Guest House, though.

No matter where you choose to stay, take a cab if you venture out at night; the extra couple of dollars is worth the security of being delivered right to your doorstep.

Attractions

If you're staying in the French Quarter, you'll find plenty of museums, historic landmarks, and other attractions close at hand, and a number of free sightseeing places (for example, **Jackson Square** or the **Moonwalk**) where you can watch the parade of life unfold before you. And if you're into this sort of thing, **Harrah's New Orleans Casino** is just across Canal Street from the **Aquarium of the Americas** and **Canal Place.** Check the listings in Chapters 17 and 18 for places of particular interest, as well as for information on senior discounts.

The **U.S. National Park Service** offers a **Golden Age Passport** that gives seniors 62 years or older lifetime entrance to U.S. national parks for a one-time processing fee of $10, which must be purchased in person at any national park facility that charges an entrance fee. (Near New Orleans, the National Park Service operates Jean Lafitte National Historic Park; see Chapter 22.) Besides free entry, a Golden Age Passport also offers a 50 percent discount on federal-use fees charged for such facilities as camping, swimming, parking, boat launching, and tours. For more information, check out www.nps.gov/fees_passes.htm or call ☎ **888-GO-PARKS.**

Weather

Whether you travel with a group (say, as part of a package tour) or on your own, some of the best advice I can give you is to be mindful of the weather. In the summer, when tourism is generally down, you won't encounter as many crowds to jostle your way through, which makes it a good time to visit. However, the heat and humidity can tire you out faster than normal, especially during the afternoons. If you're visiting in the summer, plan as many indoor activities as possible during the peak afternoon hours. When you do venture outside, keep some bottled water on hand.

If you travel with a group as part of a guided tour or package tour, make sure you know the name of your hotel. If you get lost or separated from your group, have the number of a reliable cab company on hand to take you back to your hotel. I recommend using **United Cab** (☎ **504-522-9771**), the largest and most reliable fleet in the city.

Advice for Travelers with Disabilities

A disability shouldn't stop anybody from traveling; more options and resources are available for the disabled now than ever. The following national and New Orleans–based organizations can tailor a trip to fit your specific needs:

- ✔ **Publications:** *A World of Options,* a 658-page book of resources for disabled travelers, covers everything from biking trips to scuba outfitters. You can get a copy for $35 from **Mobility International USA,** P.O. Box 10767, Eugene, OR, 97440 (☎ **541-343-1284,** voice and TTY; www.miusa.org).

  Also look for information from **Access-Able Travel Source** (www.access-able.com), a comprehensive database of travel agents who specialize in disabled travel — and also a clearinghouse for information about accessible destinations around the world.

- ✔ **Tours:** Some tour companies cater specifically to travelers with disabilities. One of the best operators is **Flying Wheels Travel** (☎ **507-451-5005;** Fax: 507-451-1685; www.flyingwheelstravel.com). They offer various escorted tours and cruises, as well as private tours in minivans with lifts.

- ✔ **Rental cars:** Many of the major car rental companies now offer hand-controlled cars for disabled drivers. With 48-hour advance notice, you can get such a vehicle at any Avis location in the United States. Most Hertz locations can do the same, provided you alert them between 24 and 72 hours before you need the vehicle.

  Wheelchair Getaways (☎ **800-642 2042** or 504-738-2634; www.wheelchair-getaways.com) rents specialized vans with wheelchair lifts and other features for the disabled. The Louisiana office is located in Metairie, a suburb between the airport and New Orleans itself.

✔ **Seeing-eye dogs:** For information on traveling with a seeing-eye dog, contact the **American Foundation for the Blind** (☎ 800-232-5463).

Building accessibility

Most of the historic sites and a few of the older hotels and restaurants in New Orleans may present problems for people with disabilities because they are exempt from the provisions of the Americans with Disabilities Act (ADA). I mention problematic places in the relevant chapters of this book, but you should call ahead and check.

All major hotels comply with the ADA, though some of the smaller hotels and most notably bed-and-breakfast establishments are either not in compliance or only partially so. Among hotels, the **Wyndham Canal Place** receives the biggest thumbs-up for accessibility, and the **Dauphine Orleans, Hotel Monteleone,** and **Royal Orleans** are also rated highly. Many major restaurants also comply, as I note in Chapter 14. If a place doesn't have a ramp, however, staffers are usually more than happy to help assist disabled patrons inside their establishments.

Other New Orleans resources

A few resources within New Orleans can make your visit easier after you've arrived in the Crescent City. The **Regional Transit Authority** (☎ 504-248-3900; www.regionaltransit.org) has lift-equipped buses available for individuals as well as for groups. If you're hearing-impaired and have a telecommunications device for the deaf (TDD), the **Louisiana Relay Service** (☎ 800-947-5277) offers a service that can connect you with non-TDD users. Travelers with disabilities can also receive assistance from **Resources for Independent Living** (☎ 504-522-1955).

The U.S. National Park Service offers a **Golden Access Passport** that gives free lifetime entrance to U.S. national parks for persons who are blind or permanently disabled, regardless of age. (Near New Orleans, the National Park Service operates Jean Lafitte National Historic Park; see Chapter 22.) You may pick up a Golden Access Passport at any national park entrance area by showing proof of medically determined disability and eligibility for receiving benefits under federal law. Besides free entry, the Golden Access Passport also offers a 50 percent discount on federal-use fees charged for such facilities as camping, swimming, parking, boat launching, and tours. For more information, surf to www.nps.gov/fees_passes.htm or call ☎ 888-GO-PARKS.

Gay and Lesbian Travelers

New Orleans is one of the most gay- and lesbian-friendly cities in the United States. You won't lack for bars, restaurants, hotels, and other businesses owned by or catering to gays and lesbians, especially in the French Quarter and the neighboring Faubourg Marigny — the center of the local gay scene.

New Orleans hosts a number of gay-themed or gay-friendly events year-round. As noted in Chapter 2, **Southern Decadence,** a major festival draw for gay and lesbian tourists and one heck of a party, takes place on Labor Day weekend. Halloween also has a sizable gay turnout, and, of course, Mardi Gras features a large (and quite enjoyable), gay celebration (see Chapter 16).

New Orleans's major gay publication is *Ambush* (☎ **800-876-1484** or 504-522-8047; www.ambushmag.com), providing excellent information on what's going on. You can find a copy in most gay-friendly establishments. In the relevant chapters of this book, I note gay-friendly choices for hotels, restaurants, and nightlife, but here are some hints:

- Best *hotel* choices for gay and lesbian travelers are the **Lafitte Guest House,** the **New Orleans Guest House,** and the **Ursuline Guest House,** all in the French Quarter. If you're willing to travel a bit farther away from the Quarter, the **Macarty Park Guest House** in Bywater is about ten minutes by cab from the Esplanade boundary of the Quarter.

- Best *restaurant* picks are **Lucky Cheng's** and the **Quarter Scene** in the French Quarter and **Feelings** and **La Peniche** in the Faubourg Marigny.

- Best gay *nightlife* choices are **The Bourbon Pub/Parade Disco,** the **Golden Lantern, Good Friends, Café Lafitte in Exile, MRB (Mississippi River Bottom), Oz,** and **Rawhide 2010,** all in the French Quarter, and **Phoenix** in the Faubourg Marigny.

New Orleans has a network of services supporting the gay community. The following organizations will connect you with gay-friendly lodgings, help with travel arrangements and offer food and entertainment recommendations.

- **The Lesbian and Gay Community Center,** 2114 Decatur St. (☎ **504-945-1103;** http://lgccno.org/)

- **Big Easy Lodging** (☎ **800-368-4876** or 504-433-2563; Fax: 504-391-1903; www.crescentcity.com/fql/)

- **French Quarter Reservation Service** (☎ **504-523-1246;** www.neworleansreservations.com)

- **Gay New Orleans Online** (www.gayneworleans.com)

Part II
Ironing Out the Details

The 5th Wave   By Rich Tennant

WHY PILOTS DON'T DRESS FOR MARDI GRAS BEFORE FLIGHTS

"That was a nasty patch of turbulence. I'd better go back and reassure the passengers."

In this part . . .

This part takes you through the various steps necessary to reach your ultimate goal — setting foot on New Orleans soil. You'll uncover the diverse options available to you, including using a travel agent, booking a package tour, and finding a super-secret airfare deal.

Of course, you'll need a place to stay once you arrive in the Crescent City, so this part also acquaints you with the different neighborhoods and lodging types. It gives you the scoop about booking a hotel room with tips on rack rates and where to find good deals. Feel free to run wild through this part's list of the city's fine, authentic, and efficient hotel choices. You also get the opportunity to tie up a few loose ends, such as the ins and outs of buying travel insurance, renting a car, making reservations, and even packing what you need for your trip. After all that, you'll be set for the next stop: New Orleans!

Chapter 5

Getting to New Orleans

. . . .

. . . .

So you're ready to come on down to the Crescent City? Before you pack your bags and throw on those Mardi Gras beads, you have to decide how to get here. Many people rush through this part of the process and end up paying for it later. But even if you know you want to fly, considering your many travel options before you book a flight can still pay off. This chapter covers the pros and cons of using a travel agent and of booking an escorted or package tour. It also mentions some things to keep in mind if you choose a more independent route, be it by plane, car, or even train.

Finding a Good Travel Agent

Word of mouth is your most valuable asset when looking for a travel agent — just like when searching for a good plumber, mechanic, or doctor. Any travel agent can find bargain airfares, hotels, or rental cars, but a good travel agent will stop you from ruining your vacation just to save a few bucks. The very best travel agents, on the other hand, can advise you on how much time to spend in one destination, find you a cheap flight that doesn't force you to change planes in Atlanta and Chicago, arrange for a competitively priced rental car, get you a better hotel room for about the same price, and even recommend a few good restaurants along the way. Doing a little homework — such as researching your destination and picking out some accommodations and attractions that interest you — will help you to get the most out of your travel agent.

You've already made a good start on your research just by picking up this book. If you feel you need even more choices than this book provides, check out *Frommer's New Orleans* (published by Wiley). If you have Internet access, look around the Web before going to your travel agent to get an idea of current airfare prices (see "Tips for getting the best airfare" later in this chapter). Armed with your guidebook and newly acquired Web information, visit your travel agent and ask him or her to arrange the trip for you.

Travel agents should manage to get you a better price than you can get by yourself because they can access more resources than even the most comprehensive Web site. They can also issue your tickets and vouchers right in the office. If your first-choice hotel is booked, they can provide you with alternatives. Feel free to come back to this book for an objective view before committing to a hotel, however.

Though travel agents work on commission, you don't pay that fee. Instead, the airlines, tour companies, and accommodations cover this cost. Unfortunately, this system leads some unscrupulous travel agents to push for certain vacations that net them the most money in commissions. However, some airlines and resorts have begun, over the past few years, to limit — or eliminate altogether — travel agent commissions. As a result, travel agents don't bother booking certain services unless a customer specifically requests them. Some travel agents have even started charging customers for their services.

Joining an Escorted Tour versus Traveling on Your Own

Do you prefer to sit in comfort while a tour guide explains everything to you and a bus driver worries about traffic? Or do you prefer renting a car and going where your whim takes you, even if you miss a few highlights? Do you like to improvise as you go or would you rather have someone plan your days for you in advance? Your answers to questions such as these determine whether you would most enjoy traveling on your own or as part of a guided tour.

Escorted tours fit some people like the proverbial glove. Tour companies take care of all the details and tell you what to see at each stop. Escorted tours also allow you to visit the maximum number of sights in the minimum amount of time with the least amount of hassle. Perhaps most importantly, you know your costs up front, and you won't stumble upon too many surprise fees.

Some people, on the other hand, need more freedom and spontaneity than a packaged tour provides. They like to discover and explore destinations alone. And if they get caught in a thunderstorm without an umbrella or discover that a recommended restaurant is closed, well, that's all just part of the adventure.

If you decide you want an escorted tour, think strongly about purchasing travel insurance, especially if the tour operator asks you to pay up front. But don't buy insurance from the tour operator! If the operator doesn't fulfill its obligation to provide you with the vacation you've paid for, it may not fulfill its insurance obligations either. Get travel insurance through an independent agency. See Chapter 9 for more information on travel and medical insurance.

Ask these few simple questions before deciding on an escorted tour:

- **What is the cancellation policy?** Do you have to pay a deposit? When is the latest you can cancel if you are unable to go? When do you have to pay? Can the operator cancel the trip if not enough people sign up? Do you get a refund if *you* cancel? Do you get a refund if *they* cancel?

- **How activity-oriented is the schedule?** Do the trip organizers try to cram 25 hours of fun into a 24-hour day? Will you have enough time to just relax by the pool or shop? Some escorted tours are not for you if the idea of getting up at 7 a.m. every day and not returning to your hotel until 6 or 7 p.m. at night makes you cringe.

- **What size is the tour group?** The larger the group, the more time you'll spend waiting for people to get on and off the bus — and the less time you'll have for seeing the sights. Tour operators may try to evade this question, because they may not know the exact size of the group until everybody has made their reservations. Nevertheless, they can give you a rough estimate.

  Another important reason for knowing the size of your tour group is that some tours require a minimum group size and may cancel the tour if not enough people sign on.

- **What exactly does the trip include?** Never assume anything. The tour may include a box lunch, but drinks may cost extra. A meal may include beer, but not wine. You may have to pay for transportation to and from the airport out of pocket. How much flexibility does the tour offer? Does the bus leave once a day, with no exceptions, or can you opt out of activities that don't interest you? Do the tour operators plan all your meals in advance? Does everyone get the same chicken cutlet for dinner, or can you choose your own entree?

A bit of judicious Web-surfing can yield a number of sites offering escorted New Orleans tours, such as New Orleans Tours (☎ **866-596-2698** or 504-592-1991; www.notours.com), which offers a variety of different packages, and Escape Holidays (www.escapeholidays.com). You can also find tours designed specifically for specialty groups; Menopausal Tours (☎ **866-468-8646;** www.menopausaltours.com), for example, caters specifically to groups of post-menopausal women.

Be aware that with escorted tours, you won't necessarily have a lot of say as to when you can take your trip. Most escorted tours adhere to a specific schedule, with a pre-determined start and end date, which will require you to plan your vacation around the tour, rather than vice-versa.

Choosing a Package Tour

Package tours differ from escorted tours; package tours are simply a way to buy your airfare and accommodations at the same time, without the uniformed tour guide thrown in. For popular destinations such as New Orleans, package tours are the smart way to go. In many cases, booking a hotel room on your own costs more than buying a package that includes airfare, hotel, and transportation to and from the airport. The prices in a package are so low because tour operators buy packages in bulk and then resell them to the public. The process is similar to buying your vacation at Sam's Club — except the tour operator is the one who buys the 1,000-count box of garbage bags and then resells them at a cost that undercuts the average neighborhood supermarket.

Like those hypothetical garbage bags, package tours can vary in quality. Some tours offer higher-class hotels than others do. Others offer the same hotels, but at lower prices. Some packages may limit your choice of accommodations and travel days. Some book charter flights, while others offer flights on scheduled airlines. Some offer both escorted and independent vacations; others allow you to add on just a few excursions or escorted day trips (also at discounted prices) without booking an entirely escorted tour.

For each destination, you can usually find one or two packagers that buy in even bigger bulk and offer better deals than the rest. Spend some time shopping around for the best package.

Finding a tour packager

The travel section of your local Sunday newspaper is a good place to start your search. Many tour packagers also advertise in the back of national travel magazines such as *Travel & Leisure, National Geographic Traveler,* and *Condé Nast Traveler.*

One of the biggest packagers in the Northeast, **Liberty Travel** (☎ **888-271-1584;** www.libertytravel.com) usually takes out a full-page ad in Sunday papers. Liberty's prices vary significantly depending on the time you travel and the hotel you pick. **American Express Vacations** (☎ **800-346-3607;** http://travel.americanexpress.com/travel/) is another option for good deals, including last-minute travel bargains.

The following sections offer some additional travel package resources for you.

Airline packages

The airlines themselves are a good resource because they often package flights with accommodations. Choose an airline on which you accumulate frequent flyer miles and that offers frequent service to your hometown. By buying your package through the airline, you can avoid disreputable packagers (which, while uncommon, do exist). You can get airline packages from **American Airlines Vacations** (☎ 800-321-2121; www.aavacations.com), **Continental Airlines Vacations** (☎ 888-898-9255; www.coolvacations.com), **Delta Vacations** (☎ 800-872-7786; www.deltavacations.com), and **US Airways Vacations** (☎ 800-455-0123; www.usairwaysvacations.com).

Train packages

If you're interested in traveling by train, check into the options offered by **Amtrak Vacations** (☎ 877-YES-RAIL [937-7245]; www.amtrak.com/services/vacations.html). They offer some standard hotel options and amenities such as car rental, as well as allow you the option of booking a return *flight* instead of going home by rail.

Hotel packages

If you already know where you want to stay, check with that hotel or resort to find out whether they offer land/air packages. Most of the biggest hotel chains, resorts, and casinos do. **Harrah's New Orleans Casino** (☎ 800-HARRAHS), for example, offers packages with lodging in many downtown hotels (unlike most casinos, the New Orleans Harrah's is not connected to any one particular hotel) for members of its Total Rewards program.

Internet packages

The Internet boasts some valuable sites for package shoppers. One comprehensive site is **Vacation Packager** (www.vacationpackager.com), an on-line clearinghouse for package companies. Input your desired destination and, if you like, select a type of activity you want to pursue on your vacation — from gambling to golf to archaeology to art festivals. The site then gives you a list of packagers specializing in the area and/or activities you've listed.

Evaluating the New Orleans packagers

Obviously, because New Orleans is an extremely popular vacation destination, you'll find no shortage of package tours — and no two are exactly alike (at least in terms of price). Some tours cater to those who want to be left to their own devices, while others target people who want a helping hand in searching out the local color. The following are just a few options:

 ✔ **Liberty Travel** (☎ 888-271-1584; www.libertytravel.com) offers fairly bare-bones packages, which I liken to big-name hotel chains. Their packages are perfectly nice if you're just looking for a room, a cheap airline ticket, and maybe an attraction or two.

✔ If you want a package tour with a bit more character, consider **Destination Management, Inc.** (DMI) (☎ **888-670-4638** or 504-524-5030; www.dmineworleans.com/dmi.htm). If Liberty Travel is like a generic, nationwide motor lodge, DMI is more like a small, independent hotel. Not a mom-and-pop establishment, mind you, but a place that offers better atmosphere and service than the national chains. DMI is a New Orleans–based company specializing in (what else?) New Orleans–specific vacation packages. DMI's packages center around different attractions and seasonal events, including Jazz Fest, Mardi Gras, the New Orleans Saints, Halloween — you name it, they've got a package for it.

✔ Last, but by no means least, **Festival Tours International** (☎ **310-454-4080;** www.gumbopages.com/festivaltours) offers a Jazz Fest tour. To further the hotel analogy, this tour is like the homey, bed-and-breakfast of New Orleans packages, with five-star service thrown in for good measure. The brainchild of Nancy Covey, this tour has atmosphere, character, culture, and slice-of-life authenticity. Unlike other packages for the New Orleans Jazz and Heritage Festival, the culture and heritage on this trip doesn't stop when you leave the event site. Covey also takes you on an insider's tour of Cajun Country, where you brush up against musicians currently stoking the musical fires of the region.

Making Your Own Arrangements

If you're the independent type who wants to create a more personal Crescent City adventure, go for it! This section helps those who want to fly solo (or with a friend) find the best deals on airfare.

Flying In

All the major airlines fly to New Orleans's Louis Armstrong International Airport (airline code MSY, for those of you booking on the Web), among them **American Airlines** (☎ **800-433-7300;** www.aa.com), **Continental** (☎ **800-525-0280;** www.continental.com), **Delta** (☎ **800-221-1212;** www.delta.com), **Northwest** (☎ **800/225-2525;** www.nwa.com), **Southwest** (☎ **800-435-9792;** www.southwest.com), and **US Airways** (☎ **800-428-4322;** www.usairways.com). The airport is in Kenner, 15 miles west of the city.

Tips for getting the best airfare

Competition among the major U.S. airlines is unlike that of any other industry. A coach seat's intrinsic value remains virtually the same from one carrier to another, yet the difference in price may run as high as $1,000.

Some people (business travelers, for example) pay the full airfare because they need the flexibility to change itineraries at a moment's notice, to purchase tickets at the last minute, or simply to get home before the weekend. You should be able to get your tickets for a fraction of this price, however, if you book long in advance, don't mind staying over Saturday night, or are willing to travel on a Tuesday, Wednesday, or Thursday. If you buy a 7-day or 14-day advance ticket, you can get your ticket for $200 to $300. Compare that price with the nearly $1,000 price tag on most flights — even the shortest hops. Obviously, planning ahead pays off in the end.

Periodically, airlines hold sales in which they lower prices on their most popular routes. Although these sales require advance purchase and enforce date-of-travel restrictions, you just can't beat the price — usually no more than $400 for a cross-country flight. Airlines tend to hold these sales during seasons of low travel volume, not in the peak summer vacation months of July and August, or around Thanksgiving or Christmas. Keep your eyes open for these sales as you plan your vacation.

Checking out consolidators

You'll see ads for *consolidators,* also known as bucket shops, in the small boxes at the bottom of the page in your Sunday travel section. Consolidators buy seats in bulk from the airlines and then sell them back to the public at prices below even the airlines' discounted rates. These prices are much better than the fares you can get yourself, and are often even lower than what your travel agent can get you. Some of the most reliable consolidators include **Cheap Tickets** (☎ **800-377-1000;** www.cheaptickets.com), **1-800-FLY-CHEAP** (www.flycheap.com), and **Travac Tours & Charters** (☎ **800-TRAV-800;** www.thetravelsite. com). **Council Travel** (☎ **800-226-8624;** www.counciltravel.com), which caters especially to young travelers, is another good choice. Despite the student angle, they do make their bargain-basement prices available to people of all ages.

Booking your travel online

You can also scour the Internet to find the cheapest fare. After all, searching through millions of pieces of data and returning information in rank order is what computers do best. Good thing, too, because the number of virtual travel agents on the Internet has increased exponentially in recent years.

Each travel-booking site has its own little quirks, but they all provide variations of the same service. Simply enter the cities you want to visit and the dates you want to fly, and the computer seeks out the lowest fares. The capability to check flights at different times or dates in hopes of finding a cheaper fare, e-mail alerts when fares drop on a route you have specified, and a database of last-minute deals that advertises super-cheap vacation packages or airfares for those who can get away at a moment's notice have all become standard features of these sites. Although the Internet holds too many travel booking sites to mention them all, a few of the most respected (and more comprehensive) ones include **Travelocity** (www.travelocity.com), **Expedia** (www.expedia.com), and **Yahoo Travel** (http://travel.yahoo.com).

The airlines themselves also offer great last-minute deals through free e-mail services called **E-savers.** Each week, you receive a list of discounted flights, which usually depart the upcoming Friday or Saturday and return the following Monday or Tuesday. Sign up with all the major airlines at one time by logging on to **Smarter Living** (www.smarterliving.com), or go to each individual airline's Web site. These sites offer schedules, flight booking, and information on late-breaking bargains.

- ✔ **American Airlines:** www.aa.com
- ✔ **Continental Airlines:** www.continental.com
- ✔ **Delta Airlines:** www.delta.com
- ✔ **Northwest Airlines:** www.nwa.com
- ✔ **Southwest Airlines:** www.southwest.com
- ✔ **US Airways:** www.usairways.com

Preparing for airport security

In the wake of the terrorist attacks of September 11, 2001, the airline industry implemented sweeping security measures in airports. Although regulations vary from airline to airline, you can expedite the process by taking the following steps:

- ✔ **Arrive early.** Arrive at the airport at least three hours before your scheduled flight.

- ✔ **Be sure to carry plenty of documentation.** A government-issued photo ID (federal, state, or local) is now required. You may need to show this at various checkpoints. With an E-ticket, you may be required to have with you printed confirmation of purchase, and perhaps even the credit card with which you bought your ticket. This varies from airline to airline, so call ahead to make sure you have the proper documentation.

- ✔ **Know what you can carry on — and what you can't.** Travelers on most airlines are now limited to one carry-on bag, plus one personal bag (such as a purse or a briefcase). The FAA frequently updates their list of restricted carry-on items at their Web site, www.faa.gov (click on "Security Tips for Air Travelers").

 ✔ **Prepare to be searched.** Expect spot-checks. Electronic items, such as a laptop or cellphone, should be readied for additional screening. Limit the metal items that you wear, such as heavy belt buckles or even underwire bras.

 ✔ **Don't make jokes.** When a check-in agent asks if someone other than you packed your bag, don't decide that this is the time to be funny. The agents will not hesitate to call an alarm.

Getting to New Orleans by Land

Of course, flying isn't everyone's cup of café au lait. Whether you're partial to ground-level scenery or just plain scared of heights, you may try driving or "training" to New Orleans.

Driving to New Orleans

New Orleans is easily accessible by car. Interstate 10 runs directly through the city from east to west, and just north of the city is Interstate 12, which also travels from east to west. From I-12, you can connect with the Lake Pontchartrain Causeway and drive south to I-10 directly in the metro area or connect with either I-55 to the west of the city or I-59 to the east of the city. Both I-55 and I-59 flow from north to south and connect with I-10. You can also access the city by U.S. highways 11, 51, 61, and 90. For help planning your route into the city, see the "Greater New Orleans" map on the inside front cover of this book.

Before you pack the trunk, however, keep this in mind: As far as sightseeing goes, New Orleans is not an easy driving city. Getting around the city isn't impossible, but at many tourist destinations, such as restaurants, nightclubs, or antiques shops, you have to fend for yourself for on-street parking. And in the French Quarter, on-street parking is as elusive as Shangri-La; even residents have perennial parking woes. In fact, finding free parking near most attractions is something of a crapshoot. Expensive commercial lots are readily available, but their locations are sometimes less than convenient.

Again, I don't want to discourage you or scare you off, especially if you have no other option. But be warned: If you drive into New Orleans (especially if you're staying in the French Quarter), you're better served to take public transportation around the Quarter and save your car for excursions outside of the district.

Riding the rails

An increasingly less popular, but still viable, option is to take to the rails. Call **Amtrak** (☎ **800-USA-RAIL** or 504-528-1610; www.amtrak.com) for specific information on train fares and schedules. Ask about senior-citizen discounts and other possible discounts when making a reservation.

Cruising into New Orleans

Don't laugh — New Orleans is all about indulging your wild side, your different streak. And taking a cruise ship into New Orleans is about as different a travel option as you can think of. (Not to mention the slow, luxurious nature of a sea cruise fits perfectly with the city's "big easy" reputation, and one of the city's most popular party tunes is the 1959 R&B hit "Sea Cruise," by local boy Frankie Ford. Coincidence? I think not.)

Seriously, though, once you've visited New Orleans, keep in mind that it is a major port city and thus is a stop for a number of cruise lines; if you miss a particular attraction during this trip, you can always catch it when your cruise ship stops here on your next major vacation. Or you could get really wacky and schedule a Caribbean cruise right in the middle of your New Orleans vacation. **Carnival** (www.carnival.com) and **Crystal** (www.crystalluxurycruises.com) lines, for example, make stops in or have cruises disembarking from New Orleans.

You'll usually disembark at the **Julia Street Cruise Ship Terminal;** if you decide to take a cruise from New Orleans — for example, on Carnival's *Holiday* or *Inspiration* — you'd board here, as well. The terminal was originally developed as part of the 1984 Louisiana World Exposition — only about five minutes on foot from the French Quarter. (For port information, call ☎ 504-522-2551.) Alternatively, many paddlewheel boats for upriver cruises and some southbound cruise ships depart from the **Robin Street Wharves.**

For more information on cruise ships as a vacation option, consider *Cruise Vacations For Dummies* (Wiley, Inc.), a handy guide to navigating the world of cruise ships. For more information on departing on a cruise from New Orleans, check out **Cruise Deals for Less** (☎ **800-330-1001** or 504-885-7245; www.cruisedealsforless.com).

Chapter 6

Deciding Where to Stay

. . . .

In This Chapter
▶ Uncovering your lodging choices
▶ Choosing the neighborhood that's right for you
▶ Knowing what you get for your money

. . . .

When it comes to lodging, many travelers simply look for the cheapest accommodations they can find. Or they choose a hotel that's central to everything (usually right on Bourbon Street), but end up paying twice as much as they have to.

To make a good all-around hotel choice that fits your needs, ask yourself what's most important to you. Is it saving money, being near the action, soaking up the city's spirit, or finding a comfortable oasis where you can unwind after a day of sightseeing? Whatever your preferences, this chapter helps you weigh your options by outlining the merits and disadvantages of staying in certain neighborhoods. It also gives you an idea of what you can expect to get, value-wise, for your dollar in New Orleans.

Picking the Place That Suits Your Style

Does a sleek, modern high-rise hotel with all the conveniences say "vacation" to you? Or do you prefer a cozy little guesthouse, with fresh muffins in the morning? Frankly, staying in an expensive "classy" hotel like you can find in just about any other city doesn't seem quite right for New Orleans (though the level of luxury at, say, the **Fairmont,** the **Windsor Court,** or **Le Pavillon** can feel appropriately sinful, if you can afford it). New Orleans demands a little more character — some of that frayed-around-the-edges mentality.

You won't have too much trouble finding atmosphere here — even in more modern areas of the city. Despite the annual influx of hundreds of thousands of visitors, New Orleans has managed to keep historic districts such as the French Quarter free of skyscraper development. The people of New Orleans have so faithfully preserved the Quarter's architectural style that determining whether a new hotel has been lovingly placed inside the shell of an older building or built from scratch isn't as easy as it sounds. Even motor hotels (which have helped alleviate the ever-present problem of on-street parking) maintain a distinctly New Orleans look.

Of course, the city does have some high-rise chain hotels, but you'll find them appropriately located in commercial sections, such as Uptown or the Central Business District. And many of them have been customized to blend in with the scenery. Whatever your preferences for a place to stay, New Orleans offers several options.

The chains: Tried and true

New Orleans has its share of national chain hotels, such as Holiday Inn, Hyatt, Marriott, Sheraton, Ramada, and Radisson. While these hotels tend to have a homogeneous, seen-one-you've-seen-'em-all quality, the best ones adapt to the color and flavor of New Orleans, both outside and inside. (Two good examples are the **Holiday Inn-Chateau LeMoyne** in the French Quarter and, to a lesser extent, the **Maison St. Charles Quality Inn** in the Lower Garden District; see these listings in Chapter 8.) These chain hotels usually attract business travelers with moderate expense accounts or families with children in tow. Many travelers prefer the consistency assured by a brand name. New Orleans features some fine chain hotels; Chapter 8 lists the best ones.

Boutique hotels: Quiet luxury

Independent hotels — also called boutique hotels — are smaller in scope. They can be family-run, mom-and-pop operations (such as the **Hotel Villa Convento** in the French Quarter), or part of a small group of hotels owned by the same company but not part of a cookie-cutter chain. Boutique hotels may target a specific niche, such as older travelers or budget-minded business travelers. They're also usually cheaper than the bigger chains (though this isn't a hard and fast rule). Independent hotels are good spots to soak up local character, but they often have fewer amenities than the chain hotels.

Motels and motor hotels: No frills

Motels are more or less like hotels, only stripped of the amenities. If you're willing to forego room service, a swimming pool, or atmosphere for a cheaper price, go with a motel. Of course, different types of motels exist — from the ubiquitous Motel 6 to seedy "no-tell motels" — but by and large, they're just places to crash. I don't recommend any lodging of this ilk in this book, concentrating instead on places with character and (usually) amenities, but you can find toll-free numbers for most of the major motel chains in any metropolitan phone book (and in this book's Appendix).

B&Bs and guesthouses:
The personal touch

Sure, some of your nicer hotels offer fine service. However, *service* and *hospitality* are not the same thing. For hospitality, head for a bed-and-breakfast (B&B). Breakfast — be it a full, belt-loosening extravaganza or (more likely) of the continental variety — is only part of the equation. After all, many hotels also offer a complimentary continental breakfast. So what sets a B&B apart? Basically, staying in a room in a B&B is a lot like being a guest in someone's home. In fact, most B&Bs *are* someone's home.

As with hotels, all B&Bs are not created equal. Some are renovated houses fully dedicated to visitors, with a small living space for the care-taker's family tucked discreetly away, and a communal kitchen where visitors socialize over breakfast. Some are lavish manses, with antique furniture and floor-to-ceiling picture windows. Such picturesque spots may offer an impressive breakfast spread and perhaps a glass of wine in the afternoon as part of the service. Generally, the more you pay, the higher the level of service and hospitality.

Of course, what's in a name and what's offered can sometimes be vastly different things. In point of fact, many places that *call* them-selves bed-and-breakfasts are actually closer to what Europeans call a *home stay* — residences that rent out extra bedrooms. That may sound all well and good, but chances are, they're neither licensed nor insured, which may not sound like a big deal until you have an accident on the stairs, or you can't find a fire extinguisher or a safe exit during a fire. When inquiring about a bed and breakfast, find out whether it belongs to the **Louisiana Bed and Breakfast Association.** All of this association's members are licensed, insured, and regularly inspected for fire safety, sanitation, and up-to-date insurance, among other concerns. Or you can call the LBBA yourself at ☎ **225-346-1857** to verify membership.

I mention a few choice B&Bs in Chapter 8, but if they interest you, call-ing a B&B reservation service is your best bet. The most reliable (and the most personable as well) is called, appropriately enough, **Bed and Breakfast, Inc. Reservation Service** (☎ **800-729-4640** or 504-488-4640; www.historiclodging.com). Other options are **Bed and Breakfast & Beyond** (☎ **800-886-3709** or 504-896-9977; www.nolabandb.com), **Bed & Breakfast and Accommodations** (☎ **888-240-0070** or 504-838-0071; www.neworleansbandb.com), and **Garden District Bed & Breakfast** (☎ **504-895-4302**).

Keep in mind that B&Bs are quite popular; regular visitors to Mardi Gras and Jazz Fest can reserve rooms up to a year in advance. So call early!

Similar to B&Bs are **guesthouses,** which are often closer in size and spirit to hotels, though the atmosphere is closer to a B&B. Like B&Bs,

native New Orleanians (or in some cases, visitors who never left) often preside over them and imbue them with a special brand of hospitality. Like B&Bs, they're often furnished with antiques and are heavy on the quaint old-world charm or cozy, homelike atmosphere. And yet again like B&Bs, guesthouses usually serve breakfast of some sort.

The difference between a B&B and a guesthouse comes down to size and, consequently, the level of service. In a B&B, you may be the only guest, or perhaps one out of six, and in intimate contact with its operators. A guesthouse, on the other hand, is often larger, and in all probability less intimate. Of course, that may be exactly what you're looking for: more intimacy than a hotel, but without having to actually talk to anyone while you're still waking up at breakfast. (At other times, the differences between a place calling itself a guesthouse and a B&B are indistinguishable; the proprietors probably just thought that the words "guesthouse" sounded better.)

The upper-crust hotels: Top of the line

You know what I'm talking about here: the cream of the crop, the five-star, super-swanky affairs that play host to world leaders, top-level rock stars, and captains of industry. The rooms are spacious and gorgeous, the staff impeccably dressed and unfailingly solicitous, and the restaurants first-rate. Needless to say, the luxurious surroundings and pampering accommodations come with a hefty price tag. But if you can afford it, these elegant hotels are worth every penny. I explore a few of these, including the relatively new **Ritz-Carlton New Orleans,** in Chapter 8.

Finding the Perfect Location

Although you probably have a specific image that comes to mind when someone mentions New Orleans, the truth is that the city has several different neighborhoods and different personalities to go with them. A series of small settlements and cities came together over time to form the New Orleans you see today. These neighborhoods retain their distinctive styles and characters.

The **French Quarter,** the **Central Business District,** and the **Garden District** represent the three main areas in which most visitors stay. You can find other options, however. The following neighborhoods should help you get an overview of the city. If you want a more detailed layout of the local neighborhoods and their boundaries (including a handy map), turn to Chapter 10.

The French Quarter

If you've never been to New Orleans, chances are the historic French Quarter is the image that you have for the city. Much of the city's action does take place here, and if you want easy access to Bourbon Street or places of historical interest, the French Quarter is exactly where you need to be. Nothing is far away as the whole section covers an area just 6 blocks wide by 13 blocks long. You'll find plenty of restaurants, shops, and sights. Unfortunately, you'll also find lots of other tourists. At least half of your fellow visitors will choose to stay there — and even those who don't will be milling around.

Because the French Quarter is New Orleans's most popular destination, and because of its relatively small size, rooms here will cost more. If you don't mind a bit of a walk or cab ride, find lodgings elsewhere and commute in to see the sights. Also, if you plan to focus your sightseeing on the Quarter, _not_ staying there may be a good idea. Many visitors to New Orleans never even leave the Quarter, which is like going to New York City and spending all your time in Greenwich Village or Times Square.

Bourbon Street

Everything I say about French Quarter lodging goes double for Bourbon Street, the center of New Orleans's party universe. Bourbon Street is pretty much a pressure-cooker of decadent, curious, and/or slumming tourists year-round (and especially during Mardi Gras). Personally, I don't recommend staying here unless you're coming to town for spring break, and you're not really planning on getting any sleep anyway. But if you're determined to stay here, you should keep a few things in mind.

- ✔ If you want to watch the free human show all night long, get a room with a balcony right on Bourbon Street — but be prepared to pay through the nose; after all, this is prime tourist real estate.

- ✔ Hotels on or near Bourbon Street will be noisy, and don't expect to get any sleep if you visit around Mardi Gras.

- ✔ The farther away from the intersection of Bourbon and Canal you get, the more reasonable hotel rates become.

- ✔ On the other hand, you have to be more careful at night the farther away from the center you get. Most hotels on the outskirts of the Quarter do have security guards, though.

The general rule about safety goes something like this — if you go north of Bourbon Street, away from the river, you enter increasingly dicey areas. Feel free to walk through these areas during the day, but take a taxi at night — particularly as you near the far border of the Quarter at Rampart Street, farther away from the crowds. You can find taxi stands throughout the Quarter.

In a nutshell, the French Quarter is right at the center of things, and getting from the Quarter to the rest of town is an easy trip. However, the Quarter can be very loud and overrun with tourists, especially on Bourbon Street.

Faubourg Marigny

Just outside the Quarter, on the other side of Esplanade Avenue, you'll find the Faubourg Marigny — a very small, very folksy neighborhood. Walking to Faubourg Marigny is easy from the Quarter, though I'd take a taxi at night. You won't find any big hotels in the Marigny, but this is the place to be if you enjoy small bed-and-breakfasts or guesthouses. Generally, the hotels closest to either Esplanade or the river have the safest locations. The Faubourg Marigny also houses the Frenchmen Street area, a small but percolating center of restaurants, music, and nightlife. Staying here does have a downside: Most of New Orleans's sights are a short walk away, and, of course, you'll have to learn how to pronounce "Faubourg Marigny" (FOE-berg MAR-a-nee).

The Central Business District

The Central Business District, which houses about 30 percent of the tourist population, is within convenient walking distance to the Quarter, the Superdome, and the Garden District. And it has readily available public transportation to the rest of the city. If you want to see Mardi Gras parades, this is the place to be — that is, if you don't mind the crowds. (If you do, Mardi Gras probably isn't your thing anyway.) Also, Canal Street features plenty of big-name shopping.

Although most hotels are located in sections that are quite safe, some are best reached at night by taxi. When traveling to and from the Quarter at night, you'll want to take a taxi, too. They're available at stands located near most of the major hotels.

The Garden District

You'll find one spectacular home after another in this, the most beautiful area in New Orleans. (Also keep your eyes peeled for one of Anne Rice's literary vampires or witches.) Take the St. Charles Streetcar for a picturesque ride through this quiet neighborhood to the Quarter (it lets you off on Canal Street at the entrance to Bourbon Street). You may not have all the big-name restaurants at your fingertips in this area, but you won't have drunken sailors howling at your window, either. What you will have is quick and convenient access to the Mardi Gras parades that trundle down St. Charles Avenue, and to great shopping along St. Charles and Magazine Street. I recommend taking a taxi at night, especially when returning from the Quarter. Many taxis regularly cruise the area, and some hotels even have taxi stands.

Mid-City

Because Mid-City is not really within walking distance of the Quarter or the city's major attractions, choosing to stay here is uncommon —

with one exception. If you come to New Orleans specifically for Jazz Fest, Mid-City provides the most convenient location to the Fair Grounds Race Course (where most of the events take place). For the other 50 non-Jazz-Fest weeks of the year, it's pretty far from the action (though City Park and New Orleans Museum of Art are nearby).

Uptown

New Orleans proper extends past the French Quarter to the Uptown area, upriver and past the Garden District. The Uptown area's northwest border forms the boundary between Orleans Parish and Jefferson Parish. If you don't have a car, staying in Uptown is not terribly convenient to most major attractions — and the Quarter is quite a long haul by foot. On the other hand, Tulane and Loyola universities are here, as is Audubon Park and Zoo. Therefore, this area could be your best bet if you're visiting a student or have an overwhelming passion for botany or zoology. It's a diverse, mostly residential area (wealthy homes coexist just a couple of blocks from less secure neighborhoods), with a good number of restaurants and shops. Here you'll find the Carrollton/Riverbend area, which boasts some very fine restaurants, and several parades wend their way through the streets during Mardi Gras. Uptown connects to the rest of the city via the St. Charles Streetcar and the Magazine bus.

Getting the Most for Your Money

Every recommended hotel in Chapter 8 uses dollar signs to help you zero in on your price limit. These symbols reflect the average of a hotel's high- and low-end rack rates. Room prices are subject to change without notice, so even the rates quoted in this book may be different than the actual rate you receive when you make your reservation. Don't be surprised if the rate you are offered is lower than the rack rates listed here; likewise, don't be alarmed if the price has crept up slightly.

Also, keep in mind that these dollar signs give broad guidelines, especially in terms of amenities. Just because two hotels charge the same rate — say, $150 a night — does not necessarily mean they both provide hair dryers, coffeemakers, and ironing boards.

> ✔ **$ (Under $75):** Accommodations at this price level may not be in the best neighborhoods, though exceptions do exist. To be safe, take a taxi to get to and from these places at night — and, in some cases, during the day. You can expect clean and relatively comfortable accommodations, though some may be on the, ah, worn side. You're likely to end up sharing a bathroom, and amenities such as telephones and televisions are a crapshoot. In some cases, the staff may not change the linen on a daily basis, so check to make sure. None of this matters anyway if you spend most of your time sightseeing.

✔ **$$ ($75–$125):** These hotels, like the really inexpensive places, are often located in marginal areas, so travel by taxi at night. Because the name of the game here is value, not luxury, don't let cracked and faded wallpaper surprise you. Room sizes may vary, but they'll be comfortable and sport amenities (telephones, private baths) that may be lacking in the previous category. You'll probably get a towel, a washcloth, and a small bar of soap, but don't expect a mint on your pillow.

✔ **$$$ ($125–$175):** The rooms are smaller than at more expensive hotels and the service aims to provide you with a nice, clean room in a safe, convenient location. Still, rooms in this category may feature some amenities usually associated with more expensive hotels. You won't have to worry about space (the rooms are comfortable), and cable TV is available, but higher-end amenities (such as hair dryers and coffeemakers) may be a question mark. The bathrooms are comfortably sized and clean. The hotel probably won't feature a restaurant, and if it does, it likely won't be of the fancy fine-dining variety. No doubt you'll find fewer conveniences, and you may have to buy any personal items from vending machines rather than just requesting them from the front desk. Also, room service (if it exists) will be slower than at fancier digs.

✔ **$$$$ ($175–$250):** Hotels with convenient locations, nice furnishings, and comfortably sized rooms fit in this category. These rooms include all the trappings of the most expensive hotels (uniformed doormen, nice furnishings, and so on), but to a lesser degree. You will see some conveniences, such as perhaps a Nintendo in every room, ironing boards along with your hair dryers, dataports for laptop computers, and maybe in-house video rentals or pay-per-view in addition to cable TV. On-site restaurants will be of a high quality, as well.

✔ **$$$$$ (Over $250):** These hotels, located in safe and convenient neighborhoods, are the cream of the crop. They offer huge rooms, elegant furnishings, and extremely comfortable bathrooms — probably larger than a regular room in a $-class hotel. Expect a mint on your freshly-turned-down bed each night. These hotels offer just about every luxurious amenity you can imagine — dataports, bathrobes, in-room video games, pay-per-view movies — though some will cost extra. You'll find individual bottles of shampoo, mouthwash, and other niceties in your room, and you may even have a minibar. These hotels will pamper you — but for a price. If the hotel includes a restaurant, you can bet it's among the best in town.

Chapter 7

Booking Your Room

*I*f you where in town you want to stay, you're ready to choose your Crescent City hotel. Before you devour the hotel listings in Chapter 8, however, you should know some of the ins and outs of booking your room. This chapter discusses rack rates and explains how you can avoid paying them. It also discusses various strategies for finding the best deal and lets you know what to do if you end up in New Orleans without a reservation.

Uncovering the Truth about Rack Rates

The maximum rate a hotel charges for a room is the rack rate. Basically, if you walk in off the street and ask for a room, this is the rate that will be quoted. Hotels will happily charge you this maximum, but don't be fooled — hardly anybody pays it. Sometimes the best way to avoid paying the rack rate is to simply ask for a cheaper or discounted rate. The response may pleasantly surprise you.

Getting the Best Room and Rate

Many factors influence the rate you pay for a room — chief among them being how you make your reservation. You can often get a better price with certain hotels if you make your reservations through a travel agent (because the hotel gives the agent a discount in exchange for steering his or her business toward that hotel). However, you don't have to use an agent to get the best deal. In addition to shopping around, which is always a wise idea, here are a few strategies you can use to help your vacation budget:

- ✔ **Call the hotel.** You may get a lower rate by making your reservation through a hotel's toll-free number rather than by calling the hotel directly. However, the central reservations people may be unaware of discount rates at specific locations. For example, a local franchise may not alert the central booking line about a special group rate for a family reunion or wedding party. To be safe, call both the local and toll-free numbers.

- ✔ **Consider a package tour.** If you're looking for a bargain, keep in mind package tours. Many of them offer deals for just travel and accommodations, so you're not locked into a rigid sightseeing itinerary. See Chapter 5 for information on package tours and some good packagers.

- ✔ **Visit in the off-season.** As occupancy rises and falls with the seasons, room rates also change. A hotel is less likely to offer discount rates if it's close to full. It may negotiate, however, if it's close to empty. In New Orleans, you'll probably find bargain rates during summer, though maybe not during the Southern Decadence festival or when a big convention descends on the town. But remember that the slowdown in summer tourism happens for a reason: Heat and humidity envelop the city.

The period between Thanksgiving and Christmas is another traditionally slow period. New Orleans can be quite pleasant at this time, especially if you're looking to avoid crowds. For more insight into seasonal and weather considerations, refer to Chapter 2.

- ✔ **Share a room with your children.** Keep your eyes peeled for hotels that let your kids stay for free in your room. Hotels may not be so quick to give you this perk, however, if your children are teenagers.

- ✔ **Ask about discounts, taxes, and service charges.** When booking a room, whether directly or through a packager, remember to take into account hotel taxes (which add almost 12 percent to your final bill) and such ill-defined fees as "occupancy rates" and other charges (see Chapter 3). If you're booking a room online, calling the hotel's toll-free number (if it has one) to double-check these charges is a good idea. If you're a member of AAA, AARP, frequent flyer programs, or any other corporate rewards program, remember to mention your membership when you get your quote — membership may shave a few dollars off your room rate.

After you make your reservation, one or two more pointed questions can go a long way toward making sure you have the best room available. You may want to request a **corner room,** as they're usually quieter, larger, and closer to the elevator; contain more windows and light than standard rooms; and don't always cost more. Also, make sure to request a room away from any renovation work, restaurants, bars, and dance clubs to make sure their noise doesn't keep you awake at night. If your room fails to satisfy you, ask at the front desk about changing rooms. They should be happy to accommodate you, within reason.

A word about smoking

If smoke bothers you, ask for a non-smoking room. If allergies, asthma, or some other condition make even the residue of smoke a problem, specify that you want a room in which smoking is *never* allowed. Most large hotels designate several rooms (or even an entire wing or floor) in which smoking is strictly forbidden.

In fact, as society's stance toward smoking has changed over the years, the number of people requiring smoking rooms has gradually decreased to where it's no longer the norm: If you need a room that allows smoking, you're much better off asking for one than assuming otherwise.

Strategies for travelers with disabilities

Not all hotels, especially older ones, meet governmental access regulations. Unfortunately, most hotels in New Orleans are older. B&Bs, small hotels, and budget hotels may also neglect the regulations. Some hotels, however, maintain special facilities (such as roll-in showers, lower sinks, and extra space in which to move around) for folks who need them. Make sure to ask for one of these accessible rooms when you make your reservation. Some chains (such as Hilton) have accessible rooms in all their hotels. Chapter 8 lists hotels that are especially good for people with disabilities. Also, see Chapter 4 for more information for travelers with special needs.

Surfing the Web for Hotel Deals

Though the major travel booking sites (such as Travelocity, Expedia, and Yahoo! Travel; see Chapter 5 for details) offer hotel booking, a Web service devoted primarily to lodging may find properties that aren't listed on more general online travel agencies. For example, some lodging sites specialize in a particular type of accommodation, such as bed-and-breakfasts, which you won't find on the more mainstream booking services. Others, such as TravelWeb, offer weekend deals on major chain properties that cater to business travelers and have more empty rooms on weekends.

> ✔ **All-Hotels** (www.all-hotels.com), though something of a misnomer, does have tens of thousands of listings throughout the world. Bear in mind that each hotel has paid a small fee ($25 and up) to be listed, so it's less an objective list and more like a book of online brochures.

✔ **Hotels.com** (www.hotels.com) lists bargain room rates at hotels in more than 50 U.S. and international cities. The cool thing is that Hotels.com pre-books blocks of rooms in advance, so sometimes it has rooms — at discount rates — at hotels that are officially "sold out." This site is notable for delivering deep discounts in cities where hotel rooms are expensive. You can find the toll-free number all over the site (☎ **800-2-HOTELS**), so call it if you want more options than the Web site lists.

✔ **InnSite** (www.innsite.com) offers B&B listings in all 50 states and more than 50 countries around the globe. You can find an inn at your destination, see pictures of the rooms, and check prices and availability. This extensive directory of bed-and-breakfasts includes listings only if the proprietor submitted one (getting an inn listed is free). The innkeepers write the descriptions, and many listings link to that inn's own Web site. Try also **BedandBreakfast.com** (www.bedandbreakfast.com).

✔ **Places to Stay** (www.placestostay.com) lists one-of-a-kind places in the United States and abroad that you may not find in other directories, with a focus on resort accommodations. Again, listing is selective. The directory may not be comprehensive, but it can give you a sense of what's available at different destinations.

✔ **TravelWeb** (www.travelweb.com) lists more than 26,000 hotels in 170 countries, focusing on chains such as Hyatt and Hilton — 90 percent of which you can book online. TravelWeb's Click-It Weekends, updated each Monday, offers weekend deals at many leading hotel chains.

No Room at the Inn?

Okay, assume that, through circumstances beyond your control, you are suddenly plopped down in New Orleans without a hotel reservation. Don't panic. Unless Mardi Gras, Jazz Fest, or one of the other larger, room-hogging events is taking place, you'll likely find several hotels with available space. First, look through the listings in Chapter 8 for hotels that strike your personal and financial fancy, and start calling them. If that doesn't yield results, you have a few options:

✔ Call **Turbotrip.com** (☎ **800-473-STAY**), the **French Quarter Reservation Service** (☎ **800-523-9091** or 504-523-1246), or one of the bed-and-breakfast agencies listed in Chapter 6.

✔ If you're stranded at one of the major French Quarter hotels and it's full, ask if they'll check around for you and see what other rooms are available. If they won't, check your luggage with them in case someone cancels a reservation while you check around on your own.

✔ Start dialing your way through the Yellow Pages, using a hotel house phone or a pay phone.

Chapter 8

New Orleans's Best Hotels

. . . .

In This Chapter

▶ Finding the hotel you want — by price and location

▶ Running down the list of the best hotels in the city

▶ Considering a few more hotel options

. . . .

This chapter offers the meat and potatoes of this part — individual hotel listings. Beginning with my reviews of these hotels (and a few bed-and-breakfasts and guest houses), I give you the information you need to make a decision on where to stay in New Orleans. I also include a list of recommended "runner-up" hotels, as well as a couple of handy indexes at the end of the chapter that list my recommended hotels by neighborhood and price.

Watch for the Kid Friendly icon, which points out those hotels that are especially good for families. The listings also note other special considerations, such as which hotels accommodate disabled travelers, which places are the most gay-friendly, which are good if you're in the mood for love, which are close to a Mardi Gras parade route, and so on.

Disabled travelers please take note: Hotels listed as wheelchair accessible may offer only a small number of these rooms, so ask about availability when you make your reservation. Also, "wheelchair accessible" does not necessarily mean that the hotel is up to the standards of the Americans with Disabilities Act — the hotel may just be accessible from the street and have an elevator and wide doorways. I try to include any special information about steps, bathroom accessibility, or other access concerns.

Keep track of the reviews that appeal to you as you read through them. Now is the time to rebel against all those teachers who told you not to write in your books by putting a check mark next to any hotel listing that you like.

French Quarter Accommodations

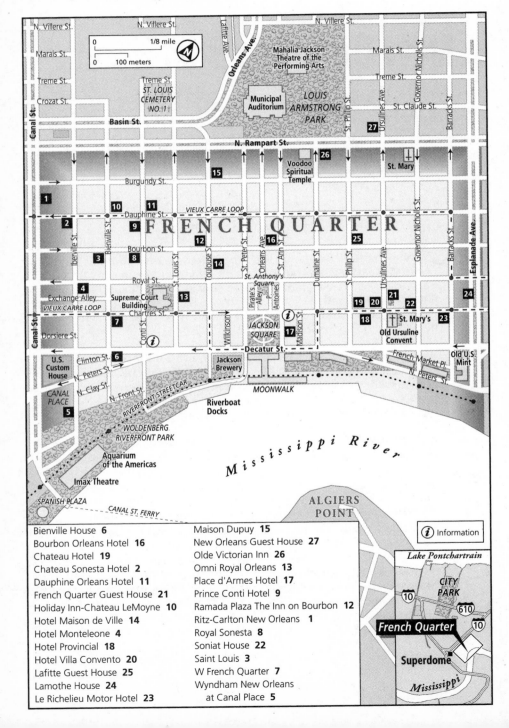

Bienville House **6**
Bourbon Orleans Hotel **16**
Chateau Hotel **19**
Chateau Sonesta Hotel **2**
Dauphine Orleans Hotel **11**
French Quarter Guest House **21**
Holiday Inn-Chateau LeMoyne **10**
Hotel Maison de Ville **14**
Hotel Monteleone **4**
Hotel Provincial **18**
Hotel Villa Convento **20**
Lafitte Guest House **25**
Lamothe House **24**
Le Richelieu Motor Hotel **23**

Maison Dupuy **15**
New Orleans Guest House **27**
Olde Victorian Inn **26**
Omni Royal Orleans **13**
Place d'Armes Hotel **17**
Prince Conti Hotel **9**
Ramada Plaza The Inn on Bourbon **12**
Ritz-Carlton New Orleans **1**
Royal Sonesta **8**
Soniat House **22**
Saint Louis **3**
W French Quarter **7**
Wyndham New Orleans
  at Canal Place **5**

New Orleans's Top Hotels from A to Z

Ambassador Hotel
$–$$$$$ Central Business District

Located in the Central Business District, the Ambassador strikes a nice balance between old-world charm and modern convenience, with a slightly artsy feel. High ceilings and exposed brick walls and beams make you feel as if you're staying in a much more expensive hotel. Room sizes are very good; bathrooms are quite spacious. In-room Nintendo and convenience to a host of French Quarter attractions (Aquarium of the Americas, Louisiana Children's Museum) make it a good bet for kids as well.

535 Tchoupitoulas St., New Orleans, LA 70130. ☎ *888-527-5271 or 504-527-5271. Internet:* www.neworleans.com/ambassador. *Parking: $20. Rack rates: $49–$289. Children 18 and under free with parent. AE, DC, DISC, MC, V. Wheelchair accessible.*

Ashton's Bed & Breakfast
$$$–$$$$ Mid-City

This restored 1860s Greek revival mansion is located in a lovely setting along Esplanade Avenue. The French Quarter is 2 miles away, a distance not worth walking, so come with a car or cab fare. Recent restoration work carefully restored many of the original fixtures and woodwork, including a leaded-glass door window and black onyx and marble fireplace mantels. Guest rooms are quite large and comfortable.

2023 Esplanade Ave., New Orleans, LA 70116. ☎ *800-725-4131 or 504-942-7048. Fax: 504-947-9382. Internet:* www.ashtonsbb.com. *Parking: free. Rack rates: $149–$179 double (includes breakfast). AE, DC, DISC, MC, V. Call regarding wheelchair accessibility.*

B&W Courtyards Bed & Breakfast
$$–$$$ Faubourg Marigny

The service and ambience of this sweet, hospitable B&B may turn you off of chain hotels forever. The owners went to ingenious lengths to convert six oddly shaped spaces into appealingly quirky guest rooms. The four rooms and two suites are all completely different (you enter one of them through the bathroom). Though room size varies, the surroundings are uniformly beautiful with two small courtyards, a fountain, and a Jacuzzi, as well as a sundeck and self-serve laundromat. Breakfast is light, but beautifully presented. They take good care of you here.

2425 Chartres St., New Orleans, LA 70117. ☎ *800-585-5731 or 504-945-9418. Fax: 504-949-3483. Internet:* www.bandwcourtyards.com. *Parking: on-street available. Rack rates: $120–$175 double. AE, DISC, MC, V.*

New Orleans Accommodations

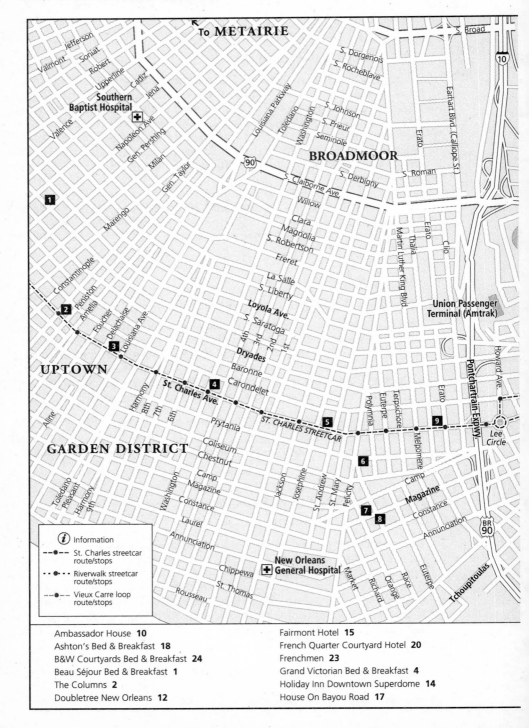

Ambassador House **10**
Ashton's Bed & Breakfast **18**
B&W Courtyards Bed & Breakfast **24**
Beau Séjour Bed & Breakfast **1**
The Columns **2**
Doubletree New Orleans **12**

Fairmont Hotel **15**
French Quarter Courtyard Hotel **20**
Frenchmen **23**
Grand Victorian Bed & Breakfast **4**
Holiday Inn Downtown Superdome **14**
House On Bayou Road **17**

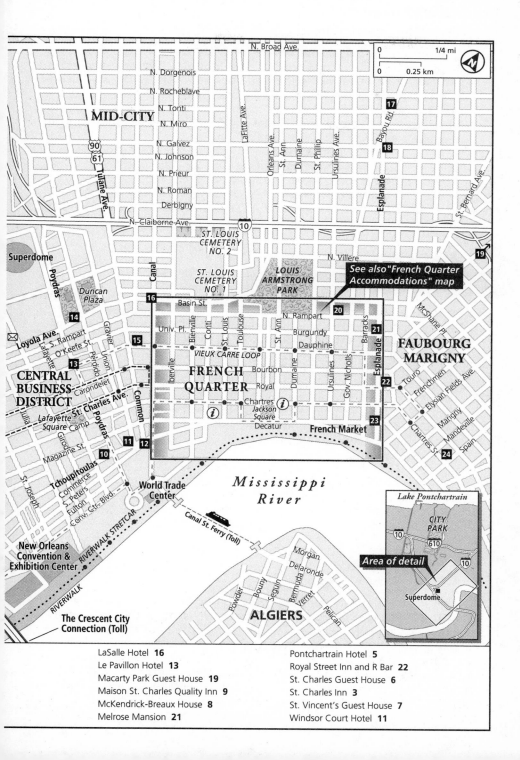

Bienville House
$$–$$$$$ **French Quarter**

This moderately priced hotel has the feel of a more expensive one, thanks in part to the antique and reproduction furniture. The elegant interior offers a striking contrast to the near-constant bustle of Decatur Street outside. Rooms are small but comfortable; some include small balconies that overlook a flagstone courtyard and pool area. Gamay, an upscale bistro featuring continental cuisine and New Orleans favorites, sits on the premises.

320 Decatur St. (4 blocks from Jackson Square), New Orleans, LA 70130. ☎ *800-535-9603 or 504-529-2345. Fax: 504-525-6079. Internet:* www.bienville house.com. *Valet parking: $11 cars; $15 sport utility vehicles. Rack rates: $89–$300 double (includes continental breakfast). AE, CB, DC, DISC, MC, V. Building and room entrances are wheelchair accessible; bathrooms are not.*

Bourbon Orleans Hotel
$$$–$$$$ **French Quarter**

Determining this lavish hotel's best feature is impossible. Is it the central location at the corner of Bourbon and Orleans, the historical pedigree, or the extravagantly decorated public spaces? The extravagance, by the way, extends to the rooms — you'll find Bath & Body Works shampoos and soaps in your bathroom, and you can order room service through your television. The double rooms are comfortable and bigger than average. The bi-level suites feature living rooms with pullout sofa beds that are good for children, who will also appreciate the hotel's outdoor pool. If possible, request a room closer to Royal Street and sidestep the clamor of Bourbon. The on-site restaurant offers good meals, and the elegant lobby features a nightly cocktail hour. Other amenities include high-speed Internet access.

717 Orleans St. (directly behind St. Louis Cathedral), New Orleans, LA 70116. ☎ *504-523-2222. Fax: 504-525-8166. Internet:* www.bourbonorleans.com. *Valet parking: $25. Rack rates: $139–$209 double. Extra person: $20. AE, CB, DC, DISC, MC, V. Wheelchair accessible.*

Chateau Hotel
$$–$$$ **French Quarter**

One of the best buys in New Orleans, this hotel sits far enough off Bourbon Street to be quiet and intimate, but is still within walking distance of virtually everything in the Quarter. Most of the rooms have antiques, giving the place a French provincial look. The rooms are a little on the dark side, but they're actually quite clean. The hotel includes a picturesque pool surrounded by a flagstone courtyard with chaise lounges. With your room fee you get a continental breakfast and newspaper. Seniors, be sure to ask about the 10 percent discount.

1001 Chartres St. (3 blocks from Jackson Square), New Orleans, LA 70116.
☎ *504-524-9636. Fax: 504-525-2989. Internet: www.chateauhotel.com. Parking: free. Rack rates: $89–$159 double. AE, CB, DC, MC, V. Wheelchair accessible, but no bars in the bathrooms.*

Chateau Sonesta Hotel
$$$–$$$$ French Quarter

Located in the former D. H. Holmes Department Store building — the 1913 facade has been retained — the Chateau Sonesta is one of the newest hotels in the Quarter. Despite the older exterior, the interior feels modern and luxurious. The rooms are large, if generic, and some feature balconies overlooking Bourbon Street. Among the noteworthy amenities are an outdoor pool, a beauty salon, and a health club. All rooms have minibars, and videos are available for rental. For those who can't escape their computers, the phones have dataports.

800 Iberville St. (at the corner of Dauphine St.), New Orleans, LA 70112. ☎ *800-SONESTA or 504-586-0800. Fax: 504-586-1987. Internet: www.chateausonesta.com. Parking: $20. Rack rates: $130–$249 double. Extra person: $40. AE, CB, DC, DISC, MC, V. Wheelchair accessible.*

The Columns
$$–$$$$ Uptown

Much like those elegant brothels of old, this place straddles the line between sophistication and seediness. Its columned porch (from whence comes the name) is a favorite meeting spot for locals, thanks to the bar inside, where jazz bands sometimes play during happy hour. The room size reminds you that this was a 19th-century home; some rooms are cozy in a way that suggests servants' quarters, while others are more expansive (one even has a private second-floor porch). Only the Pretty Baby Suite (named for the movie filmed here) features a televison, and some bathrooms contain both shower stalls and old-fashioned claw-foot tubs. All rooms, however, are clean and comfortable.

3811 St. Charles Ave. (halfway between Louisiana and Napoleon avenues), New Orleans, LA 70115. ☎ *800-445-9308 or 504-899-9308. Fax: 504-899-8170. Internet: www.thecolumns.com. Parking: on-street available. Rack rates: $110–$180 double (includes southern breakfast). AE, MC, V.*

Dauphine Orleans Hotel
$$$–$$$$$ French Quarter

This luxurious establishment is just the right blend of charming old-world history (ghosts have been sited on premises) and modern elegance, well removed from the madness of Bourbon Street. Lounge in one of the secluded courtyards or read for a spell in the guest library. A recent renovation provided the stately rooms with new furnishings and marble bathrooms. Among the eyebrow-raising amenities are a 24-hour fitness room, Nintendo for the kids, a Jacuzzi, an in-room safe for valuables, and complimentary French Quarter transportation. The staff can also hook you up with a baby-sitting service. Continental breakfast is served until 11 a.m., and complimentary tea is served every afternoon.

415 Dauphine St., New Orleans, LA 70116. ☎ *800-508-5554 or 504-586-1800. Fax: 504-586-1409. Internet:* www.dauphineorleans.com. *Valet parking: $15. Rack rates: $149–$359 double. Extra person: $15. Children under 17 free in parents' room. AE, CB, DC, DISC, MC, V. Wheelchair accessible.*

Doubletree Hotel New Orleans
$$–$$$$ **Central Business District**

Located at the foot of Canal Street, the Doubletree offers great views of the bustling Central Business District and the river. Sure, it's part of a chain, but the atmosphere is muted, pleasant, and elegant all at once. Rooms are good-sized and comfortable; bathrooms are adequate. The hotel even features a rooftop pool that the kids will enjoy, as well as a fitness center. You'll also find a nice restaurant and a breakfast cafe on the first floor. The kicker for your small fry: Nintendo in every room and delicious chocolate-chip cookies when you check in. (They're so good, you may not want to share them with the kids.)

300 Canal St., New Orleans, LA 70130. ☎ *888-874-9074 or 504-581-1300. Fax: 504-212-3315. Internet:* www.doubletreeneworleans.com. *Parking: valet, $22; self-parking next door at Harrah's Casino. Rack rates: $79–$229 double. Extra person: $20. AE, DC, DISC, MC, V. Wheelchair accessible.*

Fairmont Hotel
$$–$$$$$ **Central Business District**

Hands down, this is one of the most elegant hotels in town. Given such amenities as a high-class restaurant, rooftop pool, workout area, and beauty shop, you may never want (or need) to leave. The hotel offers a lot of local lore: Huey Long used to hold court in the Sazerac bar on the first floor (see Chapter 24 for more information on this respected gathering place). The rooms are as beautiful as you may expect for the price, and each one has its own fax machine for business travelers. A bonus for the tykes: Each room has Nintendo gear.

123 Baronne St., New Orleans, LA 70112. ☎ *800-441-1414 or 504-529-7111. Fax: 504-522-2303. Internet:* www.fairmont.com/neworleans. *Valet parking: $19. Rack rates: $99–$299 double. Children under 18 free in parents' room. AE, DC, DISC, MC, V. Wheelchair accessible.*

Frenchmen
$$–$$$ **Faubourg Marigny**

This friendly inn, which occupies two 19th-century buildings that were once grand New Orleans homes, enjoys loyal repeat business from those who've fallen for its slightly funky charms. Rooms vary in size; some are downright tiny (if that's important, ask about size when making a reservation). Some rooms have private balconies; others are loft bedrooms with a sitting area. All are individually decorated and furnished with antiques. A tropical courtyard features a pool and hot tub.

417 Frenchmen St. (across the street from the Old U.S. Mint on Esplanade), New Orleans, LA 70116. ☎ *888-365-2877 or 504-948-2166. Fax: 504-948-2258. Internet:* www.french-quarter.org. *Valet parking: $20. Rack rates: $79–$155 double (includes breakfast). AE, DISC, MC, V.*

French Quarter Courtyard Hotel
$$–$$$$$ **Central Business District**

Despite the name, the courtyard isn't the best thing about this place (though with its black fountains and grotto-like swimming pool, it is nice). The atmosphere here clinches the deal, from the large staircase that greets you upon entering to the understated look of the rooms. Exposed red brick walls, antique-reproduction beds, and hardwood floors add up to a pleasant environment and decent approximation of old-style New Orleans charm squeezed into a modern hotel setting.

1101 N. Rampart St. (a few blocks from the Quarter), New Orleans, LA 70116. Call ☎ *800-290-4233 or 504-522-7333. Fax: 504-522-3908. Internet:* www.neworleans. com/fqch. *Valet parking: $12. Rack rates: $119–$289 double. Extra person: $10. Children 18 and under free with parent. AE, DC, DISC, MC, V. Wheelchair accessible.*

Grand Victorian Bed & Breakfast
$$$–$$$$$ **Uptown**

The name pretty much sums up this elegant bed-and-breakfast; the appointments here are grand, indeed. Famed New Orleans architect Thomas Sully designed the house in 1893, and the proprietors have gone to great lengths to restore the house to its original glory. A bountiful continental breakfast is offered either in the dining room or on the porte-cochere balcony. The rooms vary in size, but are uniformly elegant with handsome antique furniture. Business travelers can avail themselves of fax and copy machines, as well as dataports for computers.

2727 St. Charles Ave., New Orleans, LA 70130. ☎ *800-977-0008 or 504-895-1104. Fax: 504-896-8688. Internet:* www.gvbb.com. *Parking: some on-street parking. Rack rates: $150–$300 double (includes breakfast; rates higher during special events). Extra person: $25. AE, DISC, MC, V. Wheelchair accessible.*

Holiday Inn–Chateau LeMoyne
$$$–$$$$ **French Quarter**

In contrast to its cousin in the Central Business District, this Holiday Inn sports an abundance of New Orleans–style character. Although the buildings are more than a century old (some of the rooms overlooking the courtyard are converted slave quarters), the historic ambience doesn't extend to the guest rooms, which are more or less standard for the chain, although comfortable. It's just around the corner from Bourbon Street, but nonetheless removed from the noise of the Quarter and convenient to Canal Street. The restaurant serves breakfast only, but you can order room service until 10 p.m. No video games in the rooms, but an outdoor heated pool and proximity to French Quarter attractions like the Aquarium of the Americas make this a good spot for the small fries.

301 Dauphine St. (just around the corner from the Deja Vu Bar & Grill), New Orleans, LA 70112. ☎ *800-747-3279 or 504-581-1303. Fax: 504-523-5709. Internet:* www.six continentshotels.com/holiday-inn. *Valet parking: $19. Rack rates: $159–$244 double. Extra person: $20. AE, CB, DC, DISC, MC, V. Wheelchair accessible.*

Holiday Inn Downtown Superdome
$$–$$$$ **Central Business District**

Accessibility is the key word when describing this hotel. Conveniently close to the Superdome and New Orleans Arena, it's a good bet for sports fans. It's also close to the city's business and financial centers, and not too far from the French Quarter (though probably farther than you'd want to walk, especially at night). Each room has a balcony and a city view, but they're standard size for the chain and decorated in typical Holiday Inn style (not that there's anything wrong with that). The hotel also features a heated pool on the roof. In-room Nintendos and movies make this a good bet for kids.

330 Loyola Ave. (across from the Louisiana Supreme Court building), New Orleans, LA 70112. ☎ *800-535-7830 or 504-581-1600. Fax: 504-522-0073. Internet:* www. holidayinndowntownsuperdome.com. *Parking: $11. Rack rates: $94–$209 double. Extra person: $15. Children 18 and under free in parents' room. AE, CB, DC, DISC, MC, V. Wheelchair accessible.*

Hotel Maison de Ville
$$$$ **French Quarter**

The Maison de Ville blends the charm and size of a B&B with the service and elegance of a five-star hotel. Antiques are abundant, and a beautiful courtyard welcomes you with a fountain and banana trees. The rooms vary in size (some are downright tiny), so ask about this when you call, as price is no indication of what you'll get. In-room amenities include bathrobes, hair dryers, and other standard fare; two-bedroom cottages and suites have coffeemakers. Continental breakfast is served on a silver tray in your room, in the parlor, or on the patio; and complimentary sherry and port are served in the afternoon and evening.

727 Toulouse St. (½ block from Bourbon St.), New Orleans, LA 70130. ☎ 800-634-1600 or 504-561-5858. Fax: 504-528-9939. Internet: www.maisondeville. com. *Valet parking: $18. Rack rates: $215–$225 double (includes continental breakfast and afternoon service of port and sherry). AE, DC, MC, V.*

Hotel Monteleone
$$$$ **French Quarter**

The largest and oldest hotel in the Quarter, the Hotel Monteleone is one of the best big hotels in New Orleans. The rooms come in a variety of styles, from smaller spaces to modern and comfortable family rooms to plush, antique-filled suites. You can likely find a room here even when the rest of the city is booked. The hotel is famous for its extravagant lobby as well as for the revolving Carousel Bar, with its pleasant view of Royal Street. Laundry, a fitness center, and a baby-sitting service top a list of amenities that also includes a heated rooftop pool and a hot tub. Often voted the city's most romantic hotel.

214 Royal St. (at the corner of Iberville), New Orleans, LA 70130. ☎ 800-535-9595 or 504-523-3341. Fax: 504-528-1019. Internet: www.hotelmonteleone.com. *Valet parking (space is limited): $15. Rack rates: $189–$230 double. Extra person: $25. Children under 18 are free in their parents' room. AE, CB, DC, DISC, MC, V.*

Hotel Provincial
$$–$$$$$ **French Quarter**

Nestled into a series of 19th-century buildings, Hotel Provincial's atmosphere (including flickering gas lamps) makes it feel smaller and more intimate than it really is, more like a guesthouse than a hotel. Rooms have the high ceilings of an earlier age and are decorated with French and Creole antiques. The hotel is located in a quiet stretch of the French Quarter, so you can wind down in peace after a day of sightseeing. Local ghost hunters swear this place is haunted because it was used as a hospital during the Civil War.

1024 Chartres St. (4 blocks from Jackson Square), New Orleans, LA 70116. ☎ 800-535-7922 or 504-581-4995. Fax: 504-581-1018. Internet: www.hotelprovincial. com. *Valet parking: $13. Rack rates: $99–$289 double. AE, CB, DC, DISC, MC, V. Wheelchair accessible.*

House on Bayou Road
$$$–$$$$$ **Mid-City**

Stepping into the luxurious quiet and elegance of this 18th-century home is like entering a time machine. The rooms and two cottages are individually decorated with antiques. The smaller cottage, which has a queen-size bed, queen sleeper sofa, and hot tub, is a perfect romantic getaway. The staff serves a complimentary full plantation breakfast, and guests can help themselves to beverages in a mini-refrigerator throughout the day.

The house occasionally offers public cooking classes, for which guests receive a discount.

2275 Bayou Rd. (1 mile from the Quarter along Esplanade; turn right at Bayou Road), New Orleans, LA 70119. ☎ *800-882-2968 or 504-945-0992. Fax: 504-945-0993. Internet:* www.houseonbayouroad.com. *Parking: Free. Rack rates: $135–$320 double (includes breakfast). AE, MC, V.*

Lafitte Guest House
$$$–$$$$ French Quarter

This erratically charming guesthouse is conveniently located on the quiet end of Bourbon Street, only a quick walk away from the action. Built in 1849, the three-story brick building features wrought-iron balconies on the second and third floors (the outside has been completely restored and looks great). Most rooms sport a Victorian air, though some are more modern than others. Rooms vary in size; the penthouse suite (room 40) takes up the entire third floor and accommodates up to six people. Breakfast is brought to your room in the morning, and guests are invited to snack on wine and cheese for a "social" in the parlor in the afternoon. Dry cleaning and baby-sitting are also available.

1003 Bourbon St. (at the corner of St. Philip), New Orleans, LA 70116. ☎ *800-331-7971 or 504-581-2678. Fax: 504-581-2677. Internet:* www.lafitteguest house.com. *Parking: $10. Rack rates: $159–$219 double (includes breakfast). Extra person: $25. AE, DC, DISC, MC, V.*

Lamothe House
$–$$$$$ French Quarter

If you don't like the shiny, homogenized feel of a chain hotel, the slightly faded, threadbare ambience of this place may be up your alley. Even the name suggests a Dickensian air of moth-eaten mustiness. A plain Creole-style facade belies the interior, which boasts a mossy, brick-lined court-yard with a fish-filled fountain and banana trees; you'll also find a swimming pool and hot-tub spa. The rooms, decorated with antiques, are worn in the right places, but not shabby. Room sizes vary according to price, so ask when reserving.

621 Esplanade Ave., New Orleans, LA 70116. ☎ *800-367-5858 or 504-947-1161. Fax: 504-943-6536. Internet:* www.new-orleans.org. *Parking: free. Rack rates: $64–$275 double (includes continental breakfast). AE, DISC, MC, V.*

Le Pavillon Hotel
$$–$$$$$ Central Business District

A unique blend of 17th-century grandeur and modern appointments makes this a truly elegant hotel. The lobby is a dazzling array of chandeliers, Oriental rugs, and detailed woodwork. Rooms of varying sizes feature original artwork and European and American antiques. Services include 24-hour room service, concierge, baby-sitting, laundry and dry cleaning, and a complimentary shoe shine. You can indulge yourself in complimentary hors d'oeuvres on weekday afternoons in the Gallery lounge, or peanut-butter-and-jelly sandwiches served with milk in the lobby each evening. Other amenities include a heated pool on the roof, a fitness center, and a whirlpool spa.

833 Poydras St., New Orleans, LA 70112. ☎ *800-535-9095 or 504-581-3111. Fax: 504-522-5543. Internet:* www.lepavillon.com. *Valet parking: $25. Rack rates: $105–$425 double. AE, CB, DC, DISC, MC, V. Wheelchair accessible.*

Le Richelieu Hotel
$$–$$$$ French Quarter

Le Richelieu, located on the Esplanade edge of the Quarter, offers convenience and tranquil old-world charm. Balconies overlooking the street or courtyard and pool accompany many rooms. You can order breakfast and lunch in the courtyard from the small in-house restaurant, or you can eat in the lounge adjacent to the pool. All rooms come with hair dryers, irons and ironing boards, and refrigerators. If you really want to go first class, ask for the VIP suite with its three bedrooms, kitchen, living area, dining area, and steam room. One of the nicest hotels in the Quarter in its price range, it's also the only hotel in the Quarter that offers free self-parking.

1234 Chartres St. (6 blocks from Jackson Square or 1 block from Esplanade), New Orleans, LA 70116. ☎ *800-535-9653 or 504-529-2492. Fax: 504-524-8179. Internet:* www.lerichelieuhotel.com. *Parking: free. Rack rates: $95–$180 double. Extra adult or child: $15. AE, CB, DC, DISC, MC, V.*

Maison Dupuy
$$–$$$$ French Quarter

This picturesque hotel, made up of several town houses, has been the site of a cotton press (the first in the U.S.), a blacksmith shop, and a sheet metal works. Today, it blends the clockwork efficiency of a large hotel with the attentive service of a B&B. You'll find desks and comfortable armchairs inside the large rooms, many of which have balconies that overlook the courtyard. On Sundays, the hotel restaurant serves a champagne and jazz brunch buffet. Dominique's Lounge is a nice place to wind down at the end of the day and enjoy award-winning cuisine. The hotel's amenities include a heated outdoor pool and Jacuzzi, an exercise room with treadmill and sauna, twice-daily maid service, and baby-sitting.

1001 Toulouse St. (2 blocks from Bourbon St.), New Orleans, LA 70112. ☎ *800-535-9177 or 504-586-8000. Fax: 504-525-5334. Internet:* www.maisondupuy.com. *Valet parking: $18 when available. Rack rates: $99–$229 double. AE, CB, DC, DISC, MC, V. Wheelchair accessible.*

Maison St. Charles Quality Inn
$$-$$$ **Lower Garden District**

From the street, you'd think this is just another chain hotel. Pull into the small covered parking lot next to the front desk, however, and you're in a distinctly New Orleans kind of place. The hotel manages to capture — or manufacture, depending on your point of view — that just-so local flavor. Accommodations are tasteful enough, and strive to replicate a guesthouse flavor; it's a pretty decent approximation, but it doesn't completely escape the hotel-chain look. Room sizes are standard, with a couple of extra-spacious ones. The amenities, which include a swimming pool and la Madeleine bakery, are chain standard.

1319 St. Charles Ave., New Orleans, LA 70130. ☎ *800-831-1783 or 504-522-0187. Fax: 504-529-4379. Internet:* www.maisonstcharles.com. *Valet parking: $12. Rack rates: $109–$159 double. Extra person: fee varies; ask when calling. AE, CB, DISC, DC, MC, V. Wheelchair accessible.*

McKendrick-Breaux House
$$$-$$$$ **Garden District**

One of the city's best B&Bs, it sits in the beautiful Garden District on a street known for its funky atmosphere and abundant dining and shopping options. The antique-filled rooms are lovely and spacious (some bathrooms are just huge). Many rooms feature artwork by local artists for sale. The public areas are gorgeous and comfortable. Amenities include a hot tub, subtropical garden (fresh flowers may be waiting in your room), and a small pond whose resident turtle comes out for feedings. The owner provides perfect personal service while still giving guests plenty of privacy.

1474 Magazine St., New Orleans, LA 70130. ☎ *888-570-1700 or 504-586-1700. Fax: 504-522-7138. Internet:* www.mckendrick-breaux.com. *Parking: free. Rack rates: $125–$195 double (includes breakfast). AE, MC, V.*

Melrose Mansion
$$$$-$$$$$ **Faubourg Marigny**

This restored mansion is intimate, romantic, and elegant — all adjectives that don't come cheap. The spacious accommodations have Victorian-era furnishings. Bed sizes, room sizes, and amenities vary; some have wet bars, Jacuzzi tubs, and separate seating rooms. A breakfast of fresh muffins, fruit, and quiche is served in the parlor or in your room. The hotel also offers a swimming pool and a menu of off-site services (Swedish massage, aromatherapy massage, manicures, and pedicures) that the courteous and friendly staff will arrange for you. Recent renovations added a ten-room annex. This is a popular place, so book as far in advance as possible.

937 Esplanade Ave. (at the corner of Burgundy), New Orleans, LA 70116. ☎ *800-650-3323 or 504-944-2255. Fax: 504-945-1794. Internet:* www.melrosegroup.com. *Parking: street parking available. Rack rates: $200–$450 double (includes champagne breakfast and cocktail hour). AE, DISC, MC, V.*

New Orleans Guest House

$$ French Quarter

This gay-friendly establishment, painted bright pink, sits just outside the Quarter, a stone's throw from Armstrong Park, Donna's, and the Funky Butt (see Chapter 23). The old Creole main house has spacious rooms, while the former slave quarters has accommodations that are even larger. Rooms in both locations are tastefully decorated with a different color scheme. The lush courtyard features a tropical garden with plenty of fresh greenery, a banana tree, and intricately carved old fountains (as well as beer and soda machines and a handy ice maker). The surrounding neighborhood is chancy at night the farther you get from Rampart.

1118 Ursulines St. (1 block outside the Quarter just across Rampart St.), New Orleans, LA 70116. ☎ *800-562-1177 or 504-566-1177. Fax: 504-566-1179. Internet:* www.neworleans.com/nogh. *Parking: Free. Rack rates: $79–$99 double (includes continental breakfast). AE, MC, V.*

Olde Victorian Inn

$$$–$$$$ French Quarter

Six distinctive Victorian period rooms (each with private bath) are tastefully decorated and whimsically appointed with lace doilies, teddy bears, and the like. The Chantilly Room is a favorite, thanks to a balcony that overlooks busy Rampart Street and Louis Armstrong Park. A cozy courtyard lies out back. Breakfasts change daily, culled from a list of some 30 menus, including Creole pancakes, crepes, and coffeecakes. The owners are happy to help with obtaining dining reservations and offer recommendations on what to see and do, and a friendly "staff" of lovable dogs lends a homey touch. Though the Olde Victorian has no parking spaces, guests are allowed to use the lot of the Best Western Landmark next door (and also avail themselves of its swimming pool).

914 N. Rampart St., New Orleans, LA 70116 ☎ *800-725-2446 or 504-522-2446. Fax: 504-522-8646. Internet:* www.oldevictorianinn.com. *Parking: available free at Best Western Landmark next door. Rack rates: $135–$225 double. AE, CB, DC, DISC, MC, V.*

Omni Royal Orleans

$$$–$$$$$ French Quarter

One of the best chain hotels in the city, its richly decorated rooms, with super-posh appointments, aren't uniform in size, so communicate your needs when reserving. The downside for families is that only a few rooms have two double beds, but the hotel will supply a roll-away bed. The rooftop swimming pool/observation deck will appeal to kids, while parents will appreciate the relatively cheap (and bonded) baby-sitting service. Amenities include terry-cloth bathrobes (upon request), umbrellas, makeup mirrors, an extensively equipped fitness center, irons and ironing boards, and emergency mending and pressing services. The hotel's Rib Room is one of the city's premier restaurants (see Chapter 14).

621 St. Louis St., New Orleans, LA 70140. ☎ 800-THE-OMNI or 504-529-5333. Fax: 504-529-7089. Internet: www.omnihotels.com. *Valet parking: $21. Rack rates: $149–$349 double. Children 18 and under free with parent. AE, CB, DC, DISC, MC, V. Wheelchair accessible.*

Pontchartrain Hotel
$$$$–$$$$$ Garden District

This local landmark is an oasis of tranquility and beauty on sprawling St. Charles Avenue. The unique romantic ambiance here is unmatched even in a city known for its atmosphere. Recent renovations have struck a nice balance between a worn, old-world feeling and a freshness of more modern hotels. Antique furnishings (including some Ming vases) contribute immeasurably to the surroundings. Rooms are comfortable and larger than most standard hotel rooms, and include cedar-lined closets and pedestal washbasins. The hotel offers 24-hour room service, complimentary shoe shine, and access to a nearby spa with health club and pool.

2031 St. Charles Ave., New Orleans, LA 70140. ☎ 800-777-6193 or 504-524-0581. Fax: 504-529-1165. Internet: www.pontchartrainhotel.com. *Parking: $13. Rack rates: $199–$600 double. Extra person: $10. AE, CB, DC, DISC, MC, V. Wheelchair accessible.*

Prince Conti Hotel
$$$ French Quarter

This small but friendly hotel boasts a congenial and helpful staff, as well as a prime location just off Bourbon Street that isn't too noisy. The rooms are very comfortable and many are furnished with antiques, but the bathrooms can be downright microscopic, with the toilet virtually on top of the sink. Travelers with kids should probably opt for the establishment's sister hotel, the Place d'Armes, which has a swimming pool and is farther removed from Bourbon Street. The Bombay Club, located on the first floor, is famous among locals for its genteel atmosphere, and serves some of the best martinis in town (see Chapter 24).

830 Conti St. (at the corner of Dauphine St.), New Orleans, LA 70112. ☎ 800-366-2743 or 504-529-4172. Fax: 504-581-3802. Internet: www.princecontihotel.com. *Valet parking: $16. Rack rates: $159 double (includes breakfast). AE, CB, DC, DISC, MC, V.*

Ramada Plaza The Inn on Bourbon Street
$$$$–$$$$$ **French Quarter**

This elegant hotel is located right on Bourbon Street. As a result, its beauty and amenities are sometimes lost on guests who just want to roll out of bed and into a bar or daiquiri shop. If you plan on sleeping while you're here (as opposed to just passing out), ask for an interior room, somewhat insulated from the street noise. But then you may not get a room with a balcony overlooking the action, which can be especially handy around Mardi Gras. (Decisions, decisions. . . .) All rooms are standard in size, yet comfortable, and have king or double beds. Amenities include a fitness room, a business center, a jewelry shop, and a concierge who can put you in touch with baby-sitting services.

541 Bourbon St. (at the corner of Toulouse), New Orleans, LA 70130. ☎ **800-535-7891** *or 504-524-7611. Fax: 504-568-9427. Internet:* www.innonbourbon.com. *Valet parking: $16. Rack rates: $205–$285 double. AE, CB, DC, DISC, MC, V. Wheelchair accessible.*

Ritz-Carlton New Orleans
$$$–$$$$$ **French Quarter**

Since opening in the fall of 2000, this newcomer to the downtown scene has quickly rivaled (some say eclipsed) the hallowed Windsor Court. A haven for visiting celebrities, the state's only five-diamond-rated hotel offers an acclaimed fine dining restaurant (Victor's), a great restaurant/bar (the French Quarter Bar), a full-service spa, a mall of shops, and the trademark ritzy accommodations for which the Ritz-Carlton chain is known. From the driveway entrance to the beautiful courtyard and rooms, the hotel makes every effort to incorporate the look and feel of the city into its own style. Afternoon tea is served every afternoon from 1:30–4:00 p.m. in the hotel's relaxing Lobby Lounge.

921 Canal St., New Orleans, LA 70112. ☎ **800-241-3333** *or 504-524-1331. Fax: 504-524-7233. Internet:* www.ritzcarlton.com/hotels/new_orleans/. *Valet parking: $25. Rack rates: $165–$395 double (penthouse suites are $4,000). AE, DC, DISC, MC, V. Wheelchair accessible.*

Royal Sonesta
$$$$$ **French Quarter**

The four-star Sonesta offers the best of both worlds: a Bourbon Street location and a gracious, classy hotel. Rooms are a bit more upscale than standard hotel rooms, but otherwise pretty typical. Many feature balconies overlooking Bourbon Street, a side street, or a courtyard with a large pool. For a good night's sleep away from the noise of the street, request an inner room. The hotel features an exercise room, business center, excellent concierge service, and room service until 2 a.m. This is the best place in the Quarter to catch a cab — they line up right at the corner.

300 Bourbon St. (3 blocks from Canal between Bienville and Conti), New Orleans, LA 70130. ☎ *800-766-3782 or 504-586-0300. Fax: 504-586-0335. Internet:* www.royal sonestano.com. *Parking: $20. Rack rates: $249–$389 double. AE, CB, DC, DISC, MC, V. Wheelchair accessible.*

St. Charles Guest House
$–$$ Lower Garden District

Character and economy are the operative words here. The property consists of three separate, connected buildings, the oldest of which dates back about 100 years. Atmospheric touches balance out a general lack of modern conveniences; rooms do not include televisions or phones, though each building has its own pay phone (including one in a fascinating antique phone booth). Owner Dennis Hilton gladly offers use of his office line for those with portable computers who want to check their e-mail. Room sizes vary, with backpacker rooms available at the very low end, though these lack air-conditioning and private baths. A continental breakfast is served in a cottage-like room that looks out on the swimming pool.

1748 Prytania St., New Orleans, LA 70130. ☎ *504-523-6556. Fax: 504-522-6340. Internet:* www.stcharlesguesthouse.com. *Parking: on-street available. Rack rates: $35–$95 double. Extra person: $10. AE, MC, V.*

Saint Louis
$$$–$$$$$ French Quarter

You'll find a splendid courtyard with a fountain at this small hotel right in the middle of the Quarter. Throughout the hotel, antique furniture, original oil paintings, and crystal chandeliers complement a Parisian–style decor. Rooms are standard yet comfortable. Most face the courtyard, though some in a new wing do not. The elegant Louis XVI restaurant, which serves fine French cuisine, serves as the main attraction, however (see Chapter 14).

730 Bienville (½ block from Bourbon St.), New Orleans, LA 70130. ☎ *888-508-3980 or 504-581-7300. Fax: 504-679-5013. Internet:* www.stlouishotel.com. *Valet parking: $16.75. Rack rates: $159–$259 double. Children under 12 free in parents' room. AE, CB, DC, DISC, MC, V. Wheelchair accessible.*

Soniat House
$$$$–$$$$$ French Quarter

Located in an 1839 home, this peaceful hotel captures all the romance of the plantation era. The rooms in this building, and in some small, adjacent buildings (one used to be the kitchen), are comfortable, though bathrooms are small. Oriental rugs, fine French and English antiques, and beautiful paintings (some on loan from the New Orleans Museum of Art) furnish the rooms. More rooms (some have Jacuzzi bathtubs) are available in the annex of suites across the street. For an additional charge of $7, you can get a continental breakfast; the large, fluffy, baked-to-order biscuits alone are worth the price.

1133 Chartres St. (across the street from the Old Ursuline Convent), New Orleans, LA 70116. ☎ *800-544-8808 or 504-522-0570. Fax: 504-522-7208. Internet:* www. soniathouse.com. *Valet parking: $19. Rack rates: $195–$285 double. Children under 13 not permitted. AE, MC, V.*

W French Quarter

$$$$$ French Quarter

Snazzy and upscale in a *nouveau-riche* kind of way, this link in the too-hip-for-school W chain places as much emphasis on style as it does on service — both, just for the record, are quite good. Lounge in the comfort of your room's patio or balcony, or mingle with other beautiful people in the Living Room, the hotel's lounge. The "Whatever/Whenever" desk goes out of its way to accommodate, and ethernet connections, Internet-access televisions, dataports, and high-tech meeting rooms keep business travelers happy. Bacco, an acclaimed Italian/Creole restaurant, is on the premises (see Chapter 14).

316 Chartres St., New Orleans, LA 70130. ☎ *800-448-4927 or 504-581-1200. Fax: 504-523-2910. Internet:* www.whotels.com/frenchquarter. *Valet parking: $29. Rack rates: $489–$514 double. Children under 16 free in parents' room. AE, CB, DC, DISC, MC, V. Wheelchair accessible.*

Windsor Court

$$$$$ Central Business District

Once voted by *Condé Nast Traveler* the best hotel in North America, the Windsor is truly magnificent — from its Italian marble and antique furnishings to its impeccable service — and about as expensive as you'd expect. The hotel is 90 percent suites, though even the smaller guest rooms are spacious. All suites feature balconies or bay windows with views of the city or river. They also have fax machines, minibars, kitchenettes, living rooms, two dressing rooms, and marble bathrooms with plush robes, a hamper, high-end personal care items, and extra hair dryers. (Ask about amenities when you call, as they are not the same in each room.) The 24-hour suite service is much more luxurious than your average room service. Conference rooms are available for business travelers. The hotel also features a resort-size pool, a health club, laundry and dry cleaning, and in-room massage. If you can afford it, this is the place to go for serious pampering. You'll also find the first-class Grill Room (see Chapter 14) and an afternoon tea with cocktails and sweets in the lobby lounge.

300 Gravier St. (1 block from Canal St.), New Orleans, LA 70130. ☎ *888-596-0955 or 504-523-6000. Fax: 504-596-4513. Internet:* www.windsorcourthotel.com.

Parking: $20. Rack rates: $350–$400 double; suites from $400. Children under 12 free in parents' room. AE, CB, DC, DISC, MC, V. Wheelchair accessible.

Wyndham New Orleans at Canal Place

$$$$$ **French Quarter**

If you're a shopper, this large, luxurious hotel is the place for you. It's situated above the elegant Canal Place Shopping Center, which you can access directly by a glass elevator from the hotel's 11th floor lobby. The rooms have fine furnishings, including marble foyers and baths. The hotel boasts spectacular views of the Quarter and the Mississippi River. Business travelers are treated to amenities such as office supplies, a coffeemaker, and use of an in-room copier/printer/fax machine.

100 Iberville St. (1 block from the Aquarium), New Orleans, LA 70130. ☎ 877-999-3223 or 504-566-7006. Fax: 504-553-5120. Internet: www.wyndham.com/canalplace. *Valet parking: $25. Rack rates: $329–$369 double. AE, CB, DC, DISC, MC, V. Wheelchair accessible.*

New Orleans's Runner-Up Hotels

This book does not have enough room to list all of the good hotels and B&Bs in New Orleans. If the suggestions in the previous section are all booked up, check out one of the options in this section. Some of these are just as charming and pleasant as the lodgings in the preceding listing, but they may be in a slightly out-of-the-way or dicey location (or I just ran out of room for them all above).

Beau Séjour Bed & Breakfast

$$–$$$ **Uptown**

1930 Napoleon Ave., New Orleans, LA, 70115. ☎ 888-897-9398 or 504-897-3746. Fax: 504-891-3340. Internet: www.beausejourbandb.com. *Parking: limited, on-street parking. Rack rates: $110–$150 double. AE, DISC, MC, V.*

French Quarter Guest House

$$–$$$ **French Quarter**

623 Ursulines St., New Orleans, LA 70116. ☎ 800-887-2817 or 504-522-1793. Fax: 504-524-1902. Parking: $6 within walking distance. Rack rates: $79–$135 double (includes continental breakfast). Extra person: $10. AE, CB, DC, DISC, MC, V.

Hotel Villa Convento

$$–$$$ **French Quarter**

616 Ursulines St. (around the corner from the Old Ursuline Convent), New Orleans, LA 70116. ☎ 800-887-2817 or 504-522-1793. Fax: 504-524-1902. Internet: www.villaconvento.com. *Parking: $6 within walking distance. Rack rates: $89–$159* *double (continental breakfast included). Extra person: $10. AE, CB, DC, DISC, MC, V.*

LaSalle Hotel

$ **Central Business District**

1113 Canal St., New Orleans, LA 70112. ☎ 800-521-9450 or 504-523-5831. Fax: 504-525-2531. Internet: www.lasallehotelneworleans.com. *Parking: $8. Rack rates: $72 double. Children under 12 free in parent's room. AE, DISC, MC, V.*

Macarty Park Guest House

$–$$ **Bywater**

3820 Burgundy St., New Orleans, LA 70117. ☎ 800-521-2790 or 504-943-4994. Fax: 504-943-4999. Internet: www.macartypark.com. *Parking: limited, free parking. Rack rates: $59–$115 double. Extra person: $15. AE, DISC, MC, V.*

Place d'Armes Hotel

$$$–$$$$ **French Quarter**

625 St. Ann St. (just behind the Presbytere), New Orleans, LA 70118. ☎ 800-366-2743 or 504-524-4531. Fax: 504-571-2803. Internet: www.placedarmes.com. *Parking: $16. Rack rates: $129–$199 double (includes breakfast). AE, CB, DC, DISC, MC, V. Wheelchair accessible.*

Royal Street Inn and R Bar

$$ **Faubourg Marigny**

1431 Royal St., New Orleans, LA 70116. ☎ 800-449-5535 or 504-948-7499. Fax: 504-943-9880. Internet: www.royalstreetinn.com. *Parking: Free on-street parking with a visitor's permit (available at check-in) and a $50 deposit. Rack rates: $90–$125 double (includes taxes and two drinks).*

St. Charles Inn

$ **Garden District**

3636 St. Charles Ave., New Orleans, LA 70115. ☎ 800-489-9908 or 504-899-8888. Fax: 504-899-8892. Internet: www.stcharlesinn.com. *Parking: Free. Rack rates: $75 double (includes breakfast). AE, DC, DISC, MC, V. Wheelchair accessible.*

St. Vincent's Guest House

$–$$ **Lower Garden District**

1507 Magazine St., New Orleans, LA 70130. ☎ 504-523-3411. Fax: 504-566-1518. Internet: www.stvincentsguesthouse.com. *Parking: Limited on-site parking. Rack rates: $59–$99 double (includes breakfast). Extra person: $10. AE, DC, DISC, MC, V. Wheelchair accessible.*

Index of Accommodations by Neighborhood

Index of Accommodations by Price

Macarty Park Guest House (Bywater)
St. Charles Guest House
    (Lower Garden District)
St. Charles Inn (Garden District)
St. Vincent's Guest House
    (Lower Garden District)

$$

Ambassador Hotel
    (Central Business District)
B&W Courtyards Bed & Breakfast
    (Faubourg Marigny)
Beau Séjour Bed & Breakfast (Uptown)
Bienville House (French Quarter)
Chateau Hotel (French Quarter)
The Columns (Uptown)
Doubletree Hotel New Orleans
    (Central Business District)
Fairmont Hotel
    (Central Business District)
Frenchmen (Faubourg Marigny)
French Quarter Courtyard Hotel
    (Central Business District)
French Quarter Guest House
    (French Quarter)
Holiday Inn Downtown Superdome
    (Central Business District)
Hotel Provincial (French Quarter)
Hotel Villa Convento (French Quarter)
Lamothe House (French Quarter)
Le Pavillon Hotel (Central Business
    District)
Le Richelieu Motor Hotel
    (French Quarter)
Macarty Park Guest House (Bywater)
Maison Dupuy (French Quarter)
Maison St. Charles Quality Inn
    (Lower Garden District)
New Orleans Guest House
    (French Quarter)
Royal Street Inn and R Bar
    (Faubourg Marigny)
St. Charles Guest House
    (Lower Garden District)
St. Vincent's Guest House
    (Lower Garden District)

$$$

Ambassador Hotel
    (Central Business District)
Ashton's Bed & Breakfast (Mid-City)
Beau Séjour Bed & Breakfast (Uptown)
Bienville House (French Quarter)
Bourbon Orleans Hotel
    (French Quarter)
B&W Courtyards Bed & Breakfast
    (Faubourg Marigny)
Chateau Hotel (French Quarter)
Chateau Sonesta Hotel
    (French Quarter)
The Columns (Uptown)
Dauphine Orleans Hotel
    (French Quarter)
Doubletree Hotel New Orleans
    (Central Business District)
Fairmont Hotel
    (Central Business District)
Frenchmen (Faubourg Marigny)
French Quarter Courtyard Hotel
    (Central Business District)
French Quarter Guest House
    (French Quarter)
Grand Victorian Bed & Breakfast
    (Uptown)
Holiday Inn–Chateau LeMoyne
    (French Quarter)
Holiday Inn Downtown Superdome
    (Central Business District)
Hotel Provincial (French Quarter)
Hotel Villa Convento (French Quarter)
House on Bayou Road (Mid-City)
Lafitte Guest House (French Quarter)
Lamothe House (French Quarter)
Le Pavillon Hotel
    (Central Business District)
Le Richelieu Motor Hotel (French
    Quarter)
Maison Dupuy (French Quarter)
Maison St. Charles Quality Inn
    (Lower Garden District)
McKendrick-Breaux House
    (Garden District)
Olde Victorian Inn (French Quarter)
Omni Royal Orleans (French Quarter)

Place d'Armes Hotel (French Quarter)
Prince Conti Hotel (French Quarter)
Ritz-Carlton New Orleans
    (French Quarter)
Saint Louis (French Quarter)

$$$$

Ambassador Hotel
    (Central Business District)
Ashton's Bed & Breakfast (Mid-City)
Bienville House (French Quarter)
Bourbon Orleans Hotel
    (French Quarter)
Chateau Sonesta Hotel
    (French Quarter)
The Columns (Uptown)
Dauphine Orleans Hotel
    (French Quarter)
Doubletree Hotel New Orleans
    (Central Business District)
Fairmont Hotel
    (Central Business District)
French Quarter Courtyard Hotel
    (Central Business District)
Grand Victorian Bed & Breakfast
    (Uptown)
Holiday Inn Downtown Superdome
    (Central Business District)
Hotel Maison de Ville (French Quarter)
Hotel Monteleone (French Quarter)
Hotel Provincial (French Quarter)
House on Bayou Road (Mid-City)
Lafitte Guest House (French Quarter)
Lamothe House (French Quarter)
Le Pavillon Hotel
    (Central Business District)
Le Richelieu Motor Hotel
    (French Quarter)
Maison Dupuy (French Quarter)
McKendrick-Breaux House
    (Garden District)
Melrose Mansion (Faubourg Marigny)
Olde Victorian Inn (French Quarter)

Omni Royal Orleans (French Quarter)
Place d'Armes Hotel (French Quarter)
Pontchartrain Hotel (Garden District)
Ramada Plaza The Inn on Bourbon
    Street (French Quarter)
Ritz-Carlton New Orleans
    (French Quarter)
Saint Louis (French Quarter)
Soniat House (French Quarter)

$$$$$

Ambassador Hotel
    (Central Business District)
Bienville House (French Quarter)
Dauphine Orleans Hotel
    (French Quarter)
Fairmont Hotel
    (Central Business District)
French Quarter Courtyard Hotel
    (Central Business District)
Grand Victorian Bed & Breakfast
    (Uptown)
Hotel Provincial (French Quarter)
House on Bayou Road (Mid-City)
Lamothe House (French Quarter)
Le Pavillon Hotel
    (Central Business District)
Melrose Mansion (Faubourg Marigny)
Omni Royal Orleans (French Quarter)
Pontchartrain Hotel (Garden District)
Ramada Plaza The Inn on Bourbon
    Street (French Quarter)
Ritz-Carlton New Orleans
    (French Quarter)
Royal Sonesta (French Quarter)
Saint Louis (French Quarter)
Soniat House (French Quarter)
W French Quarter (French Quarter)
Windsor Court Hotel
    (Central Business District)
Wyndham New Orleans at Canal Place
    (French Quarter)

Chapter 9

Taking Care of the Remaining Details

. . . .

In This Chapter

▶ Purchasing travel and medical insurance

▶ Knowing what to do in case of illness

▶ Renting a car

▶ Finding out what's happening — and being a part of it

▶ Getting the lowdown on traveler's checks

▶ Packing for New Orleans

. . . .

After you book your hotel room and flight (or make other appropriate arrangements), you may think that planning the rest of your trip is smooth sailing from there.

Not so fast, pilgrim! Before you pat yourself on the back and decide to skip ahead to the book's nightlife sections (see Chapters 23 through 25), you still need to straighten out a few final details. Finalizing these details ahead of time will save you the aggravation of dealing with them after you arrive.

Playing It Safe with Travel and Medical Insurance

You'll find that different kinds of travel insurance exist: medical insurance, trip cancellation insurance, and lost luggage insurance. You may want to invest in **trip cancellation insurance** if you paid a large part of your vacation expenses up front. For most travelers, however, paying for **medical insurance** or **lost luggage insurance** doesn't make much sense.

If sickness strikes while you're on vacation, your existing health insurance should cover you, making medical insurance redundant. (Check to see if you are fully covered when away from home, though, if you belong to an HMO.)

As for lost luggage insurance, homeowner's insurance should cover stolen luggage if your policy includes off-premises theft. Before you buy any additional coverage, make sure to check your existing policies. Also, airlines must cover $1,250 per bag on domestic flights (and $9.07 per pound, up to $635 per bag, on international flights) if they lose your luggage. Carry any valuables that exceed these price limits in your carry-on bag.

Your credit card may also offer automatic flight insurance against death or dismemberment in case of an airplane crash. Contact one of the following companies if you still want more insurance. But only buy as much insurance as you truly need. If you only want trip cancellation insurance, for example, don't feel obligated to purchase coverage for lost or stolen property. After all, trip cancellation insurance costs approximately 6 to 8 percent of the total value of your vacation, which can be a substantial amount. Among the reputable issuers of travel insurance are the following:

- ✔ **Access America,** P.O. Box 90315, Richmond, VA 23286 (☎ **866-807-3982;** Fax: 800-346-9265; Internet: www.accessamerica.com)

- ✔ **Travelex Insurance Services,** 11717 Burt St., Ste. 202, Omaha, NE 68154 (☎ **800-228-9792;** Fax: 800-867-9531; Internet: www.travelex-insurance.com)

- ✔ **Travel Guard International,** 1145 Clark St., Stevens Point, WI 54481 (☎ **800-826-1300;** Internet: www.travel-guard.com)

- ✔ **Travel Insured International, Inc.,** P.O. Box 280568, East Hartford, CT 06128-0568 (☎ **800-243-3174;** Fax: 860-528-8005; Internet: www.travelinsured.com)

Staying Healthy When You Travel

Finding a doctor you trust when you're away from home can be exceedingly difficult. When traveling, make sure you pack all your medications. If you think you may run out, also bring along a prescription for more. If you wear contact lenses, bring along an extra pair just in case you lose one. And don't forget the Pepto-Bismol for common travelers' ailments such as upset stomach or diarrhea.

If you have health insurance, check with your provider to find out the extent of your coverage outside of your home area. Be sure to carry your identification card in your wallet. And if you worry that your existing policy won't be sufficient, purchase medical insurance for more compre-hensive coverage (see the preceding section for more information).

If you suffer from such conditions as epilepsy, diabetes, or a heart con-dition, always wear a **MedicAlert identification tag** when traveling. This tag immediately alerts any doctor to your condition and allows him or her to access your medical records through Medic Alert's 24-hour hotline. For specifics, contact the MedicAlert Foundation, 2323 Colorado Ave., Turlock, CA 95382 (☎ **800-432-5378**; www.medicalert.org). Membership is $35, $15 to renew. If you do suffer from a chronic illness, make sure to consult your doctor before taking a trip.

In case of illness, ask your hotel's concierge for local doctor recom-mendations. If nothing else, get the name of the concierge's own physi-cian. Getting a recommendation in this manner is probably more accurate than calling a toll-free number to get the name of a local doctor. If your efforts to find a doctor are unsuccessful, try going to the emergency room to find out if it sponsors a walk-in clinic for non-life-threatening emergencies (or better yet, call first). At a clinic, you may not receive immediate attention, but you also won't have to fork over the cost of a visit to the emergency room — usually a minimum of $300 just for signing your name, *plus* whatever treatment you receive.

Renting a Car — If You Must

Should you rent a car in New Orleans? The short answer is no — but a qualified no. If you plan to stay in the French Quarter, a car may be more of a headache than you really need on vacation. Many of the hotels, B&Bs, and guesthouses listed in this book have a limited number of parking spaces. In addition, if you stay in an area such as Faubourg Marigny, the Quarter is still just a short walk away.

Locations without adequate parking can probably point you to a nearby garage, but these likely won't be cheap. In some cases, you may have to park on the street, which can present a big problem in the Quarter, where parking spaces are a hot commodity. (Some people swear that they don't actually exist.)

For sightseeing in the Quarter, a car is more of a hindrance than a help. All the streets are one-way, and on weekdays during daylight hours, Royal and Bourbon streets are closed to automobiles between the 300 and 700 blocks. In the Central Business District, congested traffic at peak hours and limited parking conspire to make a motorist's life diffi-cult. Also, New Orleans meter maids hand out more tickets than box-office attendants, and they're quite creative about it. Some signs marking off restricted parking spaces sit so far from the spaces themselves that you may never see them.

Now, keep in mind that New Orleans offers much more than the very small French Quarter, especially where dining and nightlife are concerned. If you stay in one of the outlying areas, such as Uptown or the Garden District, having a car becomes more feasible. You may even find a parking space near your cozy B&B.

If you do rent (or bring) a car, I suggest that you refrain from using it in the congested sightseeing areas such as the Quarter and the Central Business District and rely on public transportation instead. (See Chapter 11 for more information on seeing New Orleans by car.)

Finding the car you need at the price you want

Car rental rates vary even more than airline fares. The price depends on the size of the car, the length of time you keep it, where and when you pick it up and drop it off, where you take it, and a host of other factors. Asking a few key questions can save you hundreds of dollars.

- ✔ **Figure out the best days to rent.** For example, you may pay more on weekdays than weekends. Ask the rental company if picking up the vehicle on Friday morning is cheaper than Thursday night.

- ✔ **Check out weekly rates.** If you plan to keep the car five or more days, you may pay less for a weekly rate rather than for the daily one.

- ✔ **Make sure your pick-up (and drop-off) location is convenient *and* affordable.** Find out whether where you pick up the vehicle makes a difference in price. Some companies assess a drop-off charge if you return the car to a different renting location; others, notably National, do not.

- ✔ **Ask about specials.** Make sure to ask for any sale rates, or you may be charged the standard (higher) rate. Mention membership in AAA, AARP, and trade unions because membership in these organizations may entitle you to discounts ranging from 5 to 30 percent.

- ✔ **Remember your frequent flyer program.** Most car rentals are worth at least 500 miles on your frequent flyer account.

You'll find desks for the following rental car companies at the New Orleans airport: **Alamo** (☎ **800-GO-VALUE;** www.alamo.com), **Avis** (☎ **800-331-1212;** www.avis.com), **Budget** (☎ **800-527-0700;** www.budget.com), **Dollar** (☎ **800-800-4000;** www.dollar.com), **Hertz** (☎ **800-654-3131;** www.hertz.com), and **National** (☎ **800-227-7368;** www.nationalcar.com). Additionally, **Enterprise Rent-A-Car** (☎ **800-736-8222;** www.enterprise.com) maintains an office nearby on Airline

Drive, and **Swifty Car Rental,** a local company (☎ **504-524-7368**), operates offices throughout the metropolitan area, including one a short drive from the airport.

Surfing the Internet for a rental

As with other aspects of planning your trip, the Internet can make comparison shopping for a car rental much easier. All the major booking sites — **Travelocity** (www.travelocity.com), **Expedia** (www.expedia.com), **Yahoo Travel** (www.travel.yahoo.com), and **Cheap Tickets** (www.cheaptickets.com), for example — have search engines that can dig up discounted car-rental rates. Just enter the size of the car you want, the pick-up and return dates, and the city where you want to rent, and the server returns a price. You can even make the reservation through these sites.

Anticipating other expenses and car insurance

Most car rental companies try to bill you for *optional* charges on top of the standard rental price. You may opt to pay for a **collision damage waiver,** which covers damage in the case of an accident. Many credit card companies offer this coverage automatically, so check the terms of your credit card before you shell out money for this hefty charge (as much as $15 per day).

The car-rental companies also offer additional **liability insurance** (if you harm others in an accident), **personal accident insurance** (if you harm yourself or your passengers), and **personal effects insurance** (if someone steals your luggage from your car). If you have insurance on your car at home, that insurance probably covers you for most of these scenarios. You may want to consider the additional coverage, however, if your own insurance doesn't cover you for rentals, or if you don't have auto insurance. Also keep in mind that car-rental companies are liable for certain base amounts, depending on the state. Weigh the likelihood of getting into an accident or losing your luggage against the cost of these coverages (as much as $20 per day combined), which can significantly add to the price of your rental.

Some rental companies offer refueling packages, in which you pay up front for an entire tank of gas at a price competitive with local gas prices — but you don't get credit for any gas remaining in the tank when you return the vehicle. Otherwise, you'll pay only for the gas you use, but you must return it with a full tank or else you face charges of $3 to $4 a gallon for any shortfall.

Getting Reservations and Tickets Before You Leave Home

You won't need to make reservations or buy tickets in advance for most events in New Orleans — other than football games and special concerts, of course. If you simply must see a particular event — a production of the New Orleans Ballet, for instance — feel free to order your tickets ahead of time. You can get tickets for most events through **Ticketmaster** (☎ **504-522-5555** or www.ticketmaster.com).

If you've already booked your hotel, check with your hotel's concierge (or most reservations or front desk clerks) about acquiring tickets or reservations before you leave home; they'll be happy to try and get them for you.

Finding out what's happening at local venues

Naturally, when looking for tickets to an opera, museum exhibit, or rock concert that coincides with your visit, you can always just call the appropriate venue or organization on your own. Here's a list of some useful phone numbers:

- ✔ **Louisiana Superdome:** ☎ **504-587-3800;** www.superdome.com (see Chapter 18)

- ✔ **New Orleans Arena:** ☎ **504-587-3900;** www.neworleans arena.com (see Chapter 18)

- ✔ **Nat Kiefer University of New Orleans Lakefront Arena:** ☎ **504-280-7222;** http://arena.uno.edu

- ✔ **Saenger Theatre:** ☎ **504-524-2490;** www.saengertheatre.com (see Chapter 25)

- ✔ **Louisiana Philharmonic Orchestra:** ☎ **504-523-6530;** www.lpomusic.com (see Chapter 25)

- ✔ **New Orleans Museum of Art:** ☎ **504-488-2631;** www.noma.org (see Chapter 17)

- ✔ **New Orleans Opera Association:** ☎ **504-529-3000;** www.new orleansopera.org (see Chapter 25)

Making restaurant reservations

Remember that restaurants that do take reservations sometimes book up months in advance, so book early — as soon as you have your flight confirmed, if possible. Chapters 13, 14, and 15 give restaurant information (including notes on reservations). Some restaurants that fill up early include **Bayona, Brigtsen's, Emeril's, Grill Room,** and **Pascal's Manale.**

Researching Web sites and local sources

You'll find tons of useful information on the Internet. For the scoop on New Orleans, check out these Web sites:

- **Citysearch** (http://neworleans.citysearch.com) offers information about various entertainment options, including dining, music, and movies. It also features capsule reviews of restaurants, bars, and music venues.

- **Gay New Orleans** (www.gayneworleans.com) offers extensive information on such topics as gay-friendly hotels and Gay Mardi Gras.

- **Inside New Orleans** (www.insideneworleans.com) aims to be a one-stop online shop for locals, providing links and information for everything from news and weather to entertainment and shopping options.

- **NewOrleans.com** (www.neworleans.com) allows you to scan restaurant menus, look inside some hotels, and order free coupon books online.

- **New Orleans Online** (www.neworleansonline.com) is a function of the New Orleans Tourism Marketing Corporation; its most valuable features include a list of attractions and a database of local restaurants.

- **Satchmo.com** (www.satchmo.com) is dedicated to the late great jazz musician Louis "Satchmo" Armstrong. Its best feature is the Crescent City Connection, which offers a detailed roundup of local music events and bulletins on local music happenings.

After you get to New Orleans, you can find several good sources for uncovering what's happening around town.

- The **Times-Picayune** is one of your best bets for up-to-date information. The city's only daily paper, available at newsstands throughout the city, it features a daily entertainment section, as well as a Friday section called "Lagniappe." Its Web site (www. nola.com) offers capsule descriptions of restaurants or clubs and other helpful features.

- **Gambit Weekly** is the city's alternative weekly newspaper; it's available free most anywhere (though it can disappear fast during hot events such as Jazz Fest). It offers extensive listings for musical, artistic, and theatrical events, as well as staff picks for the best events of the week. If you can't find a *Gambit,* or would like a copy before you arrive, check out the online version at www.best ofneworleans.com.

- **OffBeat,** a local magazine dedicated to Louisiana and New Orleans music, is also available for free at any number of bars and restaurants, or by calling ☎ **504-944-4300.** It has extensive daily music listings and a monthly column on festivals in the state. You can also find the magazine online at www.offbeat.com.

- If you've come to New Orleans to hear jazz music, **WWOZ** always has the latest on the jazz scene, and regularly announces a schedule of who's playing at the major clubs that night. You can find them on your radio at **90.7 FM** or call them at ☎ **504-568-1234** or 504-568-1238. You can also listen to them online and get other information at www.wwoz.org.

Packing It Up and Heading for New Orleans

Because certain parts of New Orleans are best explored on foot, bring along a pair of comfortable walking shoes and a folding umbrella to stow in your bag. If you visit during the summer months, leave that stylish black linen number in the closet and bring light-colored cotton instead. If you plan to dine at **Antoine's,** the **Grill Room, Galatoire's,** or **Christian's** for dinner, bring along a jacket or a nice dress. These places are much more relaxed for lunch, however.

Part III
Settling into New Orleans

The 5th Wave
By Rich Tennant

"Honey, come on - that's part of the charm of New Orleans. Where else would they put a voodoo doll on your pillow instead of a mint at turndown?"

In this part . . .

*W*hew! Congratulations. After you finish all that planning, you're finally in New Orleans! Or at least, you're finally ready to arrive in New Orleans. You're probably anxious to get to work seeing the sights, learning how to pronounce all those strange words, and soaking up all the incredible and readily available food and music — not to mention savoring the experience of sleeping later than usual and ordering room service.

This part helps you get the lay of the land by outlining the various options you have to get safely to your hotel and telling you a little bit more about the city's different neighborhoods. It also gives you a whistle-stop tour of the city's public-transportation options and outlines other convenient ways of getting around. Lastly, this part discusses where you can get in touch with your money so that you're never without a continuous infusion of cash.

Chapter 10

Arriving and Getting Oriented

New Orleans can be a pretty confusing place, geographically speaking. Throw out your compass, because north, south, east, and west are meaningless in a city where the sun rises over the West Bank (which is, strictly speaking, to the east of the city). The Mississippi River replaces the magnetic poles as the focal point for getting your bearings here: Upriver is Uptown, downriver is downtown, and lakeside is toward Lake Pontchartrain.

The city began in the French Quarter, an area that covers 13 blocks between Canal Street and Esplanade Avenue, from the Mississippi River to North Rampart Street. The angular layout of the city follows the bend in the river, making directions such as north, south, east, and west pretty well useless. Consequently, you'll hear New Orleanians use the terms **riverside, lakeside, uptown,** and **downtown** in place of the traditional directions. You'll have no problem if you remember that North Rampart Street is the "lakeside" boundary of the Quarter, Canal Street marks the beginning of "uptown," and the Quarter is "downtown." (These boundaries aren't immutable, however, and some locals may use different reference points. People often refer to the Warehouse District, for example, which is on the other side of Canal Street from the Quarter, as being downtown.)

Building numbers begin at 100 on either side of Canal Street. In the Quarter, however, the numbers start at the river with 400 because the river swallowed four blocks of numbered buildings before the levee was built. Street names change when they cross Canal Street — another reminder of Canal's traditional role as the border between the old, French New Orleans (the Quarter) and the new, American New Orleans. Bourbon Street, for example, becomes Carondelet as it moves uptown.

This chapter reviews the best ways to enter the city, whether by land or by air. It also gives you the scoop on the different neighborhoods — including where to find them and what makes them unique.

Making Your Way from the Airport to Your Hotel

If you fly into New Orleans, you'll arrive at Louis Armstrong International Airport, located a good 25-minute drive from the corporate limits of New Orleans in the cozy suburb of Kenner. The airport's three-letter airport code, MSY, refers to the airport's former name, Moisant International — named for daredevil aviator John Blevins Moisant. (The SY refers to the fact that the airport sits on the site of a former stockyard.)

Moisant, as most locals still call it, is not the flashiest, most ultra-modern airport in the world; you'll probably see larger bus stations in New York, Chicago, or Atlanta. But Moisant's relative smallness is actually a blessing in disguise. The whole place is compact; all concourses are attached to a single structure, and clear signage directs you efficiently to the baggage claim area downstairs. Thus, getting around is more or less a snap. Additionally, you'll find information booths throughout the airport and in the baggage claim area. Also in the baggage claim area is a branch of the **Traveler's Aid Society** (☎ **504-525-8726**).

It's fun, it's easy: Hailing a cab

Generally, the easiest way into town if you're traveling in a group of two or more people is to take a taxi. Cabs wait in line just outside the baggage claim area, so you'll have no trouble finding one. Expect to pay around $24 for a taxi ride to the French Quarter or Central Business District for one or two people, or $10 each if your group includes more than two people. This price is more or less the same as the cost for a shuttle, and even cheaper if you're in a group of more than two or three. Taxis can hold a maximum of five passengers.

United Cab (☎ **504-522-9771**) is the largest and arguably most reliable taxi company in the city. Their taxis are usually busy handling radio calls, however, so they don't wait in line with the other taxis at the airport. Two other reputable companies are **A Service** (☎ **504-834-1400**) and **Metry Cabs** (☎ **504-835-4242**). You can also find plenty of mom-and-pop taxi operations hovering around the airport to catch your fare, most of which are reputable and won't rip you off. Still, exceptions always exist, so if you don't trust them, call one of the companies listed at the start of this paragraph.

A trip into town usually takes about 25 to 30 minutes, though that number can increase or decrease based on where you're headed and what traffic is like on Interstate 10 (I-10), the main thoroughfare into the city. Generally, you should tip between 10 and 15 percent.

Practicing safe taxis

How can you tell if an airport taxi service is legitimate? For one thing, unless you're visiting during a heavy tourist season (Jazz Fest, Mardi Gras, or a big business convention) or you're sharing a cab with other travelers, avoid any driver who attempts to negotiate with you on the price. Negotiating is common during the previously mentioned events, but outside of those times I've heard of drivers quoting one price and then demanding another when they pull up to the hotel. Also, look at the car itself. If it looks professionally painted, you're probably safer than if you approach a car that looks as if someone hand-painted the information over the door. Don't enter a cab that doesn't have a phone number on the door, and don't get into a cab if something about the driver rubs you the wrong way; another cab will come along.

Riding the magic buses

If you don't want to hail a cab, taking an airport shuttle bus into New Orleans is the next easiest option for getting into the city. Depending on your situation, taking a cab may be a more cost-effective and comfortable ride. You'll find airport shuttle information desks in the airport, staffed 24 hours a day.

For $1.50, the **Downtown/Airport Express bus** takes you to the corner of Elk's Place and Tulane Avenue — a 30- to 40-minute ride. The bus leaves from the upper level near the down ramp about every 23 minutes from 5:30 a.m. to midnight (every 12 to 15 minutes during rush hours). The **Jefferson Transit Authority** (☎ 504-818-1077) can give you more information.

For $10, the **Airport Shuttle** will take you directly to your hotel from right outside the baggage area. Taking a taxi costs about the same, or less, and is more convenient, if you have two or more passengers, however. The shuttle leaves every 10 to 15 minutes, but the ride can take up to an hour because you may have to go to several hotels before getting to your own. In comparison, a cab ride will take only about 25 to 30 minutes. Remember to reserve a spot on the shuttle if you intend to ride it back to the airport. To make your reservation, either make arrangements through your hotel's concierge or call ☎ 504-522-3500. The shuttle does offer wheelchair access.

Going with a rental car

You can find car-rental counters near the baggage claim area of the airport. (See Chapter 9 for a list of car-rental companies that maintain offices in the airport.) To navigate your trip from the airport to your hotel, read the directions in the next section and check out the "Airport Driving Routes" map in this chapter.

Airport Driving Routes

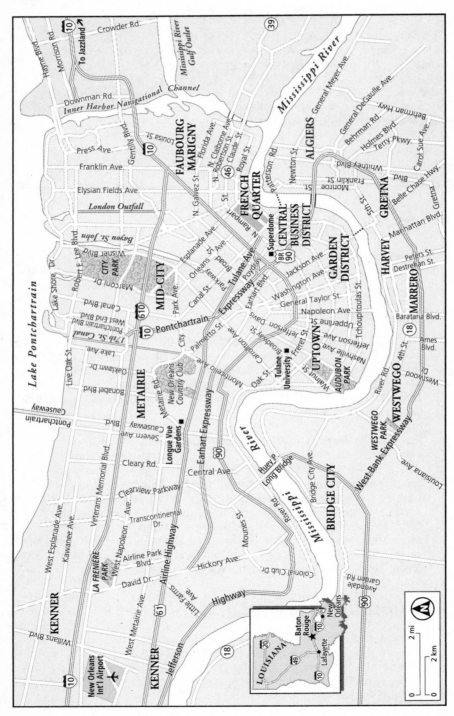

"Damn this traffic jam"

Please note that the time estimates mentioned in this chapter for getting to your destination are under optimum conditions; traffic jams, breakdowns, construction, or other disturbances can stretch your driving time. Be sure to consult your concierge, a desk clerk, or the *Times-Picayune* about any highway construction projects that may be underway during your stay and pad your timetable accordingly. If I-10 is undergoing work or just suffering a nasty traffic jam, consider alternate routes: Of these, the most direct and easiest route is to take Airline Highway (Hwy. 61 South) into or out of New Orleans.

For up-to-date information on highway construction, check out `www.dotd.state.la.us` on the Web. Even if construction is not taking place, you should always make allowances for traffic problems, especially if you're heading to the airport to catch a flight home.

Directions for driving from the airport

Follow one of the many signs at the airport to I-10 East. Take I-10 to the I-10/I-610 split, but do **not** take I-610, which branches off to your left. Continue following I-10, which branches right, until you reach the Superdome (you can't miss that). If you want to go to the French Quarter, follow I-10 to the left of the Superdome and take the Vieux Carre (French Quarter) exit. If you're trying to get to the Central Business District, stay to the right of the Superdome and exit at Loyola. If you want to reach the Garden District, stay to the right of the Superdome and take the St. Charles Avenue exit, which will drop you squarely in the Lower Garden District, right on the cusp of Lee Circle and the Central Business District. Check with your hotel for exact directions.

Getting to New Orleans by Hook or Crook (Or Car or Train)

If you drive to New Orleans, you'll probably arrive by way of one of the major thoroughfares: highways 90 or 61 or Interstate 10. To see how your route flows into the Crescent City, see the "Airport Driving Routes" map in this chapter. Both highways 90 and 61 take you right into the city. If you're following I-10, refer to the previous section, "Directions for driving from the airport," for information on specific exits and road construction.

If you're planning on chugging into New Orleans by train, you'll arrive at the **Union Passenger Terminal** (☎ **504-528-1610**) on Loyola Avenue in the Central Business District, just a few blocks from the French Quarter. After you arrive at the station, taxis will be available to take you into town. (If by some fluke they're not, you can call **United Cab** at ☎ **504-522-9771**.)

Figuring Out the Neighborhoods

Several towns and unincorporated areas extend along both the east and west banks of the Mississippi River to make up the New Orleans metropolitan area. This section gives a brief tour of some of the distinct local neighborhoods that make up the city (see the "New Orleans Neighborhoods" map in this chapter).

Small and famous: French Quarter (Vieux Carre)

Founded in 1718, the Vieux Carre (or Old Square) made up the original city of New Orleans and is now known as the French Quarter. The oldest neighborhood in New Orleans, the French Quarter lies between North Rampart Street, Esplanade, Canal, and the Mississippi River. Many people enjoy the French Quarter for the historic buildings surrounding Jackson Square (the old Ursuline Convent dates back to 1742), Bourbon Street, and the French Market. Despite its relatively small size, it boasts more restaurants and bars per square inch than any other city (which is hyperbole, of course, but not by much). During Mardi Gras, the Quarter is Party Central on the big day itself; however, you won't find parades here (the small, one-way streets don't even allow buses, much less floats), but rather throngs of revelers, exhibitionists, and people-watchers. You'll best enjoy the Quarter on foot, by buggy ride, or on an organized tour.

Commercial stuff: Central Business District

The district is roughly bounded by Canal Street on the north and the elevated Pontchartrain Expressway (I-90) to the south, between Loyola Avenue and the Mississippi River. In the midst of the high-rise buildings, watch for pleasant plazas, squares, and parks. You'll also find a few major attractions — Superdome, D-Day Museum, Louisiana Children's Museum, Confederate Museum, and World Trade Center — as well as the most elegant of the city's hotels, restaurants, and stores. The area's relative closeness to the Quarter (without the attendant crowds) is a big draw for tourists.

New Orleans Neighborhoods

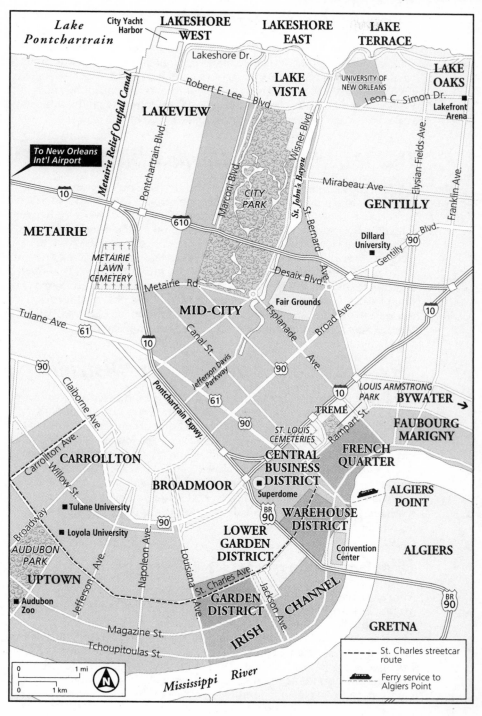

From warehouses to houses: Warehouse District

You can find this area between Julia and St. Joseph's streets within the Central Business District. Once made up almost entirely of warehouses, revitalization has turned the neighborhood into a place for artists to display their work and an upscale residential neighborhood. The Convention Center, Riverwalk Shopping Center, music clubs, hotels and restaurants, art galleries, and museums also lie in this area.

Old world charm: Garden District

Explore the Garden District — bordered by Jackson Avenue, St. Charles Avenue, Louisiana Avenue, and Magazine Street — via the St. Charles Streetcar and on foot. Originally part of the city of Lafayette, it became a fashionable residential area after the United States purchased it and wealthy Americans took up residence there. Visitors come from all over the world to view the beautiful homes and gardens along St. Charles Avenue. Unfortunately, most of the private gardens that used to flourish around the homes here (hence the name Garden District) no longer exist. Nonetheless, romance and old-world charm still rule. Anne Rice's home is located in this neighborhood, as is the world-famous restaurant **Commander's Palace** (see Chapter 14).

Hip enclave: Lower Garden District

The Lower Garden District houses a number of modest cottages, attractive churches, and some elegant town houses on Coliseum Square. Developed in the early 1800s just downriver from the Garden District, many of its streets are named for Greek Muses — though most have peculiar New Orleans pronunciations. St. Charles Avenue, Jackson Avenue, the Pontchartrain Expressway, and the Mississippi River border this area. Magazine Street is home to many small antique shops, sidewalk cafes, neighborhood bars, coffee shops, and boutiques. Exploring the area on foot is safe during the daytime, although you shouldn't stray far from Magazine Street.

Working class: Irish Channel

This area, which originally housed many of New Orleans's Irish immigrants, lies between the Garden District's Magazine Street and the Mississippi River, with its sidewise boundaries at Jackson and Louisiana avenues. Explore this part of the city on foot and with a large group of people, because it's not the safest neighborhood in town. During the 1800s, the area was a working-class neighborhood, which explains the abundance of double-shotgun cottages. (Shotgun cottages get their name because a person can stand in the front doorway and

fire a shotgun out the back without hitting anything.) Walking around
the antiques-shop district on Magazine Street and around Felicity
Street and Jackson Avenue can give you a real feel for the area.

Churches and cemeteries: Mid-City

Swampland comprised much of this area, originally called "Back O'
Town," for much of the city's early history. In the early 20th century,
however, it was drained and developed. The area, most notable for its
churches and cemeteries, stretches along Canal Street between
Esplanade, Perdido, City Park, and Derbigny (though some claim it
starts at Rampart instead of Derbigny). Some parts, notably along
Esplanade itself and City Park, can be experienced on foot; but for
safety's sake, stick with a bus or organized tour for other areas, especially the cemeteries.

Students, animals, and more: Uptown

Jackson Avenue, Claiborne Avenue, the Mississippi River, and Carrollton
Avenue bound this district, the largest area in the city. Tulane and Loyola
universities make their homes here, as do many fine mansions, the
Audubon Park/Zoo, and some churches and synagogues. Also in this area
are the legendary music club **Tipitina's** (see Chapter 23) and several fine
restaurants, such as **Pascal's Manale** (see Chapter 14). Magazine Street
runs through the district and features antiques shops, boutiques, and art
galleries. Take the St. Charles streetcar or the Magazine bus to explore,
though you may want to wander around some areas on foot.

Hip and entertaining: Faubourg Marigny

The Faubourg Marigny lies downriver from, and immediately adjacent
to, the French Quarter, bordered by Esplanade Avenue, St. Claude
Avenue, Press Street, and the Mississippi River. This area, developed
during the late 1700s, is one of the earliest suburbs. Today it houses
many Creole cottages and bed-and-breakfasts, as well as a range of residents — from bohemian to would-be suburbanite. I hate to give the
impression that the area is dangerous because overall it's very quaint
and charming, but some areas can be chancy, so you should explore
the neighborhood on foot during daylight hours. Generally, Frenchmen
Street, which is developing a reputation as a hip entertainment area, is
safe, as is most of the neighborhood close to the river. The farther
towards Rampart and St. Claude you get, the dicier it becomes.

Not backwater: Bywater

Bywater, bounded by Press Street, St. Claude Avenue, Poland Avenue,
and the Mississippi River, is just downriver from the French Quarter.

Some naysayers call this region "backwater," because it seems, at first glance, like a wasteland of light industry and run-down homes. In fact, Bywater is undergoing a renaissance. Originally, artisans, free persons of color, and communities of immigrants from Germany, Ireland, and Italy called this area home. Now artists, designers, and residents who may otherwise have gone to the suburbs occupy the area's residential housing, which includes Creole cottages and Victorian shotgun houses. Within this mix are some funky neighborhood restaurants and bars.

Creole: Algiers Point

One of the city's original Creole suburbs, Algiers Point is the only part of the city on the West Bank, and it has changed little over the decades. Here you'll find some of the best-preserved small gingerbread and Creole cottages in New Orleans. The neighborhood has begun to attract a lot of attention as a historic landmark, and makes for a nice stroll during the day, though I'd stay in the car rather than walk on foot. (Like parts of Uptown, tranquil areas can give way to less-than-desirable areas at a moment's notice.) It's also becoming a popular neighborhood for locals. A former hole-in-the-wall club called the **Old Point Bar** (see Chapter 23) has established itself as a hip musical destination, adding to the neighborhood's cachet.

Where to Get Information After You Arrive

You can find a state-run **Tourist Information Center** (☎ 504-568-5661 or 504-566-5031) in the French Quarter at 529 St. Ann St. in the historic Pontalba Buildings on the side of Jackson Square. Other information centers dot the city, many of them owned and operated by tour companies or other businesses. You can find tourist booths at these locations:

- ✔ **Canal and Convention Center Boulevard** (walk-up booth; ☎ 504-587-0739) at the beginning of the 300 block of Canal on the downtown side of the street.

- ✔ Just outside the **World Trade Center** (walk-up booth; ☎ 504-587-0734) at 2 Canal St.

- ✔ Near the **Hard Rock Cafe** (walk-up booth; ☎ 504-587-0740) on the 400 block of North Peters Street.

- ✔ **Julia and Convention Center Boulevard** (walk-up booth).

- ✔ **Poydras and Convention Center Boulevard** (walk-up booth).

- ✔ **Vieux Carre Police Station** (small tourist information desk inside the station; ☎ 504-565-7530), located at 334 Royal St.

Chapter 11

Getting Around New Orleans

. . . .

In This Chapter

▶ Hoofing it

▶ Hopping the streetcars and buses

▶ Taking taxis

▶ Getting around by car

. . . .

*A*fter you determine where you are in the city and where you want to go, you can turn your attention to the question of how you're going to get there. Whether you decide to drive, take public transportation, rely on a cab, or just hoof it, this chapter goes over strategies and helpful hints to take the travail out of traveling around New Orleans.

Traipsing Around the French Quarter

You'll probably spend most of your tourist time in the French Quarter, which is only 6 blocks wide and 13 blocks long. And most of the action in the Quarter stays in an even smaller area, with a few irregular areas along the river. Because the area is so small — and the narrow one-way streets, traffic congestion, strict traffic laws, and lack of on-street parking make driving a nightmare — I suggest you walk.

If cooped up in a car, you won't be able see the sights or hear the sounds of the French Quarter in the same way you can from your own two feet. If your feet start to ache, you can always hire a carriage and let the horse do the walking.

Use the daylight hours to explore and stick to well-lit areas with other people around after dark. Watch out for pickpockets on Bourbon Street. Avoid contact with panhandlers, and be wary of people who approach you with a "hard-luck" story — their car broke down, they need money for gas, or their purse was stolen, for example — no matter how well dressed or sincere they seem. I'm not telling you to be a bad Samaritan, but use your judgment. Also avoid people (especially kids) who want to wager with you; a common ruse is "I bet I can tell you where you got your shoes." (You got 'em on your feet.) Or, "I bet I can spell your name." (Y-o-u-r-n-a-m-e.) And, as always, use common sense when exploring any area of the city.

St. Charles Streetcar Route

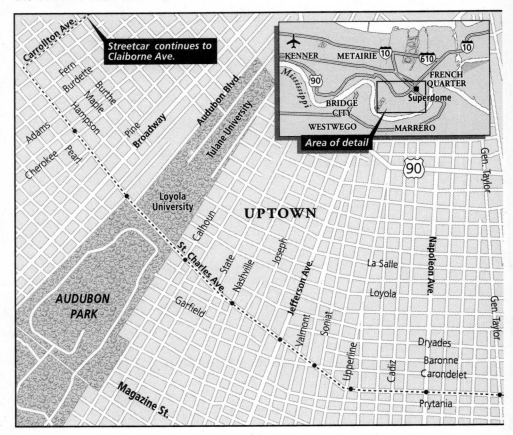

Carrollton Ave.

Streetcar continues to Claiborne Ave.

Fern
Burdette
Burthe
Maple
Hampson
Pine
Broadway
Adams
Cherokee
Pearl

Audubon Blvd.
Tulane University

KENNER   METAIRIE 10   610   10
Mississippi   90
BRIDGE CITY   Superdome   FRENCH QUARTER
WESTWEGO   MARRERO

Area of detail

90

Gen. Taylor

Loyola University

Calhoun

St. Charles Ave.

State

Nashville

Joseph

UPTOWN

Jefferson Ave.

La Salle

Loyola

Napoleon Ave.

Gen. Taylor

AUDUBON PARK

Garfield

Valmont

Soniat

Upperline

Cadiz

Dryades
Baronne
Carondelet

Magazine St.

Prytania

Riding the Lines: New Orleans's Public Transportation

New Orleans features a reliable and thorough public transportation system — streetcars and buses connect all neighborhoods that you may want to visit. Call the **Regional Transit Authority's Ride Line** at ☎ **504-248-3900** for maps, passes, and other information about streetcars or buses. Any of New Orleans's visitor information centers (including the main location at 529 St. Ann St. by Jackson Square) also have information on public transportation (see Chapter 10 for locations).

If you plan to use public transportation frequently during your stay, you should purchase a **VisiTour pass,** which entitles you to unlimited bus and streetcar rides. You can purchase them at most hotels and banks in the Quarter, Central Business District, and along Canal Street

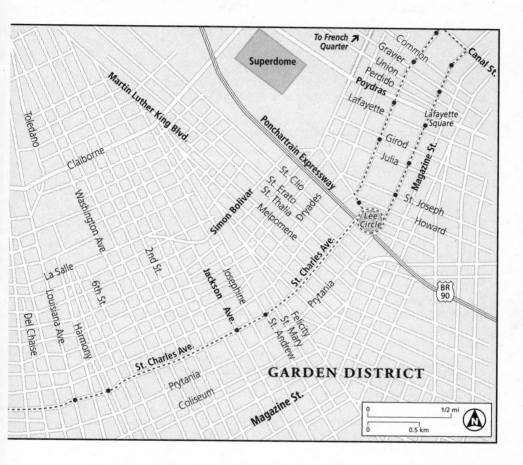

in one-day ($5) or three-day ($12) increments. Two booths also sell them: one outside the Aquarium of the Americas and the other on the 600 block of Decatur Street.

Hopping the St. Charles streetcar

The historic St. Charles streetcar line (see the "St. Charles Streetcar Route" map in this chapter) services the Central Business District, Garden District, Lower Garden District, Uptown, and Carrollton neighborhoods. The 7-mile ride from Canal Street takes you from downtown to Uptown (or vice-versa) through many historic neighborhoods, costing just $1.25 each way (exact change or a VisiTour pass is required). Chapter 21 has a list of sights to see while on the streetcar, which operates 24 hours a day and is not wheelchair accessible. The round-trip takes 90 minutes to two hours.

A streetcar with a past

Before it was electrified in 1893, the St. Charles streetcar (which began life as the Carrollton Railroad in 1835) used mule power and steam for propulsion. The St. Charles streetcar is the oldest railway system in continuous operation in the entire world. The present streetcars date from the 1920s and are listed on the National Register.

Generally, you won't wait too long for a streetcar — usually no more than half an hour. Downtown, you can board the streetcar at Canal and Carondelet (directly across Canal from Bourbon Street). You can also board at a number of designated stops along St. Charles Avenue. Like taking a bus, you can get on and off the streetcar at will, but you have to pay each time you get back on. The line ends, rather inconveniently, at Palmer Park and Playground at Carrollton and Claiborne avenues where you can transfer to a bus for 25¢.

Because the streetcar is as much a mode of public transportation as a tourist attraction, it can get pretty crowded, especially at rush hour or when school lets out in the mid-afternoon.

Riverfront seating: The Riverfront streetcar

Established during the 1984 World's Fair, the Riverfront streetcar line runs, of course, along the riverfront from the Convention Center to the far end of the French Quarter at Esplanade. The approximately 2-mile ride, which is a great way to see the river, costs $1.50 (exact change or a VisiTour pass is required). You can board, or get off, along that route at designated stops, and the streetcar is wheelchair accessible.

Getting around by bus

Buses in New Orleans may be generally more convenient than street-cars (after all, they're air-conditioned and faster), but they don't cover the same routes, and they're not anywhere *near* as picturesque. One or more bus lines connect most neighborhoods, and the fare is $1.25 (exact change or a VisiTour pass is required). Transfers cost 25¢, and buses are wheelchair accessible.

Because you're a visitor to New Orleans, you'll probably need to use only a few of the bus lines, such as **Tulane** (if you happen to stay on Tulane Avenue), **Magazine** (which runs through the Central Business

District, Lower Garden District, and Uptown between the Garden District and the Irish Channel), and **Canal Street** (which runs the length of Canal Street). Buses pick up passengers every other block or so along their routes at designated bus stops. Again, you can get more specific information from the **Regional Transit Authority's Ride Line** at ☎ **504-248-3900** or by picking up one of the excellent city maps available at the **Visitor Information Center** at 529 St. Ann Street.

Cabbing It in New Orleans

During the day, public transportation is perfectly safe, but I don't recommend taking it at night. You probably won't have any problems if you get on and off at well-lit major intersections, but I suggest a taxi if you're going somewhere not right on the line's route. A good neighborhood can take a turn for the worse in just a few short blocks.

You should be able to find an available cab without too much trouble, with the exception of busy times such as rush hour or during bad weather. If a cab is empty, driving relatively slowly, and its "On Duty" sign isn't on (if it even has one), chances are it's looking for fares. But as in most major cities, the methods and habits of New Orleans cabbies can be inscrutable. A cab may be on its way to pick up a radio call fare; also, the cabbie may be on his lunch break, he may be scrutinizing potential fares for the most lucrative ride (to the airport), or he may just not like the way you look. If you're in a hurry, your best bet is always to call ahead for a cab.

The easiest places to find a taxi include the airport, the French Quarter, and the Central Business District, but you'll also spot cabs at stands near restaurants, at all of the major hotels, and at some smaller hotels as well. If you can't find a cab on the street, call a taxi company. **United Cab** (☎ **504-522-9771**) is the largest and most reliable taxi company in the New Orleans area.

A view from the streetcar

Not only is the $1.25 streetcar ride a bargain, but it's also a fun and relaxing way to get an overview of the city. The route travels down the length of historic St. Charles Avenue (home to a number of grand residences) and takes you past great scenery and beautiful oak-lined avenues. For a guided tour of the sights, see the "Streetcar highlights" sidebar in Chapter 21. You may also want to buy a copy of *St. Charles Avenue Streetcar Line — A Self-Guided Tour* ($5.95), which gives you a wealth of information about the streetcar line itself and about the buildings along the route. You can find it at the **Historic New Orleans Collection** (at 533 Royal St. in the French Quarter) and elsewhere.

A ride for two people to most major tourist areas shouldn't cost more than $10. All taxis cost $2.50 for the first ⅙ of a mile and 20¢ for each additional ⅙ of a mile (or $1.20 per mile). If you travel at a rate less than ⅙ of a mile per 40 seconds, the cabby charges the additional 20¢ anyway. Add $1 for each additional person. The maximum number of passengers is five. You can also hire taxis for $30 an hour, though taxi companies impose a two-hour minimum and won't take you outside of the New Orleans area.

During football games, Jazz Fest, and other special events, taxi drivers usually expect you to pay $3 per person or the meter rate, whichever is greater. Special events include regularly scheduled sporting events and/or concerts at the Superdome, Saenger Theater, Fair Grounds, and most other stadiums.

In the event that you leave a wallet, piece of luggage, or other important effect in a cab when you exit, call the cab company as soon as possible. Calmly tell the dispatcher your problem, and provide him or her with your route details ("I went from the Canal Place Shopping Center to Commander's Palace"). In case of situations such as this, noting your taxi driver's name (the license should be clearly posted) and the taxi's number (which should be painted on its trunk or on another visible space) is always a good idea.

Driving Around New Orleans

Though not impossible, driving in New Orleans *is* a big hassle. Parking is an issue (except in the French Quarter, where it's more of a myth). Navigation is confusing, because street names change without warning and some streets have more twists and turns than an afternoon's worth of daytime soaps. And the other drivers . . . well, that's another story.

Avoiding the French Quarter

Before I go any further, however, absolutely the best, most essential tip I can give you about driving around New Orleans is to avoid driving in the French Quarter as much as possible. Why? Driving in the Quarter is a headache and a half. Unless you're paid to do it (that is, you're a cab driver), it's not worth the aggravation. The Quarter is small enough, with everything pretty close together, to navigate on foot.

Parking (or, not parking) in the Quarter

Driving in the Quarter is a bad idea for a number of reasons, but the biggest is parking, which is practically non-existent; even residents suffer constant parking woes. Parking spaces are scarce, and the ones that exist always seem to be occupied by people who got there before you — even if you get there at four in the morning. And if, by the grace of the Fates, you do find what seems to be an available spot, chances are it's illegal (of course, the sign pointing this fact out is probably obscured or on the other end of the street).

Keep this car talk in mind when choosing your hotel, and find out whether your hotel has parking available. If you're staying in a French Quarter hotel that has parking, well, great, but limit your car usage to any excursions you make outside of the Quarter. Wait a minute, you're saying. What if I'm staying outside the Quarter, but I want to come in to visit? Good point. My advice is to park in one of the commercial parking lots on Decatur, along the river, and walk the rest of the way. You will also see commercial lots inside the Quarter, notably for some of the bigger hotels, but they're often full. Aside from helping you to avoid the hassle of finding a parking spot, parking in one of these lots is well worth the security of knowing you won't get towed — or vandalized.

Navigating the Quarter

The streets in the French Quarter are all one-way, which can make something as uncomplicated as a simple right turn an elaborate affair. Additionally, certain tourist-heavy areas — notably Bourbon and Royal streets — are more congested than a Southern gourmand's arteries. Pedestrian traffic is thick, massive, and unrelenting, and no one shows much concern about stopping to let your car cross the street.

To complicate things, tourist traffic completely barricades the 300–700 blocks of Bourbon and Royal on weekdays during daylight hours, which turns the merely impractical into the impossible. Chartres Street is also closed on the blocks in front of the St. Louis Cathedral.

Additionally, the streets in the French Quarter are narrow with no room to pass because on-street parking takes up almost half the available driving space. The lack of space is bad enough when you're stuck in a long line of traffic trying to navigate its way across Bourbon Street, but getting stuck behind a mule-drawn buggy is even worse.

Driving outside the Quarter

Outside the French Quarter, driving is a whole different story. In the Central Business District, getting around in your car is pretty much the same as in your main downtown area back home. Parking spots (at least free ones) can be hard to come by. Traffic can and will be heavy during morning and afternoon rush hour, and probably during lunch as well. You can turn right on red throughout the city unless otherwise specified, but many streets are one-way, and many of those (most notably Tulane Avenue) do not allow left turns.

Biking it

If you're feeling especially adventurous, rent a bike and take your own tour around New Orleans, using the information in this book as a guide. **Bicycle Michael's (☎ 504-945-9505)** and **French Quarter Bicycles (☎ 504-529-3136)** are two good bets for rentals.

New Orleans stories: Carriage rides

You'll be hard pressed to resist the authentic mule-drawn carriages at Jackson Square if you have even one romantic bone in your body. The mules sport ribbons, flowers, or even a hat, and each driver fiercely competes with other drivers for the "most unique city story" award. No matter which driver you choose for the 2¼-mile ride through the French Quarter, you'll undoubtedly get a nonstop monologue on historic buildings, fascinating events of the past, and a legend or two. Look for the carriages at the Decatur Street end of Jackson Square from 9 a.m. to midnight in good weather. Most drivers charge around $8 for adults and $5 for children under 12. A private carriage tour, however, will cost you significantly more. Contact **Good Old Days Buggies** (☎ **504-523-0804**) for a private tour, including hotel or restaurant pick-up. Chapter 19 has more information on carriage tours.

If you park on a parade route, block access to someone's driveway, or break other laws, you may find your car towed away and impounded, and getting it back may cost you $100 or more. If you think your car has been towed, call the impounding lot (☎ **504-565-7235**) or the Claiborne Auto Pound, 400 N. Claiborne (☎ **504-565-7450**).

The driving situation is a little better uptown in the Garden District and other areas. You'll still encounter many one-way streets, however, and as always, free parking is hard to come by. Even if you do find a free spot, it may not be close to the attraction you're looking for. (Of course, no one guarantees that a commercial parking lot will be any more convenient.)

Avoiding local hazards: Potholes & drivers

Keep in mind that New Orleans's streets are famous for their potholes, some of which qualify as craters. Local drivers have developed a driving sixth sense; on certain streets, a sort of autopilot takes over that swerves your car this way or that to avoid wrecking your alignment on a nasty bump. Being new to the area, you won't have formed this psychic ability yet, and some potholes aren't so easy to see until after they've jolted you.

And last, but not least, are New Orleans drivers. Don't get me wrong — this is my home, and I love it — but the people here do not know how to drive. That statement is an over-generalization, of course, but for the most part, New Orleans drivers are a dangerous mixture of arrogance and cluelessness. Rubbernecking, idling in the passing lane, failure to yield or allow others to merge, and a complete lack of familiarity with turn signals are all trademarked characteristics of local drivers. Consider yourself warned.

Chapter 12

Managing Your Money

• •

In This Chapter

▶ Getting cash when you need it

▶ Knowing what to do if your wallet is stolen

▶ Keeping track of taxes

• •

*W*hoever coined the phrase "Money can't buy happiness" obviously wasn't a New Orleanian. From a hot plate of red beans and rice to a hot night of jazz, happiness is indeed for sale in the Crescent City. Of course, you need to have the money in hand. This chapter covers where to get your money (plus what to do if you lose it), and explores a couple of ways that you can unknowingly spend it — in the form of taxes of which you may or may not be aware.

Finding Cash Machines in New Orleans

As in any major American city, an automatic teller machine (or ATM) is always close at hand. They lurk like muggers on popular street corners, inside bars and hotel lobbies, and in restaurants, gift shops, and every other conceivable place where a person may need cash. During larger events such as the French Quarter Festival, you'll also likely see extra ATMs deployed along the streets like an invading force of money-spitting robots.

Though you won't have trouble finding an ATM, you may be hard pressed to find one that belongs to the same bank you use back home. Most banks in New Orleans are linked to the **Cirrus** or **Plus** networks, however, so even if your bank doesn't have a branch in New Orleans, you'll still be able to easily access your cash. To find out whether your bank belongs to one of these two networks, look on the back of your

ATM card for one of the networks' logos. Or you can call them directly at the following numbers:

- **Cirrus** (☎ **800-424-7787** or 800-4CIRRUS; `www.mastercard.com/ cardholderservices/atm/`)
- **Plus** (☎ **800-843-7587**; `www.visa.com/atms`)

For all intents and purposes, the major banking entities in New Orleans are (in alphabetical order):

- **Bank One** (☎ **800-777-8837**; `www.bankone.com/access`)
- **Dryades Savings Bank** (☎ **504-840-3920**; `www.dryadesbank. com/atm.html`)
- **Hibernia National Bank** (☎ **504-533-5361** or 504-533-3333; `www.hibernia.com/hibernia_bank/hb_contact_us.shtml`)
- **Regions Bank** (☎ **800-REGIONS** or 504-587-1888; `www. regions.com`)
- **Whitney National Bank** (☎ **877-611-9448**; `www.whitneybank. com/html/find.htm`)

Finding these banks' ATMs is easy, but their machines are by no means the only games in town. The French Quarter, in particular, is besieged with teller machines from smaller, generic banks that will more likely than not take a substantial bite out of your account in the form of an outrageous transaction fee.

Yes, Virginia, ATMs sure are convenient, but that convenience comes at a price. Like most banks these days, all of the preceding institutions charge a nominal fee for ATM transactions by non-account holders. These fees are currently pretty standard — around $2 to $2.75 for each transaction. Keep in mind that this fee is piled on top of whatever fee your own bank charges you for using another bank's ATM, or using an ATM in another city (anywhere from 50¢ to $3). Also remember that your particular bank may impose a limit on the amount of cash you can withdraw from an ATM at one time.

Because the merchants of New Orleans do *not* want you to run out of cash, you'll find 24-hour ATMs almost everywhere — particularly in the French Quarter, where commerce is as mother's milk to the resident shopkeepers, venders, artists, and street performers. The Quarter is small enough that you shouldn't have any trouble stumbling over an ATM. However, the "French Quarter ATMs" map elsewhere in this chapter shows some of the more conveniently located ATMs.

French Quarter ATMs

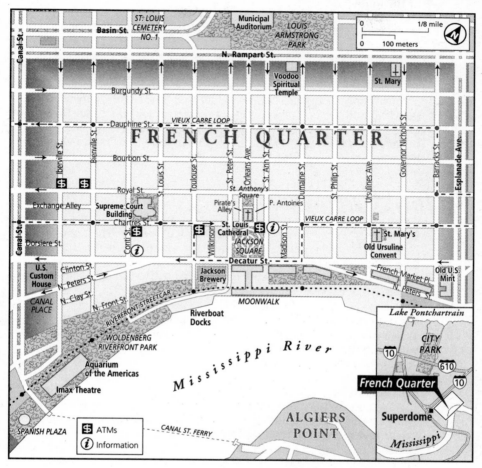

Keeping Your Money Safe (And What to Do If It's Stolen)

Almost every credit card company maintains an emergency toll-free number that you can call if someone steals your wallet or purse. The company may be able to get you a new credit card within a day or two and wire you a cash advance off your credit card immediately. Check the back of your credit card to find the issuing bank's toll-free number. Of course, if the card is stolen, you won't be able to check for the number, so make sure to write down the number elsewhere before you leave, and keep it in a safe place just in case. **Citicorp Visa's** U.S. emergency number is ☎ **800-645-6556. American Express** cardholders and traveler's check holders should call ☎ **800-221-7282** for all money emergencies. **MasterCard** holders should call ☎ **800-307-7309.**

If you opt to carry traveler's checks, be sure to keep a record of their serial numbers so that you can handle just such an emergency.

If your wallet disappears, odds dictate that you've probably seen the last of it, and the police won't likely recover it for you. Nevertheless, do call to alert the police to the theft after you cancel your credit cards, because you may need the police report number for credit card or insurance purposes later.

Taxing Matters

Taxes are a primary source for monetary confusion: When people are balancing their mental checkbooks at the end of the night, they often have a tendency to forget all of the different little taxes, surcharges, and other fiduciary paper cuts that contribute to the lightening of the wallet. All of these charges and fees add up.

Keep in mind that in New Orleans, or at least in Orleans Parish, the sales tax is a whopping 9 percent; in other words, your 99¢ hamburger actually costs $1.08. In neighboring Jefferson Parish, the sales tax is a somewhat less constricting 8½ percent.

Also be mindful of hotel taxes, which are 11¾ percent, in addition to whatever gratuitous surcharges (occupancy charges, per person rates, and so on) that your hotel tacks on to your bill. (For more straight talk on these and other hidden expenses, see Chapter 3.)

Part IV
Dining in New Orleans

The 5th Wave   By Rich Tennant

"I think I'll have the Cocoa Puffs Etouffée."

In this part . . .

Now that you're all settled in — or at least settled on when you're going, how you're getting there, and where you're staying — the time has come to get down to the meat and potatoes of your trip. Yep, I'm talking about food. After all, coming to New Orleans without sampling the cuisine is like . . . well, like coming to New Orleans without sampling the cuisine. Unthinkable! New Orleans is a city of excess, and nothing says excess like its rich, artery-clogging, sauce-laden feasts. New Orleans wasn't named the "Fattest City in America" for nothing. (It was so named in a study a few years back, but after a few meals in the Crescent City, you'll understand why the name still has meaning.)

In this part, you find information to bring you up to speed on the local dining scene, including what the locals are eating, what's good, and what's great. Then you find my picks for the city's best restaurants. Additionally, because too much is never enough, the last chapter of this part is devoted to the most important meal of the day, the snack, and the different places in New Orleans you can visit in between breakfast, lunch, and dinner. Bon appetit!

Chapter 13

Getting the Lowdown on New Orleans's Dining Scene

· ·

In This Chapter

▶ Knowing who and what are hot now

▶ Dishing up where the locals eat

▶ Discovering Cajun and Creole cuisine

▶ Finding the best places for ethnic cuisine

▶ Navigating reservation and dress-code policies

· ·

New Orleans enjoys its reputation as a Mecca for great food. The city's port-town status, unique ethnic mix, and proximity to Cajun Country all contribute to make it a combustible proving ground for exciting culinary combinations.

A recent study named New Orleans as the fattest city in the country — with good reason. Almost everything you eat here is fried or served in a rich, buttery sauce — or both. (It's also said that locals enjoy the highest self-imposed quality of life. See a connection?) If this horrifies you, you've picked the wrong place to visit. Although the city offers plenty of healthy alternatives (see Chapter 15), if you skip the decadent pleasures of a New Orleans meal, you're missing the point. Enjoy yourself; eat responsibly when you get home.

Discovering What's New, What's Hot, and Who's Who in the Kitchen

National dining trends do show up in New Orleans, but hot chefs here mostly create their own trends, employing ingredients and methods from different cuisines and coming up with some marvelous new combinations. As in Cajun and Creole cooking, fusion is a large part of what food in New Orleans is all about. Influences as varied as Spanish, Italian, West Indian, African, and Native American contribute to a wide range of choices — from creative and artistic gourmet dishes to down-home Southern cooking.

Thanks to the ubiquitous presence of celebrity chef Emeril Lagasse, Louisiana cooking has a higher profile than ever. His restaurants, **Emeril's, Nola,** and **Emeril's Delmonico,** draw large crowds looking for daring and creative Creole/New American cooking (and maybe a celebrity sighting or two).

However, Lagasse is far from the only popular chef in New Orleans. **Bayona's** Susan Spicer, **Cuvee's** Bingo Starr, and **Brigtsen's** Frank Brigtsen are just a few of the names you're likely to hear bandied about by local foodies. And one name I can almost guarantee you'll hear often in your gastronomic adventures is Brennan — with restaurants such as **Bacco** and **Brennan's,** this family is the dining scene's answer to the music scene's Neville and Marsalis dynasties.

Discovering the Top Dining Neighborhoods

How do you choose from the many excellent dining options in New Orleans? Consult the listings in Chapter 14, of course — or simply follow the locals to their favorite spots. This section presents a neighborhood-by-neighborhood breakdown of where the locals go when they want to chow down.

The French Quarter

Though the Quarter is widely regarded as tourist headquarters, it has an almost unbelievable number of standout restaurants that locals come to on a regular basis. A list of the best is much too long to run here, but a partial sampling must include classy favorites such as **Antoine's, Arnaud's,** and **Brennan's,** as well as wackier (and much cheaper) options such as **Clover Grill.** Plenty of great spots exist in between those extremes, from the contemporary fare at **Irene's Cuisine,** to the romantic ambiance and wonderful food at **Bella Luna** or Bayona. The choices are nearly endless, almost all of them commendable.

Central Business and Warehouse Districts

As I noted previously, **Emeril's** is one of the biggest names on the local scene — and with good reason. Locals also flock to the **Grill Room** for one of the most elegant dining experiences in the city. On the other end of the scale, **Mother's** exemplary sandwiches are cheap (and a calorie-counter's nightmare), and **Uglesich's** is a prime place to go for seafood (but not decor).

Garden District and Uptown

Time was, you could sum up your argument for the Garden District as a gourmet hot spot in two words: **Commander's Palace.** After all, the James Beard Association voted it best restaurant in the country a few years back — the food-industry equivalent of receiving an Oscar. But Commander's has some company these days, particularly Emeril Lagasse's reinvention of the old favorite **Delmonico.** Uptown, savvy gourmands flock to **Brigtsen's** in the Riverbend. Farther out, but worth the trip, **Upperline** serves inventive variations on Creole cuisine, while **Jacques-Imo's** has such a reputation for mouth-watering home-cooked meals that locals endure as much as an hour-and-a-half wait — the highest praise imaginable in this town.

Mid-City

Never a hotbed of culinary invention, Mid-City does boast a few stand-outs, such as the aptly named **Christian's,** serving fine French/Creole selections in a converted church. Visitors still getting over their Catholic school upbringing may have a better time at **Gabrielle,** a Creole/Cajun spot with French cafe ambience and outdoor dining. Serious steak lovers converge daily upon the original **Ruth's Chris Steak House** (where the popular chain originated) for 1½-inch-thick, USDA prime beef served on a sizzling platter.

A word on tourist spots

Aside from the really obvious tourist draws, locals don't go out of their way to avoid too many restaurants. You *will*, however, find a disproportionate ratio of tourists to locals at such Cajun-leaning establishments as **K-Paul's, Michaul's,** and **Mulate's,** which isn't necessarily a reflection on the food itself. A large proportion of tourists usually just means that a restaurant is geared more toward visitor-friendly standby dishes, while locals familiar with the basics seek out more inventive fare. (In all fairness, **K-Paul's** is arguably an exception to this rule; its high tourist count has a lot to do with Chef Paul Prudhomme's familiar name and its convenient French Quarter location.)

Eating Like a Local

Much of New Orleans cuisine rests on two regional foundations: Cajun and Creole cooking. **Cajun cooking** brought New Orleans to national attention in the early 1980s, thanks to the popularity of Chef Paul Prudhomme. Cajun descends from the households of the Acadian country folk who came from Nova Scotia to settle in rural Louisiana. In their new home, economy often dictated that these folks threw all available foods into a single pot — a tradition that brought us jambalaya, étouffée, and red beans and rice (which all true locals eat every Monday like clockwork).

Most people assume that the trademark of Cajun food is that it's prepared spicy and served piping hot. Although Cajun cuisine certainly relies on spice a great deal, its backbone is its combination of regional ingredients. And while it *is* wise to serve Cajun food steaming hot, neither the physical heat nor the spice should overwhelm the flavor.

Creole cooking is more varied and urban than Cajun food. Creole originated in the kitchens of New Orleans proper as a mix of French and Spanish cuisines. It relies heavily on high quality ingredients smothered in rich, delicate sauces, with African and Caribbean spices providing an extra kick.

New Orleans's Ethnic Eats

As if the roulette wheel of local culinary combinations wasn't enough, New Orleans, like most mid-sized cities, also offers its fair share of ethnic fare. Although I won't go into great detail, I will clue you in to a few of the best spots with this highly selective and subjective list:

- ✔ **Caribbean: Cafe Negril** (606 Frenchmen St., ☎ 504-944-4744)
- ✔ **Chinese: Five Happiness** (3605 S. Carrollton Ave., ☎ 504-482-3935)
- ✔ **Cuban: Liborio's Cuban Restaurant** (321 Magazine St., ☎ 504-581-9680)
- ✔ **Japanese: Samurai Sushi** (239 Decatur St., French Quarter, ☎ 504-525-9595) and **Wasabi** (900 Frenchmen St., ☎ 504-943-9433)
- ✔ **Mexican: Juan's Flying Burrito** (2018 Magazine St., ☎ 504-569-0000) and **Taqueria Corona** (857 Fulton St., Warehouse District, ☎ 504-524-9805; 5932 Magazine St., Uptown, ☎ 504-897-3974)
- ✔ **Mediterranean: The Moonlight Café** (1921 Sophie Wright Place, Uptown, ☎ 504-522-9919)
- ✔ **Middle Eastern: Jerusalem Restaurant** (4641 S. Carrollton Ave., ☎ 504-488-1450) and **Mona's Café** (504 Frenchmen St., ☎ 504-949-4115). See Chapter 15 for more on Mona's.
- ✔ **Thai: Basil Leaf** (1438 S. Carrollton Ave., ☎ 504-862-9001)
- ✔ **Vietnamese: Lemon Grass Café** (221 Camp St., ☎ 504-523-1200)

Ethnic food is great and all, but sometimes you just want some fried chicken and collard greens. I've saved a couple of comfort-food bastions (notably **Jacques-Imo's** and **Dooky Chase**) for the listings in Chapter 14. But here's a short list of some of the rest of the better soul food establishments in town:

  ✔ **Dunbar's Creole Cooking** (4927 Freret St., ☎ **504-899-0734**)

  ✔ **Henry's Soul Food** (2501 S. Claiborne Ave., on the corner of
     Claiborne and 2nd, ☎ **504-821-7757**; 209 N. Broad St., ☎ **504-821-8635**)

  ✔ **Zachary's** (8400 Oak St., Uptown, ☎ **504-865-1559**)

Eating Out without Losing Your Shirt

I'm sure you won't be shocked to learn that many tourist places —
especially in the French Quarter — charge inflated prices for "signature
New Orleans dishes" simply because they can. Keep in mind that many
New Orleans specialties, such as jambalaya, étouffée, red beans and
rice, muffulettas, and po' boy sandwiches, were invented as economy
measures, made with common ingredients that make them easy to prepare. Any place that charges you a lot of money for any of these is just
ripping you off. You can find incredibly tasty versions of these staples
very cheaply at any number of places, so go elsewhere.

Another way to save some dough without sacrificing the quality of
your New Orleans dining experience is to visit the city's fancier restaurants for lunch rather than dinner. Lunch menus almost always offer
more affordable versions of a particular institution's signature dishes.
This, in turn, should free you up to frequent looser, less-expensive
spots, such as Clover Grill or Franky and Johnny's (see Chapter 15), for
dinner; having stuffed yourself during the day, you'll be more likely to
eat less, which will help you sleep better as well as protect your wallet.

Conversely, you may want to skip lunch altogether, fortifying yourself
with a few snacks during your afternoon sightseeing. Of course, granola
bars and the odd piece of fruit will only take you so far, in which case
you could bend this idea slightly, maybe grabbing a Lucky Dog (see
Chapter 15) or a quick po' boy as you hoof it from one stop to another.

Dining Details

In your haste to enjoy all the fine food for which New Orleans is justly
famous, you may have overlooked one or two key considerations.
Here are some things to keep in mind before you head out on your
gastronomic adventure.

Making reservations

When a review in Chapter 14 recommends that you reserve a table at a
restaurant, it generally means for dinner. You can usually get a table for
two at lunch without having to wait too long (if at all). With a couple of
exceptions (noted in the reviews), the same goes for breakfast.

Restaurants in New Orleans do a very brisk business except during the hot summer months. Consequently, you should make reservations before you even leave home if you want to dine at a certain restaurant at a particular time. You may need to reserve a table a month or more in advance, particularly during Mardi Gras and Jazz Fest, if you want to eat at one of the most famous restaurants. If you forgot to make reservations, arrive early — before noon (or even before 11:30 a.m.) for lunch and before 6:30 p.m. for dinner.

Dressing to dine

Legends claim that Antoine's restaurant once turned away Mick Jagger because he wasn't wearing a jacket. Whether that's true or not, top-of-the-line restaurants such as **Antoine's** and **Commander's Palace** obviously require the full jacket-and-tie treatment. Other than that, though, New Orleans, being a tourist-dependent market, is pretty casual about dress codes. Most serious dining spots, such as **Olivier's,** require the much less stringent "business casual" look (a nice shirt and a jacket or blazer; jeans are usually allowed, but only if they're in good condition — if you're uncertain, call your restaurant ahead of time). Even the best restaurants allow casual wear at lunch. And obviously, no one is going to kick you out of a corner po' boy shop for wearing shorts, flip-flops, and a Hawaiian print shirt. Check the individual restaurant listings in Chapter 14 for special dress requirements.

Lighting up

When it comes to smoking in restaurants, New Orleans is slightly more lenient than the rest of the country. While many restaurants prohibit smoking or relegate it to certain sections (notably in the French Quarter, where space and atmosphere are at a premium), many others still tolerate it. If the freedom to smoke (or the freedom to enjoy a lack of smoke) is super-important, call ahead to find out a restaurant's policy.

Tips on gratuities

The **sales tax** in New Orleans is one of the highest in the country: 9 percent. Many diners use this as a handy guideline when figuring out the tip; they just take the tax and double it to get 18 percent. A general guideline for tipping is 15 to 20 percent, depending upon the level of service and quality of experience you receive.

Keep in mind that some waiters must split their tips with the rest of the wait staff *and* the kitchen staff. Don't feel obliged to reward poor service, but if the service is excellent, be generous.

Chapter 14

New Orleans's Best Dining Bets

. . . .

In This Chapter

▶ Reviewing the basics of dining in New Orleans

▶ Discovering the best restaurants in town

▶ Indexing the restaurants by location, cuisine, and price

. . . .

Grab your fork and get ready to loosen your belt a notch or two, because this chapter explores New Orleans restaurants. I start with the entree — my picks of the best and/or most popular restaurants in the city, arranged in easy alphabetical order. The price range, neighborhood, and cuisine type follow the restaurant name. After that, you can cleanse the palate with indexes that can help you figure out the best bets for your tastes and needs.

The reviews also make note of which restaurants are wheelchair accessible. Call ahead to inquire, however, because some of these places may still provide problems — tables may be packed a little too closely together, for instance.

Except for the first three weeks of December, restaurants in New Orleans are very busy from September through May. Consequently, if you simply must eat at a particular restaurant at a certain time, make your reservations at least a week in advance. Of course, the earlier you reserve your table the better. Especially around Jazz Fest and Mardi Gras, some restaurants actually fill up a month or more in advance. Even if you don't make reservations before you leave home, call and see if you can get in. People often cancel reservations at the last minute, or the restaurant may not be booked up in the first place, no matter how popular it is. Some restaurants don't take reservations at all. Long lines out front make up for this informality, however.

One further note: Even if this whole book covered nothing but New Orleans restaurants, it still couldn't do justice to the many fine establishments in the city and its outskirts. These reviews are necessarily brief and to the point (well, mostly, anyway). And because space con-straints prohibit me from highlighting every worthy establishment, this chapter is merely meant to provide a representative sampling, filled with no-brainers, conventional-wisdom choices, and necessarily selec-tive choices of my own. From Restaurant August to Belle Forché, Cobalt, and Zoe Bistrot, a whole alphabet of other fine, deserving restaurants are worth your consideration should the occasion arise.

What the $ Symbols Mean

The dining experience in New Orleans covers low-key and friendly to white-gloved formal. To let you know what to expect price-wise, the restaurant listings in this chapter are accompanied by a dollar symbol ($), which gives you an idea of what a complete meal (including appe-tizer, entree, dessert, one drink, taxes, and tip) costs per person. Most listings contain more than one symbol — for example, $–$$ — to indicate the general price range you're likely to encounter at each restaurant. Aside from price ranges, the difference between one rank-ing and the next also reflects extras such as location, reputation, type of cuisine, atmosphere, interior, service, and view.

Here's the breakdown of the dollar signs:

- ✔ **$ (dirt cheap):** You'll pay under $15 per person for a full meal at these popular places, which offer good food in a simple setting.

- ✔ **$$ (inexpensive):** Though the decor may not be designer, you can expect some delicious New Orleans food for between $15 and $25 per person.

- ✔ **$$$ (moderate):** Probably the best bets for a fine, relatively fancy dinner that doesn't cost a fortune (say, $25 to $35 dollars per person), most of these restaurants offer classy food, nice decor, and good service.

- ✔ **$$$$ (expensive):** Top food, top chefs, top service, top location, and top decor will cost you between $35 and $45 per person at some of the best restuarants in New Orleans.

- ✔ **$$$$$ (the ultimate):** These glamorous, cream-of-the-crop restau-rants have achieved world fame — either for the celebrated skills of the chef or for the atmosphere, view, and location (and fre-quently for all of the above). These restaurants will give you a unique experience to remember for the rest of your life. Also expect a memorable bill, however, more than $45 per person.

New Orleans's Top Restaurants from A to Z

Antoine's

$$$-$$$$$ **French Quarter**   **Classic French/Creole Cuisine**

An old-line experience all the way. Menu items include old-world dishes such as *pompano en papillote* (the fish is cooked in a paper bag with shrimp and lump crabmeat) and *pommes souffle* (a potato with a crispy outside and a steamy, pillowy inside). The 15 dining rooms run the gamut from plain to opulent, and some sort of caste system governs the seating process. (The front dining room is "reserved" for tourists.) Antoine's gets away with this by virtue of its place in New Orleans culinary history; it's the birthplace of Oysters Rockefeller.

713 St. Louis St. (half a block from Bourbon Street). An easy walk from anywhere in the French Quarter. ☎ *504-581-4422. Internet:* www.antoines.com. *You should make reservations a week in advance for the weekend. Main courses: $19.25–$56 (most under $25). AE, CB, DC, MC, V. Open: Mon–Sat 11:30 a.m–2 p.m. and 5:30–9:30 p.m. Jackets required after 5 p.m., but casual wear is acceptable for lunch. Wheelchair accessible.*

Arnaud's

$$-$$$$ **French Quarter**   **Creole**

Arnaud's is a classic New Orleans restaurant with a real sense of history, founded in 1918. Luckily, the quality of the food hasn't diminished with age, and neither has the decor, which features antique ceiling fans, flickering gas lamps, and dark wood paneling. The restaurant has 12 buildings connected by stairs and hallways — it sprawls leisurely over an entire city block. Specialties include shrimp Creole and trout meunière, and the filet mignon entrees are better than most steakhouse selections. For dessert, try the intimidatingly titled Chocolate Devastation. Also check out the Germaine Wells Mardi Gras Museum upstairs. Arnaud's Remoulade, a casual, more wallet-and-kid-friendly satellite, sits right around the corner on Bourbon Street.

813 Bienville (at the corner of Bourbon Street), an easy walk from anywhere in the French Quarter or Central Business District. ☎ *866-230-8891 or 504-523-5433. Internet:* www.arnauds.com. *You should make reservations a week or more in advance for the weekend. Main courses: $19.50–$34. AE, DC, DISC, MC, V. Open: Lunch Mon–Fri 11:30 a.m.–2:30 p.m.; dinner Sun–Thurs 6–10 p.m., Fri–Sat 6–10:30 p.m.; Sun jazz brunch 10 a.m.–2:30 p.m. Dress code is casual for lunch; dinner requires a jacket for men. Wheelchair accessible.*

Bacco

$$–$$$ **French Quarter** **Italian/Creole**

This relatively new addition to the Brennan portfolio pushes the Creole envelope deep into Italian territory. Though the menu is seasonal, some good bets are the Creole Italian gumbo (made with roasted goose, Italian sausage, and tasso) and *gnocchi* (potato dumplings baked with Gorgonzola cheese sauce). In lieu of your regular pepperoni pizza, experiment with the foie gras pizza topped with onions, mushrooms, mozzarella, and white truffle oil. And don't skimp on the desserts (a Brennan hallmark); the tiramisu may be the best you ever taste.

310 Chartres St. (2 blocks from Bourbon Street, 2½ blocks from Canal Street, and 2½ blocks from Jackson Square). ☎ *504-522-2426. Internet:* www.bacco.com. *You should make reservations a couple of days in advance for the weekend. Main courses: $16–$24. AE, DC, MC, V. Open: Daily 11:30 a.m.–2 p.m.; Sun–Thurs 6:30–9:30 p.m., Fri–Sat 6–10:30 p.m. Shorts and T-shirts are allowed. Wheelchair accessible.*

Bayona

$$–$$$ **French Quarter** **International**

Bayona is considered one of the city's most beloved dining experiences. Celebrity chef Susan Spicer creates unconventional dishes from different cultures (though unlike many chefs, she doesn't blend styles together; rather, each is distinct). Dishes such as grilled duck breast with pepper-jelly glaze and Pecan-crusted rabbit with Creole mustard-tasso cream sauce have consistently drawn raves from local and national publications alike. The atmosphere in this 200-year-old Creole cottage is warm and homey — the perfect background for a romantic evening.

430 Dauphine St. (1 block from Bourbon Street). ☎ *504-525-4455. Internet:* www.bayona.com. *Reservations required for dinner, recommended for lunch. Main courses: $18–$28. AE, CB, DC, DISC, MC, V. Open: Lunch Mon–Fri 11:30 a.m.–2 p.m.; dinner Mon–Thurs 6–10 p.m., Fri–Sat 6–11 p.m. Dress is business casual. A low step and small restroom may be problems for people with disabilities.*

Bella Luna

$$–$$$$ **French Quarter** **Eclectic/Continental**

Bella Luna is widely regarded as the most romantic restaurant in the city, thanks to its Italian villa decor and expansive view of the Mississippi River (which is quite breathtaking). Chef/owner Horst Pfeifer lovingly oversees an eclectic menu of (among others) Southwestern, German, Italian, and Louisiana cuisines. The menu changes throughout the year, but pasta is a specialty. Some recent favorites have included the stuffed shrimp or the pork chop with a pecan crust, horseradish mashed potatoes, and a sauce made from Abita Beer (a popular local microbrew). For dessert, try the banana bread pudding or the Key lime pie.

French Quarter Dining

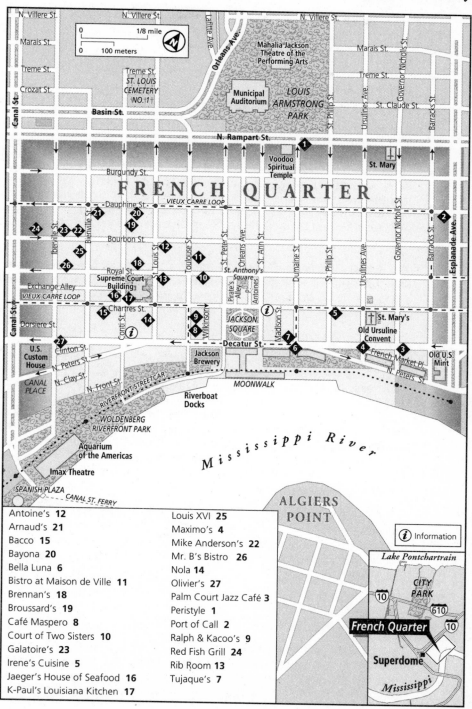

Antoine's **12**

Arnaud's **21**

Bacco **15**

Bayona **20**

Bella Luna **6**

Bistro at Maison de Ville **11**

Brennan's **18**

Broussard's **19**

Café Maspero **8**

Court of Two Sisters **10**

Galatoire's **23**

Irene's Cuisine **5**

Jaeger's House of Seafood **16**

K-Paul's Louisiana Kitchen **17**

Louis XVI **25**

Maximo's **4**

Mike Anderson's **22**

Mr. B's Bistro **26**

Nola **14**

Olivier's **27**

Palm Court Jazz Café **3**

Peristyle **1**

Port of Call **2**

Ralph & Kacoo's **9**

Red Fish Grill **24**

Rib Room **13**

Tujaque's **7**

914 N. Peters St. (1 block from Jackson Square). ☎ **504-529-1583.** *Internet: www.bellalunarestaurant.com. Reservations recommended. Main courses: $17.75–$26.50. AE, CB, DC, DISC, MC, V. Open: Mon–Sat 6–10:30 p.m., Sun 6–9:30 p.m. No jeans, shorts, sneakers, or T-shirts. The restaurant is wheelchair accessible, but restrooms are down a half-flight of stairs.*

Bistro at Maison de Ville
$$–$$$ **French Quarter** **International/Eclectic**

One of the city's best-kept secrets, the Bistro is popular among locals for many reasons, from the intimate, romantic atmosphere to the inventive dishes and extensive wine list. The leap from "intimate" to "cramped" is short here, however, and the small size can also mean a good wait (especially when the theater crowd pours in). The menu changes every three months, but, depending on the season, you're likely to encounter such options as a pan-seared foie gras appetizer served with grilled apples, perhaps followed by medallions of lamb tenderloin served atop a salad of greens, lentils, asparagus, and feta cheese.

733 Toulouse St. (in the Hotel Maison de Ville), ☎ **504-528-9206.** *Internet: www.maisondeville.com. Reservations recommended. Main courses: $19.75–$24.75. AE, DC, DISC, MC, V. Open: Daily 11:30 a.m.–2 p.m. and 6–10 p.m. Dress is casual. Not accessible for wheelchairs.*

Bluebird Cafe
$ **Uptown** **American/New American**

This unassuming spot has long been a favorite among locals seeking the best huevos rancheros in town. You'll often have to wait at least 30 minutes for a table on weekend mornings, but the breakfast is well worth it. Build your own omelet, try the buckwheat pecan waffles, or see if the huevos rancheros lives up to its rep (if you don't like your eggs runny, you can get scrambled rancheros). Burgers and similar lunch fare are satisfying, as well, and while the ambiance isn't much, it's a great place to people-watch.

3625 Prytania St. ☎ **504-895-7166.** *Reservations not accepted. All menu items are under $8. No credit cards. Open: Mon–Fri 7 a.m.–3 p.m., Sat–Sun 8 a.m.–3 p.m. Dress is casual. No ramp for wheelchairs, but the doors are wide enough to accommodate disabled visitors, and the staff will happily help you get inside with a minimum of hassle.*

Brennan's
$$$–$$$$$ **French Quarter** **French/Creole**

You've heard of Breakfast at Tiffany's? In New Orleans, the tradition is Breakfast at Brennan's. The morning repasts here have clogged generations of arteries with multicourse feasts featuring such sauce-laden options as Eggs Portuguese (poached and served in a puff pastry ladled with hollandaise). Other favorites include Eggs Benedict, Eggs Hussarde, and Trout Nancy (they're big on proper names here). Such extravagance is not without its price; spending $50 on breakfast alone is easy (Shoney's all-you-can-eat, this ain't). In spite of the cost, Brennan's is always crowded at breakfast and lunch; expect a bit of a wait, even with a reservation. Dinners are generally calmer.

417 Royal St. (1 block from Bourbon Street). ☎ *504-525-9711. Internet:* www. brennansneworleans.com. *Reservations recommended. Main courses: Dinner $28.50–$38.50. AE, CB, DC, DISC, MC, V. Open: Daily 8 a.m.–2:30 p.m. and 6–10 p.m. Jacket recommended for men at dinner. Wheelchair accessible.*

Brigtsen's

$$–$$$　**Uptown　Cajun/Creole**

The atmosphere in this converted shotgun cottage manages to be both elegant and homey. The menu changes daily, but Chef Frank Brigtsen's high consistency level ranks him as one of the best chefs in the city. Try the roast duck (a boneless half duckling served with tasty dirty rice and a sumptuous honey pecan gravy) or the garlic-roasted chicken breast. Brigtsen knows his way around rabbit (a Creole mainstay), and daily seasonal fish specials never fail to satisfy. Dessert options can include café au lait crème brûlée, homemade lemonade ice cream (an acquired taste, but one that grows on you), and homemade mint chocolate chip ice cream.

723 Dante St. (take the St. Charles streetcar; get off at the corner of St. Charles and S. Carrollton avenues and walk 3 blocks; take a taxi at night). ☎ *504-861-7610. Reservations required. Main courses: $14–$28 (early bird specials available Tues–Thurs 5:30–6:30 p.m. — full meal for $16.95). AE, DC, MC, V. Open: Tues–Sat 5:30–10 p.m. Nice casual. Steps may prove a challenge for people with disabilities.*

Broussard's

$$$–$$$$　**French Quarter　French/Creole**

The general consensus is that after a period of resting on its laurels, Broussard's is once again earning accolades as one of the Quarter's top restaurants for both food and mood thanks to such signature dishes as Oysters Broussard and Duck Normandy. If you're lucky enough to savor the garlic caraway-crusted pork rib chop (served with red lentils, onion, relish, and a wild mushroom Madeira demiglace), you'll likely agree. The nearby noise of Bourbon Street disappears beneath the quiet and elegant atmosphere. Make sure to check out the great courtyard if you're in the mood for amoré.

819 Conti St. (½ block from Bourbon Street). ☎ *504-581-3866. Internet:* www.broussards.com. *Reservations strongly recommended. Main courses: $21.50–$36. AE, MC, V. Open: Daily 5:30–10 p.m. No jeans, shorts, sneakers, or T-shirts. Wheelchair accessible.*

Café Maspero

$ French Quarter   Sandwiches/Seafood

With good reason, this place is always packed (its Decatur Street location doesn't hurt either). Café Maspero serves up seafood, grilled marinated chicken, and other familiar comfort food (though you won't find po' boys here), as well as kiddie-friendly items such as burgers and deli sandwiches — almost all of it served with fries, in impressively large portions and at ridiculously low prices. That is, low in relation to the rest of the Quarter, anyway. The café also offers a huge selection of beers, wines, and cocktails. (Don't confuse this restaurant with Maspero's Slave Exchange a few blocks away.)

601 Decatur St. (2 short blocks from Jackson Square and 3 blocks from Bourbon Street). ☎ *504-523-6250. Reservations are not accepted, and the lines can be long at times, but they usually move fast. Main courses: $4.25–$9. No credit cards. Open: Sun–Thurs 11:00 a.m.–11:00 p.m. (till midnight Fri–Sat). No dress code. Wheelchair accessible, but the crowded tables and narrow doorways make maneuvering a challenge.*

Christian's

$$$–$$$$ Mid-City   French/Creole

Located in a former church (the old altar is the waiters' station, and the sermon board out front lists the menu), this is one of the city's great French/Creole restaurants. It's not exactly close to the Quarter or Central Business District, but it's not prohibitively far, either. For appetizers, the oysters en brochette are heaven-sent (sorry); the crabmeat turnover and smoked soft-shell crabs also earned recent hosannas. The roasted duck and the gumbo are both good bets, as are daily fish specials. For dessert, ask for the chocolate espresso torte (flourless chocolate cake flavored with Grand Marnier and Kahlua in a raspberry sauce).

3835 Iberville St. (3 miles from the Quarter — take a taxi). % 504-482-4924. Reservations recommended. Main courses: $18–$30. AE, DC, MC, V. Open: Tues–Fri 11:30 a.m.–2 p.m.; Tues–Sat 5:30–9:30 p.m. Jacket and tie strongly recommended for men. Steps and closely packed tables make it problematic for people with wheelchairs.

Commander's Palace

$$$–$$$$$ Garden District   Creole

Even in a city full of top-notch, elegant restaurants, Commander's Palace evokes a knowing smile. Commander's maintains a soft spot in locals' hearts with a winning combination of stellar service (you'll be pampered by several attendants throughout your meal), a grand setting (an 1880s Victorian house with a seemingly endless series of dining rooms and a gorgeous courtyard), and outstanding food. The turtle soup is justly famous, and such bright spots as the boned Mississippi roasted quail

Mid-City Dining

Christian's **2**
Gabrielle **4**
Jacques-Imo's **1**
Ruth's Chris Steak House **3**

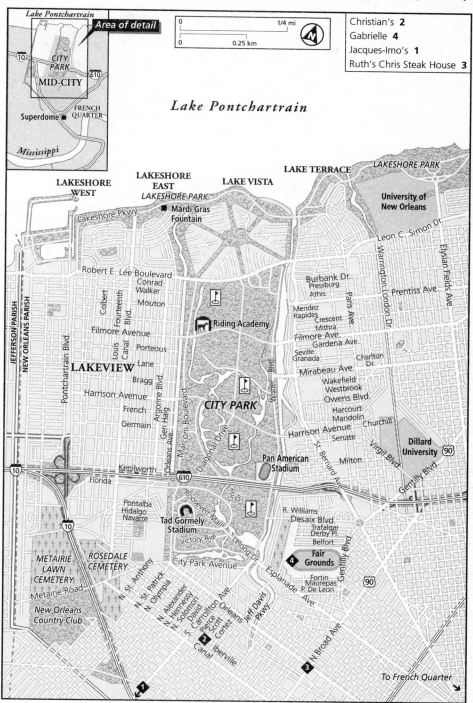

(stuffed with an awesome Creole crawfish sausage) and the mixed grill (which features lamb and rabbit sausage) light up the menu. Lastly, when the staff suggests the bread pudding soufflé for dessert, trust them.

1403 Washington Ave. (take the St. Charles streetcar to Washington and walk 2 blocks along Washington Ave. toward the river; take a taxi at night). ☎ *504-899-8221. Internet:* www.commanderspalace.com. *Reservations required. Main courses: Full brunch $22–$29; main courses $29–$32; prix-fixe $33–$40. AE, CB, DC, DISC, MC, V. Open: Mon–Fri 11:30 a.m.–2 p.m.; daily 6–10 p.m.; Jazz brunch Sat 11:30 a.m.–1 p.m., Sun 10:30 a.m.–1:30 p.m. Men must wear a jacket and tie for dinner. Wheelchairs will need to navigate over one step.*

Court of Two Sisters
$$$–$$$$ **French Quarter** **Creole**

The bottom line is that the atmosphere here — a historic building with a large, graceful courtyard filled with flowers, gurgling fountains, and a wishing well — is better than the food. A strolling jazz band serenades you during the daily jazz brunch, though most locals avoid it (the brunch, not the band) for fear of looking like tourists. The food is often impressive, but rarely spectacular. The jazz brunch boasts more than 60 dishes, including meat, fowl, fish, vegetables, fresh fruits, homemade breads, and pastries. For dinner, stick to safe bets such as the chicken Michelle or shrimp remoulade (and keep in mind that the restaurant maintains a $15 minimum for dinner). Desserts are very good, though; splurge on the pecan pie or crêpes suzette. A children's menu offers shrimp or chicken fingers, with baked potato or fries, a fruit cup or ice cream, and milk; kids 5–12 can also partake of the brunch buffet for $10.00.

613 Royal St. (1 block from Bourbon Street). ☎ *504-522-7261. Internet:* www.courtoftwosisters.com. *Reservations recommended. Main courses: $18–$30 (fixed-price meal available for $38); brunch $22. AE, CB, DC, DISC, MC, V. Open: Daily 9 a.m.–3 p.m. and 5:30–10 p.m. Shorts and T-shirts are allowed. Wheelchair accessible.*

Cuvee
$$–$$$ **Central Business District** **Creole/New American**

Chef Richard "Bingo" Starr expertly balances classic Louisiana cuisine with New American fusion at this much talked about newcomer to the dining scene. The cavernous dining room, lit by gaslight, sets a perfectly intimate mood for such creations as shrimp Mirliton Napoleon (served with a spicy shrimp remoulade sauce) and herb-crusted salmon steak. An expansive wine list complements the cuisine nicely.

322 Magazine St. ☎ *504-587-9001. Reservations recommended. Main courses: $7–$22. AE, DC, MC, V. Open: Mon–Fri 7–10 a.m., 11 a.m.–2 p.m., and 5:30–10 p.m.; Sat 7–10 a.m. and 5:30–10 p.m. Wheelchair accessible.*

Dooky Chase

$$–$$$ **Mid-City   Creole/Soul Food**

Chef Leah Chase, a local celebrity and a very sweet lady, oversees the action in this simply-yet-sumptuously decorated establishment that specializes in upscale soul food. The service is always friendly, if not always as prompt as you may like. Classic dishes such as gumbo and fried chicken are flat-out delightful, though you probably won't go wrong with more esoteric fare such as Shrimp Clemenceau, a casserole of sautéed shellfish, mushrooms, peas, and potatoes. For dessert, savor the thick, hot bread pudding with shredded coconut and pecans in a praline liqueur sauce (one of the best bread puddings in a city that excels at them).

2301 Orleans Ave. (because the neighborhood is a bit dicey, take a cab). ☎ *504-821-2294. Reservations recommended at dinner. Main courses: $10.95–$25; fixed-price 4-course meal for $25 and a "Creole Feast" for $37.50. AE, DC, DISC, MC, V. Open: Daily 11:30 a.m.–10 p.m. Dress is casual, but no shorts or tank tops. Wheelchair accessible.*

Emeril's

$$$–$$$$$ **Warehouse District   Creole/New American**

Emeril Lagasse's specialty is what he calls "New New Orleans Cuisine," using Creole tradition as a foundation while exploring bold new directions. The desserts outnumber the entrees here, and the menu changes often, but the rack of lamb and fresh duck are favorites, and the grilled, Creole-seasoned chicken is a crowd-pleaser as well. Don't miss the banana cream pie with caramel sauce, which has reduced diners to moaning and pounding on the table to document their pleasure.

800 Tchoupitoulas (8 blocks from Canal — take a taxi). ☎ *504-528-9393. Internet:* www.emerils.com. *Reservations required. Main courses: $22–$36; a 7-course degustation menu (which changes nightly) is $75. AE, CB, DC, DISC, MC, V. Open: Lunch Mon–Fri 11:30 a.m.–2 p.m.; dinner Mon–Thurs 6–10 p.m. and Fri–Sat 6–11p.m. Casual dress. Wheelchair accessible.*

Emeril's Delmonico Restaurant and Bar

$$$–$$$$$ **Lower Garden District   Creole/New American**

Emeril Lagasse's resurrection of this link in the famous Delmonico chain is arguably one of the finest restaurants in the city; it's certainly one of the most expensive. The design, like the menu, is a sumptuous blend of the old and the new. While a team of waiters takes care of the smallest details, diners sink their teeth into classic New Orleans dishes prepared with a twist. The regular menu items are pricey enough, but if you can afford it and have a few hours to kill, order the Chef's tasting menu, a fixed-price multicourse meal, which on a recent visit cost $70, plus another $50 for a matching wine for each course. Reservations here can be hard to come by; when you do book a time, show up early to enjoy a drink in the lovely downstairs bar.

1300 St. Charles Ave. % 504-525-4937. Internet: www.emerils.com. Reservations are strongly recommended. Main courses: $18–$30; fixed-price $50–$70. AE, DC, DISC, MC, V. Open: Lunch Mon–Fri 11:30 a.m.–2 p.m.; dinner Sun–Thurs 6–10 p.m. and Fri–Sat 6–11 p.m.; brunch Sun 10:30 a.m.–2 p.m. Jackets are recommended for men; the dress is business casual, which means no jeans or shorts. Wheelchair accessible.

Gabrielle

$$–$$$$ **Mid-City** **French/Creole/Cajun**

This small, intimate restaurant recalls a Parisian sidewalk café. The ever-changing menu, which features crowd-pleasing gumbos, homemade sausages, rabbit, and seafood dishes, has lately become one of the city's standouts. A typically tasty (and inventive) entree is the slow-roasted duck with orange sherry sauce, served with wild mushrooms and red and yellow peppers atop a bed of shoestring potatoes. As for desserts, the Peppermint Patti — a concoction made of chocolate cake, peppermint ice cream, and chocolate sauce — has proven quite popular.

3201 Esplanade Ave. (2½ miles from the Quarter — take a taxi). ☎ 504-948-6233. Reservations recommended. Main courses: $18–$32. AE, CB, DC, DISC, MC, V. Open: Tues–Sat 5:30–10 p.m.; lunch on Fridays only, Oct–May, 11:30 a.m.–2 p.m. Casual dress. The restaurant is wheelchair accessible, but the restroom is not.

Galatoire's

$$–$$$$ **French Quarter** **French**

One of the classiest restaurants in New Orleans, generations of families have stood in line here: Galatoire's does not accept reservations, and even made the Duke and Duchess of Windsor wait for a table — or so local legend has it. An ongoing debate rages about this place, however: Is Galatoire's still the best, or is it coasting on its reputation? Those in the know (including those who have made Sunday dinner here a tradition) say to order the trout amandine without sauce, or the red snapper or redfish topped with sautéed crabmeat meunière from the à la carte menu, and you'll be persuaded this staunchly traditional spot is still a contender.

209 Bourbon St. (located in the second block of Bourbon Street, an easy walk from anywhere in the Quarter or the Central Business District). ☎ 504-525-2021. Internet: www.galatoires.com. Reservations not accepted. Main courses: $13.50–$27. AE, DC, DISC, MC, V. Open: Tues–Sun 11:30 a.m.–10 p.m. Men must wear jackets for dinner and on Sunday. The restaurant is wheelchair accessible, but the restrooms can be a problem.

Gautreau's

$$–$$$$ **Uptown**   **Contemporary Louisiana**

The candlelight and nostalgic photographs set a more romantic mood than the building (an old converted neighborhood drugstore) may suggest. The upscale menu changes every few weeks; appetizers have included duck confit and eggplant crisps, and the grilled hanger steak (similar to flank) was a recent hit, though you may want to try the roasted chicken, served with wild mushrooms, garlic potatoes, and green beans. Try the triple-layer cheesecake (with chocolate, pecan, and almond layers) for dessert, or if it's available, the tarte tatin (apples and sun-dried cherries with a strawberry sorbet).

1728 Soniat St. (take the St. Charles streetcar and walk 2½ blocks down Soniat away from the river; take a taxi at night). ☎ *504-899-7397. Reservations recommended. Main courses: $17.50–$34. DC, DISC, MC, V. Open: Mon–Sat 6–10 p.m. A few steps make the small restrooms inaccessible to wheelchairs.*

Grill Room

$$$–$$$$$ **Central Business District**   **International**

An exceptionally high level of service, food quality, and comfort makes the Grill Room (on the second floor of the Windsor Court Hotel) an unforgettable dining experience — at a price you won't soon forget, either. The menu changes frequently and can include such fancy fare as moderately blackened filet of halibut, chilled oysters with frozen champagne ginger granita (champagne seasoned with ginger, which has been frozen into a sorbet), or a rich roasted goose. Though you can indulge your wine-drinking habits and pay upwards of $18,000 for a double magnum (a quadruple-sized bottle) of 1961 Chateau Petrus, wine starts at just $20 a bottle. Eating here is an extravagant experience, but not necessarily excessive.

300 Gravier St. (one block from Canal). ☎ *504-522-1992. Internet:* www.windsor courthotel.com. *You should make reservations a week or two in advance. Main courses: $28–$39 (3-course lunch specials $25). AE, DC, DISC, MC, V. Open: Daily 7–10:30 a.m., Mon–Sat 11:30 a.m.–2 p.m., Sun–Thurs 6–10 p.m., and Fri–Sat 6–10:30 p.m.; brunch Sun 9 a.m.–2 p.m. Jacket required and tie recommended at dinner. Wheelchair accessible.*

Herbsaint

$$–$$$$ **Central Business District**   **French/New American**

Acclaimed local chef Susan Spicer opened this cozy, happening space in the fall of 2000, instantly enhancing her already rosy reputation as the mastermind behind the popular restaurants Bayona (see its review elsewhere in this chapter) and Cobalt. The decor is suitably minimal, assuring no distractions from the adventurous cuisine. Offerings such as

New Orleans Dining

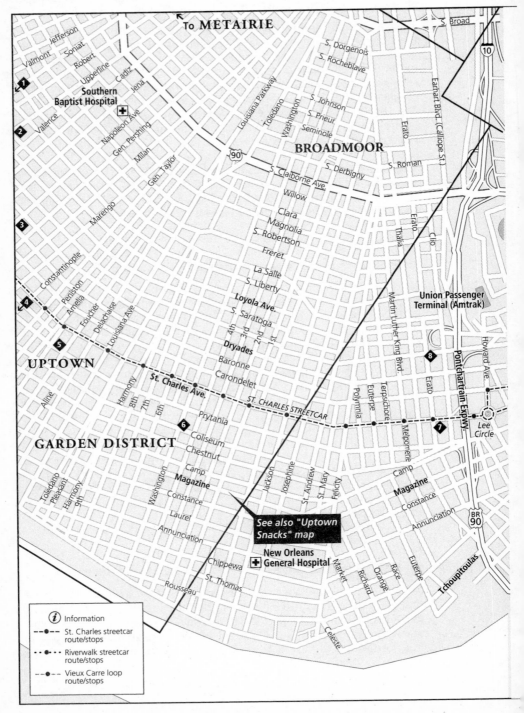

To METAIRIE

Jefferson
Valmont
Soniat
Robert
Upperline
Cadiz
Jena

Southern
Baptist Hospital

Valence

Napoleon Ave.
Gen. Pershing
Milan
Gen. Taylor

Marengo

Constantinople
Peniston
Amelia
Foucher
Delachaise
Louisiana Ave.

UPTOWN

St. Charles Ave.

Aline
Harmony
8th
7th
6th

Prytania

Coliseum
Chestnut
Camp
Magazine

GARDEN DISTRICT

Toledano
Pleasant
Harmony
9th

Washington
Constance
Laurel
Annunciation

Chippewa
St. Thomas

Rousseau

S. Dorgenois
S. Rocheblave

Louisiana Parkway
Toledano
Washington
S. Johnson
S. Prieur
Seminole

BROADMOOR

S. Derbigny
S. Roman

S. Claiborne Ave.
Willow
Clara
Magnolia
S. Robertson
Freret
La Salle
S. Liberty
Loyola Ave.
S. Saratoga
4th
3rd
2nd
1st
Dryades
Baronne
Carondelet

ST. CHARLES STREETCAR

Jackson
Josephine
St. Andrew
St. Mary
Felicity

See also "Uptown
Snacks" map

New Orleans
General Hospital

S. Broad

10

Earhart Blvd. (Calliope St.)
Erato
Thalia
Clio

Martin Luther King Blvd.

Union Passenger
Terminal (Amtrak)

Erato

Pontchartrain Expwy.

Howard Ave.

Lee
Circle

Polymnia
Euterpe
Terpsichore
Melpomene

Camp
Magazine
Constance
Annunciation

BR
90

Market
Orange
Richard
Race
Euterpe

Tchoupitoulas

Celeste

ⓘ Information

--●-- St. Charles streetcar
route/stops

--●-- Riverwalk streetcar
route/stops

--●-- Vieux Carre loop
route/stops

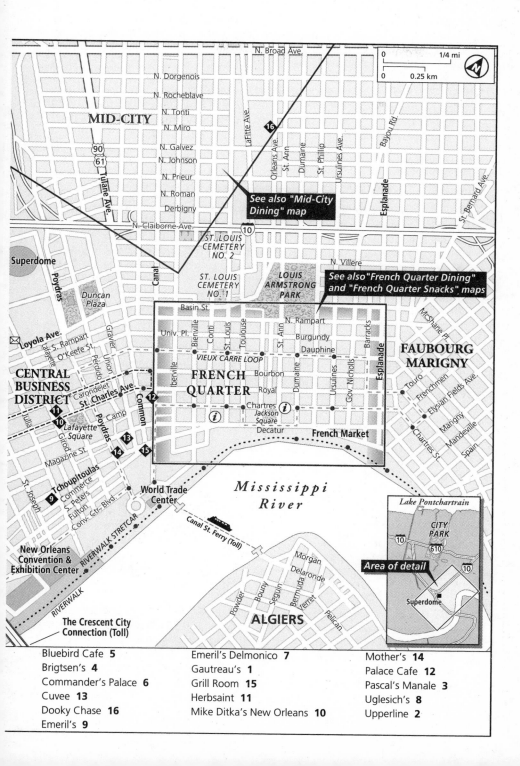

Bluebird Cafe **5**	Emeril's Delmonico **7**	Mother's **14**
Brigtsen's **4**	Gautreau's **1**	Palace Cafe **12**
Commander's Palace **6**	Grill Room **15**	Pascal's Manale **3**
Cuvee **13**	Herbsaint **11**	Uglesich's **8**
Dooky Chase **16**	Mike Ditka's New Orleans **10**	Upperline **2**
Emeril's **9**		

braised lamb shanks, duck confit, and fried frogs' legs dot a menu that veers between Gallic familiarity and New American experimentation. Try an obscure but pleasant selection from the offbeat wine list, and satisfy your curiosity by enjoying a chocolate beignet for dessert.

701 St. Charles Ave. ☎ *504-524-4114. Internet:* www.herbsaint.com. *Reservations recommended. Main courses: $14–$18. AE, DISC, MC, V. Open: Lunch Mon–Fri 11:30 a.m.–2:30 p.m., Mon–Sat 5:30–10:30 p.m. Dress is business casual. Wheelchair accessible.*

Irene's Cuisine
$$–$$$ **French Quarter** **Italian/French Provencal**

Many locals swear by this small restaurant, located on the corner of a parking garage. Despite a brisk pace, the dark atmosphere (the waiters carry flashlights for a reason) can be really romantic. Start off with an appetizer of grilled shrimp served with just-so crunchy, panéed oysters. Follow that up with rack of lamb (served with a port wine sauce and herb garlic potatoes) or roasted chicken Rosmario, draped in a luxuriant rosemary gravy. Fish fans should consider the daily fish specials, which an acquaintance of mine raves about often. For dessert, the bread pudding with roasted pecans is a crunchy, creamy pleasure.

539 St. Philip St. (3 short blocks from Jackson Square and 1 block from Decatur Street). ☎ **504-529-8811.** *Reservations not accepted (go early to avoid a wait). Main courses: $14–$19. AE, MC, V. Open: Sun–Thurs 5:30–10:30 p.m. and Fri–Sat 5:30– 11 p.m. Dress is casual to dressy. Wheelchair accessible.*

Jacques-Imo's Café
$$–$$$ **Uptown** **Creole/Soul Food**

Say it with me: JOCK-a-moe's. People will gladly wait over an hour for a seat at this somewhat claustrophobic cafe just to bear down on some of the tastiest Southern soul food imaginable. You can take the easy out and order tender, incredibly moist fried chicken or the stuffed pork chop, and no one would blame you. But the menu has a creative, experimental bent that's well worth pursuing. A seafood-stocked Cajun bouillabaisse is an unexpected treat, as is the savory shrimp and alligator cheesecake appetizer in a rich, spicy cream. If you can find the room (and if you can, my hat's off to you), try the coffee bean crème brûlée dessert.

8324 Oak St. (2 blocks from Carrollton Avenue). ☎ **504-861-0886.** *Reservations accepted for parties of five or more. Main courses: $11–$20. AE, DISC, MC, V. Open: Mon–Thurs 5:30–10 p.m. and Fri–Sat 5:30–10:30 p.m. Wheelchair accessibility is a problem, though you can roll down a less-than-nice-looking alleyway to the back dining areas. Present plans include expansion into an empty space next door, which will have full wheelchair access.*

Jaeger's House of Seafood

$$–$$$ French Quarter   Seafood

Andrew Jaeger is by all accounts an excellent chef, and this award-winning restaurant is indeed a good place to go for seafood. But I'd forego the red beans and rice or crawfish étouffée; they're a little pricey, and you can find much more authentic (not to mention flavorful) versions elsewhere. Instead, try the crab cakes (not my thing, but my companion raved) or one of the daily fish specials, which are generally more consistent. The wait service is polite and attentive, though the waiter I had during one visit was a bit pushy.

622 Conti St. ☎ 504-522-4964. Internet: www.andrewjaegers.com. *Reservations recommended for dinner. Main courses: $14.95–$27. AE, DC, MC, V. Open: Daily 6 p.m. to midnight. Dress is casual. Wheelchair accessible, with an elevator.*

K-Paul's Louisiana Kitchen

$$$–$$$$ French Quarter   Cajun

The hoopla about Cajun cooking started from Chef Paul Prudhomme's restaurant, which offers upscale (and high-priced) takes on traditional Cajun fare. The menu, which changes daily and features a variety of extra-hot interpretations of the Cajun tradition, is known for its blackened redfish and Cajun martini. Also try the chicken and rabbit from its own farm, fiery gumbo, and Cajun popcorn (fried crawfish tails). If it's available for dessert, order the sweet potato pecan pie with Chantilly cream. You won't find a children's menu as such, but several items are kid-compatible and non-spicy.

416 Chartres St. (between Conti and St. Louis streets). ☎ 504-524-7394. Internet: www.kpauls.com. *Reservations suggested for upstairs dining room only; otherwise you have to wait in a sometimes hour-long line. Main courses: Dinner $25–$35.95. AE, DC, DISC, MC, V. Open: Mon–Sat 5:30–10 p.m. Wheelchair accessible. Dress is business casual.*

Louis XVI

$$$–$$$$$ French Quarter   French

A premier example of New Orleans dining at its most formal, Louis XVI emphasizes meticulously prepared French food with fastidious attention to detail. The subdued and romantic room complements the cuisine, which is rich with sauces and traditional flavors. The menu guides you toward specialties such as beef Wellington or rack of lamb. The staff prepares and lights aflame many of the attention-grabbing desserts right at your table.

730 Bienville (½ block from Bourbon Street in the Saint Louis Hotel). ☎ 504-581-7000. Internet: www.louisxvi.com. *Reservations recommended. Main courses: $18–$34. AE, CB, DC, MC, V. Open: Daily 7–11 a.m. and 6–10 p.m. Dress is business casual. Wheelchair accessible.*

Maximo's

$$–$$$$ French Quarter   Italian

If you suffer from a little Creole cooking overload, Maximo's is a fine place to go for Italian food. The solid fare slants heavily toward pasta (usually more than a dozen pastas are offered each day). The specialty of the house is penne Rosa, topped with sun-dried tomatoes, garlic, arugula, and shrimp, and it's pretty good. Other dependable choices are the veal scallopine or the veal T-bone cattoche, which is served pan-roasted with garlic and fresh herbs. The desserts are serviceable as well, and the wine list features an excellent selection.

1117 Decatur St. (4 blocks from Jackson Square). ☎ *504-586-8883. Reservations recommended. Main courses: $9–$28.95. AE, DC, DISC, MC, V. Open: Daily 6–10 p.m. Casual dress. Wheelchair accessible.*

Mike Anderson's Seafood

$$–$$$ French Quarter   Seafood

This seafood restaurant is strategically located on Bourbon Street to attract tourists, and its comfortable seafood dishes reflect that reality without suffering a plain, lowest-common-denominator quality. You'll get seafood any way you want it — broiled, fried, baked, or even raw. You'll also find étouffée, jambalaya, and daily specials to choose from. Specialties include the crawfish bisque and crawfish étouffée, and the Guitreau (fresh fish fillets topped with crawfish tails, shrimp, and mushroom caps sautéed in butter, white wine, and spices). When raw oysters are in season, you can get them for just 25¢, Monday through Thursday until 6 p.m. A reasonably priced kids' menu offers catfish, burgers, shrimp, chicken, and crawfish tails.

215 Bourbon St. (2 blocks from Canal St.). ☎ *504-524-3884. Internet:* www.mike andersons.com. *Reservations not accepted (expect to wait 15 minutes or longer for a table). Main courses: $10.95–$21.95. AE, DC, DISC, MC, V. Open: Sun–Thurs 11:30 a.m.–10 p.m., Fri–Sat 11:30 a.m.–11 p.m. Casual dress. Not accessible for wheelchairs.*

Mike Ditka's New Orleans

$$–$$$$ Central Business District   New American/International/ Steakhouse

Mike Ditka's is an odd animal — part steakhouse, part sports bar, and despite the ever-present image of Da (former Saints) Coach, it's obviously striving for a fine-dining reputation. You'll find cigars, steaks, and "Ditka's Draft" beer, but also a solicitous and accommodating wait staff and a fair-to-middling menu stocked with seafood and other New Orleans options. A trendy lunch menu of fried-oyster burritos and Cobb salads is offset by such dinnertime entrees as lobster risotto (a bit tougher than it should be) or New York strip steak (same play: hard on the outside, but nice and tender within), and starters such as a duck "cigar" spring roll with jalapeno-ginger sauce.

600 St. Charles Ave. between Lafayette and Girod. ☎ *504-569-8989. Reservations recommended. Main courses: $15–$29. AE, DC, DISC, MC, V. Open: Mon–Thurs 7 a.m.–10 p.m., Fri–Sat 7 a.m.–11 p.m. Dress is business casual. Wheelchair accessible.*

Mother's

$–$$ Central Business District Sandwiches/Creole/Short Order/ Breakfast

Mother's overstuffed, mountainous po' boys have tipped quite a few scales over the years. The long lines and lack of atmosphere are minor qualms in the face of the Ferdi special — a giant roll stuffed with baked ham, roast beef, gravy, and other bits of beef debris that's just as delightfully, mouth-wateringly sloppy as it sounds. Mother's also offers "the world's best baked ham," as well as seafood platters, serviceable fried chicken, Creole offerings (gumbo, jambalaya), and of course, po' boys. Chicken strips are available for the kids, and most of the sandwiches and breakfast dishes are kid-friendly as well.

401 Poydras St. (easy walk from anywhere in the Quarter or Central Business District). ☎ *504-523-9656. Internet:* www.mothersrestaurant.com. *Reservations not accepted. Menu selections: $1.75–$16.50. AE, MC, V. Open: Mon–Sat 5 a.m.–10 p.m. and Sun 7 a.m.–10 p.m. No dress code. Wheelchair accessible.*

Mr. B's Bistro

$$–$$$ French Quarter Contemporary Creole

This popular bistro boasts white-glove-level service in a casual atmosphere. Regulars convene here daily for modern, spicy interpretations of Creole classics. The crab cakes are as good as they get, the andouille sausage is superb (order anything it comes with), and the Gumbo Ya-Ya is a hearty, country-style blend of chicken and andouille sausage (my favorite kind; I recommend it gladly). The Cajun barbequed shrimp are large and plump, and served with their heads on in a rich butter sauce. If you come on Sunday, show up early for the jazz brunch, and let yourself be serenaded into a languid torpor.

201 Royal St. (1 block away from Bourbon or Canal St.). ☎ *504-523-2078. Internet:* www.mrbsbistro.com. *Reservations recommended. Main courses: $16–$28. AE, DC, MC, V. Open: Mon–Sat 11:30 a.m.–3 p.m., Sun–Fri 5:30–10 p.m. and Sat 5–10 p.m.; brunch Sun 10:30 a.m.–3 p.m. Dress is business casual. Wheelchair accessible.*

Nola

$$$–$$$$ French Quarter Creole/New American

Of chef Emeril Lagasse's restaurants, this is the cheapest and most casual. Though some diners complain about slow, impersonal service, the unique entrees keep them coming back. For starters, the Caribbean-style grilled free-range chicken (with a brown sugar-cayenne rub served with sweet potato casserole, guacamole, and fried tortilla threads) is delicious; the grilled double-cut pork chop is a favorite, served with pecan-glazed sweet potatoes and a Creole mustard caramelized onion reduction sauce. Of course, the menu is subject to frequent experimentation, so you can never predict what will be available when you come. The chicory coffee crème brûlée is a dessert treat.

534 St. Louis (2½ blocks from Bourbon). ☎ *504-522-6652. Internet:* www.emerils.com. *Reservations recommended. Main courses: $20–$32. AE, DC, DISC, MC, V. Open: Mon–Sat 11:30 a.m.–2 p.m.; Sun–Thurs 6–10:30 p.m. and Fri–Sat 6–11 p.m. Dress is business casual. Wheelchair accessible.*

Olivier's

$$–$$$ **French Quarter   Creole**

Chef Armand Olivier comes from a family famous for its Creole cooking, and the menu is filled with dishes originated by family members, going back to his great-great-grandmother. The Creole Rabbit is a version of a popular 19th-century Creole staple, braised and simmered in gravy to keep it moist and served with a rich oyster dressing. The beef Bourguignon is also good, with tenderloin tips simmered into a thick roux and served with pasta. The bread pudding dessert is fabulous. The service is highly professional and classy, and the decor is the same without being too fancy.

204 Decatur St. ☎ *504-525-7734. Internet:* www.olivierscreole.com. *Reservations are recommended. Main courses: $12.95–$18.95. Open: Daily 11 a.m.–10 p.m. AE, DC, DISC, MC, V. Dress is casual. Wheelchair accessible.*

Palace Café

$$–$$$ **French Quarter   Contemporary Creole**

Palace Café, owned by restaurateur Dickie Brennan, is a gorgeous bistro right in the thick of the Canal Street bustle. Some locals refer to this place as "Commander's Palace Lite," but that's a cheap dismissal of its charms. The menu is subject to seasonal changes, but keep an eye peeled for the oyster pan roast, the shrimp remoulade, or the smoked chicken and andouille sausage étouffée. The wonderful dessert menu features white chocolate bread pudding and café au lait crème brûlée. This place can get noisy, though.

605 Canal St. (an easy walk from anywhere in the Quarter). ☎ *504-523-1661. Internet:* www.palacecafe.com. *Reservations recommended. Main courses: $18.95–$24.95. AE, DC, DISC, MC, V. Open: Mon–Fri 11:30 a.m.–2:30 p.m.; daily 5:30–11 p.m.; brunch Sat–Sun 10:30 a.m.–2:30 p.m. Dress is business casual. Wheelchair accessible.*

Palm Court Jazz Café

$$–$$$ **French Quarter**   **Creole**

People know the Palm Court more for its excellent jazz entertainment than for its decent food (see Chapter 23). You can't go wrong if you stick to traditional fare such as crawfish pie or shrimp Creole. Avoid the high-priced versions of economy dishes such as jambalaya or red beans and rice, however. The place is usually crowded with tourists, the entrees are a little pricey, and service can be slow. But the great traditional jazz should keep you from noticing.

1204 Decatur St. (5 blocks from Jackson Square and a safe walk). ☎ *504-525-0200. Internet:* www.palmcourtjazz.com. *Reservations strongly recommended. Main courses: $14–$19.50; 3-course special $25. AE, DC, DISC, MC, V. Open: Dinner Wed–Sat 7–11 p.m. Dress is elegant casual. Wheelchair accessible.*

Pascal's Manale

$$–$$$ **Uptown**   **Italian/Seafood/Steaks**

This Uptown favorite bills itself as an Italian–New Orleans steak house, but that doesn't quite do justice to the slightly eccentric selection. Pascal's most popular item is its barbecued shrimp (a local favorite that originated here), which are actually soaked in a rich, irresistible, spicy butter sauce, not barbecued. (They're also served with their heads on, so be forewarned if you don't like them that way.) Among other dishes, the combination pan roast features chopped oysters and crabmeat in a blend of shallots, parsley, and seasonings. Even with reservations, you may find a bit of a wait.

1838 Napoleon Ave. (take the St. Charles streetcar to Napoleon and walk 3 blocks away from the river — take a taxi at night). ☎ *504-895-4877. Internet:* www.new orleansrestaurants.com/pascalsmanale. *Reservations recommended. Main courses: $10.95–$23.95. AE, CB, DC, DISC, MC, V. Open: Mon–Fri 11:30 a.m.– 10 p.m., Sat 4–10 p.m., and Sun 4–9 p.m. (closed Sun Memorial Day weekend through Labor Day). Dress is business casual. Wheelchair accessible.*

Peristyle

$$–$$$$ **French Quarter**   **French/Italian/New American**

This romantic restaurant is a local sentimental favorite. The menu changes seasonally, so ask about the availability of creative, talked-about dishes such as pan-seared foie gras or crabmeat and roasted beet salad. The desserts (such as an incredibly rich quenelles of sweetened goat's cheese, served with fresh berries) are equally striking.

1041 Dumaine St. (3 blocks from Bourbon St. — take a taxi for safety). ☎ *504-593-9535. Reservations recommended. Main courses: $22–$27. AE, MC, V. Open: Tues–Thurs 6–10 p.m. and Fri–Sat 6–11 p.m.; lunch on Fri only 11:30 a.m.– 2:30 p.m. Dress is business casual. The front step is a bit steep (about 6 inches), but once inside, navigating via wheelchair is easy.*

Port of Call

$–$$ French Quarter Hamburgers

This character-filled, nautical-themed restaurant and bar is famous for its burgers, which locals generally agree are the best in town. They certainly are huge, weighing in at a half-pound without condiments or the accompanying baked potato (sorry, no fries). Steaks are another specialty, though I've found thickness and juiciness levels to vary. The place really gets jumping late at night when the restaurant is dark and crowded, and attentive service is at a premium, but it's busy most all the time. For extra atmosphere, sit and eat at the bar.

838 Esplanade Ave. (take a taxi for safety). ☎ *504-523-0120. Reservations are not accepted. Menu items: $6–$19. AE, MC, V. Open: Sun–Thurs 11–1 a.m. and Fri–Sat 11–2 a.m. No dress code. Not accessible for wheelchairs.*

Ralph & Kacoo's

$–$$ French Quarter Creole/Seafood

The New Orleans branch of this restaurant chain is usually crowded at all hours, though you'll seldom have to wait longer than 15 to 20 minutes, which you can spend at the bar (a full-sized replica of a fishing boat) downing drinks and raw oysters and people-watching. The food is worth the wait for the onion rings alone, though the hush puppies and fried crawfish tails have also proven popular. This restaurant is a solid, dependable (if not adventuresome) choice for seafood; the portions are large, the prices reasonable, and the fixings fresh. A kids' menu offers burgers and grilled cheese sandwiches and a shrimp boat.

519 Toulouse St. (2½ blocks from Bourbon St. and around the corner from Jackson Square). ☎ *504-522-5226. Internet:* www.ralphandkacoos.com. *Reservations recommended for 15 or more. Main courses: $9–$19. AE, DC, DISC, MC, V. Open: Sun–Thurs 11:30 a.m.–9 p.m. and Fri–Sat 11:30 a.m.—10 p.m. Casual dress. Wheelchair accessible.*

Red Fish Grill

$–$$$ French Quarter Seafood

If you're looking for a relaxed experience, the atmosphere at this Brennan outpost may prove too noisy for your tastes, but the selections are very agreeable. The gumbo is among the best you'll find, and the sweet potato catfish served with an andouille cream sauce is as unique as it is good. The desserts are absolutely sinful; try the signature dessert dish, Bananas Foster Up, a twist on the New Orleans classic bananas Foster that features a martini glass lined with caramel sauce and comes with vanilla ice cream, brown sugar sabayon, and banana beignets (yes, banana beignets).

115 Bourbon St. (½ block from Canal St.). ☎ *504-598-1200. Internet:* www.red fishgrill.com. *Reservations limited. Main courses: $8.95–$17.95. AE, MC, V. Open: Daily 11 a.m.–3 p.m. and 5–11 p.m. Dress is casual. Wheelchair accessible.*

Rib Room

$$$$–$$$$$ French Quarter   Steaks/Seafood

The arched windows, high ceilings, and wood and brick atmosphere of the Rib Room are reminiscent of a conservative British men's club, though it's hard to act genteel when tackling one of the signature filets, sirloins, and other meat dishes. The chefs slow-roast the restaurant's specialty, prime rib, on a rotisserie over an open flame. Spit-roasted lamb, spit-roasted jumbo shrimp, and other hearty dishes round out the menu. This is a good alternative for those tired of seafood or sauce-heavy Creole fare (though trading those rich creamy sauces for juicy, artery-hardening steak isn't much of a trade-off).

621 St. Louis St. (1 block from Bourbon Street in the Omni Royal Orleans Hotel). ☎ 504-529-7045. Reservations recommended. Main courses: $32–$68. AE, DC, DISC, MC, V. Open: Daily 6:30 a.m.–10:30 p.m. Dress is business casual. Wheelchair accessible.

Ruth's Chris Steak House

$$$–$$$$$ Mid-City   Steaks

This is the original location of the national upscale steak house chain. Local politicians and wheeler-dealers come here to seal deals over delicious, sizzling platters of prime beef, and reporters come to watch them, conveniently taking the opportunity to partake of same. Corn-fattened, custom-aged beef is prepared a number of ways here, cut into filets, strips, rib-eyes, and porterhouses — none too tough and all beautifully prepared. The restaurant does offer other selections such as lobster, veal, chicken, or fish, but steak is the name of the game here.

711 N. Broad St. (take a taxi). ☎ 504-486-0810. Internet: www.ruthschris.com. Reservations recommended. Main courses: $17.95–$65. AE, DC, MC, V. Open: Sun–Fri 11 a.m.–11 p.m. and Sat 4–11 p.m. Dress is business casual. Wheelchair accessible.

Tujague's

$$$–$$$$ French Quarter   Creole

Opened in 1856, Tujague's (pronounced *two-jacks*) is one of the oldest restaurants in New Orleans. It's a favorite institution among New Orleanians, but its simple, traditional charms aren't for everyone. The restaurant features no printed menu; instead, the waiters recite the limited but changing daily selections. Options frequently include the signature beef brisket with horseradish sauce (*very* spicy), shrimp remoulade (with a spicy mustard sauce), and a daily fish special.

823 Decatur St. (1 short block from Jackson Square). ☎ 504-525-8676. Internet: www.tujaguesrestaurant.com. Reservations recommended. Main courses: 6-course meal with choice of 4 entrees (no choice for the other courses) $29.95–$35.95 (4-course lunch $6.50–$13.95). AE, CB, DC, DISC, MC, V. Open: Daily 11 a.m.–3 p.m. and 5–11 p.m. Casual dress. Wheelchair accessible.

Uglesich's

$–$$ Warehouse District   Seafood

From the outset, you may be puzzled as to why many locals sing the praises of this tiny, crowded, and greasy neighborhood spot. You'll almost always encounter a long line to place your order, and the additional waits for a table and your food can test even the most patient of souls. But everything becomes clear when you're presented with divine seafood dishes that prompt many locals to bow to "Ugly's" as the best spot in town. With choices such as fried green tomatoes with shrimp remoulade, fried oysters with blue cheese dressing, and all kinds of trout, the food is worth the wait.

1238 Barrone St. at Erato St. (from St. Charles Ave., turn left at Erato — away from the river). ☎ *504-523-8571. Reservations not accepted, but expect a line anywhere around lunchtime. Main courses: $9–$16. No credit cards. Open: Mon–Fri 10 a.m.– 4 p.m., and occasionally on Sat during cooler months; closed July and first 2 weeks of August. Casual dress. Not accessible for wheelchairs.*

Upperline

$$–$$$ Uptown/University   Eclectic/Creole

Nestled in a largely residential section of Uptown, Upperline is every bit as inventive as bigger names such as Commander's Palace or Emeril's (just on a smaller, low-key scale). The tiny, charming house makes for an intimate environment, the better to enjoy imaginative dishes at prices that are, by fancy restaurant standards, downright reasonable. Standbys include their fried green tomatoes with shrimp remoulade sauce and fried sweetbreads (keep in mind that the menus are seasonal). You may be lucky enough to catch one of their special menus — such as an all-garlic selection. The staff is so friendly, they even recommend dishes at other restaurants on their menu.

1413 Upperline St. (take the St. Charles streetcar to the Upperline stop). ☎ *504-891-9822. Internet:* www.upperline.com. *Reservations required. Main courses: $18.50–$24.50. AE, DC, MC, V. Open: Wed–Sat 5:30–9:30 p.m. Dress is casual. Not accessible for wheelchairs.*

Index of Restaurants by Cuisine

American/New American

Bluebird Cafe (Uptown, $)
Cuvee (Central Business District, $$–$$$)
Emeril's (Warehouse District, $$$–$$$$$)
Emeril's Delmonico (Lower Garden District, $$$–$$$$$)

Herbsaint (Central Business District, $$–$$$$)
Mike Ditka's New Orleans (Central Business District, $$–$$$$)
Nola (French Quarter, $$$–$$$$)
Peristyle (French Quarter, $$–$$$$)

Breakfast

Bacco (French Quarter, $$–$$$)
Bluebird Cafe (Uptown, $)
Brennan's (French Quarter, $$$–$$$$$)
Court of Two Sisters (French Quarter, $$$–$$$$)
Grill Room (Central Business District, $$$–$$$$$)
Mother's (Central Business District, $–$$)
Rib Room (French Quarter, $$$$–$$$$$)

Cajun

Brigtsen's (Uptown, $$–$$$)
Gabrielle (Mid-City, $$–$$$$)
K-Paul's Louisiana Kitchen (French Quarter, $$$–$$$$)

Contemporary Louisiana/French Provencal

Gautreau's (Uptown, $$–$$$$)
Herbsaint (Central Business District, $$–$$$$)
Irene's Cuisine (French Quarter, $$–$$$)

Creole

Antoine's (French Quarter, $$$–$$$$$)
Arnaud's (French Quarter, $$–$$$$)
Bacco (French Quarter, $$–$$$)
Brennan's (French Quarter, $$$–$$$$$)
Brigtsen's (Uptown, $$–$$$)
Broussard's (French Quarter, $$$–$$$$)
Christian's (Mid-City, $$$–$$$$)
Commander's Palace (Garden District, $$$–$$$$$)
Court of Two Sisters (French Quarter, $$$–$$$$)
Cuvee (Central Business District, $$–$$$)
Dooky Chase (Mid-City, $$–$$$)
Emeril's (Warehouse District, $$$–$$$$$)
Emeril's Delmonico (Lower Garden District, $$$–$$$$$)
Gabrielle (Mid-City, $$–$$$$)

Jacques-Imo's (Uptown, $$–$$$)
Mother's (Central Business District, $–$$)
Mr. B's Bistro (French Quarter, $$–$$$)
Nola (French Quarter, $$$–$$$$)
Olivier's (French Quarter, $$–$$$)
Palace Café (French Quarter, $$–$$$)
Palm Court Jazz Café (French Quarter, $$–$$$)
Ralph & Kacoo's (French Quarter, $–$$)
Tujaque's (French Quarter, $$$–$$$$)
Upperline (Uptown, $$–$$$)

French

Antoine's (French Quarter, $$$–$$$$$)
Brennan's (French Quarter, $$$–$$$$$)
Broussard's (French Quarter, $$$–$$$$)
Christian's (Mid-City, $$$–$$$$)
Gabrielle (Mid-City, $$–$$$$)
Galatoire's (French Quarter, $$–$$$$)
Herbsaint (Central Business District, $$–$$$$)
Louis XVI (French Quarter, $$$–$$$$$)
Olivier's (French Quarter, $$–$$$)
Peristyle (French Quarter, $$–$$$$)

International/Eclectic

Bayona (French Quarter, $$–$$$)
Bella Luna (French Quarter, $$–$$$$)
Bistro at Maison de Ville (French Quarter, $$–$$$)
Cuvee (Central Business District, $$–$$$)
Grill Room (Central Business District, $$$–$$$$$)
Mike Ditka's New Orleans (Central Business District, $$–$$$$)
Upperline (Uptown, $$–$$$)

Italian

Bacco (French Quarter, $$–$$$)
Irene's Cuisine (French Quarter, $$–$$$)
Maximo's (French Quarter, $$–$$$$)
Pascal's Manale (Uptown, $$–$$$)
Peristyle (French Quarter, $$–$$$$)

Sandwiches/Hamburgers

Bluebird Cafe (Uptown, $)
Café Maspero (French Quarter, $)
Mother's (Central Business District, $–$$)
Port of Call (French Quarter, $–$$)

Seafood

Café Maspero (French Quarter, $)
Gabrielle (Mid-City, $$–$$$$)
Jaeger's House of Seafood (French Quarter, $$–$$$)
Mike Anderson's Seafood (French Quarter, $$–$$$)
Mother's (Central Business District, $–$$)
Olivier's (French Quarter, $$–$$$)
Pascal's Manale (Uptown, $$–$$$)
Ralph & Kacoo's (French Quarter, $–$$)
Red Fish Grill (French Quarter, $–$$$)

Rib Room (French Quarter, $$$$–$$$$$)
Uglesich's (Warehouse District, $–$$)

Short Order

Bluebird Cafe (Uptown, $)
Mother's (Central Business District, $–$$)

Soul Food

Dooky Chase (Mid-City, $$–$$$)
Jacques-Imo's Café (Uptown, $$–$$$)

Steaks

Mike Ditka's New Orleans (Central Business District, $$–$$$$)
Pascal's Manale (Uptown, $$–$$$)
Rib Room (French Quarter, $$$$–$$$$$)
Ruth's Chris Steak House (Mid-City, $$$–$$$$$)

Index of Restaurants by Price

$

Bluebird Cafe (American/New American, Uptown)
Café Maspero (Sandwiches/Seafood, French Quarter)
Mother's (Sandwiches/Creole/Short Order/Breakfast, Central Business District)
Port of Call (Hamburgers, French Quarter)
Ralph & Kacoo's (Creole/Seafood, French Quarter)
Red Fish Grill (Seafood, French Quarter)
Uglesich's (Seafood, Warehouse District)

$$

Arnaud's (Creole, French Quarter)
Bacco (Italian/Creole, French Quarter)
Bayona (International, French Quarter)
Bella Luna (Eclectic/Continental, French Quarter)

Bistro at Maison de Ville (International/Eclectic, French Quarter)
Brigtsen's (Cajun/Creole, Uptown)
Cuvee (Creole/New American, Central Business District)
Dooky Chase (Creole/Soul Food, Mid-City)
Gabrielle (French/Creole/Cajun, Mid-City)
Galatoire's (French, French Quarter)
Gautreau's (Contemporary Louisiana, Uptown)
Grill Room (Central Business District)
Herbsaint (French/New American, Central Business District)
Irene's Cuisine (Italian/French Provencal, French Quarter)
Jacques-Imo's (Creole/Soul Food, Uptown)
Jaeger's House of Seafood (Seafood, French Quarter)
Maximo's (Italian, French Quarter)

Mike Anderson's Seafood (Seafood, French Quarter)

Mike Ditka's New Orleans (New American/International/Steakhouse, Central Business District)

Mother's (Sandwiches/Creole/Short Order/Breakfast, Central Business District)

Mr. B's Bistro (Creole, French Quarter)

Olivier's (Creole, French Quarter)

Palace Café (Creole, French Quarter)

Palm Court Jazz Café (Creole, French Quarter)

Pascal's Manale (Italian/Seafood/Steaks, Uptown)

Peristyle (French/Italian/New American, French Quarter)

Port of Call (Hamburgers, French Quarter)

Ralph & Kacoo's (Creole/Seafood, French Quarter)

Red Fish Grill (Seafood, French Quarter)

Uglesich's (Seafood, Warehouse District)

Upperline (Eclectic/Creole, Uptown)

$$$

Antoine's (Creole/French, French Quarter)

Arnaud's (Creole, French Quarter)

Bacco (Italian/Creole, French Quarter)

Bayona (International, French Quarter)

Bella Luna (Eclectic/Continental, French Quarter)

Bistro at Maison de Ville (International/Eclectic, French Quarter)

Brennan's (French/Creole, French Quarter)

Brigtsen's (Cajun/Creole, Uptown)

Broussard's (French/Creole, French Quarter)

Christian's (French/Creole, Mid-City)

Commander's Palace (Creole, Garden District)

Court of Two Sisters (Creole, French Quarter)

Cuvee (Creole/New American, Central Business District)

Dooky Chase (Creole/Soul Food, Mid-City)

Emeril's (Creole/New American, Warehouse District)

Emeril's Delmonico (Creole/New American, Lower Garden District)

Gabrielle (French/Creole/Cajun, Mid-City)

Galatoire's (French, French Quarter)

Gautreau's (Contemporary Louisiana, Uptown)

Grill Room (International, Central Business District)

Herbsaint (French/New American, Central Business District)

Irene's Cuisine (Italian/French Provencal, French Quarter)

Jacques-Imo's (Creole/Soul Food, Uptown)

Jaeger's House of Seafood (Seafood, French Quarter)

K-Paul's Louisiana Kitchen (Cajun, French Quarter)

Louis XVI (French, French Quarter)

Maximo's (Italian, French Quarter)

Mike Anderson's Seafood (Seafood, French Quarter)

Mike Ditka's New Orleans (New American/International/Steakhouse, Central Business District)

Mr. B's Bistro (Creole, French Quarter)

Nola (Creole/New American, French Quarter)

Olivier's (Creole, French Quarter)

Palace Café (Creole, French Quarter)

Palm Court Jazz Café (Creole, French Quarter)

Pascal's Manale (Italian/Seafood/Steaks, Uptown)

Peristyle (French/Italian/New American, French Quarter)

Red Fish Grill (Seafood, French Quarter)

Ruth's Chris Steak House (Steaks, Mid-City)

Tujaque's (Creole, French Quarter)

Upperline (Eclectic/Creole, Uptown)

$$$$

Antoine's (Creole/French, French Quarter)

Arnaud's (Creole, French Quarter)

Bella Luna (Eclectic/Continental, French Quarter)

Brennan's (French/Creole, French Quarter)

Broussard's (French/Creole, French Quarter)

Christian's (French/Creole, Mid-City)

Commander's Palace (Creole, Garden District)

Court of Two Sisters (Creole, French Quarter)

Emeril's (Creole/New American, Warehouse District)

Emeril's Delmonico (Creole/New American, Lower Garden District)

Gabrielle (French/Creole/Cajun, Mid-City)

Galatoire's (French, French Quarter)

Gautreau's (Contemporary Louisiana, Uptown)

Grill Room (International, Central Business District)

Herbsaint (French/New American, Central Business District)

K-Paul's Louisiana Kitchen (Cajun, French Quarter)

Louis XVI (French, French Quarter)

Maximo's (Italian, French Quarter)

Mike Ditka's New Orleans (New American/International/Steakhouse, Central Business District)

Nola (Creole/New American, French Quarter)

Peristyle (French/Italian/New American, French Quarter)

Rib Room (Steaks/Seafood, French Quarter)

Ruth's Chris Steak House (Steaks, Mid-City)

Tujaque's (Creole, French Quarter)

$$$$$

Antoine's (Creole/French, French Quarter)

Brennan's (French/Creole, French Quarter)

Commander's Palace (Creole, Garden District)

Emeril's (Creole/New American, Warehouse District)

Emeril's Delmonico (Creole/New American, Lower Garden District)

Grill Room (International, Central Business District)

Louis XVI (French, French Quarter)

Rib Room (Steaks/Seafood, French Quarter)

Ruth's Chris Steak House (Steaks, Mid-City)

Chapter 15

On the Lighter Side: Snacks and Meals on the Go

. . . .

In This Chapter

▶ Finding a fast sandwich or burger

▶ Shooting oysters

▶ Getting healthy food in the land of deep-fry

▶ Exploring street food, pizza, 24-hour snack joints, and other hangouts

▶ Enjoying coffee, tea, or a sweet treat

. . . .

Snacking is a great American pastime, and New Orleans is nothing if not a city of traditions. So the fact that New Orleans is stuffed to the gills with snack food should come as no surprise — from Lucky Dog (hot dogs and sausage sold by street vendors in giant hot dog-shaped carts) to the city's twin sandwich staples, the po' boy and the muffuletta. This chapter takes you on a whistle-stop tour of some of the best places to go for these delights, as well as bar food, late-night munchies, beignets, and other sugary confections. It also cracks open the shell on the subject of oysters, and gives you my two cents on the longstanding debate as to the best burger in town.

Which Sandwich Is Which?

Heroes, hoagies, subs, clubs — a sandwich is a sandwich, right? Well, maybe where *you* come from. But as with everything even tangentially related to food, in New Orleans we take our sandwiches pretty seriously. After all, you can get a sandwich, or you can get a stuffed shrimp po' boy, a muffuletta, or even a juicy burger from Port of Call or Clover Grill. Call them whatever you want, though. To paraphrase Shakespeare, a po' boy by any other name would taste as delicious.

New Orleans Snacks

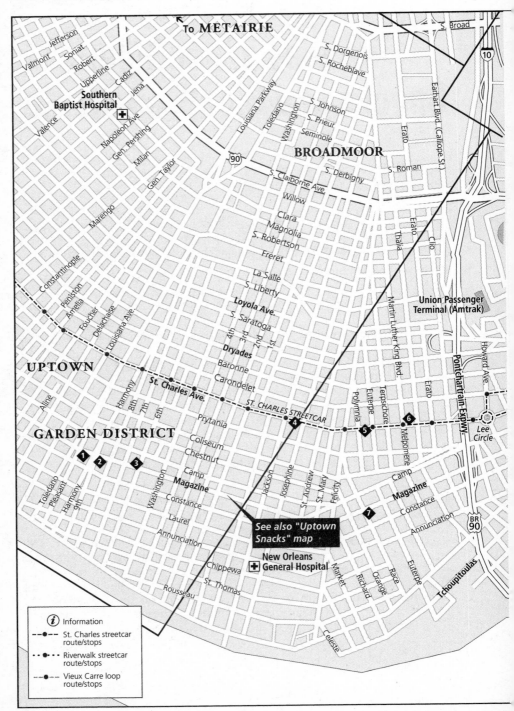

To METAIRIE

Jefferson
Valmont
Soniat
Robert
Upperline
Cadiz
Jena

Southern
Baptist Hospital

Napoleon Ave.
Gen. Pershing
Milan

Valence

Gen. Taylor

S. Broad

S. Dorgenois
S. Rocheblave

S. Johnson
S. Prieur
Seminole

Louisiana Parkway
Toledano
Washington

BROADMOOR

Erato

Earhart Blvd. (Calliope St.)

S. Derbigny
S. Roman

Marengo

90

S. Claiborne Ave.
Willow

Clara
Magnolia
S. Robertson

Freret

La Salle
S. Liberty

Loyola Ave.
S. Saratoga

Erato

Thalia

Clio

Union Passenger
Terminal (Amtrak)

Constantinople
Peniston
Amelia
Foucher
Delachaise
Louisiana Ave.

4th
3rd
2nd
1st

Dryades

Baronne

Carondelet

Martin Luther King Blvd.

Howard Ave.

Pontchartrain Expwy.

UPTOWN

St. Charles Ave.

Harmony
8th
7th
6th

Prytania

ST. CHARLES STREETCAR

4

Polymnia

Euterpe

5

Terpsichore

6

Melpomene

Lee
Circle

GARDEN DISTRICT

Aline

Coliseum
Chestnut

Camp.

Magazine

1 2 3

Toledano
Pleasant
Harmony
9th

Washington
Constance

Laurel

Annunciation

Jackson
Josephine

St. Andrew
St. Mary
Felicity

Camp

Magazine

Constance

7

Annunciation

Euterpe

Race

Orange

Richard

BR
90

See also "Uptown
Snacks" map

New Orleans
General Hospital

Chippewa
St. Thomas

Rousseau

Celeste

Market

Tchoupitoulas

(i) Information

St. Charles streetcar
route/stops

Riverwalk streetcar
route/stops

Vieux Carre loop
route/stops

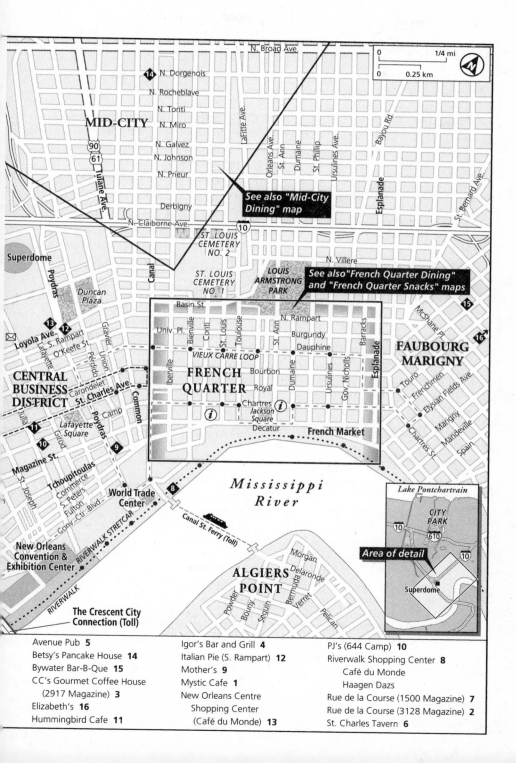

Avenue Pub **5**

Betsy's Pancake House **14**

Bywater Bar-B-Que **15**

CC's Gourmet Coffee House
(2917 Magazine) **3**

Elizabeth's **16**

Hummingbird Cafe **11**

Igor's Bar and Grill **4**

Italian Pie (S. Rampart) **12**

Mother's **9**

Mystic Cafe **1**

New Orleans Centre
Shopping Center
(Café du Monde) **13**

PJ's (644 Camp) **10**

Riverwalk Shopping Center **8**
Café du Monde
Haagen Dazs

Rue de la Course (1500 Magazine) **7**

Rue de la Course (3128 Magazine) **2**

St. Charles Tavern **6**

Savoring the muffuletta experience

Italian cold cuts and cheese stuffed into round Italian bread and slathered with olive salad dressing: This is a *muffuletta* (say muff-ah-*let*-ah, or to be more colloquially accurate, muff-ah-*lot*-ah). That description may not do it justice; getting excited about any sentence that contains the words *cold cuts* is difficult. Trust me on this, though; this local fixture is delicious and quite filling. Half of a muffuletta makes a great meal, and a quarter makes a nice, filling snack. One person cannot (or should not, at least) eat a whole one. As with many foods in New Orleans, arguments abound as to who makes the best. I think I'll stay out of that particular debate, but here are a couple of places to help you decide for yourself.

- ✔ **Central Grocery** (923 Decatur St., ☎ **504-523-1620**) makes the most likely winner in the great muffuletta debate. The place probably invented the muff, so if you have just one, have it here. You can also buy many New Orleans spices and other deli items here as well.

- ✔ **Napoleon House** (500 Chartres St., ☎ **504-524-9752**) is the sole seller of *hot* muffulettas. Some locals find the very idea blasphemous, but others swear by it. This European-style cafe also serves other sandwiches, soups, jambalaya, and similar moderately priced fare. The bar is a popular late-night hangout. Try the Pimm's Cup, an oddly likable mix of lemonade, 7-Up, and Pimm's No. 1 — it's the bar's signature drink. Classical music lends some romantic ambience.

Feasting on po' boys: Lots of fun and fixin's

The other signature sandwich of New Orleans, the *po' boy*, takes its name from the idea that it's the only food a "po' boy" can afford. As a matter of fact, though not much different in structure from a hero or a sub, it's fixed in the minds of many locals as *the* premier New Orleans sandwich. The sandwich is not all that complicated; take a long, skinny loaf of French bread, slice it open lengthwise, and stuff it with just about anything you can imagine. Roast beef po' boys are great, especially if you have a little debris gravy dripping out the sides. Ham and cheese is a standard, and smoked sausage is also good. Seafood is a reliable standby; fried fish, soft-shell crab, oysters, and shrimp are all popular ingredients. Weird as it may sound, many people actually seem to enjoy french-fry po' boys; that's right, a sandwich of french fries between two slices of bread — and hopefully some of that naughty brown gravy. (Hey, anything goes, right?)

French Quarter Snacks

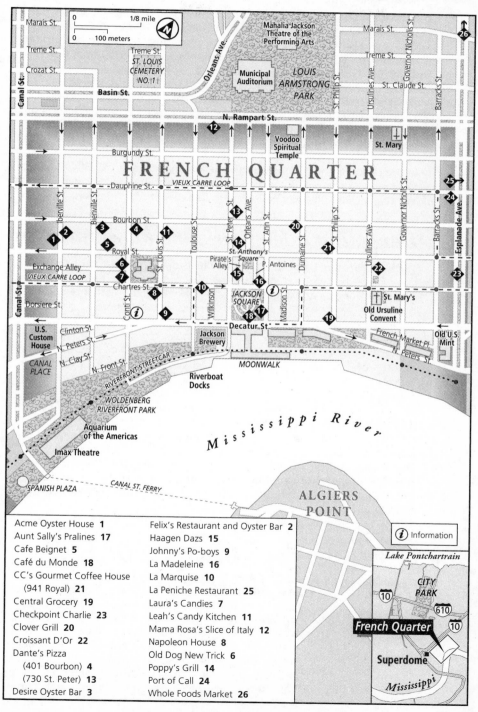

Acme Oyster House **1**
Aunt Sally's Pralines **17**
Cafe Beignet **5**
Café du Monde **18**
CC's Gourmet Coffee House
  (941 Royal) **21**
Central Grocery **19**
Checkpoint Charlie **23**
Clover Grill **20**
Croissant D'Or **22**
Dante's Pizza
  (401 Bourbon) **4**
  (730 St. Peter) **13**
Desire Oyster Bar **3**

Felix's Restaurant and Oyster Bar **2**
Haagen Dazs **15**
Johnny's Po-boys **9**
La Madeleine **16**
La Marquise **10**
La Peniche Restaurant **25**
Laura's Candies **7**
Leah's Candy Kitchen **11**
Mama Rosa's Slice of Italy **12**
Napoleon House **8**
Old Dog New Trick **6**
Poppy's Grill **14**
Port of Call **24**
Whole Foods Market **26**

i Information

Obviously, po' boys aren't exactly health food. The best sandwiches have fried fixings or thick sauces (or both). They are also a *teensy* bit messy; you're just not getting the proper New Orleans experience if your shrimp, roast beef, or whatever isn't spilling out of the sides of your overstuffed sandwich. (I'm not suggesting that we're barbarians here; we wipe stray fixings off of our faces just like you do at home — we're just less self-conscious about it.)

Mother's (401 Poydras St., ☎ 504-523-9656; see Chapter 14) serves up a fine po' boy as does the **Napoleon House** (see the preceding section). For the most popular po' boy spot in the Quarter, however, head to **Johnny's Po-boys** (511 St. Louis St., ☎ 504-524-8129).

In the Uptown area, **Domilise's** (5240 Annunciation St., ☎ 504-899-9126) has been serving po' boys, as well as other hot dishes, for over 75 years. Try the "Peacemaker," a half-shrimp, half-oyster combination.

Becoming a New Orleans burgermeister

When discussing hamburgers, those fast-food approximations have their place, but we all know that the best burgers aren't mass-produced. The best burgers are thick, juicy, and made to order with any and all trimmings your heart — and your arteries — may desire.

In New Orleans, sports, politics, and current events are popular conversation topics. But those discussions are nothing compared to the amount of discourse spent on the merits of different New Orleans burger spots. The truth is that many places in town make excellent burgers. When you get right down to the nitty-gritty, however, this is a two-burger race between the **Port of Call** (838 Esplanade Ave., ☎ 504-523-0120; see Chapter 14) and the **Clover Grill** (900 Bourbon St., ☎ 504-598-1010). Both places make big burgers; the Port of Call's is a half a pound, while the Clover Grill's weighs in at a trim third of a pound. And both places keep their burgers juicy (the Clover cooks its burgers under a hubcap, believe it or not, to seal in the juices). I've enjoyed many from both places, but in the long run, my heart belongs to Port of Call.

The World Is Your Oyster (Or Is the Oyster Your World?)

In my experience, people new to the art of oyster shooting — slurping a raw oyster, often dressed with ketchup and horseradish, right out of its shell and letting it slide, virtually unchewed, right down the gullet — soon curse themselves for not trying the activity sooner. Oyster shooting may *sound* unappetizing, but you should definitely try it once; it can sometimes be the right alternative to a heavy, sauce-laden meal. The following oyster bars also offer fried oysters, shrimp for peeling and dipping, and, when they're in season, plenty of boiled crawfish:

- ✔ **Acme Oyster House** (724 Iberville St., ☎ 504-522-5973) offers some *serious* oysters. Get 'em raw, fried, or in overstuffed po' boys.

- ✔ **Felix's Restaurant and Oyster Bar** (739 Iberville St., ☎ 504-522-4440) offers Creole dishes, but specializes in oysters and fried seafood.

- ✔ **Desire Oyster Bar** (300 Bourbon St., ☎ 504-586-0300) is a tad less authentic than the previous two, but the convenient location (it's part of the Royal Sonesta Hotel) keeps the place hopping.

These places should get you started. Refer to the cuisine index in Chapter 14 for some good seafood restaurants to visit after you suck down your fill of oysters. Keep in mind that a good fried oyster achieves that just-so, delicate balance of a crunchy outside and a soft, chewy center. Happy slurping!

Restaurant Rescue for Vegetarians

If you're a vegetarian traveler, I won't patronize you by telling you how much great stuff you're missing out on (nobody likes that), but I will say that your options in New Orleans *are* limited. If you can cook a food in animal fat, New Orleanians do. Ham and sausage even lurk in the red beans and rice. Nevertheless, a few places in town cater to the vegetarian market (though most of them aren't *exclusively* vegetarian), and do a decent job of it, too.

- ✔ **Old Dog New Trick** (517 Frenchmen St., ☎ 504-522-4569) calls itself "vegan friendly." Although the cafe does offer dishes with cheese (and some with tuna), the cooks happily make them without. *Gambit Weekly* readers voted the food here as the best vegetarian fare in town.

- ✔ **Mystic Cafe** (3244 Magazine St., ☎ 504-895-7272) does include meat in some dishes (after all, the restaurant is technically Mediterranean). Nevertheless, the whole-grain, high-quality options give vegetarians and the heart-conscious plenty from which to choose.

- ✔ **Whole Foods Market** (3135 Esplanade Ave., ☎ 504-943-1626), a local favorite for organic produce and vegetarian specialties, offers all items to go.

- ✔ **Mona's Café** (504 Frenchmen St., ☎ 504-949-4115) is an unpretentious spot where people from all walks of life converge for Middle Eastern fare such as gyros, falafel, and the baba ganuj eggplant dip, with much to satisfy vegetarians with international palates.

Aside from these places, call ahead and ask if a particular restaurant that interests you features vegetarian entrees; a good number of them do. (Central Grocery, for example, offers a mean vegetable muffuletta.)

Lucky Dogs: Street Fare

A tradition in New Orleans since 1948, Lucky Dog carts became famous when spoofed in the Pulitzer Prize–winning book *Confederacy of Dunces*. You can find the carts that sell Lucky Dogs (which are basically hot dogs) on street corners throughout the French Quarter and Central Business District. (The carts spread out to other locations throughout the city during special events.) Spotting the carts is easy because they look like giant hot dogs.

Lucky Dogs are the perfect food for late-night revelers with a blood-alcohol volume of .05% or higher, and the carts are conveniently located throughout the Quarter to accommodate those who stumble out of nearby bars. A regular or foot-long hot dog or sausage dressed with the works (including chili) goes for less than $5.

A "Pizza" the Pie

If you're in the mood for a regular old cheese-and-pepperoni pizza, or perhaps something a bit more gourmet, stop by one of these places:

- **Café Roma** (3340 Bienville St., Mid-City, ☎ **504-827-2300**)
- **Dante's Pizza** (730 St. Peter St., ☎ **504-523-2683;** and 401 Bourbon St., ☎ **504-561-8670**)
- **Figaro's Pizzerie** (7900 Maple St., ☎ **504-837-5816** or 504-866-0100)
- **Italian Pie** (417 S. Rampart St., ☎ **504-522-7552;** and 5538 Magazine St., ☎ **504-894-0005**)
- **Mama Rosa's Slice of Italy** (616 N. Rampart St., ☎ **504-523-5546**)
- **Reginelli's** (741 State St. at the corner of Magazine, ☎ **504-899-1414**)

These Are the People in Your Neighborhood

For me, nothing quite tops people-watching at a diner or neighborhood joint, observing the ebb and flow of regular Janes and Joes in the tidal pool of the working world. The everyday give-and-take of greasy-spoon

Uptown Snacks

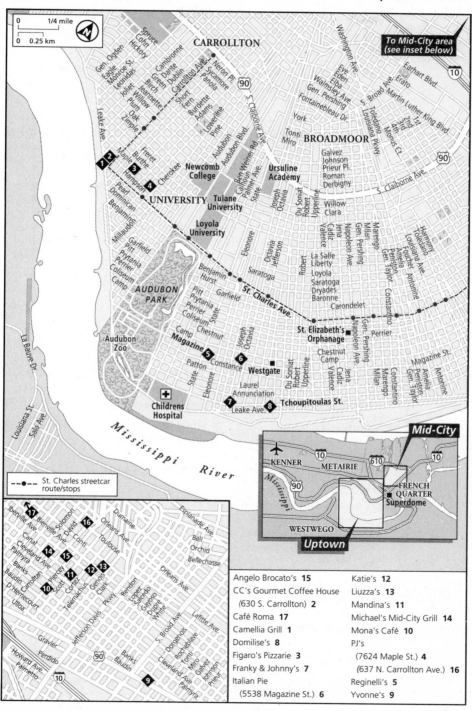

Angelo Brocato's **15**

CC's Gourmet Coffee House
  (630 S. Carrollton) **2**

Café Roma **17**

Camellia Grill **1**

Domilise's **8**

Figaro's Pizzarie **3**

Franky & Johnny's **7**

Italian Pie
  (5538 Magazine St.) **6**

Katie's **12**

Liuzza's **13**

Mandina's **11**

Michael's Mid-City Grill **14**

Mona's Café **10**

PJ's
  (7624 Maple St.) **4**
  (637 N. Carrollton Ave.) **16**

Reginelli's **5**

Yvonne's **9**

waitresses interacting with accountants, mechanics, and eccentrics is as fascinating to me as watching native tribal rituals is to an anthropologist. What follows, then, is a short and highly subjective list of neighborhood spots with just as much, if not more, emphasis on character and atmosphere as on good food:

- ✔ **Betsy's Pancake House** (2542 Canal St., ☎ 504-822-0213) serves breakfast food, as you may imagine, but also a filling variety of lunch specials; my favorite is the hamburger steak smothered in onions.

- ✔ **Bywater Bar-B-Que** (3162 Dauphine St., ☎ 504-944-4445) is the perfect place to harden your arteries with some prime barbecue. It also serves a decent burger and great pizza.

- ✔ **Elizabeth's** (601 Gallier St. at Chartres, ☎ 504-944-9272; also in Bywater) is a virtual thesaurus of neighborhood-joint adjectives: fun, funky, folksy, and down-home. This spot has some of the best breakfast food around, as well as mouth-watering lunches, most all reasonably priced. Elizabeth's serves breakfast and lunch only, Tuesday through Saturday.

- ✔ **Franky and Johnny's** (321 Arabella St. just off Tchoupitoulas, Uptown, ☎ 504-899-9146) specializes in boiled seafood, but just about any of the sandwiches are rewarding.

- ✔ **Katie's** (3701 Iberville St., ☎ 504-488-6582) is notable both for its purple exterior and for the fine, filling neighborhood-joint fare served within.

- ✔ **Liuzza's** (3636 Bienville St., ☎ 504-482-9120) may be the mother of all neighborhood restaurants. Hot plate lunches, po' boys, and daily specials are the name of the game here.

- ✔ **Mandina's** (3800 Canal St., ☎ 504-482-9179) aspires to some odd cross between stuffy upper-crust establishment and regular-Joe hangout. The sandwiches are good, but the real draws are daily specials such as red beans and rice or beef stew, as well as Italian and seafood dishes.

- ✔ **Michael's Mid-City Grill** (4139 Canal St., ☎ 504-486-8200) is a favorite of local movers and shakers, as well as the after-work crowd. If you're bucks up, you may want to splurge for the Big Bucks burger; it costs $125, but it comes with a "free" bottle of Dom Perignon.

- ✔ **Yvonne's** (2544 Gravier St., ☎ 504-821-9393) is in a somewhat dicey neighborhood, but some nice folks run and frequent it. Although it's a little too well lighted for my taste, the small, close tables put you in the middle of what seems like a whole other world.

After Hours Appetizers: Nocturnal New Orleans Noshing

In a 1999 issue of *Rolling Stone,* the *Times-Picayune's* resident music writer named the **Clover Grill** the best place in town to eat at four in the morning, and it is indeed a great spot for exactly that. Also in the French Quarter, **Poppy's Grill** and **Café du Monde** (800 Decatur St. at Jackson Square, ☎ **504-525-4544**) are a couple of other reliable 24-hour snacking destinations. But don't limit your options to them, nor to the French Quarter. In fact, chances are good you can find some late-night nourishment wherever you happen to be in New Orleans in the pre-dawn hours.

- **Clover Grill** (900 Bourbon St., ☎ **504-598-1010**) is a fun 24-hour diner known for its juicy burgers (cooked under a hubcap to seal in the flavors). Breakfast is served around the clock in a cheeky, whimsical atmosphere. This gay-friendly hangout also offers good shakes, malts, a painfully sweet icebox pie, and lots of coffee.

- **Hummingbird Cafe** (804 St. Charles Ave., ☎ **504-561-9229**) can satisfy your middle-of-the-night red beans and rice cravings. It offer lots of other options, too. Its funky, seedy atmosphere attracts a broad range of characters; a great American novel is just waiting to be written here.

- **Poppy's Grill** (717 St. Peter St., ½ block from Bourbon St., across from Pat O'Brien's, ☎ **504-524-3287**) is owned by the same folks who run Clover Grill, so the same light-hearted attitude prevails ("dancing in the aisles only"). It serves the same fabulous shakes, burgers, and other diner fare. That's not to say that Poppy's doesn't have its own special qualities, however. For a true Poppy original, try the steak and eggs platter for $9.99, biscuits and gravy for $2.99, vodka cocktails from $3.25, or a 20-ounce beer for $2.25.

- The down-home snacks and meals at **La Peniche Restaurant** (1940 Dauphine St., ☎ **504-943-1460**) can really hit the spot. This gay-friendly spot in the Faubourg Marigny has great half-pound hamburgers and homemade desserts; if the Oreo pie doesn't cause you to moan in ecstasy, call your mortician, because you must be dead.

- At **Checkpoint Charlie** (501 Esplanade Ave., ☎ **504-949-7012**), you can enjoy decent bar food (including a breakfast sandwich) while soaking up alternative, jazz, or blues-tinged rock and roll (you can also do your laundry at the same time). See Chapter 23 for more details.

- The **Avenue Pub** (1732 St. Charles Ave., ☎ **504-586-9243**) is a homey little place in the Lower Garden District. As the name suggests, it's a neighborhood bar, and it serves decent burgers 24 hours a day.

✔ A few blocks farther down, **Igor's Bar and Grill** (2133 St. Charles Ave., ☎ **504-522-2145**) also offers 24-hour food, including the "world-famous" Igor burger, a good jukebox, and plenty of local atmosphere (and, again, self-serve laundry). It's also a good place to shoot pool.

✔ Near the Avenue Pub, the **St. Charles Tavern** (1433 St. Charles Ave., ☎ **504-523-9823**) is also open 24 hours. The fare ranges from burgers to red beans and rice to Creole omelettes (stuffed with shrimp Creole). Don't be surprised if you find a short wait for a table even after 2 a.m.

✔ Situated in the Riverbend area in Uptown, **Camellia Grill** (626 S. Carrollton Ave., ☎ **504-866-9573**) is a throwback to the kind of old-style neighborhood diners you occasionally see on television. It's not open around the clock, but it does stay open until the wee hours most nights. On weekend mornings, people line up outside the door for the famous pecan waffles.

Great Places for Coffee

Though New Orleans is not known as the coffee capital of the Western World, you can still find quite a few great places to get a jolt of the jumping bean.

✔ Open 24 hours, the original **Café du Monde** (800 Decatur St. at Jackson Square, ☎ **504-525-4544**) makes a great café au lait — strong New Orleans coffee flavored with chicory to make it less bitter and mixed with an equal portion of scalded milk. This prime place for people-watching has been around since 1862. (A handful of Café du Monde satellites are scattered about the city and suburbs.)

✔ **Rue de la Course** is your basic bohemian spot, modeled after 17th-century European coffeehouses, with cool, friendly college kids and locals hanging out and lingering over the morning paper. A handful of these exist in the metropolitan area, including one at 1500 Magazine St. (☎ **504-529-1455**) and another at 3128 Magazine St. (☎ **504-899-0242**).

The Sweet Science

I've said it before and I'll say it again: Part of the point of the whole New Orleans experience is letting yourself go, succumbing to certain culinary cravings and temptations that you wouldn't necessarily acknowledge at home. Sooner or later, chances are you're going to give in to a treat that's either rolled in sugar or boiled in fat — more than likely, both. To make the decision easy for you, this section runs down some of the options available.

Quick-stop java shops

The presence of two ubiquitous local coffee institutions in New Orleans is akin to that of Starbucks in the rest of the country (we have those too, by the way). **CC's Gourmet Coffee House** and **PJ's** both have multiple locations throughout the metropolitan area. Of the two, I'm partial to **PJ's**, with its funkier atmosphere.

Some of the more centrally located CC's locations include the following:

- 2917 Magazine St. (☎ 504-891-2115)
- 941 Royal St., in the Quarter (☎ 504-581-6996)
- 2800 Esplanade Ave. (☎ 504-482-9865)
- 630 S. Carrollton Ave., Uptown (☎ 504-865-0027)

Some of their more popular PJ's locations are the following:

- 7624 Maple St., Uptown (☎ 504-866-7031)
- 637 N. Carrollton Ave., Mid-City (☎ 504-482-4847)
- 644 Camp St., Warehouse District (☎ 504-529-3658)

Beignets: Sweet treats

Beignets (pronounced *ben-YAYS*) are pieces of dough, fried fresh and covered with lots of powdered sugar. Novices may be tempted to shake some of the sugar off. Don't mess with it; the sugar tastes great, especially after the heat of the freshly baked beignet melts it. If anything, you'll end up adding *more* powdered sugar, courtesy of sugar shakers likely to be conveniently located. **Café du Monde** (800 Decatur St. at Jackson Square, ☎ 504-525-4544) is Beignet Central. They're a steal at three for about $1, and because the place is open 24 hours (every day but Christmas), you can satisfy your craving at any time. Other non-24-hour Café du Mondes are at the Riverwalk Shopping Center (1 Poydras St., ☎ 504-587-0841) and the New Orleans Centre Shopping Center (1400 Poydras St., by the Superdome, ☎ 504-587-0842).

Café du Monde definitely holds the beignet advantage in most peoples' minds, but **Cafe Beignet** (334-B Royal St., ☎ 504-524-5530) is a nice coffeehouse-type place in its own right. Competing with Café du Monde's atmosphere and tradition is difficult, but sample the wares at Cafe Beignet anyway, just to be fair. You'll be glad you did.

La patisserie

If you want to pretend that you're grabbing a snack back in French Colonial days, drop by one of these spots for a pastry. Although each of these places offers seating, you may want to take your pastry to nearby Jackson Square to soak up some local color.

- ✔ **La Marquise** (625 Chartres St., ☎ **504-524-0420**) makes a great place to take a leisurely breakfast or an afternoon break. It offers all sorts of delicious pastries and sandwiches.

- ✔ **Croissant D'Or** (617 Ursulines St., ☎ **504-524-4663**), only a few blocks away from La Marquise, provides the daily fresh-baked pastries for both locations. Ask the staff for the history behind the old "Ladies' Entrance" sign on the sidewalk.

- ✔ **La Madeleine** (547 St. Ann St. at Jackson Square, ☎ **504-568-0073**) serves delectable French pastries and other light menu items. It also maintains a location in the Garden District, attached to the Maison St. Charles Quality Inn (see Chapter 8).

Candy the New Orleans way

The one word you need to know when discussing homegrown New Orleans–style sugary snacks is **pralines** (pronounced *PRAW-leens,* not *PRAY-leens*). Give these tasty confections (made with brown sugar and pecans) a try and you may become addicted. At **Aunt Sally's Pralines** (810 Decatur St., ☎ **800-642-7257** or 504-944-6090), you can watch the staff making the famous local candy. **Laura's Candies** (600 Conti St., ☎ **800-992-9699** or 504-525-3880) offers not just pralines, but fudge and golf-ball-size truffles as well. Some people cast their vote for best praline to **Leah's Candy Kitchen** (714 St. Louis St., ☎ **504-523-5662**), and because they stay open until 10 p.m., they win the late-night candy-craving vote by default.

We all scream for ice cream

You can find ice cream carts throughout the French Quarter, especially around Jackson Square. **Haagen Dazs Ice Cream Parlors** are located at 621 St. Peter St. (☎ **504-523-4001**) and in the Riverwalk Shopping Center (1 Poydras St., ☎ **504-523-3566**). An outpost of **Ben & Jerry's** is right on Jackson Square (537 St. Ann St., ☎ **504-525-5950**).

For a really special treat, head to the delightful **Angelo Brocato's** (214 N. Carrollton Ave. in Mid-City, ☎ **504-486-0078**). Their creamy and rich gelato will make you an instant fan of Italian ice cream.

Part V
Exploring New Orleans

The 5th Wave   By Rich Tennant

In this part . . .

You have at least one foolproof way to work off all the sinful food you savor in New Orleans — sightseeing! Nothing helps the digestion like a vigorous workout, after all, and you'll get more than that simply deciding which of New Orleans's many sights and attractions you want to see — to say nothing of actually *visiting* them! The first chapter covers all things Mardi Gras. Then, this part runs through the absolute, top of the tops, must-see attractions, followed by a comprehensive list of other places that may be worth your while, helpfully sorted into categories of interest. Next, you find information on one way of seeing the sights you've picked — the guided tour.

And then comes the shopping. New Orleans is a city of excess; that especially holds true for shopping. Whether you want to browse the familiar brand-name department stores or comb through funky boutiques in the city's diverse shopping areas, this part familiarizes you with the lay of the land.

Lastly, you find some helpful suggestions on how to structure your time, in case you're still having trouble figuring out what to see first and how to go about it. First, this part suggests some great itineraries for taking in the sights, and then throws in a couple of side trips you may enjoy, if you've got the time and energy. Just make sure you get back to town by sundown; New Orleans always offers plenty to do at night (which is, incidentally, covered in the next part).

Chapter 16

The Big Attraction: Mardi Gras

● ●

In This Chapter

▶ Discovering the roots of Mardi Gras

▶ Enjoying the mayhem

▶ Avoiding the rip-offs

▶ Taking in Mardi Gras with the family

● ●

*M*ost people who've never experienced it — or perhaps have only seen pictures of the revelry on television — can be forgiven if they think that Mardi Gras is just some weird yearly excuse for people to go crazy. This — believe it or not — religious holiday offers a bit more than the chance to party (although you can do that too).

Mardi Gras always falls 46 days before Easter. If you're not a math whiz (or just can't find your calendar), don't fret. The dates for the next four years are

✔ March 4, 2003

✔ February 24, 2004

✔ February 8, 2005

✔ February 28, 2006

What It Means to Mardi Gras

Mardi Gras is no less than the biggest party thrown on the North American continent. You could write volumes about its rich and colorful history (and indeed, many people have). Revelers flock to the city from all over the country — and the world — while some locals, who don't feel like fighting the crowds, hightail it out of town for the final few days.

Understanding its religious origin

Mardi Gras is the culmination of Carnival (and don't get the two terms confused). *Mardi Gras* is French for "Fat Tuesday," though the term generally applies to the final two weeks of *Carnival* (from *carnisvale,* or "farewell to flesh," which begins on January 6, the 12th night of Christmas). The idea of Mardi Gras is to cram as much celebrating as you can into this final frenzied fortnight; on Ash Wednesday, the Christian season of Lent begins, with its 40 days of fasting and repentance. Of course, not all celebrants on the streets during Mardi Gras are strict religious adherents; some are here for the party.

I love a parade

During the two weeks of Mardi Gras, the party most often takes place on city streets in the form of parades thrown by *krewes,* organizations of men and women dressed in full costume who ride on colorful papier-mâché floats. These parades include spectacularly decorated floats (some people work year-round on these things), with marching bands and horseback riders interspersed throughout. Krewe members and their floats usually focus on a central theme. Riders on each float wave and dispense beads, doubloons, and other trinkets (ranging from plastic pitchforks to cups to women's undergarments) to the crowds below. See the "Mardi Gras Parade Routes" map for some of the major parades that take place over the last days of Carnival.

Most krewes are hierarchies, with one member serving as king, and several others making up the royal court. (Some krewes, such as Endymion and Bacchus, recruit celebrities from film, television, music, and sports to act as their kings.) Many krewes have roots in private, exclusive organizations, with agendas ranging from the socially aware to purely pleasurable.

And everyone loves a party

Despite the elitism of some krewes, Mardi Gras is generally an inclusive and unifying event, bringing together the city's disparate populations for one long party. The lower French Quarter even offers a gay-friendly celebration between St. Ann Street (the unofficial boundary that marks the gay section of the Quarter) and Esplanade Avenue, where the Quarter ends. On Mardi Gras day, gays and lesbians converge around noon in front of the **Rawhide Bar and Lounge,** at St. Ann and Burgundy, to see (and be seen in) outrageous costumes and to compete for the much sought-after Bourbon Street Award.

Mardi Gras Parade Routes

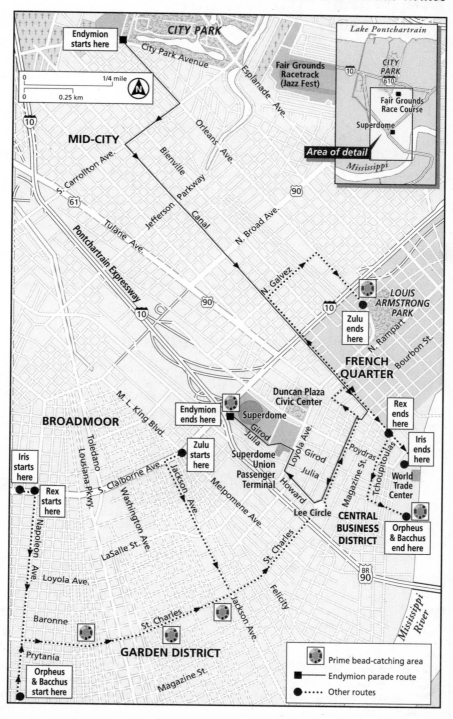

The Mardi Gras Mambo: Some Useful Tips

Despite the anything-goes atmosphere that pervades Mardi Gras, you should keep in mind some basic rules, customs, and bits of common sense.

Deciding whether to drive

If you drive a car to New Orleans, *never* park along a parade route for at least two hours before or after a parade. You'll see signs telling you the parade dates and times all over the place. If you choose to ignore these warnings, your car will be towed. The best bet for getting to Mardi Gras parades is to walk or take public transportation. Even for people who know how to get around, traffic is impossible, so if you must drive, give yourself plenty of time.

If you don't have to drive, don't. You can always call a cab, even on the Fat Tuesday itself. The number for **United Cab,** the city's largest and most well known cab fleet, is ☎ 504-522-9771.

Keeping your perspective

Though the doubloons, beads, and other throws that krewes toss are basically worthless, people act as if they are throwing gold, or tossing packages of food into a famine-ravaged mob. Normally rational human beings will stampede one another for some plastic beads or a plastic cup. Grown adults scramble on all fours after these things, often competing with children. Though the parades are usually all in fun, they can get nasty. Don't laugh. I've seen it happen.

Anticipating crowd control

Mardi Gras probably calls up images of drunken orgies and large rambunctious crowds. I can't vouch for the orgies, but the crowds are everywhere — particularly on Bourbon Street. This street, especially from the 500 block to the 1000 block, represents the worst (some would say the best) of Mardi Gras. People pack themselves in the streets like sardines in a can. Thankfully, the New Orleans Police Department, which is great at controlling crowds, doesn't let the situation get too out of hand.

Obviously, if you like to be in the eye of the storm, the French Quarter is the only place to be on Mardi Gras day. But if you're claustrophobic or hate elbowing your way through dense crowds, your best bet (aside from staying home) is to stake a position in the back, along a sidewalk

Mardi huh? What those strange words mean

Talking the talk and walking the walk are critical if you plan to go to New Orleans during Mardi Gras. With these terms, you'll talk the talk like a pro. Walking the walk, on the other hand, is entirely up to you.

- **Ball** or **Tableau Ball:** Krewes throw these themed, masked balls. Themes change from year to year.

- **Boeuf Gras** (fattened calf): The calf represents ritual sacrifice, as well as the last meal eaten before Lent. It's also the symbol of Mardi Gras and the first float of the Rex parade.

- **Carnival:** A celebration beginning January 6 (the 12th night after Christmas) and ending Mardi Gras day.

- **Court:** A krewe's king, queen, and attendants.

- **Doubloon:** Krewes throw these metal coins during parades. They feature the logo of the krewe on one side and its theme for a particular year on the other.

- **Fat Tuesday:** Otherwise known as Mardi Gras, the last day before Ash Wednesday, which is the first day of Lent.

- **Favor:** Krewe members give these souvenirs, which feature the krewe's logo and date, to people who attend their ball.

- **Flambeaux:** Flaming torches carried by paraders.

- **King Cake:** An oval, sugared pastry decorated with purple, gold, and green (Mardi Gras colors) that contains a small doll representing the baby Jesus.

- **Krewe:** The traditional word for a Carnival organization.

- **Lagniappe** (pronounced *lan-YAP*): Loosely means "a little extra," and refers to any small gift or token — even a scrap of food or a free drink.

- **Mardi Gras:** French for "Fat Tuesday." Technically, if you say "Mardi Gras day," you're really saying "Fat Tuesday day."

- **Rex:** Latin for "king." The King of Carnival is Rex.

- **Second Line:** A group of people that follows a parade, dancing to the music. Also a musical term that specifies a particular shuffling tempo popularized in much New Orleans music.

- **Throws:** Inexpensive trinkets thrown from floats to parade watchers, including doubloons, mini-footballs, plastic swords, tridents and spears, and all sorts of knick-knacks. The most coveted throws are the gilded coconuts of the Zulu Social Aid and Pleasure Club.

or storefront. Or, of course, you can partake of a parade in the Uptown or Mid-City area (see Chapter 10), where the streets will still be crowded, but much less crazy.

As a more practical consideration, keep in mind that large crowds translate into packed restaurants. Depending on where you are, your chances of walking in off the street and being seated without a reservation dwindle to zero. If you have a particular destination in mind, call ahead earlier in the day to be safe.

Though parades are central to Mardi Gras, things don't end when the last float rolls by. Much of the crowd simply relocates to another spot, such as a bar, to continue partying (especially during the two weekends of Carnival). Club owners usually book exciting, party-friendly acts, even on Sunday and Monday nights when many spots would otherwise be dark. And I don't need to tell you that the action on Bourbon Street rolls ever onward. If you base your dream image of New Orleans on the constant street party scenes you've seen in the movies, Mardi Gras is your time.

How Not to Get Ripped Off

The large crowds of Mardi Gras are, naturally, ripe for pickpockets, troublemakers, and other unsavory types. Nothing attracts a potential criminal like a clueless touristy-looking type. Here are some common-sense tips to avoid becoming an easy mark:

- ✔ Keep your money where a pickpocket can't reach it and don't keep it all in one pocket.
- ✔ Take no more than one credit card to a parade.
- ✔ Keep your ID separate from your money and credit card.
- ✔ Don't leave anything of value in your car.
- ✔ Stay with the crowd and steer clear of side streets. Unless you know your way around, you can easily wander into a dangerous neighborhood.

In the event that you are robbed or encounter other trouble, keep these numbers handy: For all emergencies, ☎ **911**; for the New Orleans police (non-emergency), ☎ **504-821-2222.**

All hail Rex (not the dog)

The identity of Rex (the King of Carnival) is kept secret until the day before Mardi Gras. To be named King of Carnival is the ultimate honor for a New Orleanian, usually signifying his prominent standing and work in the community. The king is almost always an older man; his queen is always a young debutante. The krewe of Rex parade always ends in an elaborate tradition: The parade stops at Gallier Hall for a toast from the mayor before moving to Canal Street, where Rex gives a speech, toasts his queen, and presents her with a big bouquet of roses.

Mardi Gras, Family-Style

On Fat Tuesday, the French Quarter is no place to bring your kids. The further into the Quarter you go, the raunchier the costumes become. You'd be amazed what people get away with. Also, many young women (and some not-so-young) are prone to lift up their shirts and bare their breasts at the slightest provocation. (Increasingly, men are flashing their private parts as well.) Although this practice originated as an incentive to get float riders to throw beads, it's evolved (or devolved) beyond that. In recent years, I've witnessed bartering sessions in the middle of the Quarter, whereby women consent to flash their breasts for camera-toting tourists in return for a free drink, a pair of beads, or even just an appreciative hoot.

Recently, the police announced a crackdown on this behavior, promising to arrest anyone violating exposure and decency laws. And while they've certainly put their money where their mouths are, this is one "tradition" that doesn't look to be going anywhere anytime soon.

For a family-friendly Mardi Gras experience, check out the parades in other parts of the city, most notably the parade route along **St. Charles Avenue** uptown. Also, the suburbs are increasingly becoming a haven for families. Although it's a bit of a drive, you'll find a much more G-rated experience (okay, maybe PG-13) if you decamp along one of the major suburban parade routes. **Veterans Highway** in Metairie (on the East Bank of Jefferson Parish), the **Westbank Expressway** (one of the main thoroughfares across the river, on the West Bank of Jefferson Parish), or **St. Bernard Parish** (just north of the city proper) make good spots. Compared to the bacchanalia on Bourbon Street, these suburban areas offer a whole other world. Sure, some drinking and partying goes on, but for the most part, they're good for a family outing.

Your kids are sure to enjoy the Mardi Gras experience; costumes, crowds, and parades are quite a stimulant. Make sure your kids get plenty of sleep the night before, so they won't tire out early. Mardi Gras certainly won't bore them, but it can make for a long day. Avoid spending the kids' college fund on overpriced Mardi Gras food by bringing snacks and drinks with you. Also, decide on a meeting place in advance in case someone gets lost or separated.

Where to Get More Information

For more information on just about any aspect of Mardi Gras, check out *Arthur Hardy's Mardi Gras Guide*. This "Mardi Gras bible" gives you the lowdown on all parades and events in the metropolitan area, and usually contains a couple of interesting and informative articles on various aspects of Mardi Gras. You can pick it up almost anywhere in the city (it usually comes out right after Christmas) or order a copy by calling ☎ 504-838-6111.

Mardi Gras Indians

Groups (or "tribes") of African-American men who dress in elaborate Native American costumes are called "Mardi Gras Indians." The costumes are their pride and joy, and they put serious work into them, usually taking a whole year to put one together. Feathers, sequins, headdresses — the costumes are unbelievable. Some people say that the tradition originally developed as a way of showing thanks to Native Americans who helped escaped slaves. The Indian parades never follow an organized route, but roam at will. Fights used to break out when two different tribes met on the street, but today the tribes just engage in an elaborate call-and-response ceremony instead. (Some Mardi Gras Indian tribes are also musical groups. The most popular these days is the Wild Magnolias, who have played and recorded albums with such luminaries as Dr. John, Bruce Hornsby, and Robbie Robertson.)

Chapter 17

New Orleans's Top Sights

Sure, the food is great and the music is an embarrassment of riches, but the thing about New Orleans that charms many people is its unique sense of character and identity. This chapter presents a selective, alphabetical list of the top places where you can soak up the best of the Crescent City, while also having a good time and maybe learning something along the way.

This chapter starts with the main attractions. (Chapter 18 offers some "not-so-main" attractions, though they're all worth considering.) Watch for the Kid Friendly icon, which points out sights of particular interest if you've got kids along. At the end of this chapter, indexes list the attractions by location and type (museums, parks, and so on). Use these indexes when, for example, you emerge from the Aquarium of the Americas and say, "What else is there to do around here?" Just turn to the location index, find the French Quarter section, and get a list of other nearby attractions.

Hitting the Highlights from A to Z

Aquarium of the Americas
French Quarter

This stylish, entertaining, and winningly educational aquarium — one of the top ten in the country — features breathtaking exhibits that make you feel as if you're walking under water or gazing at a tropical rain forest. The aquarium features an interactive, hands-on activity area for kids, along with popular exhibits of penguins (fed daily at 11 a.m. and 4 p.m.)

and sharks (fed on Tuesdays, Thursdays, and Saturdays at 1 p.m.). Aquarium volunteers in blue or green shirts will answer your questions and steer you in the right direction if you're lost. Give yourself 1½ to 2 hours to see the aquarium.

One Canal St. (at the Mississippi River). ☎ *800-774-7394 or 504-581-4629. Internet:* www.auduboninstitute.org. *Open: Sun–Thurs 9:30 a.m.–6 p.m., Fri–Sat 9:30 a.m.–7 p.m. Admission: $13.50 adults, $10 seniors, $6.50 children 2–12, children 2 and under get in free. Parking: 3-hour complimentary parking in the Hilton New Orleans Riverside parking lot with ticket stub. Wheelchair accessible.*

Armstrong Park
French Quarter

This spot, once the only place where slaves could congregate, used to be called Congo Square. (Congo Square still exists inside the park.) Transformed into a public park and dedicated to jazz legend Louis Armstrong, the park offers visitors stately sycamores, peaceful lagoons, and rolling grassy knolls. You can also find the **Municipal Auditorium** and the **Mahalia Jackson Theater for the Performing Arts** (see Chapter 25). The park entrance is just outside the Quarter in the Faubourg Tremé neighborhood at St. Ann and Rampart streets. The area is safe during the day, but I don't recommend venturing into it at night, unless you go as part of a large group or during an event. Give yourself 30 to 60 minutes to visit the park.

On N. Rampart Street, between Toulouse and St. Phillip streets, facing the French Quarter. Open: seasonal hours. Admission: free. Wheelchair accessible.

Audubon Park
Uptown

This 340-acre public park is one of the most beautiful and tranquil spots in the city. A refuge for nature lovers, it's also a busy social thoroughfare; bicyclists, joggers, and dog walkers come to enjoy the atmosphere and the scenery. Tucked into this sprawling expanse of land are tennis courts, riding and jogging paths, a public golf course, resident populations of squirrels and birds, and hundreds of centuries-old live oaks. Come here to have a picnic, indulge in some exercise, or just contemplate the nature of the universe — but don't stay after dark. Allow 30 to 60 minutes for an appreciative stroll.

6500 St. Charles Ave. (across from Tulane and Loyola universities, nestled between St. Charles Avenue and Magazine Street). Take the St. Charles Streetcar and get off in front of the park. ☎ *504-581-4629. Open: Daily 6 a.m.–10 p.m. Admission: free. Wheelchair accessible.*

A New Orleans IMAX experience

Next door to the Aquarium of the Americas is the IMAX Theatre (☎ 800-774-7394 or 504-581-4629), with large-screen 3-D documentaries (past shows have featured everything from dinosaurs to the Rolling Stones) that are sure to delight the small fry. You can purchase tickets separately for $7.75 for adults and $5.00 for children 2–12 years old ($6.75 for seniors 65 and up), or save a couple of bucks with the aquarium/IMAX combination admission. Shows run hourly from 10 a.m.–8 p.m. The theater is wheelchair accessible.

Audubon Zoo
Uptown

More than 1,800 animals, including some rare and endangered species, make their home in this sprawling maze of carefully constructed lagoons, waterfalls, and vegetation. Situated inside Audubon Park on the bank of the Mississippi River, the zoo features an array of exhibits, including a replica of a Louisiana swamp and the **Butterflies in Flight** exhibit (you walk through an airy, enclosed environment where more than 1,000 butterflies live freely — one or two may land on you to say hi). The zoo boasts a white alligator, two white Bengal tigers, and a host of other exotic animals, and the **Jaguar Jungle** exhibit is a stunning acre-and-a-half replica of an ancient Mayan city filled with spider monkeys, macaws, iguanas, and other creatures; low-lying fog adds an air of mystery. Give yourself two to four hours to thoroughly enjoy the zoo.

6500 Magazine St. Take the St. Charles Streetcar and get off at the park entrance. A free shuttle through the park runs every 20 minutes. If you prefer, take the Magazine Street bus and get off at the zoo. ☎ 800-774-7394 or 504-581-4629. Internet: www.auduboninstitute.org. *Open: Daily 9:30 a.m.–5 p.m.; open till 6 p.m. weekends in the summer. Last ticket sold one hour before closing. Closed Mardi Gras day, the first Friday in May, Thanksgiving, and Christmas. Admission: $9 adults, $5.75 seniors (over 65), and $4.75 children 2–12. Parking: free. Wheelchair accessible.*

Bourbon Street
French Quarter

As you walk along Bourbon Street, between the 100 and 1000 blocks, you'll feel like you've just crashed the world's largest ongoing, open-air frat party. This is New Orleans Party Central, for better or for worse, and at night it's definitely not a kids' attraction — unless you're a kid between the ages of 21 and 100. Bourbon Street is an odd mix of the authentic and the contrived, with its carnival-style barkers trying to lure you into strip clubs, its buggy drivers ferrying tourists, and its requisite street performers and scam artists competing for your attention (and your money). Most, if not all, bars on Bourbon Street (which is blocked off for pedestrians only) stay open until the wee, wee hours — some well into the morning. You can even take an alcoholic drink with you for a stroll — as long as you carry it in a plastic "go-cup." During the daylight hours, Bourbon Street becomes more relaxed and can almost look deserted. Only restaurants, T-shirt and souvenir shops, and a few bars stay open during the day. Depending on the ages of your children and your definition of family values, you may want your kids to see Bourbon Street only in daylight — or not at all. With the kids during the day, allow about an hour for a visit. If you're a bigger kid looking to cut loose at night, well, take your time.

Cabildo
French Quarter

The Cabildo, where the Spanish government turned over the Louisiana Purchase to the United States in 1803, was built in 1795 as the Spanish seat of government. Worthwhile exhibits cover all aspects of life in early Louisiana, including antebellum music, mourning and burial customs, and the changing roles of women in the South. Each room seems more interesting than the one before. Allow at least an hour for your visit.

701 Chartres St. (at St. Ann Street on Jackson Square; 2 blocks from Bourbon Street). ☎ *800-568-6968 or 504-568-6968. Internet:* http://lsm.crt.state. la.us/site/cabex.htm. *Open: Tues–Sun 9 a.m.–5 p.m. Admission: $5 adults, $4 students and seniors, free for children under 12. Wheelchair accessible, though the elevator is small.*

Cruising from A(quarium) to Z(oo)

You can purchase a combination ticket for admission to both the Aquarium of the Americas and the Audubon Zoo, with a riverboat ride on the sternwheeler *John James Audubon* taking you between the two. Combination admissions for all three (cruise, aquarium, and zoo) are $31 (adults) and $15.50 (children 2–12). Combination admissions are also available for cruise and zoo ($22 adults, $11 kids) or cruise and aquarium ($24 adults, $12 kids). Trips depart from the Riverwalk (in front of the aquarium) at 10 a.m., noon, 2 p.m., and 4 p.m., and from the zoo at 11 a.m., 1 p.m., 3 p.m., and 5 p.m. (Call ☎ 504-586-8777 for more information or to confirm schedule.)

New Orleans Attractions

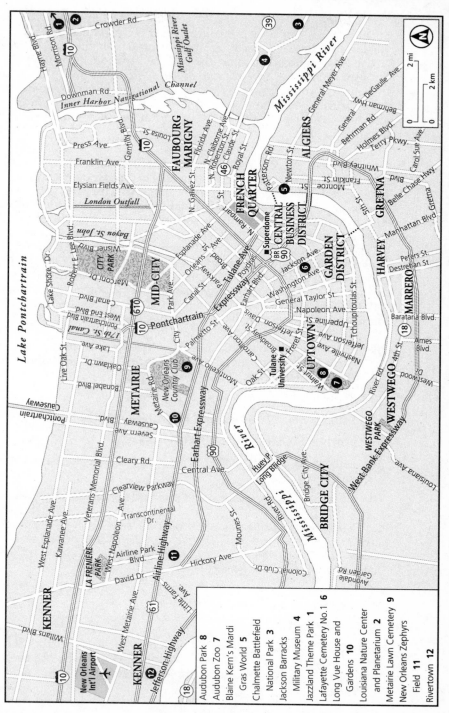

Audubon Park **8**
Audubon Zoo **7**
Blaine Kern's Mardi
 Gras World **5**
Chalmette Battlefield
 National Park **3**
Jackson Barracks
 Military Museum **4**
Jazzland Theme Park **1**
Lafayette Cemetery No.1 **6**
Long Vue House and
 Gardens **10**
Louisiana Nature Center
 and Planetarium **2**
Metairie Lawn Cemetery **9**
New Orleans Zephyrs
 Field **11**
Rivertown **12**

City Park
Mid-City

At 1,500 acres, City Park is the fifth largest urban park in the country and shelters the largest collection of mature live oaks in the world. Give yourself at least an hour to explore the park, two to three if you have children or want to linger at two or more of the spots listed here. (Much longer, of course, if you're going to play 18 holes of golf.) If you plan to visit the **New Orleans Museum of Art** (☎ **504-488-2631;** see listing later in this chapter), which is located on the park grounds, allow another hour to an hour and a half.

The **Carousel Gardens** (☎ **504-483-9356**) in City Park. The gardens house one of the country's few remaining carved wooden carousels. Two miniature trains take riders on a 2½-mile trip through the park. Also check out the small Ferris wheel and wading pool. Admission is $2, single-ride tickets are $1, and $10 buys you unlimited rides; children under two are free. The **Botanical Garden** (☎ **504-483-9386**) offers visitors 12 acres of gardens, fountains, ponds, and sculptures, plus a horticultural library and a gift shop. Open Tuesday through Sunday from 10 a.m. to 4:30 p.m., admission is $5 adults, $2 children, but children under 12 can get in free with a parent. Offering 26 larger-than-life storybook exhibits, **Storyland** (☎ **504-483-9381**) is great for children. Admission is $2.00, free for kids under two. Other features of the park include the following:

- Four 18-hole public golf courses with lessons by PGA pros, electric carts, rentals, pro shop, and restaurant (☎ **504-483-9396**), plus a 100-tee driving range (☎ **504-483-9394**)
- Softball center (☎ **504-483-9422**)
- Pedal boats (☎ **504-483-9371**) for the 8 miles of lagoons
- Thirty-six tennis courts (☎ **504-483-9383**)
- Fishing (☎ **504-483-9371**) in the park's lagoons for bass, catfish, and perch
- Horseback rides, lessons, and pony rides (☎ **504-483-9398**)

City Park is located all the way up Esplanade Avenue out of the French Quarter. Take the Esplanade bus from the French Quarter and get off at the park. ☎ *504-482-4888. Internet:* www.neworleanscitypark.com. *Open: sunrise–sunset. Parking: free. Wheelchair accessible.*

French Market
French Quarter

This nexus of local trade, located right next to the river (from St. Phillip Street to the edge of the Quarter at Esplanade Avenue), has been a fixture since the early 1700s. Its shops, flea market, and farmer's market are

French Quarter Attractions

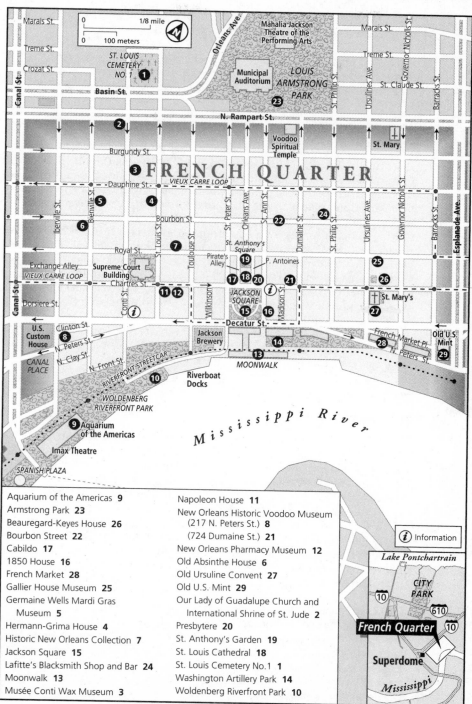

still neat places to shop for souvenirs, gifts, T-shirts, jewelry, arts and crafts, and fresh produce. Finish your shopping spree by indulging in some beignets at **Café du Monde,** located right along the market. Give yourself at least 30 to 60 minutes to wander the market.

The French Market stretches along Decatur and N. Peters streets from St. Ann to Barracks. Open: most shops from 10 a.m.–6 p.m. daily. The Farmer's Market and Café du Monde are open 24 hours. Admission: free. Wheelchair accessible.

Jackson Square
French Quarter

Historically, Jackson Square served New Orleans as the place of execution, military parade ground, and town square. Today, beautiful landscaping, trees, benches, and a fountain make this square one of the more popular public places in the city. Just outside the iron fence, artists set up shop on the sidewalk while mules stand along Decatur Street, patiently waiting to take tourists for a trip around the Quarter. Consult a tarot card reader or a psychic while watching clowns, street musicians, and mimes vie for your tips. You can grab some ice cream, a soft drink, or another snack from a street vendor, or head for one of the restaurants located on each corner of the square. Allot 30 to 60 minutes to look around — considerably more if you decide to run away and join the street mimes.

The square fronts the 700 block of Decatur Street and is bounded by Chartres, St. Ann, and St. Peter streets. Internet: www.jackson-square.com. *Open: seasonal hours, but usually from dawn to dusk. Admission: free.*

Jazzland Theme Park
New Orleans East

This 140-acre theme park opened in May 2000. Jazz and Louisiana are the dominant motifs, with rides and attractions such as Lafitte's Pirate Ship, Voodoo Volcano, the Big Easy (a giant, 90-foot Ferris wheel), and the Mardi Gras Menagerie carousel. The park boasts two thrill-packed roller coasters, Zydeco Scream (a boomerang coaster that drops into reverse toward the end) and the Mega Zeph (a 4,000-foot-long coaster — the park's signature ride). The park also includes a bayou-themed section with alligators and Cajun crafts and dancing. A definite family attraction, Jazzland presents enough history and New Orleans themes to almost qualify as informative. Thrill-junkies of all ages should allow between four hours and a full day, depending on your level of addiction.

12301 Lake Forest Boulevard (at the intersection of I-10 and I-510, approximately 12 miles from the Central Business District; off I-10, take exit 246A South onto I-510, then Lake Forest Boulevard East). ☎ **504-253-8100.** *Internet:* www.jazz landthemepark.com. *Open: Daily Memorial Day–mid-August, weekends only in spring and fall. Admission: $32 adults and children taller than 4 feet, $25 children under 48", $25 seniors 60 and up, free for children 2 and under. Parking: $5. Wheelchair accessible.*

Central Business District/Warehouse District Attractions

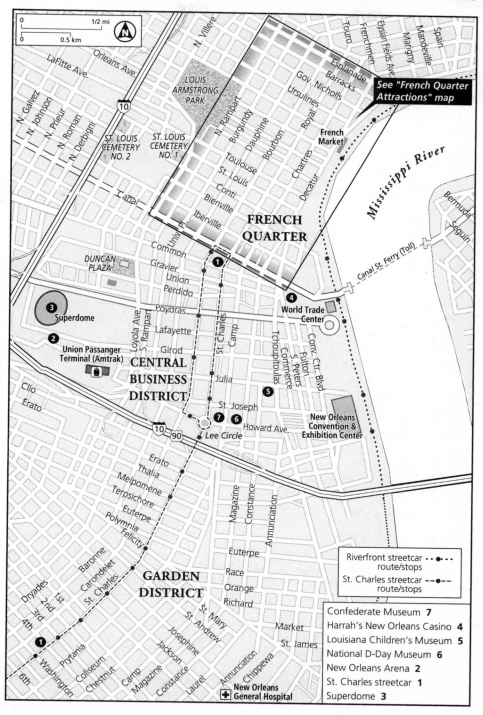

0   1/2 mi
0   0.5 km

LaFitte Ave.
Orleans Ave.
N. Galvez
N. Johnson
N. Prieur
N. Roman
N. Derbigni
10
ST. LOUIS CEMETERY NO. 2
ST. LOUIS CEMETERY NO. 1
LOUIS ARMSTRONG PARK
N. Villere
N. Rampart
Burgundy
Dauphine
Toulouse
St. Louis
Conti
Bienville
Iberville
Esplanade
Barracks
Gov. Nicholls
Ursulines
Royal
Chartres
Decatur
Bourbon
French Market
Touro
Frenchmen
Elysian Fields Ave.
Spain
Mandeville
Marigny
Mississippi River
Bermuda
Seguin

Canal
Univ.
Common
Gravier
Union
Perdido
Poydras
DUNCAN PLAZA
Loyola Ave.
S. Rampart
St. Charles
Camp
Lafayette
Girod
Julia
St. Joseph
Howard Ave.
Lee Circle
Tchoupitoulas
Fulton
S. Peters
Commerce
Conv. Ctr. Blvd.
FRENCH QUARTER
World Trade Center
Canal St. Ferry (Toll)

1
4
3 Superdome
2 Union Passanger Terminal (Amtrak)
CENTRAL BUSINESS DISTRICT
7 **6**
5
New Orleans Convention & Exhibition Center

Clio
Erato
10 90
Erato
Thalia
Melpomene
Terpsichore
Euterpe
Polymnia
Felicity
Baronne
Carondelet
St. Charles
Dryades
1st
2nd
3rd
4th
6th
Prytania
Coliseum
Chestnut
Camp
Magazine
Constance
Laurel
Washington
Magazine
Constance
Annunciation
Euterpe
Race
Orange
Richard
St. Mary
St. Andrew
Josephine
Jackson
Chippewa
Annunciation
Market
St. James
GARDEN DISTRICT
New Orleans General Hospital

Riverfront streetcar route/stops
St. Charles streetcar route/stops

Confederate Museum **7**
Harrah's New Orleans Casino **4**
Louisiana Children's Museum **5**
National D-Day Museum **6**
New Orleans Arena **2**
St. Charles streetcar **1**
Superdome **3**

See "French Quarter Attractions" map

Louisiana Children's Museum
Warehouse District

Kids can really indulge themselves in this interactive museum. With plenty of hands-on exhibits that open up the worlds of science and nature, the real fun is playing grown-up. Kids can be chefs, tugboat captains, or even TV anchors in a simulated television studio. Kids will find plenty of activities and exhibits, from a pint-sized grocery store to a "challenges" exhibit where they shoot hoops from a wheelchair and visit a math and physics lab. Allow 90 minutes to 2 hours.

420 Julia St. (four blocks from the Convention Center). ☎ *504-523-1357. Internet: www.lcm.org. Open: Tue–Sat 9:30 a.m.–4:30 p.m. (Mon 9:30 a.m.–4:30 p.m. in Jun–Aug), Sun noon to 4:30 p.m. Admission: $6, children under 1 free. Parking: Hourly lots nearby. Wheelchair accessible.*

Louisiana Nature Center and Planetarium
New Orleans East

The Nature Center sits in Joe Brown Park, a 68-acre stretch of Louisiana forest. Guided walks are given every day except Monday; a nature film runs on weekdays; and the weekends offer special activities such as canoeing, bird watching, and arts-and-crafts workshops. The center features changing exhibits, 3 miles of trails available for public use, and a wheelchair-accessible wooden walkway. The planetarium offers shows on Saturday and Sunday, and usually a laser rock show on Friday and Saturday nights.

Nature Center Drive in the Joe Brown Memorial Park. Take I-10 to Exit 244. Pass Plaza Shopping Center and turn left onto Nature Center Dr. Or catch the Lake Forest Express bus at Canal and Basin (2 blocks from French Quarter), get off at Lake Forest Blvd. and Nature Center Dr., walk 3 to 4 blocks. ☎ *800-774-7394 or 504-246-5672. Internet: www.auduboninstitute.org. Open: Tues–Fri 9 a.m.– 5 p.m., Sat 10 a.m.–5 p.m., Sun noon to 5 p.m. Admission: $5 adults, $4 seniors, $3 children (2–12). Parking: free. Wheelchair accessible.*

Moonwalk
French Quarter

Although the name conjures images of Michael Jackson doing his patented dance move, the Moonwalk is a great place for a romantic stroll with a great view of the Mississippi River. From the Moonwalk, you can watch river traffic coming into and going out of the second busiest port in the world. Named for Mayor Moon Landrieu, during whose administration it was built, the Moonwalk is directly across the street from Jackson Square. Allow 10 to 15 minutes for general sightseeing, or more if you're looking for *amoré.*

Jackson Square. ☎ *504-587-0738. Open: 24 hours a day, but go before midnight for safety's sake. Admission: free. Wheelchair accessible.*

National D-Day Museum
Central Business District

This one-of-a-kind, three-story museum houses many thought-provoking exhibits relating to D-Day, the day (June 6, 1944) when the Allies stormed the beaches of Normandy and changed the course of World War II. The museum includes a 110-seat theater playing the Oscar-nominated documentary, *D-Day Remembered.* The museum also features exhibits devoted to other beach landings and amphibious invasions during the war. Allow one to two hours for the curious, at least half a day for serious history buffs.

945 Magazine St. (at Howard Avenue in the Warehouse District; enter on the Howard Avenue side). ☎ **504-527-6012.** *Internet:* www.ddaymuseum.org. *Open: Daily 9 a.m.–5 p.m. (excluding Thanksgiving, Christmas, New Year's, and Mardi Gras day). Admission: $10 adults, $6 seniors, $5 children under 18, children under 5 free. Parking: On-street and hourly lots available nearby. Wheelchair accessible.*

New Orleans Historic Voodoo Museum
French Quarter

This museum, now with two locations, dedicates itself to voodoo and Marie Laveau (Voodoo Queen of New Orleans from 1796 to 1881), providing a dim, atmospheric, and titillating look at the world of zombies and *gris-gris* that owes more to Hollywood than serious museums. You'll see artifacts, talismans, and potions all peculiar to this blend of African and Christian religions. The people who run the place are practitioners, and you may catch a genuine voodoo priestess on site, giving readings or making personal *gris-gris* bags; you may even see a staged ritual (call for schedules). You can also catch a tour here to visit Congo Square as well as Marie Laveau's tomb at St. Louis Cemetery No. 1. The newer, now-primary location, on N. Peters Street, is larger, and each museum offers a different collection emphasizing the same theme. Give yourself 30 to 45 minutes to see each location; at either location you visit, you also receive a ticket to the other.

217 N. Peters St. and 724 Dumaine St. ☎ **504-522-2223** *and* **504-523-7685.** *Internet:* www.voodoomuseum.com. *Open: Daily 10 a.m.–8 p.m. Admission: $7 adults, $5.50 seniors, $3.50 children. French Quarter tour $22, cemetery tour $22, tour of the Undead $22. Wheelchair accessible, though the narrow entry door may be a tight fit.*

New Orleans Museum of Art
Mid-City

Set in peaceful City Park, New Orleans's premier fine arts museum has a 35,000-piece permanent collection of European paintings, sculpture, and decorative glassware. You'll also find ever-changing art exhibits from North and South America, Asia, and Africa. Traveling international exhibits come through regularly, bringing paintings by Claude Monet and

Edgar Degas, eggs by Fabergé, and who knows what else. NOMA always has special exhibits and tours for kids. Allow one to two hours, plus transportation.

1 Collins Diboll Circle (take the Esplanade bus and get off in front of the museum). ☎ *504-488-2631. Internet:* www.noma.org. *Open: Tue–Sun 10 a.m.–5 p.m. Admission: $6 adults, $5 seniors, $3 children 3–17; free to Louisiana residents Thurs 10 a.m. to noon. Parking: free. Wheelchair accessible.*

Old U.S. Mint
French Quarter

This huge Greek Revival building now belongs to the Louisiana State Museum, but it used to mint money for both the United States and the Confederacy. These days, it plays host to a large exhibit showcasing New Orleans jazz. The museum features a comprehensive collection of pictures, musical instruments (including Louis Armstrong's first trumpet), and other artifacts that trace the development of jazz. Joint tours of the Mint and two or more of the other Louisiana State Museum properties, such as the Presbytere and the Cabildo, are available; call the number below for more information. Allow an hour, maybe more for serious jazz buffs.

400 Esplanade. ☎ *800-568-6968 or 504-568-6968. Internet:* http://lsm.crt.state.la.us/site/mintex.htm. *Open: Tue–Sun 9 a.m.–5 p.m. Admission: $5 adults, $4 seniors and students, free for children under 12. Wheelchair accessible.*

Presbytere
French Quarter

This building was begun as a home for the Spanish clergy, but it took many years to finish and wound up being used as a courthouse instead. Today, it's a branch of the Louisiana State Museum and home of a Mardi Gras exhibit, which features colorful costumes and interactive displays on the history of the festival. Allow about an hour.

751 Chartres St. (on Jackson Square). ☎ *800-568-6968 or 504-568-6968. Internet:* http://lsm.crt.state.la.us/site/presbex.htm. *Open: Tue–Sun 9 a.m.–5 p.m. Admission: $5 adults, $4 seniors and students, free for children under 12. Wheelchair accessible.*

St. Charles Streetcar
Central Business District

The oldest continually operating streetcar system in the world, the St. Charles streetcar began in 1835 as a mule-drawn railway and was electrified in 1893. In one of those quirky little convergences of tradition and modernity that New Orleans is so famous for, the streetcar is both a

Mid-City Attractions

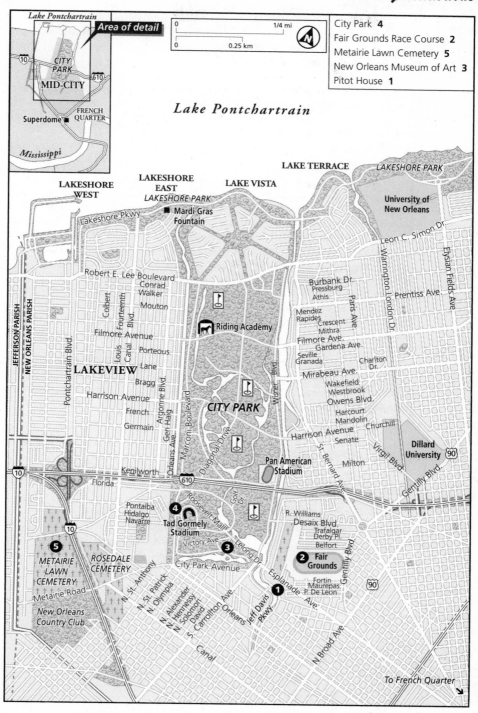

City Park	**4**
Fair Grounds Race Course	**2**
Metairie Lawn Cemetery	**5**
New Orleans Museum of Art	**3**
Pitot House	**1**

national historic attraction *and* a functioning arm of the New Orleans public transit system. See Chapters 11 and 21 for information on the St. Charles route and attractions along the line. The round-trip is about 15 miles and takes about 1½–2 hours. If you're in the neighborhood, you should also check out the Riverfront streetcar (see Chapter 11), which runs — where else? — along the river.

☎ *504-248-3900. Internet:* www.regionaltransit.org. *Admission: $1.25 each way (exact change required); a VisiTour pass provides unlimited rides on street-cars or buses at a cost of $5 for 1 day or $12 for 3 days. Ask at your hotel for the nearest VisiTour pass vendor.*

St. Louis Cathedral
French Quarter

Said to be the oldest continuously operating cathedral in the United States, the St. Louis Cathedral dates from 1794, though the church was largely rebuilt in the 1850s. Not much to look at on the inside, it has quite an interesting history, the third building to stand on this spot. The first church was destroyed by a hurricane in 1722, and the second by the great fire of 1788; it's said that the bells of the cathedral were kept silent for religious reasons (it was Good Friday), and so they didn't ring out to alarm folks of the fire, which went on to destroy over 800 buildings. Be sure to check out the beautiful stained glass windows and mural depicting the life of King Louis IX, the cathedral's patron saint.

615 Pere Antoine Alley (at Jackson Square). ☎ *504-525-9585. Internet:* www.saintlouiscathedral.org. *Open: Tours are given Mon–Sat 9 a.m.– 5 p.m. and Sun 2 p.m.–5 p.m. Admission: Entry and tours are free, but donations are requested. Wheelchair accessible.*

Index of Top Attractions by Neighborhood

French Quarter
Aquarium of the Americas
Armstrong Park
Bourbon Street
Cabildo
French Market
Jackson Square
Moonwalk
New Orleans Historic Voodoo Museum
Old U.S. Mint
Presbytere
St. Louis Cathedral

Central Business District/Warehouse District
Louisiana Children's Museum
National D-Day Museum
St. Charles Streetcar

Mid-City
City Park
New Orleans Museum of Art

New Orleans East
Jazzland Theme Park
Louisiana Nature Center and
   Planetarium

Uptown
Audubon Park
Audubon Zoo

Index of Top Attractions by Type

Historic Attractions and Churches
Armstrong Park (French Quarter)
Cabildo (French Quarter)
French Market (French Quarter)
Jackson Square (French Quarter)
Old U.S. Mint (French Quarter)
St. Charles Streetcar (Central Business
   District)
St. Louis Cathedral (French Quarter)

Museums
Louisiana Children's Museum
   (Warehouse District)
National D-Day Museum (Warehouse
   District)
New Orleans Historic Voodoo Museum
   (French Quarter)

New Orleans Museum of Art (Mid-City)
Presbytere (French Quarter)

Parks and Gardens
Audubon Park (Uptown)
Audubon Zoo (Uptown)
City Park (Mid-City)
Moonwalk (French Quarter)
Nature Center and Planetarium
   (New Orleans East)

Miscellaneous Attractions
Aquarium of the Americas (French
   Quarter)
Bourbon Street (French Quarter)
Jazzland Theme Park (New Orleans
   East)

The Top Sights to See with Your Kids

Aquarium of the Americas (French
   Quarter)
Audubon Zoo (Uptown)
City Park (Mid-City)
Jazzland Theme Park (New Orleans
   East)

Louisiana Children's Museum
   (Warehouse District)
Louisiana Nature Center and
   Planetarium (New Orleans East)
New Orleans Museum of Art (Mid-City)

Chapter 18

More Cool Things to See and Do

. . . .

In This Chapter

▶ Checking out more sights, attractions, and activities for children and teenagers

▶ Traveling deep into the past

▶ Doing the outdoors thing

▶ Going gambling

. . . .

While Chapter 17 gives you the big-name highlights, this chapter presents a list of some other places you may consider, depending on your interests. For locations, see the maps in Chapter 17 unless directed elsewhere.

Especially for Kids

It goes without saying that touring New Orleans with your small fry in tow will be a drastically different experience from the one you'd have coming alone or with your significant other. But that doesn't mean that you have to sacrifice for the sake of the kids: finding attractions that hold appeal for all age groups is easier than you think. For example, a romantic riverboat ride (see Chapter 19) will also appeal to the young 'uns — just in a different way. Following are some kid-tested sights that you'll likely find interesting as well.

Blaine Kern's Mardi Gras World
Algiers

If your visit doesn't coincide with Mardi Gras season, this place gives you a taste of what the whole thing is about. You'll see people building and/or decorating a Mardi Gras float (this is where most of the floats in the city are made). You can watch a Mardi Gras film and even get your picture taken in a Mardi Gras costume. On top of all that, you get complimentary king cake and coffee. Budget around two hours to get here, take the tour, and find your way back to the Quarter.

223 Newton St., Algiers Point. (Take the Canal St. Ferry — free for pedestrians — and a van will meet you, take you to the site, and bring you back. Van reservations only needed for parties of 15 or more.) ☎ *800-362-8213 or 504-361-7821. Internet:* www.mardigrasworld.com. *Open: Daily 9:30 a.m.–4:30 p.m. (closed some holidays). Admission: $13.50 adults, $10 seniors (over 62), $6.50 children under 12. Parking: free. Wheelchair accessible.*

Chalmette Battlefield National Park
Chalmette

This is the site of the historic Battle of New Orleans, where General Andrew Jackson and a ragtag band staged a desperate defense of the city against the British. This last major battle of the War of 1812 actually took place *after* the war was officially over — the participants just hadn't yet received word. Replica cannons, a reconstructed bunker, and the Chalmette Monument, which honors the battle's fallen soldiers, create a sense of history underlined by the collection of battlefield memorabilia housed in the visitors' center. Also on the ground is the Chalmette National Cemetery, which holds the bodies of 14,000 Union soldiers who died during the Civil War (as well as the bodies of American soldiers from every subsequent American war). Oddly enough, only one combatant from the Battle of New Orleans rests here. To see the park, give yourself at least an hour, plus 30 to 60 minutes to get to and from the park.

8606 W. Saint Bernard Hwy., Chalmette (about 7 miles down river from New Orleans). No public transportation is available. A taxi from the French Quarter will cost about $15 each way for 1 or 2 people (add 75¢ for each additional person). ☎ *504-589-4430. Open: Daily 9 a.m.–5 p.m. Admission: free. Parking: free.*

Musée Conti Wax Museum
French Quarter

The climate control here makes this a good place to escape from the heat. As you'd expect, you'll see the requisite Haunted Dungeon with its monsters and scenes from well-known horror tales. You'll also find a large section devoted to Louisiana legends such as Andrew Jackson, Marie Laveau, Napoleon Bonaparte, Huey Long, Pete Fountain, Louis Armstrong, and even a Mardi Gras Indian. Allow 30 to 60 minutes, unless you're procrastinating to beat the heat.

917 Conti St., near the corner of Burgundy. ☎ *800-233-5405 or 504-581-1993. Internet:* http://get-waxed.com. *Open: Mon–Sat 10 a.m.–5 p.m, Sun noon to 5 p.m. Admission: $6.75 adults, $6.25 seniors (over 62), $5.75 children 4–17, free for children under 4. Parking: On-street and hourly lots within one block. Wheelchair accessible.*

Rivertown
Kenner

Offering a nice little tourist area along the banks of the Mississippi River, the city of Kenner sits about 10 miles northwest of the French Quarter. A sort of town within a city, Rivertown is a great family spot for visitors, with a multitude of kid-friendly attractions. (Note: All of the Rivertown attractions below share the same telephone number: ☎ 504-468-7231.)

- ✔ Kids will love the six working train layouts at the **Louisiana Toy Train Museum** at 519 Williams Blvd.

- ✔ The planetarium and observatory at the **Freeport McMoRan Daily Living Science Center** (409 Williams Blvd.) is also worth a visit. Shows run at 2 p.m. Tuesday through Friday, with three shows on weekends. On Thursday through Saturday, 7:30 to 10:30 p.m., you can view the night sky.

- ✔ If your child likes magic, puppet shows, mimes, and stories, visit the **Children's Castle** at 503 Williams Blvd.

- ✔ Kids, as well as sports fans of all ages, will get a kick out of seeing memorabilia and film clips of the New Orleans Saints NFL franchise at the **Saints Hall of Fame** at 415 Williams Blvd.

- ✔ You can see many animals, as well as a small aquarium, at the **Louisiana Wildlife Museum,** 303 Williams Blvd. The museum also features tales of everyday life from 1750 to 1850 told by people in period costume.

- ✔ Finally, the **Mardi Gras Museum of Jefferson Parish** (407 Williams Blvd.) caters to those people who didn't come during Mardi Gras, didn't visit Mardi Gras World, or just can't get enough Mardi Gras fun.

All museums are within a 3-block area and an easy walk from each other. ☎ *504-468-7231. Internet:* www.rivertownkenner.com. *Open: Tue–Sat 9 a.m.– 5 p.m. Admission to each: $3 for adults, $2.50 for seniors and children under 12. A multiticket pass is also available at $15 for adults, $11 for seniors, $9 kids (pass doesn't include the Children's Castle). Parking: free. All museums are wheelchair accessible.*

Especially for Teens

Most teenagers admit to a fondness for hanging out in that great social organism, the mall. If your teen fits in this category, the **Riverwalk, Canal Place,** and **Jax Brewery** shopping centers (see Chapter 20) are good bets for shopping or just hangin' around.

If your kid likes vampires, that ultimate Goth magnet — the cemetery — will almost certainly attract him or her. The cemeteries of New Orleans are attractions in their own right, filled with elegant statuary, crypts, and tombs, but youngsters find them especially appealing. (For information on guided cemetery tours, see Chapter 19.) This section lists some popular local haunts.

Lafayette Cemetery No. 1
Garden District

It may not be as old as St. Louis Cemetery No. 1, but this place still features its share of large above-ground tombs. Anne Rice fans take note: This is also the family burial place of the fictional vampire Lestat. The cemetery has figured into many books and films, including the movie version of *Interview with a Vampire*. The famous **Commander's Palace** restaurant sits right across the street from the cemetery. Touring the cemetery alone is unsafe. Only visit here on a guided tour (see Chapter 19) or in a large group. Allow 30 to 60 minutes.

1400 block of Washington Avenue. Open: Mon–Fri 7:30 a.m.–2:30 p.m., Sat 7:30 a.m. to noon. Admission: free. Wheelchair accessible.

Metairie Lawn Cemetery
Metairie

The largest of all New Orleans cemeteries, Metairie is also the youngest (built after the Civil War). You'll find some of the most amazing tombs in the city in this, the most beautiful of the city's cemeteries. Pick up a free cassette-tape tour (with player) at the office. Unlike most of the other cemeteries in New Orleans, you can tour the cemetery from your car or walk safely through it. Give yourself an hour.

5100 Pontchartrain Blvd. The Canal Street bus will take you from the French Quarter to the cemeteries at the end of Canal Street. From there, the Metairie Cemetery is only a block or two (ask the driver), but you'll have to walk several more blocks from the street to the office. ☎ 504-486-6331. Open daily 8 a.m.–5 p.m. Admission: free. Wheelchair accessible.

New Orleans Pharmacy Museum
French Quarter

Louis Dufilho, the first licensed pharmacist in the United States, opened an apothecary shop here in 1823; the Creole-style town home also served as his residence, and he supposedly grew herbs for his medicines in the courtyard. The museum opened in 1950, and it features lots of voodoo potions, giant syringes, bone saws, leeches, and other medical instruments, as well as a cosmetics counter (old-time pharmacists also manufactured makeup and perfumes). Although you may not learn as much as you'd hoped for, you'll at least develop an appreciation for modern medicine. Allow 15 to 30 minutes.

514 Chartres St. (2 blocks from Bourbon Street). ☎ *504-565-8027. Internet:* www.pharmacymuseum.org. *Open: Tue–Sun 10 a.m.–5 p.m. Admission: $2 adults, $1 seniors and students, children under 12 free. Wheelchair accessible.*

St. Louis Cemetery No. 1
French Quarter

This "city of the dead" is the oldest extant cemetery in the city (it was founded in the late 1700s) and features large tombs, monuments, and smaller, unmarked niches that resemble baker's ovens. People still leave gifts at the tomb of Marie Laveau to pay their respects and perhaps to ask for supernatural aid. The place is fascinating. Only visit here in a large group or on an organized tour because the neighborhood is in a high-crime district. For this reason (and to avoid the errant ghoul or vampire), come only during daylight. Allow 30 to 60 minutes.

400 block of Basin Street (4 blocks from Bourbon Street). ☎ *504-482-5065. Open: Mon–Sat 9 a.m.–3 p.m., Sun 9 a.m. to noon. Admission: free, but organized tours are not. Call Save Our Cemeteries at* ☎ *504-525-3377 for information on taking a tour. Wheelchair accessible for the most part, but some spots may pose problems.*

Especially for History Buffs

If it hasn't dawned on you yet that New Orleans is a city steeped in historical significance, you just haven't been paying attention. Almost all of the sights in this chapter have historic value, but here are a few that die-hard History Channel buffs shouldn't miss.

1850 House, Lower Pontalba Building
French Quarter

The beautifully restored Pontalba Apartments (as they're locally known) were built in 1849, originally as individual town houses. The Baroness Pontalba built them in an effort to combat the deterioration of the older part of the city. Take a look at the private courtyard, servants' quarters, and huge rooms with their high ceilings, marble fireplaces, and authentic period furniture to get a fascinating look at the lifestyles of the rich and famous, 19th-century style. Allow 15 to 30 minutes.

523 St. Ann St. (on Jackson Square). ☎ *800-568-6968 or 504-568-6968. Internet:* http://lsm.crt.state.la.us/site/1850ex.htm. *Open: Tues–Sun 9 a.m.–5 p.m. Closed state holidays. Admission: $3 adults, $2 seniors and students, free for children under 12. Not accessible for wheelchairs.*

Beauregard-Keyes House
French Quarter

This lovely house, built in 1826, is named for two of its most famous tenants: Confederate General Pierre Gustave Toutant Beauregarde, who resided here after the Civil War, and author Frances Parkinson Keyes, who wrote many of her novels here, including the most famous, *Dinner at Antoine's*. Take a gander at the twin staircases, the Doric columns, and the "raised cottage" architecture, and try to imagine what life was like when this place was a boardinghouse during the Civil War. The house itself is not wheelchair accessible, but the beautiful garden adjoining the house is. Allot 45 to 75 minutes to peruse the house.

1113 Chartres St. (2 blocks from Bourbon Street). ☎ 504-523-7257. Open: hourly tours depart Mon–Sat 10 a.m.–3 p.m. Admission: $5 adults, $4 seniors, students, and AAA members, $1.50 children under 13.

Confederate Museum
Warehouse District

Billed as the oldest museum in Louisiana, this place has displayed Civil War artifcats since 1891. The memorabilia includes uniforms, photographs, guns, battle flags, swords, and personal belongings of Gen. Robert E. Lee, Gen. P. G. T. Beauregard, and Confederate president Jefferson Davis. The museum houses the second-largest collection of Confederate memorabilia in the country. A visit to the museum takes about 30 to 60 minutes.

929 Camp St. (take the St. Charles streetcar to Lee Circle and walk one block to Camp Street). ☎ 504-523-4522. Internet: www.confederatemuseum.com. Open: Mon–Sat 10 a.m.–4 p.m. Admission: $5 adults, $4 students and seniors, $2 children under 12. Parking: On-street and hourly lot nearby. Not accessible for wheelchairs.

Gallier House Museum
French Quarter

Noted architect James Gallier once resided in this house, which people say served as the model for a location in Anne Rice's vampire books. The house was thoroughly modern back in 1857 — it has hot and cold running water and a bathroom. The guided tour gives you a great look at mid-19th-century New Orleans life. Allow an hour to explore this modern miracle.

1132 Royal St. (1 block from Bourbon Street). ☎ 504-525-5661. Open: Mon–Sat 10 a.m.–3:30 p.m. Admission: $5; free for children under 8. Not accessible for wheelchairs.

Germaine Wells Mardi Gras Museum
French Quarter

This museum, which houses the Mardi Gras gowns worn between 1910 and 1960 by former Arnaud's owner Wells, sits atop Arnaud's restaurant (see Chapter 14). Give yourself 15 to 20 minutes to peruse the costumes.

813 Bienville St. (½ block from Bourbon Street). ☎ *504-523-5433. Internet:* www.arnauds.com/museum.html. *Open: during restaurant hours. Admission: free. Not accessible for wheelchairs.*

Hermann-Grima House
French Quarter

Cooking demonstrations are held in the period kitchen of this 1832 house every Thursday from May through October. The interior of the house depicts funeral customs of the time, except during December, when the house gets decorated for a "Creole style" Christmas. Tours cover both the house and the stable. Joint tours of this property and the Gallier House museum are available; call for details. Allow 30 to 60 minutes, or two hours or more for the combined tour.

820 St. Louis St. (½ block from Bourbon Street). ☎ *504-525-5661. Open: Mon–Sat 10 a.m.–3:30 p.m. Admission: $5; free for children under 8. Wheelchair accessible, but call ahead so that workers can put out the portable ramp.*

Historic New Orleans Collection
French Quarter

If you want the lowdown on the evolution of New Orleans, visit this complex of buildings (one of which dates from 1792) where you'll see art, maps, and original documents from Louisiana's past. The collection's research center provides a treasure trove of research materials. You can find the research center in a beautifully restored courthouse and police stations at 410 Charles St. The exhibits change periodically. Allow 30 to 60 minutes.

533 Royal St. (1 block from Bourbon Street). ☎ *504-523-4662. Internet:* www.hnoc.org. *Open: Tue–Sat 10 a.m.–4:30 p.m. Admission: free. Guided tours cost $4 and are given at 10 a.m., 11 a.m., 2 p.m., and 3 p.m. Wheelchair accessible.*

Jackson Barracks Military Museum
Holy Cross

Generals Robert E. Lee and Ulysses S. Grant served here prior to the Civil War; now it serves as headquarters for the Louisiana National Guard. The reason to visit is the military museum, where a chronological history traces the involvement of Louisiana soldiers in major wars and skirmishes from the American Revolution through Desert Storm. You'll also see flags, guns, artillery pieces, uniforms, and other military hardware on display among the museum's artifacts. Allot 60 to 90 minutes to see the museum and to get there from the Quarter.

6400 St. Claude Ave. (take the St. Claude bus and get off in front of the museum). ☎ *504-271-6262, ext. 242. Open: Mon–Fri 7:30 a.m.–4 p.m. Admission: free. Parking: free. Wheelchair accessible.*

Lafitte's Blacksmith Shop and Bar
French Quarter

Records verify this building's existence since 1772 (though many insist that it's much older and is, in fact, the oldest building in the Mississippi Valley). According to legend, the pirate Jean Lafitte and his brother Pierre used it as a front for their illegal activities, posing as blacksmiths while selling ill-gotten pirate booty (and, some say, slaves). Since 1944, it's been a bar, a haunt of Tennessee Williams, among others. Kids can't go inside, but you can get an excellent view of the dark interior through the open doorway. Only budget a couple of minutes here, unless you plan to have a drink or two.

941 Bourbon St. ☎ *504-523-0066. Open: daily 11 a.m.–"until" (New Orleans term for no set closing time). Admission: no cover charge. Part of it is not accessible to wheelchairs.*

Napoleon House
French Quarter

People claim that Mayor Nicholas Girod's home was offered to the exiled Napoleon Bonaparte as a refuge, but Napoleon died before the scheme got off the ground. Some doubt the veracity of this tale, claiming that the building was built after Napoleon's death. Whatever the truth, the building's been trading on this near brush with glory ever since, and it's become a favorite spot of bohemian locals in recent decades. Today, the Napolean House bar and cafe provides patrons with a dark and quiet atmosphere. Unless you want to grab a drink or a bite to eat, only allow yourself a few minutes here. Kids are also welcome.

500 Chartres St. (at the corner of Chartres and St. Louis streets, 2 blocks from Bourbon Street and Jackson Square). ☎ *504-524-9752. Open: Daily 11 a.m.–1 a.m. Admission: no cover. Wheelchair accessible.*

Old Absinthe House
French Quarter

According to legend, Andrew Jackson and the Lafitte brothers (pirates Jean and Pierre) met in this 1806 building to plan the Battle of New Orleans. The drink for which the bar is named is illegal these days, so the bar serves anisette instead — which tastes like absinthe but, thankfully, doesn't cause brain damage. Stop here for a few minutes to look around, or longer if you're going to drink. Because it's a bar, kids are not allowed inside.

240 Bourbon St. ☎ *504-523-3181. Internet:* www.oldabsinthehouse.com. *Open: Daily from 9:30 a.m. Admission: no cover. Wheelchair accessible.*

Old Ursuline Convent
French Quarter

This structure is said by some to be the oldest building of record in New Orleans and the entire Mississippi Valley, as well as the only surviving building from the French colonial period in what is now the United States. Erected between 1745 and 1752, it was once run by the Sisters of Ursula, who had the first girls-only school in the country. In 1831, the state assembly met here. Today, it houses a Catholic archive with documents that go back to 1718. Give yourself 60 to 75 minutes to see the place.

1100 Chartres St. (2 blocks from Bourbon Street). ☎ *504-529-3040. Open: tours run Tues–Fri 10 a.m.–3 p.m. on the hour (closed for lunch at noon); Sat–Sun 11:15 a.m., 1 p.m., and 2 p.m. Admission: $5 adults, $4 seniors, $2 students, children under 8 free. Not accessible for wheelchairs.*

Our Lady of Guadalupe Church and International Shrine of St. Jude
French Quarter

Erected in 1826 across the street from St. Louis Cemetery No. 1, Our Lady served as a convenient place to hold funerals for victims of yellow fever and other diseases. It's also said to be the oldest church in New Orleans. Our Lady serves as a shrine to both St. Jude (saint of impossible causes) and a guy called St. Expedite. Legend claims that this saint's statue showed up at the church in a crate, marked only with the word "expedite" stamped on the outside. The name stuck, and today people know him as the saint to whom you pray when you want things in a hurry (I'm not making this up). Allow 15 minutes.

411 N. Rampart St. (3 blocks from Bourbon St.). ☎ *504-525-1551. Internet:* www.saintjudeshrine.com. *Open: Daily 7 a.m.–7 p.m. Admission: free. Wheelchair accessible.*

Pitot House
Mid-City

James Pitot, the first mayor of incorporated New Orleans, moved this beautiful house in 1810, which was originally built on a different spot in the late 1700s. This excellent example of an 18th-century, West Indies–style plantation home features wide galleries and large columns. Seeing the house takes one to two hours, plus transportation time.

1440 Moss St. (near City Park). ☎ *504-482-0312. Open: Wed–Sat 10 a.m.–3 p.m. Admission: $5 adults, $4 seniors and students, $2 children under 12. Parking: free. The first floor is wheelchair accessible, but the second floor is not.*

Parks and Gardens

New Orleans boasts a number of areas of interest to fans of the out-doors. Whether you're looking for spacious parks (check Chapter 17 for some of the city's best) or impressive gardens, here are a few choice selections.

Longue Vue House and Gardens
Metairie

Natural and formal gardens, gorgeous fountains, and tranquil ponds form the backdrop for this beautiful Greek Revival mansion, which sits at the end of an oak-lined drive just minutes from downtown New Orleans. Check out the interior of the house to get a look at the beautiful antiques, rice-paper wall coverings, Oriental carpets, and other lovely touches. Families will want to check out the Discovery Garden, a ½-acre interactive garden for children of all ages. A visit here takes one to two hours plus transportation time.

7 Bamboo Rd. Catch the Canal Street bus at any stop on Canal (every other corner) and get off at the cemeteries; take the Metairie Road bus, get off at Bamboo Road, and walk ½ block. ☎ *504-488-5488. Internet:* www.longuevue.com. *Open: Mon–Sat 10 a.m.–4:30 p.m., Sun 1 p.m.–5 p.m. Closed most holidays. Admission: $10 adults, $9 seniors, $5 children and students; children under 5 free. Parking: free. Wheelchair accessible, though parts of the garden are wild and may be rough going.*

St. Anthony's Garden
French Quarter

The garden, located directly behind St. Louis Cathedral (see Chapter 17), is named for Pere Antoine, a popular rector who served New Orleans in the late 18th and early 19th centuries. Legend claims that many duels were fought here in the past. Now, however, the main attraction comes at night, when a huge shadow of Christ appears against the back of the church — thanks to a statue and a carefully placed spotlight. The garden is not open for tours, but you can easily catch a glimpse of it from Royal Street, Pirates' Alley, or Pere Antoine's Alley.

Washington Artillery Park
French Quarter

This spot and Jackson Square have long been two of the most popular places for tourists, as well as gathering points for young people. Street performers often run through their routines for tips in front of the steps leading to the top of the levee (which double as seats for a small amphitheater). This place had fallen into disrepair for awhile, but the Audubon Institute prettied it up a few years ago, re-landscaping the area, reopening the public restrooms, and providing a tourist information center.

Just west of the French Market, along the riverfront. ☎ *504-587-0738. Admission: free. Wheelchair accessible.*

Woldenberg Riverfront Park
French Quarter

This park, which features almost 20 acres of green grass, open space, and hundreds of trees and shrubs, makes a great place for an afternoon break along the Mississippi River. This area has historically been the city's promenade; nowadays it stretches from the Moonwalk to the Aquarium of the Americas and features works by popular local artists.

Riverfront behind the 500 block of Decatur Street. ☎ *504-587-0738. Open: dawn to 10 p.m. Admission: free. Wheelchair accessible.*

For the Sporting (or Betting) Type

Granted, the Crescent City isn't a sports Mecca on the order of, say, Chicago or New York, but it does sport some areas of interest for gamers and fans of major- and minor-league franchises, including the NFL's New Orleans Saints and the NBA's New Orleans Hornets.

Fair Grounds Race Course
Mid-City

One of the oldest racetracks in the country, this course has hosted Pat Garrett, Frank James (brother of Jesse and a betting commissioner), and Generals Ulysses S. Grant and George Custer, among others. The racing season runs from Thanksgiving Day to late March. The New Orleans Jazz and Heritage Festival (a.k.a. Jazz Fest) is also held here every year during the last weekend of April and the first weekend of May.

1751 Gentilly Blvd., Mid-City (approximately 10 minutes by car from the Central Business District and the French Quarter). ☎ *504-944-5515. Internet: www.fgno. com. Parking: free; valet $4. Open: first post time is 12:30 p.m. and last race around 4:37 p.m. Admission: during racing season, $4 for the clubhouse, $1 for the grand-stand; during the off-season (off-track betting only), $1. Wheelchair accessible.*

Harrah's New Orleans Casino
Central Business District

Because gambling is a hot-button issue around here, I'm neither advocating nor condemning it as an attraction, family or otherwise. Nevertheless, this place is *huge,* both in terms of its size and its impact (for good or ill) on the local community. You may want to take a look at it for those reasons alone.

*512 S. Peters St. ☎ **800-VIP-JAZZ** or 504-533-6000. Internet: www.harrahs.com/ our_casinos/nor/. Open: 24 hours. Parking: valet and garage parking are available; call the information number for prices and other details. The casino is wheelchair accessible.*

New Orleans Arena
Central Business District

This arena shares many facilities with its neighbor and older sibling, the Superdome, including parking spaces, power, water, and staff. Smaller than the Superdome but larger than other area venues, it hosts sporting events (including some Tulane University basketball home games), concerts, and other touring events. The arena is also the new home of the New Orleans Hornets NBA team, which relocated from Charlotte at the end of the 2001–02 basketball season.

*1501 Girod St. (next to the Superdome, even though the street names are different). ☎ **504-587-3663**. Internet: www.neworleansarena.com. Wheelchair accessible.*

New Orleans Zephyrs Field
East Jefferson

Although New Orleans may not host a major league baseball team, it does have the Zephyrs — the AAA-class farm team of the Houston Astros. Since their arrival in New Orleans in the 1990s, the Zephyrs have become a popular team among jaded local sports fans (it helps that the Zephyrs won the 1998 AAA World Series, giving the city a winning team).

*6000 Airline Dr., East Jefferson (approximately 9 miles from the French Quarter, on the way to the airport). Take the Airline bus and get off by the stadium. ☎ **504-734-5155**. Internet: www.zephyrsbaseball.com for game times and admission.*

Superdome
Central Business District

One of the largest buildings in the world in terms of diameter (680 feet), the Superdome provides a climate-contolled environment for 76,000 New Orleans Saints fans or over 100,000 concert-goers. The Superdome also hosts trade shows and conventions. (Note: As of this writing, tours of the Superdome facility had been suspended as a security measure following the terrorist attacks of September 11, 2001, but may be reinstated by the time you read this. Be sure to call the facility beforehand to inquire about tours.)

*1500 Poydras. Take the Poydras bus and get off in front of the Superdome. ☎ **504-587-3808** or 504-587-3663.*

Chapter 19

Seeing New Orleans by Guided Tour

To tour or not to tour? That is the question. Personally, I'm on the (wrought-iron) fence on this issue. You can get an entertaining overview of the city (or of a specific part of it, such as the French Quarter or the Garden District) by taking a guided tour. Depending on the tour operator you choose, you'll definitely see some good sights, (hopefully) be entertained by your guide, and, if you're not careful, learn a thing or two before the end.

The decision to take a guided tour basically comes down to your answer to one question: Do you enjoy setting off into the unknown with nothing but your guidebook and some sun block, or do you prefer exploring with a little extra security, structure, and comfort — and don't mind looking like a tourist? If you're the adventurous type, a tour may not be for you. If you would rather see the sights in the company of a licensed professional, however, a guided tour gives you a few hours to do nothing more than look and listen.

Bear in mind, however, that as often as not, your tour will offer more entertainment value than historical significance. I mention some exceptions in this chapter, but most tours here are Show Biz, baby. They all mean well, and most of them even have their facts right, but you'll definitely get your daily allowance of drama, intrigue, history, and innuendo — New Orleans's rich history holds more soap opera than Aaron Spelling can ever invent.

Help! I've been de-toured

If you're interested in taking a tour, keep your eyes open. Some hotel concierges have been known to take kickbacks from certain tour operators to steer business exclusively to them. Obviously, not every concierge is on the take, but your best bet would be to book any tours directly through the operator; no reputable operator will force you to go through a third party.

If you can't find sufficient tour information at your hotel, call or visit the **State Office of Tourism** (529 St. Ann St., right on Jackson Square; ☎ **504-568-5661**). Aside from offering a multitude of booklets, brochures, and other such material, they also have someone from the New Orleans Convention and Visitor's Bureau on hand to give you the straight dope on tours and attractions, and to steer you towards a reputable tour that's right for your budget, needs, or time frame. For more information on tourist offices, see Chapter 10.

Nevertheless, tours are still a lot of fun — like settling down for a couple hours of prime-time TV. They can also provide the perfect compromise for those days when you're trying to balance your aching feet against the urge to get out and see some sights. General orientation tours and specialty tours make up the two main types of guided tours. You'll find information on both types in this chapter.

Time versus Info: General Orientation Tours

If you only have limited time, but still want the rundown on what's old, what's new, what's borrowed, and especially what's blue (as in "rhythm and"), consider a general orientation tour. Riding around the city on a half-hour carriage tour, you get a condensed New Orleans history lesson, learn about the local architecture, find the good clubs, and see the attractions. However, general information is all that you'll get. Walking tours and bus tours may take a little longer, but with a thorough guide, you'll walk away feeling like you're a part of things.

Cooling off with a bus tour

If you can't take the heat, a bus tour — where you can see the sights without leaving the air conditioning — is just your cup of iced tea. Aside from seeing the whole city, you can also take a tour that goes outside of town to plantations or swamps. Licensed guides narrate these tours, and buses come variously equipped with TVs and VCRs, stereo sound, bathrooms, cellular phones, and equipment for travelers with disabilities. (If a particular amenity is important to you, make sure to ask for the appropriate bus ahead of time.)

One of the oldest and most reliable tour companies, **New Orleans Tours** (☎ 504-592-0560) offers city and neighborhood tours by bus, as well as riverboat cruises, swamp tours, plantation tours, walking tours, nightlife tours, jazz tours, and combination tours. For more options, check out these other tour companies as well:

- ✔ **Custom Bus Charters** (☎ 504-528-1865)
- ✔ **Dixieland Tours** (☎ 800-489-8747)
- ✔ **Gray Line** (☎ 800-535-7786 or 504-587-0861)
- ✔ **Hotard** (☎ 504-528-9433)

Strolling the Quarter

Because the French Quarter is the oldest and arguably most interesting part of New Orleans, most tourists focus on this area. No large buses are allowed in the Quarter (though you will see smaller buses and vans), so walking is your best option for getting around.

Strolling around the French Quarter on your own is the best way to see the area. Traveling on your own gives you the freedom to linger in a pastry shop or park, stop to watch street entertainers, poke your head in all the cute stores you find, admire the local architecture, or follow your nose into off-the-beaten-path nooks and crannies. Chapter 21 lists several itineraries for walking tours that you can take on your own. If you still feel like you want to bring someone along to tell you what you're seeing, contact **Friends of the Cabildo** (☎ 504-523-3939), a non-profit group that gives two-hour walking tours of the French Quarter. Cost is $10 for adults, $8 for seniors and students, and free for kids 12 and under.

Because the French Quarter and other parts of New Orleans are part of the Jean Lafitte National Park, you can also get a free tour from the **National Park Service.** The service offers only one tour each day at 10:30 a.m. and each person must pick up his or her own ticket. The tickets are given out, starting at 9:00 a.m. each morning on a first-come, first-serve basis. For more information, stop by the **Visitor's Information Center** at 419 Decatur St. or call ☎ 504-589-2636.

University of New Orleans professor Kenneth Holditch (who really knows his stuff) leads the **Heritage Literary Tours** (732 Frenchmen St., ☎ 504-949-9805). He gives a general tour centered around the literary legacy of the French Quarter (which has played host to a considerable number of famous and colorful writers over the years), as well as a more specialized tour dealing with Tennessee Williams. If you arrange it in advance, he can (probably) design a tour for you around a specific author. He's a character in his own right, and his tours are fun and informative and loaded with anecdotes. Tours are $20 for adults and $10 for students.

Riding in style: Carriage tours

Like bus tours, a carriage tour may or may not be up your alley. Riding through the French Quarter in a mule-drawn carriage certainly gives you a more intimate experience than riding around in a bus with 50 or 60 other name-tag-wearing passengers. It can also be quite romantic (if you can block out the, er, nature smells). But again, carriage tours are pretty conspicuous, and not exactly the brightest move if you're focused on blending in with the surroundings. But if you want one, go for it! Throw caution to the winds. A good carriage driver can show you the highlights of the Quarter in just 30 minutes; spend an hour touring, and you'll feel like a native.

Carriage rides stay in the Quarter, and no one guarantees the veracity of the information you receive. But hey, *caveat emptor* and all that, right? Some drivers are licensed tour guides, though most are not. Nevertheless, each one has his or her area of expertise. Some have eaten their way through the city, some are historians, and others pride themselves on knowing the location of every bar. One driver may regale you with ghost stories, another may tell you jokes, and a third may not say anything. Talk to the driver for a minute and try to gauge his personality before getting into the rig.

Most of the carriages in the Quarter line up along Decatur Street at Jackson Square and at carriage stands at the corners of Royal and St. Louis, Bourbon and Conti, or Bourbon and Toulouse. Also keep your eyes open for carriages cruising throughout the Quarter or parked on a corner waiting for a fare.

You'll see two types of carriages: the large hard-topped, bus-like models that you share with anybody else that comes along, and the smaller convertible models that you hire individually for your party. Generally, carriages have abandoned the per-person rates, charging $50 for a half-hour ride and $105 for an hour (the latter price includes picking you up from your hotel).

If your tour lasts appreciably less than 30 minutes, your driver is giving you a "zip tour." If this is the case, confront the driver about this and find out if the tour can be extended. If the driver won't comply, complain to the driver's boss. If the driver refuses to give you the boss's name, write down the driver's name (if you know it), the company name, and the carriage number (on its side or back), and call the city's **Taxicab Bureau** (☎ 504-565-6272) to complain.

If you want a carriage to pick you up, call one of the following licensed carriage companies:

- Royal Carriages (☎ 504-943-8820)
- Good Old Days Buggies (☎ 504-523-0804)
- Mid-City Carriages (☎ 504-581-4415)
- Old Quarter Tours (☎ 504-944-0446)

Filling a Niche: Specialty Tours

Specialty tours are obviously good bets if you're interested in comprehensive information on a particular subject. And they're better for sounding learned when you get back home. You can spout off the very general, touristy info you got on a basic orientation tour, and everyone will know you're probably just parroting some tour guide. But if you're able to expound at length about, say, the history of jazz, they're more likely to be impressed.

Gay old New Orleans

The Bienville Foundation's **Gay Heritage Tour** (☎ 504-945-6789) is a 2½-hour tour that shows you the city from a gay-friendly perspective. You'll explore the Quarter and hear about such figures as Tennessee Williams, Clay Shaw, and Ellen DeGeneres. Robert Batson, the knowledgeable and personable tour guide, also explains the importance of various gay landmarks. The $20 tour leaves from Alternatives (a gay-targeted gift shop at 909 Bourbon St.); days and times vary seasonally (the tour doesn't run during August or December), so be sure to call for information.

Discovering New Orleans's African-American heritage

If you want to delve into New Orleans's history of Africans and African Americans, contact **African American Heritage Tours** (☎ 504-288-3478). Tours include trips to plantations, Xavier University (the first Black Catholic university in the United States), and a narrative on historic sites such as Liberty Bank, which was founded by African Americans.

Hepcats unite: Jazz tours

Photographer for the *Times-Picayune* and well-known local jazz historian John McCusker leads **John McCusker's Jazz Tours** (☎ **504-282-3583**). He takes visitors on a bargain-priced ($25), 2½-hour van tour every Saturday morning that traces the history of New Orleans jazz. He points out the spots where jazz was born, where it matured, and where performers such as Louis Armstrong were born or played their music.

Thirst for blood: Vampire and ghost tours

If you're up for a cemetery tour, **Magic Walking Tours** (☎ **504-588-9693**) will oblige. The fearless can even go on a vampire hunt. If you're really lucky, your guide may even let you carry the wooden stake and mallet.

Haunted History Tours (☎ **504-861-2727**; www.hauntedhistorytours. com) offers vampire tours and tours of the cemeteries. You can also opt for the Haunted History Tour itself, which details various ghost stories and legends in the Quarter. The tour will entertain you, but don't put too much stock in the "facts" here.

Fun with the dead: Cemetery tours

Many cemeteries are simply not safe unless you're with an organized group. I strongly advise against wandering through any cemetery (especially St. Louis No. 2) alone or without an official tour.

The members of **Save Our Cemeteries** (☎ **504-525-3377**), a non-profit organization, do more to restore and maintain New Orleans' cemeteries than anyone else. Their tours are a good crash course for newcomers to the subject.

Fred Hatfield (☎ **504-891-4862**), a semi-retired native New Orleanian, has spent his whole life in the neighborhood of **Lafayette Cemetery No. 1.** Consequently, he's done extensive research on the people buried there, as any good neighbor would do. His combination walking tours of the Garden District and Lafayette No. 1 take about two hours and cost $14 per person (minimum of 4 people); he also gives individual tours of the cemetery for $9 (minimum of 4 people). He's usually home, so give him a call.

Many visitors have raved about the wealth and quality of information they receive from **Historic New Orleans Walking Tours** (☎ **504-947-2120**; www.tourneworleans.com). Here you can find a number of French Quarter tours, including tours for history and "mystique," as well as the following cemetery tours:

✔ The **Cemetery/Voodoo Tour** takes you to the tomb of Marie Laveau and to an actual voodoo temple. You'll get the straight facts about voodoo's West African religious roots and its modern-day practitioners. In short, it's long on the authentic and short on the wink-wink-nudge-nudge sensationalism you may get elsewhere; you'll also see other famous burial sites and hear the stories of some legendary locals.

✔ The **Garden District/Cemetery Tour** tours this historic neighborhood (pointing out the homes of such notables as Anne Rice and Trent Reznor) as well as Lafayette Cemetery No. 1.

No petting the gators: Swamp tours

Swamp tours can be a great deal of fun; you see some incredible scenery and wildlife, you're out on the water, and you get a feel for what it's like to live out on the bayous. Your guide may call alligators up to the boat for a little snack of chicken, but be careful to keep your hands inside the boat, because gators can't always tell the difference.

You can find plenty of swampland within the metro area worth exploring, but the really isolated swamp areas lie three hours outside of the city.

✔ **Dr. Paul Wagner,** a well-known swamp ecologist and a national conservationist, gives excellent tours of the Honey Island Swamp area. His **Honey Island Swamp Tours** (☎ **504-242-5877** or 504-641-1769) cost $20 per person.

✔ **Gator Swamp Tours** (☎ **800-875-4287** or 504-484-6100) also has good tours of the Honey Island Swamp, approximately 40 minutes east of New Orleans; they charge $20 per adult and $10 for children under 12.

✔ **Cypress Swamp Tours** (☎ **504-581-4501**) tours the Bayou Segnette area (near Westwego, on the West Bank across the Crescent City Connection) for $22 per adult and $12 for children under 12.

✔ **Jean Lafitte Swamp Tours** (☎ **504-689-4186**) tours the Bayou Aux Carpes, a patch of private land flush with all sorts of wildlife near the intercoastal canal, just 20 minutes from the Crescent City Connection; charges are $20 for adults and $10 for children under 12.

Ask when calling about the length of each tour, whether the tours are private or public, and how many people are allowed on one tour; you won't want one that's too crowded.

Other tour companies operate in the Atchafalaya Basin, a vast swamp about 2½ hours west of New Orleans, between Baton Rouge and Lafayette. These include **McGee's Landing** (☎ **337-228-2384**) and

Angelle's Swamp Tours (☎ 337-228-8567). The basin is pretty big, so the good tours will take more time; you may want to budget your afternoon around it.

Shopping for old stuff: Antique tours

Macon Riddle's Antique Tours (☎ 504-899-3027; www.neworleans antiquing.com) provides an enthusiastic and educational way to see New Orleans's antique districts. Macon Riddle will pick you up at your hotel, take you on a customized antique shopping tour, and even make lunch reservations for you. She'll even take care of shipping your antique finds home for you. The experience is like having your own antiquing personal trainer. The cost is $100 per hour with a 3-hour minimum.

Dinner on the Water: Riverboat Cruises

Riverboat cruises are extremely popular in New Orleans, as you may expect. Gambling cruises, however, are a thing of the past (riverboat casinos rarely leave the dock, because most gamblers want to be able to come and go at will). You'll still find harbor cruises, dinner and dancing cruises, river cruises, and combination cruises where you also visit the Audubon Zoo or Chalmette Battlefield. The riverboats themselves come in several different forms: steam- or diesel-powered, with their paddle wheels on the side or on the stern, and so forth. From personal experience, I can tell you that standing at the railing of a riverboat at night, watching the water flow beneath you, is a very romantic experience. Companies and boats offering riverboat tours include the following:

- ✔ **Creole Queen Paddle Wheel Tours** (☎ 800-445-4109 or 504-524-0814)
- ✔ **New Orleans Steamboat Co.** (☎ 504-586-8777)
- ✔ **John James Audubon** (☎ 800-233-BOAT or 504-586-8777)

Chapter 20

A Shopper's Guide to New Orleans

. . . .

. . . .

*V*acation shopping is an odd thing. You'd think that spending yet *more* money is the last thing a vacationer would want to do. But for whatever reason, whether trying to find that perfect memento of their trip or suddenly deciding to redecorate their home with antiques, vacationers *shop* — a *lot*.

This chapter explores shopping in New Orleans from a couple different angles. It runs through the big-name stores and looks at the major shopping areas, some of which feature antique shops and art galleries. At the end of the chapter is an index of stores to help you find what you're looking for.

Surveying the Shopping Scene: Imported Goods and Other Cool Stuff

New Orleans has a nice advantage over other American cities for the shopping vacationer: As an international port, the city has access to a variety of imported items. If you can name it, you can probably find it in New Orleans. Selection is not limited to things such as home furnishings, pottery, and designer clothing — also on hand is quite a bit of imported fine jewelry. Don't neglect the locally crafted jewelry, however: Some local designers work with such innovation and creativity that their shops seem more like art galleries.

New Orleans Shopping

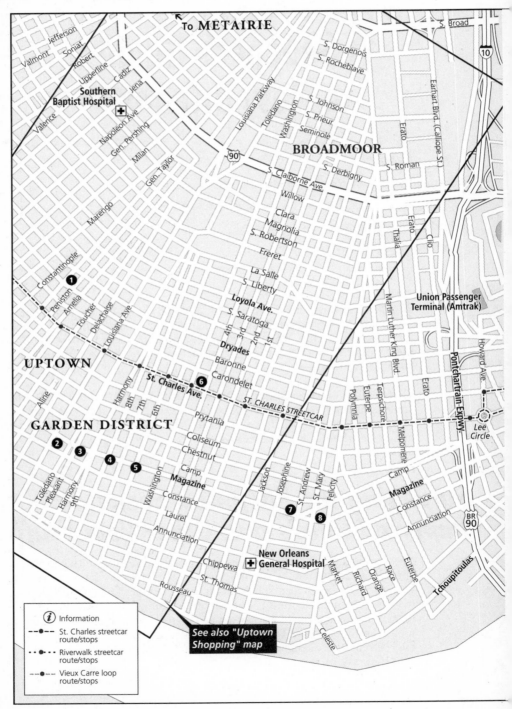

To METAIRIE

Jefferson
Valmont
Soniat
Robert
Upperline
Cadiz
Jena

Southern
Baptist Hospital

Valence
Napoleon Ave.
Gen. Pershing
Milan
Gen. Taylor

Marengo

Constantinople
Peniston
Amelia
Foucher
Delachaise
Louisiana Ave.

UPTOWN

Aline

Harmony
8th
7th
6th

St. Charles Ave.

GARDEN DISTRICT

Toledano
Pleasant
Harmony
9th

Washington

Prytania

Coliseum

Chestnut

Camp

Magazine

Constance

Laurel

Annunciation

Chippewa

St. Thomas

Rousseau

S. Broad

10

S. Dorgenois
S. Rocheblave

Louisiana Parkway

Toledano
Washington
Seminole

S. Johnson
S. Prieur

BROADMOOR

S. Claiborne Ave.
S. Derbigny
S. Roman

Willow

Clara
Magnolia
S. Robertson

Freret

La Salle
S. Liberty

Loyola Ave.
S. Saratoga
4th
3rd
2nd
1st

Dryades

Baronne

Carondelet

ST. CHARLES STREETCAR

Prytania

Jackson
Josephine
St. Andrew
St. Mary
Felicity

New Orleans
General Hospital

Earhart Blvd. (Calliope St.)

Erato

Erato
Thalia

Clio

Martin Luther King Blvd.

Union Passenger
Terminal (Amtrak)

Euterpe
Terpsichore
Melpomene

Polymnia

Erato

Howard Ave.

Pontchartrain Expwy.

Lee
Circle

Camp
Magazine
Constance
Annunciation

Market
Richard
Orange
Race
Euterpe

BR
90

Tchoupitoulas

Celeste

- ❶
- ❷ ❸ ❹ ❺
- ❻
- ❼ ❽

ⓘ Information
●—●— St. Charles streetcar
route/stops
●••●••• Riverwalk streetcar
route/stops
●─●─ Vieux Carre loop
route/stops

*See also "Uptown
Shopping" map*

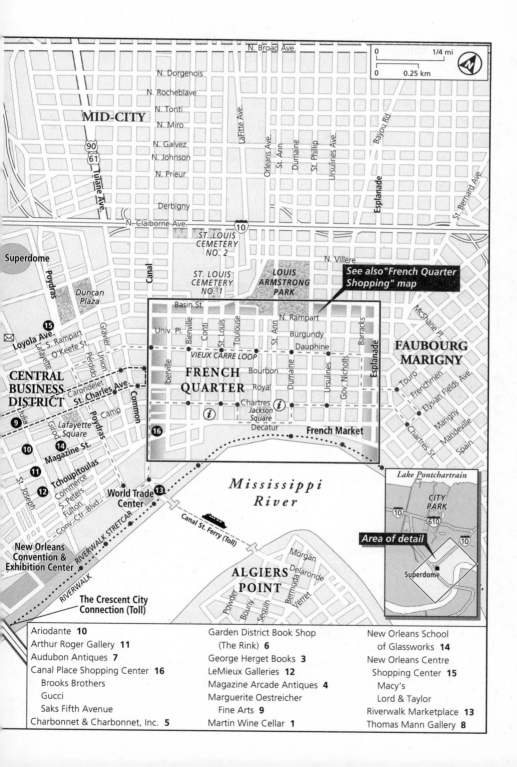

If you're shopping for antiques or contemporary art, you'll find plenty on Royal and Magazine streets. Royal Street boasts the finest, most expensive goods; Magazine Street promises more bargain-basement finds. Also in that area, and on Julia Street, are the city's art galleries. (I cover these areas individually later in this chapter.)

Shop hours vary, but, on the average, most are open Monday through Saturday from 10:00 a.m. to 5:00 p.m., with quite a few shops open later on Saturday night and Sunday afternoon. The French Quarter's souvenir shops, not missing a trick, often remain open until 11:00 p.m. every day of the week. As a general rule, call ahead for hours before setting out.

A word on sales tax: Weigh your options carefully if buying a large, expensive item. Because sales tax in New Orleans is 9 percent, you may save money by having the item shipped to you at home. Of course you'll pay for shipping and handling instead of the sales tax, but the difference may be to your favor.

A program called **Louisiana Tax-Free Shopping** benefits shoppers who hail from other countries. If you are not from the United States, look for store windows with this program's logo; these merchants give you a tax refund voucher that you can cash in, either at the airport or by mail. To take advantage of this program, you need a valid foreign passport and round-trip airline ticket. Call ☎ **504-568-5323** for details.

Checking Out the Big-Name Stores (And Shopping Areas)

As corporate America has made inroads here during the last half-century, local homegrown institutions have found it difficult to compete with the deep pockets of the big-name corporations. As a result, New Orleans is now almost exclusively the province of the big-name corporate chains. Here's a list of the big players:

- ✔ **Macy's:** New Orleans Centre, 1400 Poydras St. (☎ **800-456-2297** or 504-592-5985; www.macys.com); open Monday to Saturday from 10 a.m. to 9:30 p.m., and Sunday from 11 a.m. to 7 p.m.

- ✔ **Lord and Taylor:** New Orleans Centre, 1400 Poydras St. (☎ **504-581-5673;** www.lordandtaylor.com); open Monday to Friday from 10 a.m. to 8 p.m., Saturday from 9 a.m. to 8 p.m., and Sunday from noon to 6 p.m.

- ✔ **Brooks Brothers:** Canal Place Shopping Center, 300 block of Canal Street (☎ **504-522-4200;** www.brooksbrothers.com); open Monday to Saturday from 10 a.m. to 7 p.m., and Sunday from noon to 6 p.m.

- **Saks Fifth Avenue:** Canal Place Shopping Center, 300 block of Canal Street (☎ **504-524-2200;** www.saksfifthavenue.com); open Monday to Saturday from 10 a.m. to 7 p.m., and Sunday from noon to 6 p.m.

- **Gucci:** Canal Place Shopping Center, 300 block of Canal Street (☎ **504-524-5544;** www.gucci.com); open Monday to Saturday from 10 a.m. to 6 p.m., and Sunday from noon to 6 p.m.

These big-name stores, of course, need a place to house their wares, and New Orleans offers plenty of alternatives for shoppers hoping to meet all their shopping needs under one roof. In addition to the Canal Place Shopping Center (see the "Canal Street" section, later in this chapter), the following shopping areas are good choices for a little mall-browsing:

- **Jackson Brewery:** Just across from Jackson Square (600 Decatur St.; ☎ **504-566-7245;** www.jacksonbrewery.com), the old **Jax Brewery** is now a complex of shops, cafes, restaurants, and entertainment spots. Look for gourmet and Cajun and Creole foodstuffs, fashions, toys, hats, crafts, pipes, posters, and souvenirs. You'll also find a huge **Virgin Megastore** (☎ **504-671-8100**). The Brewery hours are Sunday to Thursday from 10:00 a.m. to 9:00 p.m., and Friday to Saturday from 10:00 a.m. to 10:00 p.m. Note that many shops in the Brewery close at 5:30 or 6:00 p.m.

- **New Orleans Centre:** This place (1400 Poydras St.; ☎ **504-568-0000;** www.neworleanscentre.com) offers upscale department stores, such as **Lord and Taylor** and **Macy's,** plus three levels of specialty shops, restaurants, and a huge food court. Add on the fancy office tower and you get plenty of foot traffic in this spacious environment. Hours are Monday to Saturday from 10:00 a.m. to 8:00 p.m., and Sunday from noon to 6:00 p.m.

- **Riverwalk Marketplace:** Actually a covered mall running along the river from Poydras Street to the Convention Center (1 Poydras St.; ☎ **504-522-1555;** www.riverwalkmarketplace.com), this is a popular venue that's also quite atmospheric. Take a break from shopping and just watch the river roll by or the occasional free entertainment. Among the more than 100 specialty shops are such big hitters as **Eddie Bauer, The Sharper Image,** and **Banana Republic**, plus several eateries.

Searching Out the Best Shopping Neighborhoods

The trick to shopping in New Orleans is in knowing where to go. The major shopping areas you'll want to visit are the French Quarter, Central Business District, Warehouse District, and along Magazine Street, both in the Garden District and the Uptown area. The best strategy for shopping in these neighborhoods is to just wander around and see which shops catch your eye. Submitted for your approval, then, is this rundown of the city's best shopping areas, and a little data about what you'll find in each one.

The French Quarter

This section breaks down some of the Quarter's more prominent shopping streets — Bourbon, Decatur, and Royal. But first, I take a quick look at some of the noteworthy shops found elsewhere in the Quarter.

- ✔ **Billy Bob's Chinese Laundry** (225 N. Peters St.; ☎ 504-524-5578) recently moved from its original location on Magazine Street, which the owners discovered had actually *been* a Chinese laundry in 1866 (incredibly enough, *after* the current owners had named the place). It's a fun, funky store for contemporary men's and women's clothing; check out the T-shirt selection, a cut above what you'll find on Bourbon Street.

- ✔ **Bookstar** (414 N. Peters St.; ☎ 504-523-6411) is a link in the national book-selling chain, offering the latest best-sellers and everything else you'd expect.

- ✔ **Faulkner House Books** (624 Pirates Alley; ☎ 504-524-2940) is in the one-time home of Nobel Prize–winner William Faulkner, who wrote his early works *Mosquitoes* and *Soldiers' Pay* here. The one room (and hallway) of this private home may be small in comparison to chain bookstores, but it boasts possibly the finest selection per square foot of any bookstore on the planet. The stock tends to be highly collectible and literary, including a large collection of first-edition Faulkners and rare and first-edition classics by other authors.

- ✔ **Kaboom** (915 Barracks St.; ☎ 504-529-5780) is a used bookstore with stock that trends primarily toward fiction, but a little digging here will likely turn up some real gems.

- ✔ **Latin's Hand** (1025 N. Peters St.; ☎ 504-529-5254) features hammocks, dresses, jackets, sandals, and leather goods, all imported from places such as Brazil, El Salvador, Guatemala, Bolivia, and Mexico.

- ✔ **Record Ron's** (239 Chartres St.; ☎ 504-522-2239) is a local music landmark. Before his death, "Record Ron" was a beloved media presence for years. At the store that bears his name are thousands of CDs, cassettes, 45s, and LPs covering all the bases from classic rock and jazz to Cajun, zydeco, R&B, and the blues. You can also pick up T-shirts, posters, sheet music, music memorabilia, and jewelry.

- ✔ **Tower Records** (408 N. Peters St.; ☎ 504-529-4411) is, yes, part of the well-known national chain, but this location distinguishes itself by way of an extensive collection of local and regional music.

French Quarter Shopping

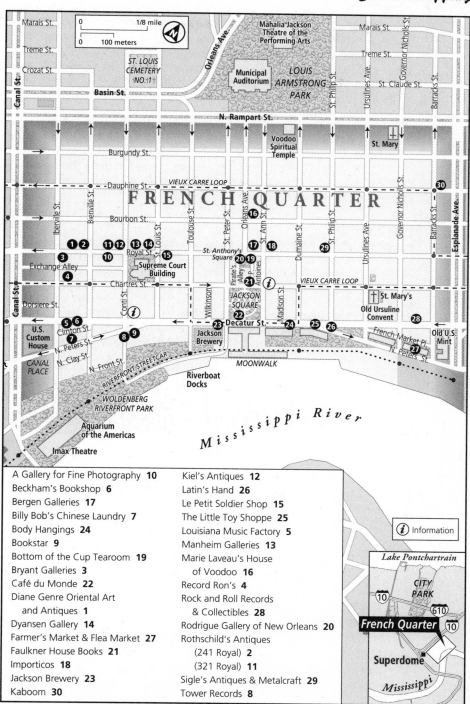

Bourbon Street

If you're looking for silly slogan T-shirts or the usual trinkets and souvenirs, here's as good a place as any. Of course, most of the stuff will be of the "My Grandma Went to Bourbon Street and All I Got Was This Stupid T-Shirt" variety, and if you're seen buying that kind of stuff, forget about trying to blend in: You've just slapped the scarlet "T" (for tourist) on your shirt, and it ain't coming off. (On the plus side, it's one of the few places in the world you can window-shop while carrying a large plastic cup full of booze.)

If you're looking for something a little different, **Marie Laveau's House of Voodoo** (739 Bourbon St., ☎ 504-581-3751), a popular attraction in the French Quarter, is a good place to find a voodoo doll (though hopefully you won't need one). The resident psychic and palm reader can give you a reading as well.

Canal Street

Longtime fans of and visitors to New Orleans may remember when Canal Street was *the* place to shop. Nowadays, the **Canal Place Shopping Center,** located at the foot of Canal Street (365 Canal St.; ☎ 504-581-5400), represents the extent of the Canal Street shopping experience — but it's a plush one, with polished marble floors, a landscaped atrium, fountains, and pools. This mall features more than 50 shops. It's open Monday to Wednesday from 10:00 a.m. to 6:00 p.m.; Thursday from 10:00 a.m. to 8:00 p.m.; Friday and Saturday from 10:00 a.m. to 7:00 p.m.; and Sunday from noon to 6:00 p.m.

Decatur Street

One of the French Quarter's main drags, Decatur Street runs along the river and gets a lot of foot traffic. Although the main attraction is the **Jax Brewery** (which I'll mention in more detail shortly), you'll also find a number of worthwhile shops for serious collectors and enthusiasts. Among the best are the following:

- ✔ **Beckham's Bookshop** (228 Decatur St.; ☎ 504-522-9875) is a real treasure trove for book and music lovers alike, with two levels of old editions, rare secondhand books, and thousands of classical LPs. You may get lost wandering the musty, Byzantine aisles.

- ✔ **Body Hangings** (835 Decatur St.; ☎ 800-574-1823 or 504-524-9856), in case you're wondering, refers to cloaks, which are this store's specialty. A selection of capes and scarves is also available.

- ✔ **The Little Toy Shoppe** (900 Decatur St.; ☎ 504-522-6588) presents strikingly beautiful dolls, as well as wooden toys from Germany, stuffed animals, tea sets, and miniature cars and trucks.

- ✔ **Louisiana Music Factory** (210 Decatur St.; ☎ 504-586-1094; www.louisianamusicfactory.com) offers a large selection of regional music, including Cajun, zydeco, R&B, jazz, blues, and gospel. The Factory also sells reference books, posters, and T-shirts, and occasionally provides live in-store performances. More than just a record store, it's an integral part of the city's music community.

✔ **Rock and Roll Records & Collectibles** (1214 Decatur St.; ☎ 504-561-5683), despite its name, has a lot more than just rock and roll on sale here. The owners claim to have the biggest and best collection of vinyl anywhere, and that includes 45s and 78s. Indeed, the collection even takes up valuable floor space. There's just no telling what you can find here.

Julia Street

Julia Street, from Camp Street down to the river and along some of its side streets, is your best bet for contemporary art galleries in New Orleans. Of course, some of the works are a bit pricey, but collectors can get some good deals and casual viewers can take in lots of fine art. While on Julia Street, be sure to check these places out:

✔ **Ariodante Contemporary Craft Gallery** (535 Julia St.; ☎ 504-524-3233) features hand-crafted furniture, glass, ceramics, jewelry, and decorative accessories.

✔ **Arthur Roger Gallery** (432 Julia St.; ☎ 504-522-1999) has played a large role in nurturing the local art community and developing ties to the New York art scene. Regional exhibits have shared this space with more far-flung shows, and the gallery represents a number of prominent artists.

✔ **LeMieux Galleries** (332 Julia St.; ☎ 504-522-5988) showcases the work of local and regional craftspeople as well as contemporary artists from Louisiana and the Gulf Coast.

✔ **Marguerite Oestreicher Fine Arts** (626 Julia St.; ☎ 504-581-9253) has consistently been a showcase for emerging artists, with a focus on contemporary painting, sculpture, and photography.

Taking it to the street (market)

New Orleans's premier street market is the French Market (☎ 504-522-2621), a complex of shops that begins on Decatur Street across from Jackson Square. In the market, you can find candy, cookware, fashions, crafts, toys, New Orleans memorabilia, candles — all manner of goodies. Also in the complex are **Café du Monde** (☎ 504-581-2914) and the **Farmer's Market** and **Flea Market** (☎ 504-596-3420), which are located in the 1200 block of North Peters. Hours are from 10:00 a.m. to 6:00 p.m. (Café du Monde is open 24 hours.)

Magazine Street

Running from Canal Street to Audubon Park, Magazine Street offers about 6 miles of almost 150 shops, some in 19th-century brick store-fronts, others in quaint, cottage-like buildings. Overall, it's a very unique, funky stretch. Because it's a less ritzy area of the city, you can usually find some bargains here. Look for antiques, art galleries, bou-tiques, crafts, and dolls.

I'm not pointing a finger at any of the antiques dealers or shops here, but in general, it helps to be discerning when looking at antiques. You never know; someone could have passed off an everyday household item as a priceless family heirloom. And as the song says, you better shop around. Some places ask entirely too much money for their wares, when a little digging can find you something very similar at a much more reasonable price.

Following are some noteworthy shops, from art galleries to antiques stores and more:

✓ **Audubon Antiques** (2025 Magazine St.; ☎ **504-581-5704**) stocks everything from curios to authentic antique treasures spread out over two floors.

✓ **Beaucoup Books** (5414 Magazine St.; ☎ **504-895-2663**) is another popular independent bookseller with a strong emphasis on local and regional reference books.

✓ **Berta's and Mina's Antiquities** (4138 Magazine St.; ☎ **504-895-6201**) showcases self-taught Louisiana folk artist Nilo Lanzas (or "NL"), whose work is on display in collections all over the United States and Europe.

✓ **Charbonnet & Charbonnet, Inc.** (2728 Magazine St.; ☎ **504-891-9948**) is the place to go for country pine; they've got beautiful English and Irish pieces on display, and custom furnishings are also built on site.

✓ **George Herget Books** (3109 Magazine St.; ☎ **504-891-5595**) has more than 20,000 rare and used books on every subject you can think of.

✓ **Magazine Arcade Antiques** (3017 Magazine St.; ☎ **504-895-5451**) offers an excellent selection of 18th- and 19th-century furnishings as well as music boxes, dollhouse miniatures, porcelain, antique toys, and a host of other treasures. Budget a fair amount of time for this place.

✓ **New Orleans School of Glassworks and Printmaking Studio** (727 Magazine St.; ☎ **504-529-7277**) features blown-glass sculp-tures, lampworking, bronze pours, printmaking, and bookbinding. The heart of the activity here is a state-of-the-art, 800-pound fur-nace. Visitors can commission glass, hand-bound books, or prints,

Uptown Shopping

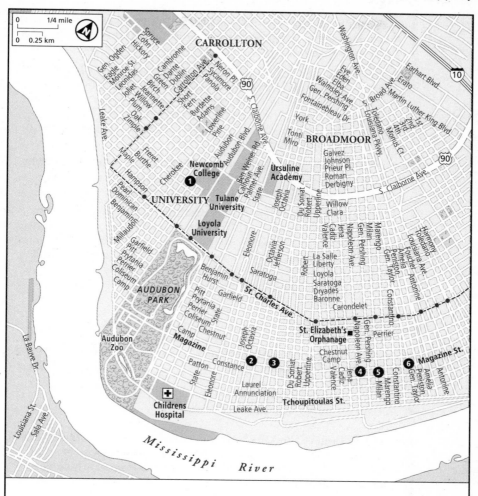

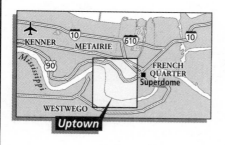

Beaucoup Books **2**
Berta's and Mina's Antiquities **5**
Mushroom Rock and Roll Records **1**
Shadyside Pottery **6**
Uptown Costume and Dancewear **4**
Westgate—The Original Necrotorium **3**

- - - ● - - - St. Charles streetcar route/stops

as well as watch daily demonstrations of glassblowing, glass painting, metal sculpture, and other arts.

✔ At **Shadyside Pottery** (3823 Magazine St.; ☎ 504-897-1710), you can witness the creation of *raku*, a particular type of pottery that has a cracked look.

✔ **Thomas Mann Gallery I/O** (1812 Magazine St.; ☎ 504-581-2113) features "techno-romantic" jewelry designer Thomas Mann, who claims a lot of the credit for bringing contemporary jewelry and sculpture to New Orleans. This store/gallery seeks to "redefine contemporary living" via its eclectic collection of jewelry, lighting, and home furnishings.

✔ **Uptown Costume & Dancewear** (4326 Magazine St.; ☎ 504-895-7969) is the place to go for spooky monster masks, hats, wigs, makeup, and all kinds of mischievous mask wear.

✔ **Westgate — The Original Necrotorium** (5219 Magazine St.; ☎ 504-899-3077; www.westgatenecromantic.com) celebrates the inner Goth, a one-stop shop for death-related items, including "necromantic" art and jewelry (featuring lots of skeletons and other death images). The book section offers titles on (can you guess?) death and the undead.

Royal Street

Along Royal Street, you can find many fine art galleries and shops selling antiques, jewelry, perfume, and candy, as well as shops for coin and stamp collectors.

First, here are some sites of general interest:

✔ **The Bottom of the Cup Tearoom** (732 Royal St.; ☎ 504-523-1204) is supposedly the oldest tearoom in the United States. You can have someone read your tarot cards or tea leaves or build your astrological chart; you can also get a reading from "pure clairvoyant psychics." I can't vouch for their accuracy, but they're sure a lot cheaper than those 1-900 psychic lines. Offered for sale are books, jewelry, crystal balls, tarot cards, crystals, and healing wands.

✔ **Importicos** (736 Royal St.; ☎ 504-523-3100) features an international selection of hand-crafted silver jewelry; pottery; textiles; leather, wood, stone, and metal items; and teak, mahogany, and wrought-iron furniture.

✔ **Le Petit Soldier Shop** (528 Royal St.; ☎ 504-523-7741), as its name implies, sells miniature soldiers made by local artists. Armies represent a span from ancient Greece up to Desert Storm, and you can find quite a few miniatures that resemble major figures in military history, such as Eisenhower, Grant, Lee, Hitler, and Napoleon. Also available is a good-sized collection of medals and decorations.

For antiques, you'll want to check out these places:

- **Diane Genre Oriental Art and Antiques** (431 Royal St.; ☎ 504-595-8945) is a nice change of pace if you've looked at too many European antiques. It offers East Asian porcelains, 18th-century Japanese woodblock prints, and Chinese and Japanese textiles, scrolls, screens, engravings, and lacquers.

- **Kiel's Antiques** (325 Royal St.; ☎ 504-522-4552) was established in 1899 and is still a family business. It houses a considerable collection of 18th- and 19th-century French and English furniture, chandeliers, jewelry, and other items.

- **Manheim Galleries** (403–409 Royal St.; ☎ 504-568-1901) showcases a huge collection of Continental, English, and Oriental furnishings, along with porcelain, jade, silver, and fine paintings.

- **Rothschild's Antiques** (241 and 321 Royal St.; ☎ 504-523-5816 or 504-523-2281) is not only an antiques store but also a full-service jeweler; look for antique and custom-made jewelry among the more standard offerings of antique silver, marble mantels, porcelains, and English and French furnishings.

- **Sigle's Antiques & Metalcraft** (935 Royal St.; ☎ 504-522-7647) is the place if you are a big fan of the lacy ironwork that distinguishes French Quarter balconies. Sigle's offers some of its antique ironwork already converted into more packable household items, such as planters.

If you're in the mood for fine art, check out these galleries:

- **Bergen Galleries** (730 Royal St.; ☎ 800-621-6179 or 504-523-7882; www.bergenputmangallery.com) boasts the South's largest selection of posters and prints. It also specializes in New Orleans, Louisiana Cajun, African-American, and Jazz fine art. The service here is extremely personable.

- **Bryant Galleries** (316 Royal St.; ☎ 800-844-1994 or 504-525-5584; www.bryantgalleries.com) represents a number of American and European artists. Look for glasswork, graphic art, and bronzes depicting jazz themes. The staff is quite friendly here.

- **Dyansen Gallery** (433 Royal St.; ☎ 504-523-2902) features graphics, sculpture, and other contemporary art by the likes of LeRoy Neiman and others.

- **A Gallery for Fine Photography** (322 Royal St.; ☎ 504-568-1313; www.agallery.com) offers rare photographs and books from the 19th and 20th centuries, with an emphasis on New Orleans and Southern history and contemporary culture. The owner calls it "the only museum in the world that's for sale"; indeed, the place really *is* like a museum of photography.

- The **Rodrigue Gallery of New Orleans** (721 Royal St.; ☎ 504-581-4244) features the now-famous blue dogs of Cajun artist George Rodrigue, who began painting blue portraits of his late dog for a children's book in 1984. Now his work has achieved international renown, hanging in galleries in Munich and Yokohama. Take a trip down here to see this canine pop icon in home territory.

Uptown

I've already covered a good bit of Uptown ground on Magazine Street, but here are a few more sites of interest:

- **Garden District Book Shop** (2727 Prytania St.; ☎ 504-895-2266) is a popular independent bookstore beloved by local fans. Anne Rice has used it as a starting point for a number of her book-signing tours; they usually keep a number of signed Rice books on hand. However, you'll find much more than that here.

- **Martin Wine Cellar** (3827 Baronne St.; ☎ 504-899-7411) carries an expansive selection of wines, spirits, and champagnes for unexpectedly reasonable prices. Also on hand are preserves, coffees, teas, crackers, biscotti, cookies, and cheeses.

- **Mushroom Rock and Roll Records** (1037 Broadway St.; ☎ 504-866-6065), located on Fraternity Row in the university area in the heart of Uptown, is a hip little place that is good for alternative music. As if that weren't enough, frugal students enjoy the comprehensive collection of used CDs (though they're not arranged in any particular order, so happy digging) and a large selection of T-shirts and other paraphernalia.

Index of Stores by Merchandise

Antiques

Audubon Antiques
Charbonnet and Charbonnet, Inc.
Diane Genre Oriental Art and Antiques
Kiel's Antiques
Magazine Arcade Antiques
Manheim Galleries
Rothschild's Antiques
Sigle's Antiques & Metalcraft

Art galleries

A Gallery for Fine Photography
Arthur Roger Gallery
Bergen Galleries
Berta's and Mina's Antiquities
Bryant Galleries

Dyansen Gallery
LeMieux Galleries
Marguerite Oestreicher Fine Arts
New Orleans School of Glassworks and
    Printmaking Studio
Rodrigue Gallery of New Orleans
Shadyside Pottery

Books

Beaucoup Books
Beckham's Bookshop
Bookstar
Faulkner House Books
Garden District Book Shop
George Herget Books
Kaboom

Clothing stores

Brooks Brothers
Gucci
Lord and Taylor
Saks Fifth Avenue

Costumes and masks

Uptown Costume & Dancewear

Crafts

Ariodante Contemporary Craft Gallery

Department stores

Macy's
Lord and Taylor
Saks Fifth Avenue

Fashion

Billy Bob's Chinese Laundry
Body Hangings

Food and drink

Café du Monde
Martin Wine Cellar

Jewelry and gifts

Importicos
Latin's Hand
Thomas Mann Gallery I/O

Markets

Farmer's Market
Flea Market
French Market

Record stores

Louisiana Music Factory
Mushroom Rock and Roll Records
Record Ron's
Rock and Roll Records & Collectibles
Tower Records

Shopping centers

Canal Place Shopping Center
Jax Brewery
New Orleans Centre
Riverwalk Marketplace

Spooky stuff

Bottom of the Cup Tearoom
Marie Laveau's House of Voodoo
Westgate — The Original Necrotorium

Toys

Le Petit Soldier Shop
The Little Toy Shoppe

Chapter 21

Five Great New Orleans Itineraries

• •

In This Chapter

▶ Spending one, two, or three days in New Orleans

▶ Experiencing the historical, romantic, and spooky highlights of the French Quarter

▶ Knowing what to look for while riding the St. Charles streetcar

• •

I don't know about you, but I'm not one of those people who likes to make super-detailed plans before I start something. I like leaving a little — sometimes a lot of — wiggle-room, whether I'm exploring a new city or cleaning my apartment.

But though I've given a lot of lip service to exploring New Orleans on your own, the truth is, you do need some structure. However, that doesn't mean you can't have fun. Why not arrange your day around spooky, supernatural sights or romantic hot spots? This chapter presents suggestions for themed itineraries, as well as suggestions on what to do if your time is limited. It covers where to go, what to look for, and how much time to budget for each stop. It also tips you off to some good places for meals and snacks along the way.

New Orleans in One Day

Face it. If you're only in New Orleans for one day, you're not going to be able to see and do everything worth seeing and doing. So how do you solve this dilemma? Spend the whole day in the French Quarter. As much as I stress throughout this book that New Orleans is more than this historic district, I'd never advise you not to take in the Quarter's sights. It *is* the single most popular attraction in the city, after all, and it certainly contains a lot of culture, history, and lore in its small (6 blocks wide and 13 blocks long) confines.

New Orleans in One Day

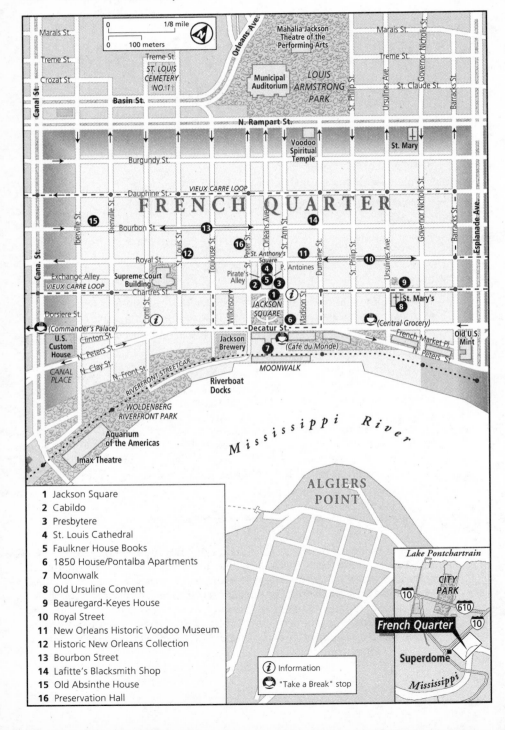

1 Jackson Square
2 Cabildo
3 Presbytere
4 St. Louis Cathedral
5 Faulkner House Books
6 1850 House/Pontalba Apartments
7 Moonwalk
8 Old Ursuline Convent
9 Beauregard-Keyes House
10 Royal Street
11 New Orleans Historic Voodoo Museum
12 Historic New Orleans Collection
13 Bourbon Street
14 Lafitte's Blacksmith Shop
15 Old Absinthe House
16 Preservation Hall

To get into the spirit of things, take your time getting started in the morning with a visit to **Café du Monde** (see Chapter 15) for **beignets** (fried squares of dough dripping with powdered sugar), washed down with a **café au lait.** After lingering for a bit at Café du Monde, begin the day's touring with a 30–60-minute stop at historic **Jackson Square.** While in the neighborhood, check out the **Cabildo** and the **Presbytere** (see Chapter 17), allowing roughly an hour for each. Then wander over to the **St. Louis Cathedral,** on the north side of the square at 721 Chartres (see Chapter 17), for a short 15-minute go-through. Afterward, pop in at **Faulkner House Books** (see Chapter 20) for a little bit of literary history and maybe to buy a rare first-edition hardback or two. You may also want to take a gander at the beautifully restored **Pontalba Apartments** (formally known as **1850 House, Lower Pontalba Building;** see Chapter 18) at 523 St. Ann St.; allow about one hour.

Right about now, you'll realize that all you had for breakfast was the rough equivalent of three very sugary donuts. My suggestion is to forego an actual sit-down restaurant and roll some sightseeing into your lunch; stroll down to Decatur Street and sample a **muffuletta** (one of New Orleans's premier sandwiches) at **Central Grocery** (see Chapter 15). Take your sandwich across the street, wander along the **Moonwalk** and eat by the banks of the Mississippi River.

After lunch, a little walking will help the digestive process. Wind your way up Ursuline to the **Old Ursuline Convent** and tour the oldest surviving building in the Mississippi Valley (see Chapter 18). Allow about an hour before wandering over to the **Beauregard-Keyes House** across the street; plan to spend about 45 minutes to an hour at this literary landmark (see Chapter 18).

Next, walk westward down **Royal Street,** checking out the shops along the way, to the **New Orleans Historic Voodoo Museum,** for some history from a slightly different cultural slant (see Chapter 17); take a good hour. If you have enough energy for one more hour-long stop, visit the **Historic New Orleans Collection** (see Chapter 18) for a nice wrap-up of the history you've been seeing all day.

Steel yourself for a pre-dinner stroll down **Bourbon Street.** Stop in at **Lafitte's Blacksmith Shop and Bar** (Chapter 18) for a pre-dinner drink, and darned if you won't absorb some more history in the process. To continue the historical theme, you can trudge down to the **Old Absinthe House** (Chapter 18) to sip an anisette and imagine what it must have been like back in the day of Andrew Jackson and Jean Lafitte.

For dinner, only one place is worth considering if you've only got one day in town. **Commander's Palace** (see Chapter 14) is widely considered one of the best restaurants in the country; it's a regular stop for visiting celebrities, who come to relax in the luxurious dining rooms (all sporting a bit of New Orleans flair). The restaurant is a bit pricey, but the experience is worth the cost.

Make a pit stop at your hotel to recharge your batteries, because you haven't had the complete New Orleans experience until you've heard some music. Start out in the Quarter, first heading to **Preservation Hall** (see Chapter 23) for incredibly authentic, traditional jazz. Then head back to **Bourbon Street,** which by now should be in full, raunchy swing.

New Orleans in Three Days

Okay, so say you've got more than just one day to spend in New Orleans. Great! Whether you've got one or two extra days, this itinerary maps out where you should go and what you should do. (If you're in town for more than three days, you may consider taking a day to get away from it all with one of the day trips in Chapter 22.)

For **day one** of this itinerary, see the preceding section to get most of the historic French Quarter out of your system. Start **day two** by adhering to my New Orleans Golden Rule: Get out of the Quarter!

If you're staying in the French Quarter, have breakfast at the breezy and friendly **Clover Grill** (see Chapter 15). From there, head down to Decatur Street for a glimpse of the Mississippi River and to look for souvenirs at **Jax Brewery.** Allow about an hour to 90 minutes. Next, cross Canal Street and head into the **Warehouse District,** specifically toward **Julia Street,** a bustling corridor of art galleries (see Chapter 20). Stop in for a late-morning snack at the **True Brew Coffee House** (see Chapter 25), and take a gander at the theater space while munching on a pastry.

From there make your way by streetcar, auto, or other propulsive means (*not* by foot) to the **Garden District.** You can take a walking tour (see Chapter 19) or stroll around on your own to admire the stately, crumbling elegance of the gorgeous manses, especially those along St. Charles Avenue and Prytania Street. Closer to the river, along **Magazine Street,** the elegance gives way to a loose and funky vibe. Here you'll find more art galleries and some antiques shops (see Chapter 20). Allow at least two hours to explore the district.

For lunch, the Garden District offers several great options. I recommend that you head to **Franky & Johnny's** (just off Magazine at Arabella Street; see Chapter 15) for filling sandwiches and New Orleans staples. After which, take the bus to **City Park** (see Chapter 17) and spend a little time enjoying its tranquil charms. While you're there, you're obligated to wander the halls of the **New Orleans Museum of Art** (see Chapter 17). Allow about two hours for the park and the museum.

Take a cab from the park along grand old Esplanade Avenue and gaze at the sort-of-funky neighborhood close to the park, which is home to the Fair Grounds Race Course. If you're feeling a little peckish, the

Whole Foods Market (see Chapter 15) is a great place for an ultra-healthy snack. Esplanade takes you right up to the border of the French Quarter.

After a little downtime at your hotel — or additional French Quarter touring for the truly hearty — treat yourself to a quintessential (and fairly cheap) French Quarter dining experience — slurping down raw oysters at **Acme Oyster House** (see Chapter 15). If seafood isn't your thing, head to the Quarter's edge and grab a burger at **Port of Call** (see Chapter 15). Either way, you'll dine relatively cheaply, and rub elbows with some down-to-earth locals.

After that, get ready for some music. Digest and unwind with a drink at a local watering hole; I recommend **Molly's at the Market** (see Chapter 24), a homey hangout rich in atmosphere, charm, and friendliness. Next, hop across Esplanade to **Frenchmen Street** (see Chapter 23) for a whirlwind tour of jazz, funk, and world music. You can easily spend an evening at just one of these clubs, but I recommend that you stroll from place to place. After a couple hours, head over to **Fritzel's European Jazz Pub** (Chapter 23) to catch a late-night jam session before collapsing into bed.

After using day two to sample the city's charms beyond the French Quarter (though you've really only scratched the surface), treat **day three** as a reward, indulging in some of the more touristy, but no less entertaining, sights, including the hedonistic pleasures of a breakfast at **Brennan's** (see Chapter 14). Allow about an hour to savor the experience. From there, head over to **Riverwalk Marketplace** (Chapter 20) to finish up any last-minute shopping, followed by a tour of the breathtaking **Aquarium of the Americas** (Chapter 17). Allow one to two hours to take it all in (closer to two to include a film at the **IMAX Theater**).

Next, take a riverboat cruise aboard the sternwheeler *John James Audubon,* which deposits you at the world-renowned **Audubon Zoo** (see Chapter 17). If your plentiful Brennan's breakfast has begun to wear off, grab lunch (or at least a snack) at the zoo. Allow about two hours. Next, travel back to the French Quarter by riverboat or by the **St. Charles streetcar,** which provides a scenic glimpse of the city's grandest boulevard (see the sidebar "Streetcar highlights" for a list of sights to see along the way).

Return to your hotel to rest up for another signature New Orleans dining experience — dinner at **Antoine's** (see Chapter 14). After dinner, take a leisurely last stroll through the Quarter, making sure to stop at **Pat O'Brien's** (see Chapter 24), where the expansive courtyard, complete with flaming fountain, may be touristy, but it's also charming. Then wind your way to the Rampart Street border of the Quarter, where you'll finish the night with some great, authentic New Orleans music — and more than a little atmosphere — at **Donna's Bar and Grill** and the **Funky Butt** (Chapter 23).

New Orleans in Three Days

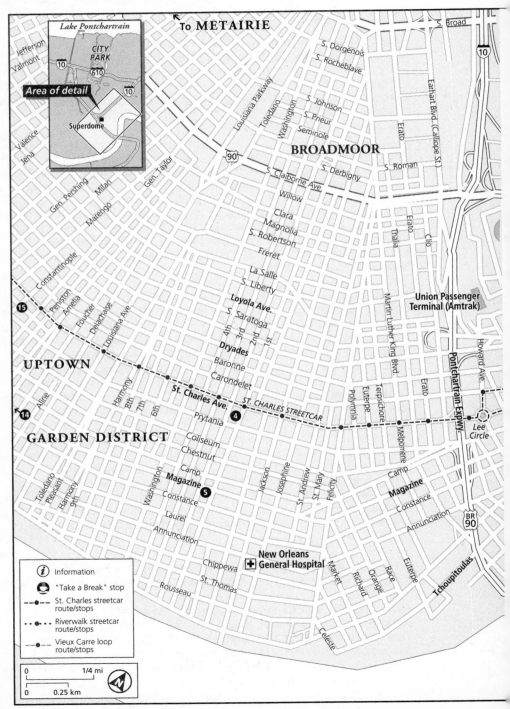

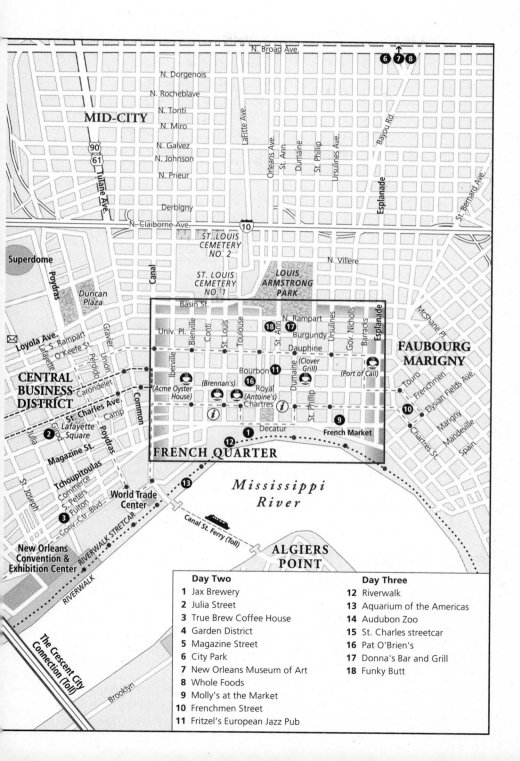

Day Two	Day Three
1 Jax Brewery	**12** Riverwalk
2 Julia Street	**13** Aquarium of the Americas
3 True Brew Coffee House	**14** Audubon Zoo
4 Garden District	**15** St. Charles streetcar
5 Magazine Street	**16** Pat O'Brien's
6 City Park	**17** Donna's Bar and Grill
7 New Orleans Museum of Art	**18** Funky Butt
8 Whole Foods	
9 Molly's at the Market	
10 Frenchmen Street	
11 Fritzel's European Jazz Pub	

Streetcar highlights

Taking the St. Charles streetcar? Watch for these sights along the way. (For a map of the streetcar route, see Chapter 11.) When traveling from the French Quarter through the Garden District toward Audubon Park, note that odd-numbered addresses are on the right, even-numbered addresses on the left.

- ✔ After passing Julia and St. Joseph streets, you'll go around Lee Circle. That's General Robert E. Lee atop the massive column. Note that he's facing north so that his back won't be to the Yankees. The statue was erected in 1884.

- ✔ At 2040 St. Charles is La Tour Eiffel. If it looks like the Eiffel Tower in Paris, that's because it actually was a part of the tower, built in Paris as an upper-level restaurant and then moved to New Orleans and reassembled in 1936. It now houses the Red Room (see Chapter 24), an upscale supper club with cabaret music and live jazz.

- ✔ The Columns Hotel (1883), located at 3811 St. Charles, was the location of a Storyville bordello in the movie *Pretty Baby.*

- ✔ Does the Palmer House at 5705 St. Charles look familiar? If you've seen *Gone With the Wind,* it should. It's a replica of Tara.

- ✔ Audubon Park (extending all the way from St. Charles to the Mississippi River) was the site of the 1884 World's Industrial and Cotton Centennial Exposition. The renowned Audubon Zoo is on the far side of the park.

- ✔ After passing Tulane University and the old St. Mary's Dominican College (now Loyola's Broadway campus), you enter what used to be the town of Carrollton, named for General William Carroll, a commander at the Battle of New Orleans. Carrollton was founded in 1833 and incorporated in 1845. New Orleans annexed the city in 1874.

- ✔ After the streetcar turns right onto Carondelet, look ahead and a little to the left. The tall building with the cupola at 325 Carondelet is the Hibernia Bank Building (1921), the tallest building in the city until 1962. The cupola is lit at night in colors that change with the seasons.

New Orleans in Three Days for Families

As I note earlier, the dynamics of your visit will be very different if you're bringing the family along than if you come alone or with an adult friend. Happily, more than enough diversions are available that should appeal to grown-ups and little ones alike.

On **day one,** start with a breakfast at **Café du Monde** (see Chapter 15), followed by a brief walk through the French Quarter, taking in **Jackson Square** and maybe a historic home or two. But you'll spend the majority of the morning enjoying the many delights of the **Aquarium of the Americas** (see Chapter 17), allowing one to two hours before a brief lunch either on site or at one of many nearby restaurants. After lunch, take the *John James Audubon* sternwheeler to the **Audubon Zoo** (see Chapter 17), where you'll while away the afternoon (allow at least two hours) ooh-ing and aah-ing at the wildlife on display. Take the **St. Charles streetcar** to wind your way back toward downtown, disembarking near Lee Circle, the Quarter a short hop away by cab. Grab a bite at **Café Maspero** (see Chapter 14) and retire to your hotel to rest up for the next day. If you or the kids get restless, a **carriage ride** (see Chapter 19) is a pleasant way to enjoy the sights of the French Quarter.

On **day two,** after breakfast at **Mother's** or **Clover Grill,** a cheerful gay-friendly establishment (see Chapter 15), take the Canal Street Ferry (it's free, and departs from the foot of Canal Street every quarter hour; a pedestrian-only commuter boat also runs at 15-minute intervals) to **Blaine Kern's Mardi Gras World** (see Chapter 18), where you'll spend the morning (about two hours round-trip) looking at floats-in-progress and learning a little bit about the crazy party we call Carnival. Afterward, the ferry takes you back to the Quarter (it costs a dollar this way), where you can do a bit more walking around, taking in the **Moonwalk** and the Mississippi, and perhaps even the open-air **French Market** (see Chapter 20). Take your time, but budget some time to have a quintessential New Orleans lunch courtesy of **Central Grocery** (see Chapter 15) before heading down gorgeous Esplanade Avenue to **City Park** (see Chapter 17). Here you can enjoy the **New Orleans Museum of Art** and the park's **Carousel Gardens** (see Chapter 17), allowing about two and a half to four hours, depending on your stamina, before hopping a cab back to your hotel and dinner at **Remoulade** (309 Bourbon St., ☎ **504-523-0377**), a kid- and budget-friendly cousin to the legendary **Arnaud's.** Squeeze in a bit more strolling in the evening if you like, but be sure to rest up for the following day.

Day three starts with a leisurely jazz brunch at **Court of Two Sisters** (see Chapter 14) before stopping by the **New Orleans Historic Voodoo Museum** (see Chapter 17) for an entertaining look at this much-misunderstood religion. If you think your tots may be more scared than amused, take a short hop to the Warehouse District for the much safer **Louisiana Children's Museum** (see Chapter 17). Either way, allow about an hour.

Follow it up with some shopping and a quick lunch at **Jax Brewery** (or the **Riverwalk Marketplace,** if you went to the Children's Museum). Then, assuming you've come during the right time of year, reward your brood for putting up with all the historical stuff with a fun-filled afternoon at **Jazzland Theme Park** (see Chapter 17). If Jazzland's closed when you visit, a jaunt out to the **Louisiana Nature Center** (see Chapter 17) is a good substitute.

New Orleans in Three Days for Families

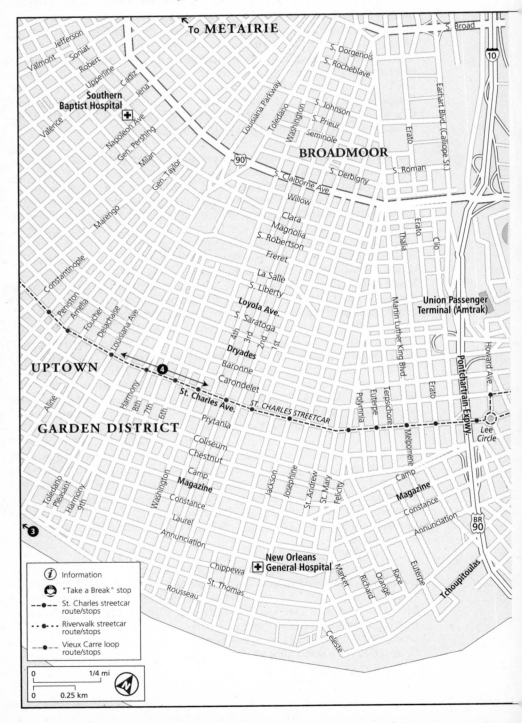

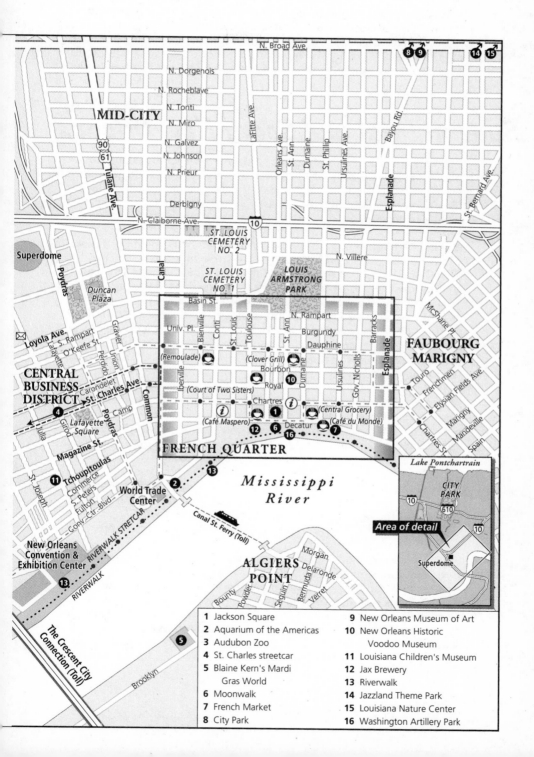

1 Jackson Square
2 Aquarium of the Americas
3 Audubon Zoo
4 St. Charles streetcar
5 Blaine Kern's Mardi Gras World
6 Moonwalk
7 French Market
8 City Park
9 New Orleans Museum of Art
10 New Orleans Historic Voodoo Museum
11 Louisiana Children's Museum
12 Jax Brewery
13 Riverwalk
14 Jazzland Theme Park
15 Louisiana Nature Center
16 Washington Artillery Park

You've probably gorged on goodies at Jazzland, so go easy on dinner and walk off some of those calories, enjoying one last look at the French Quarter by night, perhaps enjoying a final, lingering gaze out over the Mississippi by **Washington Artillery Park** (see Chapter 18). Then take time for souvenir packing and sleep before heading back home.

Supernatural and Scary New Orleans

In addition to its great music and food, New Orleans boasts atmosphere galore. This itinerary explores the city's darker side, inasmuch as you *can* explore it during the day. Voodoo, graveyards, psychics — they're all here. And they're all easily squeezed into a single day's (and night's) sightseeing.

As befits a tour of things associated with the night, you have the option of sleeping in (a natural New Orleans pastime in its own right). When you do roll out of bed, make your first stop a quick one at **Our Lady of Guadalupe Church and International Shrine of St. Jude** (see Chapter 18). Say a quick prayer to St. Expedite, in preparation for your next stop, an organized tour of **St. Louis Cemetery No. 1** (see the listing in Chapter 18 for the lowdown on a tour by **Save Our Cemeteries,** as well as Chapter 19 for more detailed cemetery-tour information). You'll probably find a tour getting underway around 10 or 10:30 a.m., so plan your time accordingly.

Afterwards, head over to the **New Orleans Pharmacy Museum** at 514 Chartres St., between St. Louis and Toulouse streets (see Chapter 18; note that it's closed Mondays). If you don't think a pharmacy can be spooky and supernatural, take a look at the leeches and the drill once used to relieve headaches. Allow 15 to 30 minutes.

With all that morbidity, you've probably built up a good appetite, right? If so, you'll find a number of good restaurants in the area, including **Napoleon House, Café Maspero,** and the **Court of Two Sisters** (see Chapters 14 and 15), which sport a suitably Gothic atmosphere.

Sufficiently refreshed, you can take a brief pause and head over to **Body Hangings** on Decatur Street (see Chapter 20). Peruse their selection of cloaks and capes before making your way to the one and only **New Orleans Historic Voodoo Museum** (see Chapter 17). Poke around for a spell, scope the artifacts, tip your hat to the resident snakes, and spend about 30 minutes before heading to **Marie Laveau's House of Voodoo** (see Chapter 20). Have your palm read, talk to a psychic, and buy a voodoo doll to give to (or take care of) a friend back home; allow half an hour.

Supernatural and Scary New Orleans

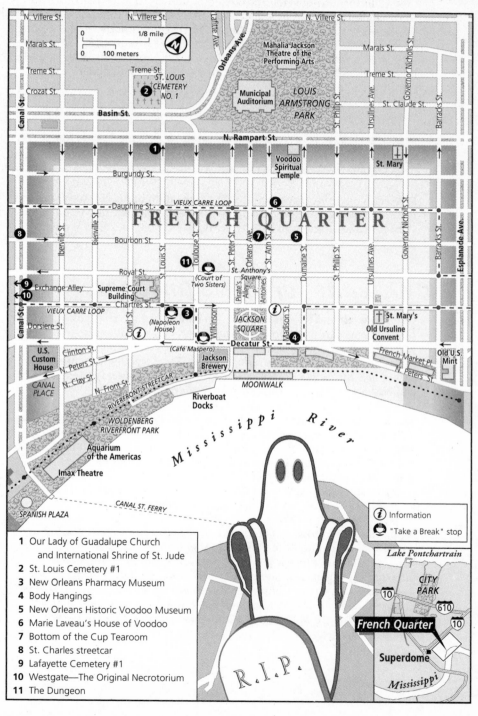

N. Villere St.   N. Villere St.   N. Villere St.
Marais St.   Marais St.
Treme St.   Treme St.   Treme St.
Crozat St.   ST. LOUIS   St. Claude St.
                 2 CEMETERY
                     NO. 1
Basin St.

Mahalia Jackson
Theatre of the
Performing Arts

Municipal   LOUIS
Auditorium   ARMSTRONG
                 PARK

0   1/8 mile
0   100 meters

N. Rampart St.

Burgundy St.   Voodoo   St. Mary
                                  Spiritual
                                  Temple

Dauphine St.   VIEUX CARRE LOOP   **6**

FRENCH QUARTER

Bourbon St.   **7**   **5**

Toulouse St.
11   St. Anthony's
                         Square
Royal St.   (Court of
St. Louis St.   Two Sisters)

9 Exchange Alley   Pirate's
10   Alley
         Supreme Court   Antoines
         Building
         Chartres St.

VIEUX CARRE LOOP   **3**   JACKSON   St. Mary's
Dorsiere St.   (Napoleon Wilkinson SQUARE   Old Ursuline
                 House)   Convent

U.S.   Clinton St.   (Café Maspero) Decatur St. **4**   Old U.S.
Custom   Mint
House   N. Peters St.   Jackson   French Market Pl.
         N. Clay St.   Brewery
CANAL   N. Front St.   N. Peters St.
PLACE
                              MOONWALK

              Riverboat
              Docks
WOLDENBERG
RIVERFRONT PARK

Aquarium
of the Americas

Imax Theatre

CANAL ST. FERRY

SPANISH PLAZA

Mississippi   River

(i) Information
(T) "Take a Break" stop

Lake Pontchartrain

CITY
PARK
10   610

French Quarter   10

Superdome

Mississippi

1 Our Lady of Guadalupe Church
   and International Shrine of St. Jude
2 St. Louis Cemetery #1
3 New Orleans Pharmacy Museum
4 Body Hangings
5 New Orleans Historic Voodoo Museum
6 Marie Laveau's House of Voodoo
7 Bottom of the Cup Tearoom
8 St. Charles streetcar
9 Lafayette Cemetery #1
10 Westgate—The Original Necrotorium
11 The Dungeon

R.I.P.

Next, head one block riverward to the **Bottom of the Cup Tearoom** (see Chapter 20; note that it's closed Sundays) to have your fortune told. Then, take a taxi or walk down Royal Street to Canal Street and hop the **St. Charles streetcar.** Get off at Washington Street and go one block south to **Lafayette Cemetery No. 1** (see Chapter 18). This cemetery is generally safe for exploring as long as you're with a few people. If you want to take an organized tour, contact the organizations in Chapter 19.

Finally, if you're up for it, get onto Magazine Street for a jaunt down to this tour's souvenir shop, **Westgate — The Original Necrotorium** (see Chapter 20; note that it's closed Sundays and Mondays). It's filled with "necromantic" art and jewelry, peppered with images of skeletons and other things associated with death.

Regarding nightlife, though it doesn't open until midnight, the **Dungeon** (Chapter 24) is an essential stop. It isn't really spooky, but if you enjoyed Westgate and/or have an affinity for the Goth subculture, you'll find plenty of friends here.

New Orleans for Honeymooners

Of course, almost anything you do in New Orleans, from antique shopping to binge drinking on Bourbon Street, can be romantic — if you're with the right person. However, this itinerary is specifically designed to enhance, or maybe induce, some *amoré.* I've foregone the must-see sights and historic attractions in favor of a leisurely day in the French Quarter, with plenty of time to stop and smell the roses.

This itinerary assumes a late start (especially if you're on your honeymoon). When you do get moving, start your day with a jazz brunch at **The Court of Two Sisters** (see Chapter 14); allow about an hour. Next, saunter down **Royal Street** and browse among antiques shops and art galleries (see Chapter 20), keeping an eye out for that special piece of bedroom furniture you need for the new house. Spend as much time as you like; this isn't a day for rushing from place to place.

Next head down toward the river and browse the **French Market** for some souvenirs and tokens of your affection for each other; allow at least a half hour, more if you're really interested in all the cheap jewelry displays. You can follow that, if you like, by taking in the action at **Jackson Square** (see Chapter 17). Depending on how early or late you ate breakfast, you can grab an optional lunch (or a quick romantic snack) at **Café du Monde** or **La Marquise** just off the square (see Chapter 15).

New Orleans for Honeymooners

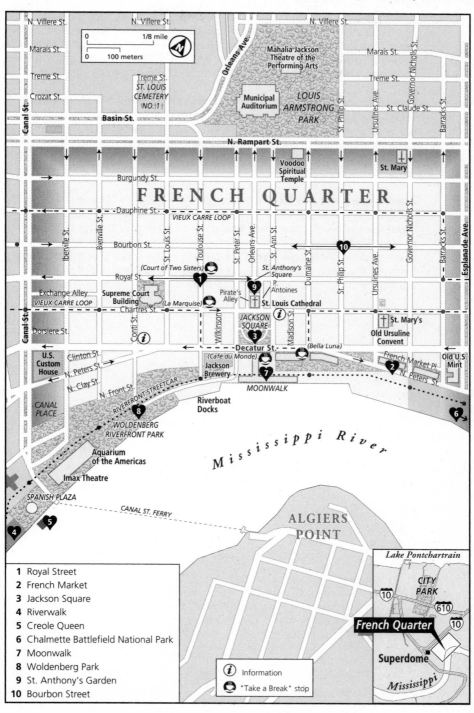

1 Royal Street
2 French Market
3 Jackson Square
4 Riverwalk
5 Creole Queen
6 Chalmette Battlefield National Park
7 Moonwalk
8 Woldenberg Park
9 St. Anthony's Garden
10 Bourbon Street

i Information

🌀 "Take a Break" stop

Ease into the afternoon with a leisurely **carriage tour** of the French Quarter (see Chapter 19); allow about half an hour. Then stroll to the **Riverwalk Marketplace** (see Chapter 20) for a bit of exploring before boarding the 2 p.m. *Creole Queen* paddle wheeler for a riverboat cruise (see Chapter 19). It'll take you seven miles downriver to **Chalmette Battlefield National Park** (see Chapter 18), where you can enjoy a brief walking tour before the return trip upriver, arriving back at 4:30 p.m.

Continue your river motif with a relaxed stroll along the **Moonwalk** and **Woldenberg Riverfront Park** (see Chapter 17 for both). Watch the sun set before making your way to **Bella Luna** (see Chapter 14), whose commanding river view makes this one of the most romantic restaurants in the city; wedding proposals are almost as common as appetizers here.

After dinner, feel free to stroll through any section of the Quarter that catches your fancy (yes, even Bourbon Street); you may want to take a quick look at **St. Anthony's Garden** (see Chapter 17). After that, stroll to your heart's content: Enjoy a bit more of the Mississippi River, or saunter down **Bourbon Street** for a taste of the city's naughtier pleasures, before calling it a night and retiring to the pleasure of one another's company.

Chapter 22

Exploring Beyond New Orleans: Three Great Day Trips

● ●

In This Chapter

▶ Spending a day in Cajun Country

▶ Taking a sightseeing tour of remarkable plantation homes

▶ Getting back to nature — without driving all day to do it

● ●

*A*s you may have figured out by now, New Orleans has more than enough historical, cultural, musical, culinary, and atmospheric attractions to sustain you through a number of visits. You could probably spend your next three or four vacations in the Crescent City and not get to explore everything on your list. Having acknowledged that, sometimes you just need to get away from it all. This chapter offers three relaxing day trips to help clear your head. Each requires a bit of a drive from the French Quarter and the New Orleans city limits. So gas up the car, get out your maps, and hit the road.

Discovering Cajun Country

This day trip takes you to Lafayette, the heart of Cajun Country, where you discover the food, culture, and music of this unique region.

The **Lafayette Parish Convention and Visitors Commission** (P.O. Box 52066, Lafayette, LA 70505, ☎ **800-346-1958** in the United States, 800-543-5340 in Canada, or 337-232-3737; fax: 337-232-0161) can give you the scoop on all Lafayette has to offer. If you plan to come out this way, call them for a brochure. They may even persuade you to extend your stay.

Before getting started, a polite warning: Creoles, zydeco musicians, and non-Cajun residents don't much care for the "Cajun Country" label. Also, many citizens of Acadian descent aren't too wild about it either, especially in large urban centers such as Lafayette. While the people here are proud of their heritage, some of them bristle at the rather touristy simplification of the term. If you drive through Lafayette, you'll find that it's a city like any other. You won't have to abandon your car and paddle through dense swamp to get to a hotel or restaurant, nor will you encounter fiddle-playing *Deliverance* extras on every street corner and front porch.

Getting to Lafayette

Lafayette (167 miles — give or take a few — west of New Orleans) is a straight shot from New Orleans on Interstate 10 west. Drive in the mid- to late morning so that you don't get caught in rush-hour traffic in Baton Rouge or Lafayette — or New Orleans, for that matter.

Taking a tour of Cajun Country

Sure, the New Orleans area offers some authentic swamp tours, but the Atchafalaya Basin holds the distinction of being the third-largest swamp in the United States. How can you beat that? (Well, except by visiting the two larger swamps, but how much swamp do you need, really?) A boat tour is a great way to experience this mystical region. **Angelle's Atchafalaya Basin Swamp Tours** (Whiskey River Landing, P.O. Box 111, Cecilia, LA 70521, ☎ **337-228-8567**) operates tours in glass-bottomed boats or smaller, open boats. To get to the swamp from I-10, take Exit 115 to Henderson, go through Henderson to the levee, and turn right. The landing is the fourth exit on the left. Fares are $12 for adults, $10 for seniors (55 and up), and $6 for children. Departures are at 10 a.m., 1 p.m., and 3 p.m. daily (weather permitting).

Seeing the sights of Cajun Country

The sights in this day trip will wet your feet in the bayous of the Cajun experience. What's a bayou, exactly? Coming from the Choctaw word meaning "small stream," a *bayou* is a sluggish offshoot of a lake or river that flows through swampland — and an integral part of swampland culture.

Where in the world is Cajun Country?

Cajuns are the descendants of Acadians, settlers who were forced out of their established colony in Nova Scotia in the mid-18th century. Arriving in the French colony of Louisiana, they found themselves in relative isolation, farming in the low-lying wetlands and developing their own distinct culture. You need to leave New Orleans two to three hours behind to experience some true Cajun culture — that's how long it'll take you to drive to Lafayette. You'll find the culture — food, music, and lifestyle — that developed as the Acadians mingled with their neighbors and became an integral part of Louisiana life and lore.

Discovering Cajun Country

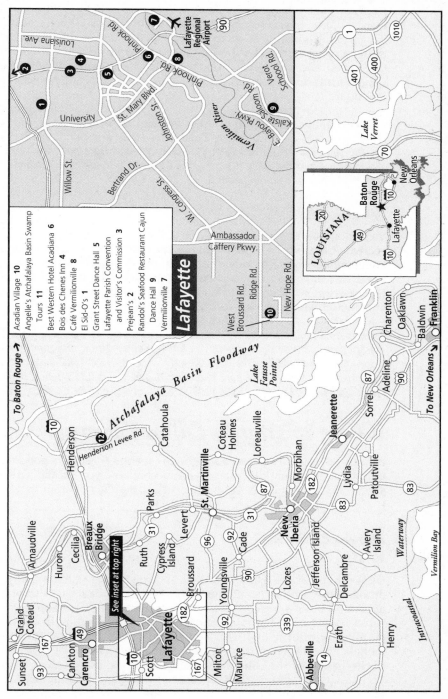

Lafayette

Acadian Village **10**
Angelle's Atchafalaya Basin Swamp Tours **11**
Best Western Hotel Acadiana **6**
Bois des Chenes Inn **4**
Café Vermilionville **8**
El Sid-O's **1**
Grant Street Dance Hall **5**
Lafayette Parish Convention and Visitor's Commission **3**
Prejean's **2**
Randol's Seafood Restaurant Cajun Dance Hall **9**
Vermilionville **7**

Acadian Village

Acadian Village is a reconstructed — reassembled would be a better word — Cajun bayou community in which houses have been transported from their original location to this site beside a sleepy bayou. If you're the exploring type, take the footpath and venture along the banks of the bayou and the houses on its banks. Peek inside to glimpse the Cajun furniture. The gift shop sells Cajun handicrafts and books. Allow 1 to 2 hours.

200 Greenleaf Dr. Take I-10 from Lafayette to Exit 97. Go south on La. 93 to Ridge Road, then take a right on Ridge Road followed by a left on West Broussard. ☎ *800-962-9133 or 337-981-2364. Fax: 337-988-4554. Internet:* www.acadian village.org. *Open: Daily 10 a.m.–5 p.m. Admission: $7 adults, $6 seniors, $4 children 6–14; free for children under 6.*

Vermilionville

Vermilionville is a small village on Bayou Vermilion that attempts to recreate Cajun life as it existed in the 18th and 19th centuries. Costumed staff members demonstrate crafts from the period. Shows feature Cajun music and dancing, and the restaurant serves up authentic Cajun fare. A bit contrived in a tourist-trap kind of way, Vermilionville is fun and informative nonetheless. Allow 1 to 2 hours.

300 Fisher Rd. Take I-10 from Lafayette to Exit 103A. Get on the Evangeline Thruway going south and keep going until you get to Surrey Street and then follow the signs. ☎ *866-99-BAYOU or 337-233-4077. Fax: 337-233-1694. Internet:* www. vermilionville.org. *Open: Tues–Sun 10 a.m.–4 p.m. Closed most major holidays. Admission: $8 adults, $6.50 seniors, $5 students; free for children under 6.*

Where to stay in Cajun Country

If you want to enjoy the area's nightlife (see the "Passing a good time: Cajun Country nightlife" sidebar in this chapter), you should plan to spend the night in Lafayette, rather than make the two-hour drive back to New Orleans.

Bois des Chenes Inn
$$–$$$

Once the center of a 3,000-acre cattle and sugar cane plantation, this plantation home is now a small but lovely bed-and-breakfast. With only five accommodations here — two suites in the main plantation home and three rooms in the carriage house — each room has been lovingly restored and furnished with Louisiana French antiques. Room rates include not only a Louisiana-style breakfast but a bottle of wine and tour of the house as well. Also available are nature and birding trips into Atchafalaya Swamp, as well as guided fishing and hunting trips. These adventures are conducted by the inn's owner, a retired geologist.

338 N. Sterling St., Lafayette, LA 70501. ☎ *337-233-7816. Internet:* www.members. aol.com/boisdchene/bois.htm. *Parking: free. Rates: $100–$150 double. Rates include breakfast. Extra person $30. AE, MC, V.*

Best Western Hotel Acadiana
$$–$$$$

The Hotel Acadiana offers great value for your vacation dollar, providing all the conveniences you'd expect to find in a large chain hotel, including a complimentary airport shuttle. The hotel's restaurant, Bayou Bistro, serves great Cajun food, and the hotel itself is located close to Lafayette's sights.

1801 W. Pinhook Rd., Lafayette, LA 70508. ☎ *800-874-4664 in Louisiana, 800-826- 8386 in the United States and Canada, or 337-233-8120. Fax: 337-234-9667. Internet:* www.bestwestern.com/hotelacadiana. *Parking: free. Rates: $79–$210 double. AE, DC, DISC, MC, V.*

Where to dine in Cajun Country

Although all of these restaurants have their merits — and very strong ones at that — if you have time for only one, I recommend Prejean's.

Café Vermilionville
$$–$$$

For the best of Louisiana cuisine, check out Café Vermilionville, where they throw a little Cajun into the menu to round things out. With plenty of fresh seafood on the menu, specialties include Creole bronze shrimp and the unique Louisiana Crawfish Madness, which is crawfish tails prepared according to the mood of the chef: au gratin, étouffée, fried, or in crawfish beignets (yes, crawfish beignets).

1304 W. Pinhook Rd., Lafayette. ☎ *337-237-0100. Internet:* www.cafev.com. *Reservations recommended. Main courses: $17–$26. AE, DC, DISC, MC, V. Open: Mon–Fri 11 a.m.–2 p.m. and Mon–Sat 5:30–10 p.m.*

Prejean's
$–$$

While in the heart of Cajun Country, treat yourself to a night at Prejean's, *the* spot for nouvelle Cajun cooking. While it gives the appearance of being simply another family restaurant, the bill of fare reveals this place to be one of the finest restaurants in Acadiana, with some of the best ingredients and recipes you'll find in Cajun cuisine. Highlights include crawfish enchiladas, crawfish étouffée, shrimp, grilled or fried oysters, gumbo, and alligator. Kids can dine on burgers or chicken fingers. Also a treat is the Cajun music, playing nightly at 7 p.m.

Passing a good time: Cajun Country nightlife

While in Lafayette, I strongly advise you to check out some of the local nightlife. A visit to El Sid-O's (1523 Martin Luther King Dr. in Lafayette), which is a hot spot for zydeco music, is an essential stop. The place is run by Sid Williams, whose brother Nathan is an acclaimed zydeco musician and leader of the popular group, Nathan and the Zydeco Cha-Chas. The decor may not be very fancy, but that just adds to the aura of authenticity (though not quite as authentic as an old-time roadhouse). A lot of zydeco history has gone down between these walls. Call ☎ 337-235-0647 to find out who's playing.

Grant Street Dance Hall (113 W. Grant St. in Lafayette) is the place where out-of-town rock bands are most apt to play when they pass through town (unless they're stadium-sized acts filling the nearby Cajundome). Local bands also call this place home, from alternative-rock outfits to Cajun and brass bands. Call ☎ 337-237-8513 or visit www.grantstdancehall.com for information.

3480 I-49 North, Lafayette (next to the Evangeline Downs Racetrack). ☎ *337-896-3247. Internet:* www.prejeans.com. *Reservations strongly recommended. Main courses: $12–$24; children's menu $3.50–$8.95. AE, CB, DC, DISC, MC, V. Open: Sun–Thurs 11 a.m.–10 p.m. and Fri–Sat 11 a.m.–11 p.m.*

Randol's Seafood Restaurant Cajun Dance Hall

$–$$

For the full Cajun experience, go to Randol's and enjoy a little Cajun music with your cuisine. Randol's serves up seafood fresh from the bayou, prepared any way you want it: fried, steamed, blackened, or grilled. The house specialty is a seafood platter guaranteed to fill you up: It includes a cup of seafood gumbo, fried shrimp, fried oysters, fried catfish, stuffed crab, crawfish étouffée, deviled crab, and coleslaw. With live music every night at 7:00 p.m., you can take in a few dances before, during, and after your meal.

2320 Kaliste Saloom Rd., Lafayette. ☎ *800-962-2586 or 337-981-7080. Fax: 318-981-7083. Internet:* www.randols.com. *Reservations for 20 or more only. Main courses: $7.95–$15.95. MC, V. Open: Mon–Fri 5–10 p.m. and Sat–Sun 5–11 p.m.*

Plantations along the Great River Road

Once the focal point of a self-sustaining community, plantation homes flourished in Louisiana from the 1820s to the beginning of the Civil War.

While dozens of grand, beautiful homes once dotted the landscape (particularly around the Mississippi River, because the homes were generally built near riverfronts), today the number has dwindled to a relative few. This trip meanders along the river between New Orleans and Baton Rouge, stopping at a number of stately plantation homes along the way.

Getting to the plantations

This trip follows Interstate 10 west of New Orleans. Driving times and directions are given with each plantation listing. The plantations are listed in the order in which they appear on the "Plantations along the Great River Road" map, running north from New Orleans along the Mississippi River. Keep in mind that the river winds a bit, so some distances may be deceiving.

Taking a plantation tour

All plantations listed in this section offer guided tours. Most present engaging historical details about the homes and their owners; I especially recommend those for Laura and Destrehan Manor. Except where otherwise noted, tours generally last between 30 to 45 minutes. Some plantations schedule tours continuously (that is, a tour begins whenever a group arrives asking for one) or every 15 minutes or so; the Oak Alley, Tezcuco, and Houmas House tours begin on the half-hour. See the individual listings for admission prices.

Seeing the sights

Because the houses are spread apart and individual visits can take some time, it's unlikely that you'll see all the homes in a single day. My advice is to pace yourself and find out how far you get by mid-day (or even mid-morning). With a home or two under your belt, go through the list and concentrate on the ones that appeal to you the most. If you only have time for two or three, Laura, Oak Alley, and Madewood can be seen in one day at a comfortable pace. Allow 1 to 1½ hours for each visit, 2½ hours if you're a serious enthusiast.

With the exception of Destrehan Manor, with an elevator to the second floor, these plantation homes will be rough going for those traveling in wheelchairs.

Destrehan Manor

The oldest plantation open to the public in the Lower Mississippi Valley, and the site of some of the largest live oaks in the country, Destrehan Manor was built in 1787 by a free person of color and restored using some of the earliest methods of construction. (In a nice touch, one room has

Plantations along the Great River Road

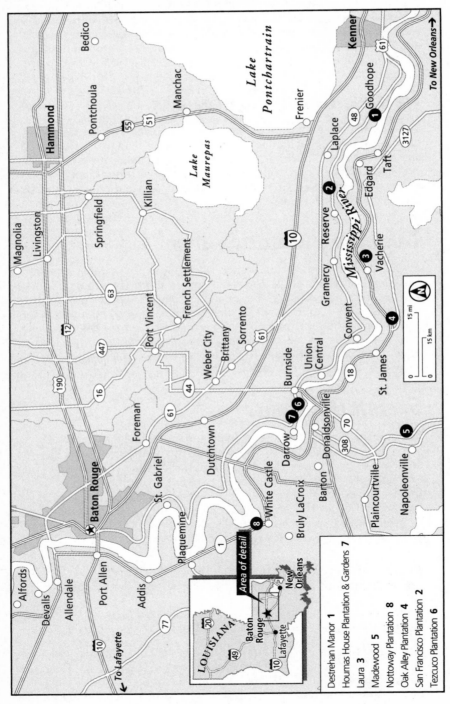

Destrehan Manor **1**

Houmas House Plantation & Gardens **7**

Laura **3**

Madewood **5**

Nottoway Plantation **8**

Oak Alley Plantation **4**

San Francisco Plantation **2**

Tezcuco Plantation **6**

been deliberately spared the renovation process, allowing a glimpse of the true ravages of age.) An appearance in the movie version of *Interview with a Vampire*, along with its proximity to New Orleans, has made this a popular attraction. Guided tours start every 20 minutes.

13034 River Rd. (P.O. Box 5), Destrehan, LA, 70047 (approximately 25 miles from New Orleans). Take I-10 West to Exit 220 (I-310 South), stay on I-310 for about 6 miles, exit onto River Road, and turn left at the light. ☎ 985-764-9315. Fax 985-725-1929. Internet: www.destrehanplantation.org. *Open: Daily 9 a.m.–4 p.m. Admission: $10 adults, $5 teenagers, $3 children 6–12; free for children under 6.*

San Francisco Plantation

From an architectural point of view, this home's interest lies in its resemblance to a ship: The broad galleries are reminiscent of a ship's double decks, and atop two sets of stairs is a broad main portal much like one that leads to a steamboat's grand salon. English and French 18th-century furniture and paintings are featured as part of the restoration. The contrast between the plantation and its neighbor, a huge oil refinery practically in its backyard, is a bit jarring, but oddly enough adds some poignant perspective on how much the times have changed.

2646 La. 44 (P.O. 950), Garyville, LA 70051 (approximately 35 miles from New Orleans). Take I-10 West to U.S. 51 (23 miles). Turn south and continue for 3 miles to ST44, and then go west for 5 miles. ☎ 888-322-1756 or 985-535-2341. Fax: 985-535-5450. Internet: www.sanfranciscoplantation.org. *Open: Daily Mar–Oct 9:30 a.m.–5 p.m. and Nov–Feb 9:30 a.m.–4 p.m. Closed major holidays and Mardi Gras. Admission: $10 adults, $5 students 13–18, $3 children 6–12; free for children under 6.*

Laura: A Creole Plantation

This is the belle of the ball, the one plantation home you should definitely see. You'll find an authentic, informative atmosphere, rather than the touristy feel you may get from other homes. You'll get a comprehensive view of daily life on a plantation in the 18th and 19th centuries; you'll also peruse a cultural history of Louisiana Creoles, and get an entertaining glimpse of a Creole family. The house is a classic Creole home, somewhat plain on the outside but filled with history on the inside, including more than 375 original artifacts covering a 200-year period in the lives of one family. Basic tours last about an hour. Special 90-minute tours, which must be scheduled in advance, focus on subjects such as "Women on the Creole Plantation" and "Plantation Slaves, Artisans, and Folklore."

2247 La. 18, Vacherie, LA 70090 (about 60 miles from New Orleans). Take I-10 West about 28 miles from New Orleans to Exit 194 (Gramercy). Cross the bridge and turn left onto Highway 18 (River Road); travel about 4 more miles. ☎ 888-799-7690 or 225-265-7690. Internet: www.lauraplantation.com. *Open: Daily 9 a.m.–5 p.m. Closed major holidays. Admission: $10 adults, $5 students 6–17; free for children under 6.*

Oak Alley Plantation

Originally named Bon Sejour, the most popular plantation home in Louisiana gets its current name from its quarter-mile alleyway of live oaks. Along with Laura and Madewood, this is the best bet for those wishing to abridge this trip into a "best of" tour, offering exactly what the word "plantation" conjures up. A non-profit foundation runs the place, and authentically costumed guides lead tours. The mansion has been lovingly restored, though its furnishings range from antiques to modern. You can stay the night here (it also serves as a bed-and-breakfast), with rates from $105 to $135. On site is a restaurant open for breakfast and lunch.

3645 La. 18, Vacherie, LA 70090 (60 miles from New Orleans). Take I-10 West to the Gramercy exit (#194). Turn left on Highway 641 (South), and follow the highway, which turns into Highway 3213. Continue over the Veteran's Memorial Bridge. Turn left onto Highway 18 and drive 7½ miles to the plantation. ☎ 800-44-ALLEY or 225-265-2151. Fax: 225-265-7035. Internet: www.oakalleyplantation.com. *Open: Daily Mar–Oct 9 a.m.–5:30 p.m. and Nov–Feb 9 a.m.–5 p.m. Closed Jan 1, Thanksgiving, Dec 25. Admission: $10 adults, $5 students, $3 children 6–12; free for children under 6. No credit cards accepted.*

Madewood

Another must-see stop on this route, Madewood is an imposing two-story Greek Revival mansion with a bit of history behind it (surprise, surprise!). The owner commissioned it solely for the purpose of outdoing his brother, who had a grand house of his own. The construction took eight years, including four just to cut the lumber and make the bricks. In a cruel twist of fate, the owner died of yellow fever just before the house's completion. It was bought and saved from disrepair in 1964, and photos of the laborious restoration process are a revelation. You can stay overnight, either in the main house for $225, or in a more secluded raised cottage.

4250 La. 308, Napoleonville, LA 70390 (approximately 72 miles from New Orleans). Take I-10 West from New Orleans to Exit 182 (Donaldsonville). Cross the Sunshine Bridge onto La. 70; follow it to Spur 70. Follow signs that say "Bayou Plantations," turn left onto Highway 308, and then travel south about 6 miles. ☎ 800-375-7151 or 985-369-7151. Fax: 985-369-9848. Internet: www.madewood.com. *Open: Daily 10 a.m.–4 p.m. Closed holidays. Admission: $6 adults, $4 children and students.*

Tezcuco Plantation

About an hour outside of New Orleans by car rests this tiny home, one of the last plantations built before the Civil War. In contrast to its outward appearance, the rooms are pretty grand. Overnight accommodations are available in two small cabins, done up in a rustic ski-lodge style with wood-burning fireplaces, or in the main house. Rates go from $65 to $180 per night and include breakfast and wine.

3138 La. 44, Darrow, LA 70725 (approximately 50–55 miles from New Orleans). Take I-10 West to exit 179 (Burnside/Gonzales). Take a right, which curves left onto

Highway 44, and travel 5½ miles. ☎ *877-567-3334 or 225-562-3929. Fax: 225-562-3923. Internet:* www.tezcuco.com. *Open: Daily Mar–Nov 9 a.m.–5 p.m. and Dec–Feb 10 a.m.–4 p.m. Admission: $9 adults, $8 seniors, $7 children 13–17, $4 children 5–12; free for children 4 and under.*

Houmas House Plantation & Gardens

With its grand live oaks, magnolias, and formal gardens, this place is the very definition of a plantation home. The structure is actually two houses joined together; the original was built in 1790, and in 1840 a larger, Greek Revival–style house was built next to it (some time in the intervening years, a roof was built over both, joining them together). This bit of architectural jury-rigging is worth a look, as long as you're making a day of it anyway.

40136 La. 942 Burnside, LA 70725 (58 miles from New Orleans). Take I-10 from New Orleans or Baton Rouge, exit onto La. 44 to Burnside, turn right on La. 942. ☎ *888-323-8314 or 225-473-7841. Fax: 225-474-0480. Internet:* www.houmashouse.com. *Open: Daily Feb–Oct 10 a.m.–5 p.m. and Nov–Jan 10 a.m.–4 p.m. Closed holidays. Admission: $10 adults, $6 children 13–17, $3 children 6–12; free for children under 6.*

Nottoway Plantation

The last stop on this tour is a comparative stone's throw (about 25 miles) from Baton Rouge. The house has a formidable presence, with 22 enormous columns and its original slate roof. Sixty-four rooms cover more than 54,000 square feet, including a grand ballroom, beautiful archways, and original crystal chandeliers. You can have lunch or dinner in the restaurant, and stay overnight in one of the restored bedrooms for between $125 and $250 a night; the rate includes a full plantation breakfast, a wake-up tray of muffins, juice, and coffee, and a house tour.

30970 Mississippi River Rd. (P.O. Box 160), White Castle, LA 70788 (69 miles from New Orleans). From New Orleans, follow I-10 West to the La. 22 exit, then turn left on La. 70 across Sunshine Bridge; exit onto La. 1 and drive 14 miles north through Donaldsonville. From Baton Rouge, take I-10 West to the Plaquemine exit, then La. 1 south for 18 miles. ☎ *866-LASOUTH or 225-545-2730. Fax: 225-545-8632. Internet:* www.nottoway.com. *Open: Daily 9 a.m.–5 p.m. Last tour begins at 4:30 p.m. Closed Dec 25. Admission: $10 adults, $4 children under 13; free for children under 5.*

Where to stay and dine among plantations

For accommodations at a plantation, see the preceding listings for Oak Alley Plantation, Tezcuco Plantation, Madewood, and Nottoway Plantation.

For dining, see the preceding listings for Oak Alley Plantation (lunch), Tezcuco Plantation (lunch), and Nottoway Plantation (lunch and dinner).

Two noteworthy eateries near Houmas House and Tezcuco plantations are **The Cabin** (5405 Highway 44 at the intersection of Highway 22, in Burnside, approximately 3 miles from Houmas House; ☎ 225-473-3007; www.thecabinrestaurant.com) and **Hymel's** (8740 Highway 44, in Convent, approximately 8 miles south of Burnside; ☎ 225-562-7031).

New Orleans Nature Getaway

This trip takes you a whole world away from the other experiences in this book, and gets you back to New Orleans in time for dinner. Grab breakfast in your hotel or at one of your favorite local morning spots before driving across the Mississippi River on the Crescent City Connection to the West Bank. Spend the morning at **Barataria Preserve** followed by lunch at an atmospheric restaurant overlooking **Bayou des Familles** in nearby Crown Point. Then spend the afternoon communing with alligators on a swamp tour before heading back to New Orleans for another great meal.

Getting back to nature

In New Orleans, get on I-10 East heading toward the Mississippi River and the West Bank. (Yes, it's the West Bank, though it's directly *east* of New Orleans. Go figure.) Cross the Crescent City Connection; after you're over, it becomes the West Bank Expressway, an elevated thoroughfare that connects a good deal of the West Bank. Go to exit 4B, Barataria Boulevard, and get off, turning left at the second stoplight onto Barataria Blvd. Then drive about 9 miles to Barataria Preserve.

Taking a swamp tour

Lil' Cajun Swamp and Shrimping Tours (Hwy. 301, just outside Jean Lafitte National Park, next to Frank's Boat Launch; ☎ 800-725-3213 or 504-689-3213; www.lilcajunswamptours.com) offers a tour of the local waterways, including Bayou Barataria. The tour is roughly two hours long, and admission is $17 adults, $15 seniors, $13 children 4–12, and free for children under 4. Tour times are 10 a.m. and 2 p.m. The boat is wheelchair accessible, but the bathrooms are not.

Seeing the sights

The **Barataria Preserve** is a branch of the **Jean Lafitte National Historical Park and Preserve,** which encompasses several locations around the state. The preserve sprawls over approximately 20,000 acres of hardwood forest, cypress swampland, and fresh water marshlands, with 8 miles of hiking trails (including 2½ miles of boardwalk) and waterways, preserving a representative sample of the environment of the delta, including bayous, swamps, marshes, and natural levee forests.

New Orleans Nature Getaway

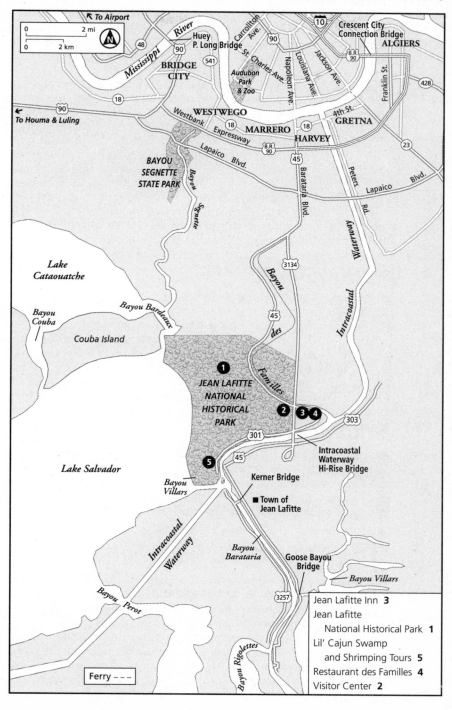

Jean Lafitte Inn **3**

Jean Lafitte
    National Historical Park **1**

Lil' Cajun Swamp
    and Shrimping Tours **5**

Restaurant des Familles **4**

Visitor Center **2**

The preserve is filled with wildlife, while also preserving evidence of prehistoric human settlements (archaeologists have unearthed village sites along the bayous dating back some 2,000 years). In fact, the area offers evidence of human agrarian evolution in miniature, with traces of colonial farming, plantation life, and commercial enterprises such as logging, trapping, hunting, and fishing, and oil and gas exploration.

The trails and waterways make it a natural spot for hiking and exploration, and for getting some perspective on the peoples who settled this area, which was a delta formed by the Mississippi River some 2,500 years ago. You can easily lose yourself here, either taking a "natural history walk," striking out on your own along the pathways, or exploring the 9 miles of canoe trails (closed to motorized boats and accessible by three canoe launch docks; see canoe rental information later in this section), as well as 20 miles of waterways accessible to all types of craft. Picnic tables are scattered throughout, and fishing (with a valid Louisiana fishing license) and even hunting and trapping (by permit only) are allowed; the marshes are dotted with recreational hunting and fishing camps. In short, it's perfect for clearing your mind of all the history, hedonism, and clutter you may have accumulated during your visit to New Orleans.

Head to the **visitor center** (6488 Barataria Blvd. in Marrero, ☎ 504-589-2330, www.nps.gov/jela/Barataria Preserve.htm), where you can get your bearings before heading out and exploring this preserved wilderness. The center also offers exhibits and films. Trails in the preserve are open daily from 7 a.m. to 7 p.m. (during daylight savings hours) and 7 a.m. to 5 p.m. (standard time), and the visitor center is open daily from 9 a.m. to 5 p.m. (closed on Christmas Day). No admission fee is required, though donations are accepted at the visitor center. The visitor center, restrooms, and the Bayou Coquille Trail are all wheelchair accessible.

Canoe rentals are available at **Jean Lafitte Inn** (☎ 504-689-3271), located next to the park just off Barataria Boulevard (before you get to the Lafitte/LaRose Highway, which you cross on your way to Restaurant des Familles, mentioned later in this chapter). Rentals are $25 for the day and must be returned by dark; canoes are launched into the preserve.

Where to dine

For lunch, check out **Restaurant des Familles** ($$–$$$; 7163 Barataria Blvd., Marrero, LA 70072; ☎ 504-689-7834). The restaurant is open Tuesday through Saturday for lunch and dinner (as well as Sunday for brunch). Offerings include an array of seafood and Cajun and Creole dishes served in an extremely scenic setting. Enjoy outdoor dining as well as indoor dining in a glass-walled room overlooking the picturesque **Bayou des Familles.** (The restaurant accepts American Express, Discover, MasterCard, and Visa.)

Part VI
Living It Up After the Sun Goes Down: New Orleans Nightlife

The 5th Wave   By Rich Tennant

"I asked for a seat near the steel drum, but I don't see any steel drum."

In this part . . .

New Orleans after dark is nothing like New Orleans during the day. The experience is completely different with its own landmarks, history, and etiquette. Luckily, I know my way around a watering hole or two, and happily share my expertise in this part of the book.

A discussion of the city's nightlife has to start with music, particularly jazz, and this part certainly covers the best spots to go, whether you want the quickie tourist experience or something more authentic. It also ferrets out the best spots for real-deal Cajun and zydeco, and visits the city's best bars (stopping to refuel along the way). To wrap up, this part delves into the local theater and performing arts scenes — hey, you need something to do before all the bars open, right? So get out your highlighter and *laissez le bon temps roulet* (let the good times roll).

Chapter 23

New Orleans's Music Scene

. . . .

In This Chapter

▶ Uncovering the best jazz clubs

▶ Finding other premier clubs in the city

▶ Stomping along with Cajun and zydeco music

▶ Getting your rock-and-roll fix

. . . .

*N*o self-respecting discussion of New Orleans's nightlife can afford to skip over the city's vibrant music landscape. Music is pretty much a part of daily life in New Orleans: From brass-band street parades to jazz funerals, locals have found ingenious ways to work their beloved music into their everyday lives. And the city's reputation as a capital city of jazz ensures that you won't suffer for a lack of unique musical experiences, from down-home traditional Dixieland to cutting-edge contemporary jazz.

Of course, when it comes to music, New Orleans is much more than just the city that jazz built. The city's early contributions to rhythm and blues, funk, and rock and roll reverberate everywhere, from the world-renowned Tipitina's to the modern brass sounds spilling out of the Maple Leaf. But New Orleans isn't just trading on its storied past. The Crescent City boasts a creative music scene, with top-notch performers mixing the area's trademark indigenous styles together in intriguing new combinations. Whether you're a rhythm-and-blues buff, a Cajun connoisseur, a rock fan, or simply looking to jazz up your vacation, this chapter introduces you to the prime spots you need to know to truly experience New Orleans music on the (ahem) scale that it deserves.

Getting All Jazzed Up

New Orleans is often referred to as the birthplace of jazz. Some say the genre was born (or at least incubated) in the brothels of old Storyville (New Orleans's now-vanished, but still-legendary, red-light district), where the city's innovative young musicians entertained the clients, increasing the number of ears exposed to the unique new form of music.

New Orleans Music/Nightlife

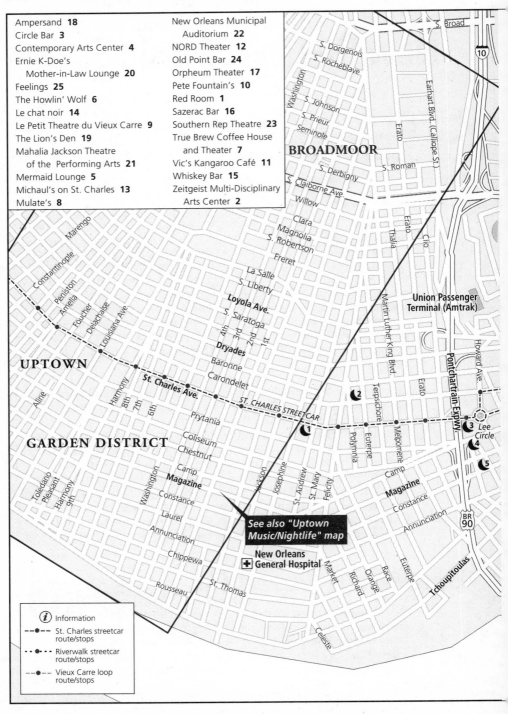

Ampersand **18**
Circle Bar **3**
Contemporary Arts Center **4**
Ernie K-Doe's
 Mother-in-Law Lounge **20**
Feelings **25**
The Howlin' Wolf **6**
Le chat noir **14**
Le Petit Theatre du Vieux Carre **9**
The Lion's Den **19**
Mahalia Jackson Theatre
 of the Performing Arts **21**
Mermaid Lounge **5**
Michaul's on St. Charles **13**
Mulate's **8**

New Orleans Municipal
 Auditorium **22**
NORD Theater **12**
Old Point Bar **24**
Orpheum Theater **17**
Pete Fountain's **10**
Red Room **1**
Sazerac Bar **16**
Southern Rep Theatre **23**
True Brew Coffee House
 and Theater **7**
Vic's Kangaroo Café **11**
Whiskey Bar **15**
Zeitgeist Multi-Disciplinary
 Arts Center **2**

BROADMOOR

UPTOWN

GARDEN DISTRICT

Union Passenger
Terminal (Amtrak)

Lee
Circle

See also "Uptown
Music/Nightlife" map

New Orleans
➕ General Hospital

ℹ Information

- - ●- - St. Charles streetcar
route/stops

·· ●·· Riverwalk streetcar
route/stops

- - ●- Vieux Carre loop
route/stops

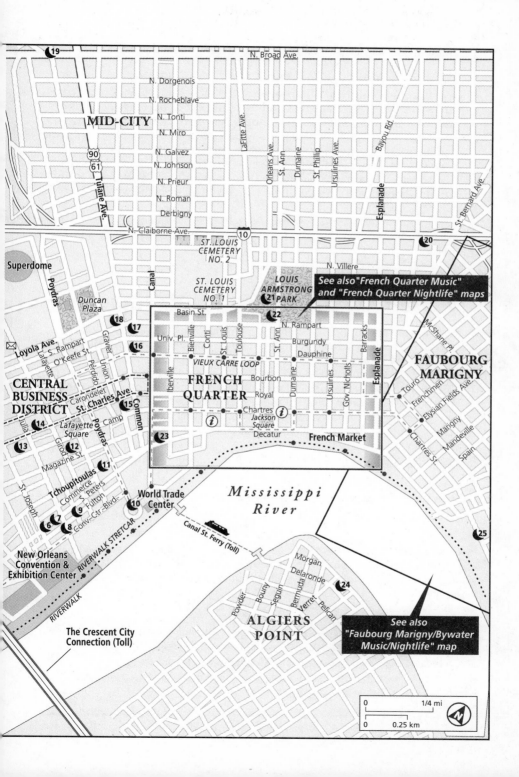

N. Broad Ave.

N. Dorgenois
N. Rocheblave
N. Tonti
MID-CITY
N. Miro
N. Galvez
N. Johnson
N. Prieur
N. Roman
Derbigny

LaFitte Ave.

Orleans Ave.
St. Ann
Dumaine
St. Phillip
Ursulines Ave.

Bayou Rd.

Esplanade

St. Bernard Ave.

90
61
Tulane Ave.

N. Claiborne Ave.

10

20

Superdome

Poydras

Duncan
Plaza

Canal

ST. LOUIS
CEMETERY
NO. 2

ST. LOUIS
CEMETERY
NO. 1

LOUIS
ARMSTRONG
21 PARK

N. Villere

See also "French Quarter Music"
and "French Quarter Nightlife" maps

Loyola Ave.
S. Rampart
O'Keefe St.

Gravier

Perdido
Union

18
17
16

Basin St.
Univ. Pl.
Bienville
Conti
St. Louis
Toulouse

N. Rampart
Burgundy
Dauphine
St. Ann

22

Barracks

McShane Pl.

**FAUBOURG
MARIGNY**

**CENTRAL
BUSINESS
DISTRICT**

Carondelet
St. Charles Ave.

Common

Poydras

15

Iberville

**FRENCH
QUARTER**

VIEUX CARRE LOOP

Bourbon

Royal

Chartres
Jackson
Square

Dumaine

Ursulines

Gov. Nicholls

Esplanade

Touro
Frenchmen
Elysian Fields Ave.

Chartres St.

Marigny

Mandeville

Julia
14

Lafayette
Square

Camp

Girod

Magazine St.

13
12
11

Decatur

French Market

Spain

St. Joseph

Tchoupitoulas
Commerce
S. Peters
Fulton
Conv.-Ctr.-Blvd.

9

23

**New Orleans
Convention &
Exhibition Center**

RIVERWALK STREETCAR

6 7

10

World Trade
Center

Canal St. Ferry (Toll)

*Mississippi
River*

25

RIVERWALK

**The Crescent City
Connection (Toll)**

Morgan
Delaronde

Powder
Bouny
Seguin
Bermuda
Verret
Pelican

24

**ALGIERS
POINT**

See also
"Faubourg Marigny/Bywater
Music/Nightlife" map

0   1/4 mi
0   0.25 km

N

This may or may not be true, but in a city as steeped in romance and mystique as New Orleans, the verity of such a claim is largely beside the point. It *sounds* right, and it fits the city's freewheeling image.

Of course, it doesn't hurt that New Orleans is one of the world's foremost jazz laboratories, where some of the most important players continue to challenge themselves and their audiences by steering the form into new, unexplored areas. Sure, some New York clubs such as the Knitting Factory and the Village Vanguard get a lot more of the spotlight, but invariably, many (if not most) of the players on those stages call New Orleans home, getting their feet wet in the local clubs. New Orleans jazz musicians form the backbone of the modern jazz world, and many are recognized and enthusiastically received all over the world.

"Just what is jazz?" you may ask. As native New Orleanian Louis Armstrong once said, "If you got to ask what it is, you'll never get to know." So save your questions; by the time you've danced your way through these clubs, you'll no longer have to ask.

Preserving the strains of Dixieland jazz

Preservation Hall (726 St. Peter St.; ☎ **800-785-5772** or 504-522-2841; www.preservationhall.com) is run by a non-profit group dedicated to the preservation of jazz. Shows start at 8:30 p.m. and end around midnight, with 35-minute sets and about a 10-minute break after each set. The band will play requests if you make a decent offering, but try not to be the fifth person in a row to request "When the Saints Go Marching In." Keep in mind that you'll find minimal seating, no air-conditioning, and no food or drinks. Still, you'll almost certainly enjoy yourself, and the kids should love it, too. A selection of tapes and CDs is for sale if you find you can't get enough of the music. Admission is $5.

A lesson in jazz

From the moment the mercurial Buddy Bolden began playing his cornet around town near the end of the 19th century (widely regarded as the starting point of jazz history), New Orleans has enjoyed a reputation as one of the nation's premier music cities. Since then, clubs in the French Quarter have fostered such jazz greats as Louis Armstrong, Jelly Roll Morton, and Sidney Bechet, as well as contemporary musicians Harry Connick, Jr., several members of the Marsalis family, and other talented folks. More recent decades have seen the New Orleans music scene broaden well beyond its jazz roots, with musicians such as the Neville Brothers and Dr. John melding unique local sounds and customs together to form rhythm and blues, a direct precursor to rock and roll. But it all started with jazz, which makes it a perfect starting point here, as well.

French Quarter Music

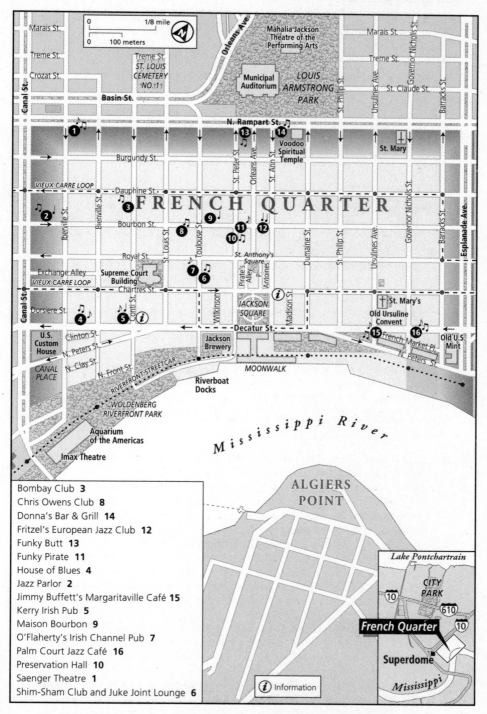

Bombay Club **3**

Chris Owens Club **8**

Donna's Bar & Grill **14**

Fritzel's European Jazz Club **12**

Funky Butt **13**

Funky Pirate **11**

House of Blues **4**

Jazz Parlor **2**

Jimmy Buffett's Margaritaville Café **15**

Kerry Irish Pub **5**

Maison Bourbon **9**

O'Flaherty's Irish Channel Pub **7**

Palm Court Jazz Café **16**

Preservation Hall **10**

Saenger Theatre **1**

Shim-Sham Club and Juke Joint Lounge **6**

Greenwich Village south: The Frenchmen Street scene

If Bourbon Street is New Orleans's answer to Times Square, then Frenchmen Street is its analog to Greenwich Village (albeit a very, very small one). For whatever reason, Frenchmen Street is the epicenter of hip, funky, bohemian spots, especially in terms of music (and now enjoying a renaissance as a nightclub and restaurant center). Its small strip of clubs is one of the focal points of New Orleans's music scene, where everything from jazz to Latin music to gritty, down-home funk is stretched like Play-doh into new, innovative shapes. Here's a brief rundown of the landmarks:

✔ **Café Brasil:** The heart of this strip, this corner nightclub runs the gamut from Latin and Brazilian music and Afro-Cuban funk to avant-garde jazz and danceable ethno-musical amalgams. During Mardi Gras and Jazz Fest in particular, crowds spill into the street and stay well into the dawn. (See listing in Chapter 24.)

✔ **Checkpoint Charlie:** Aptly named, this outpost on Esplanade is your entry into the Frenchmen area. It's sort of a cross between a biker bar and a college hangout, with a focus on homegrown rock acts. (See listing later in this chapter.)

✔ **Snug Harbor:** The city's premier jazz room, it offers a mix of traditional jazz and more experimental contemporary stuff, from acclaimed local masters such as Ellis Marsalis (father to Wynton and Branford) to internationally renowned touring acts. (See the listing later in this chapter.)

✔ **Blue Nile Cafe:** This newly opened club focuses on an eclectic and diverse lineup of local music, from avant-garde rock to modern jazz and more. (See its listing elsewhere in this chapter.)

The sign outside **Maison Bourbon** (641 Bourbon St.; ☎ **504-522-8818**) proclaims that the place is "Dedicated to the Preservation of Jazz," which means that Dixieland jazz is the only item on the musical menu. Despite being located on Bourbon Street, this is not a tourist trap. No children are allowed, so if you are with kids and want them to get a taste of some Dixieland, simply stand outside the bar — you can hear and see everything just fine. Records and CDs are available for purchase. Show times vary; it's open from 2:30 p.m. to 12:15 a.m. Monday through Thursday, and from 3:30 p.m. to 1:15 a.m. Friday through Sunday. Though you won't face a cover charge, a one-drink minimum is enforced.

The **Palm Court Jazz Café** (1204 Decatur St.; ☎ **504-525-0200;** www.palmcourtjazz.com), like Preservation Hall, offers old-style jazz played by old-style musicians — but the Palm Court also has air-conditioning, food (which can be a little pricey; see Chapter 14), and drinks. You may want to make reservations. Music is played from 8 to 11 p.m., Wednesday through Sunday. Diners are charged a small "music fee," while those who opt to stand at the bar to enjoy the same show pay nothing more than the cost of their drinks.

For jazz with a little different slant, try **Fritzel's European Jazz Club** (733 Bourbon St.; ☎ 504-561-0432; http://expage.com/page/ fritzels). Fritzel's is known for late night (or early morning) jam sessions: Musicians who have finished playing their sets at other jazz clubs often come here to take turns running through old-time traditional jazz. An oasis among the sanitized jazz spots in the French Quarter, this place boasts an agreeable German beer-house décor, with a one-drink minimum per set instead of a cover charge. Come here way after midnight, order a German beer, and watch some talented musicians compare notes (children not allowed). Music starts at 9:30 p.m. and runs late.

The **Blue Nile** (534 Frenchmen St. in the Faubourg Marigny, ☎ 504-948-BLUE [2583]) is a relative newcomer to the New Orleans music landscape, occupying a building that formerly housed the jazz-themed Tin Roof Cafe and before that, the eclectic Dream Palace, a long-beloved institution. The proprietors seem to be aiming for a vibe and roster similar to the Dream Palace, booking a varied mix of local bands of different genres. Shows begin at 10 p.m.; call for a specific evening's cover charge.

In praise of contemporary jazz

In comparison with Preservation Hall and the Palm Court, **Snug Harbor** (626 Frenchmen St.; ☎ 504-949-0696; www.snugjazz.com) is more in line with the times. Located in Faubourg Marigny, just outside the French Quarter, this is one of the prime spots for modern jazz in the city. The place enjoys a very good reputation; among local musicians and fans, a show at this small, often-crowded spot is shorthand for class. Drinks, sandwiches, and a full dinner service are available. The cover charge varies according to the performer, but is usually between $8 and $20. Shows begin nightly at 9 and 11 p.m.

Jazz Fest–quality music and food from the Brennan family (thanks to the **Red Fish Grill** right next door) are the twin draws of the **Jazz Parlor** (125 Bourbon St.; ☎ 504-410-1000), formerly the ambitious Storyville District. Jazz is the order of the day, obviously, and despite the Parlor's prime Bourbon Street real estate, it's the real deal, not watered-down tourist bait. Show times are generally 5, 7:30, and 11 p.m., with a one-drink minimum per person per set.

Sweet Lorraine's (1931 St. Claude Ave., ☎ 504-945-9654) aims to be a throwback to the days when jazz clubs lined the streets. This establishment offers a program of modern and traditional jazz. Not in what you'd call the safest neighborhood, and parking is a bit chancy, so take a cab. The cover varies from $5 to $15. Show times vary, but generally start at 10 p.m. and midnight.

Faubourg Marigny/Bywater Music/Nightlife

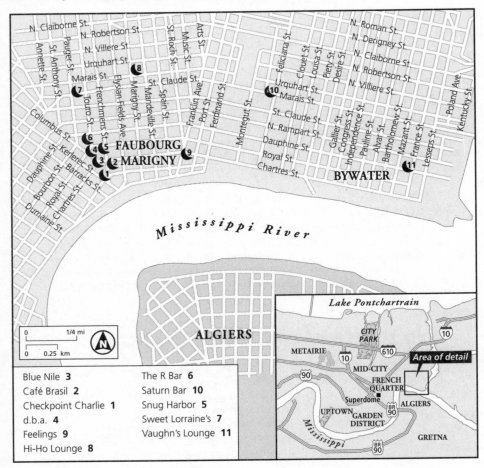

Blue Nile **3**	The R Bar **6**
Café Brasil **2**	Saturn Bar **10**
Checkpoint Charlie **1**	Snug Harbor **5**
d.b.a. **4**	Sweet Lorraine's **7**
Feelings **9**	Vaughn's Lounge **11**
Hi-Ho Lounge **8**	

Toe-tapping to the top brass

Donna's Bar & Grill (800 N. Rampart St.; ☎ **504-596-6914**) is known as "Brass Band World Headquarters," the only place in town where you can reliably expect to hear brass band music (picture a cross between marching-band music and jazz) on a regular basis. Only three blocks from Bourbon Street at North Rampart and St. Ann, Donna's has a funky hole-in-the-wall vibe that's relaxed and unpretentious. The crowds often follow bands onto the street for a second-line parade. Because the neighborhood can be dicey, take a cab if you're concerned about safety — it's worth the trip. Show times are 10 p.m. Thursday through Monday (closed Tuesday and Wednesday). The average cover is $5.

Takin' it to the streets: Jazz traditions

Jazz in New Orleans has some traditions that seem a little odd at first. For one, you occasionally see musicians marching in a street parade, complete with a brass band — even when it isn't Carnival season. Consider it part of the culture. Like their cousins, the Mardi Gras Indian parades (see Chapter 16), these spontaneous outbursts keep the music connected to its roots in the city's streets. As authentic as seeing a jazz band perform in a club can be, there's no substitute for witnessing this joyous ceremony, as jazz or brass band musicians strengthen their ties to the street communities from whence they sprang. After you've been here awhile, a brass-band parade through the streets in the middle of a weekend afternoon seems as natural as going to the grocery (or "makin' groceries," as the phrase goes here).

Another popular jazz tradition you may see moving through the streets is the jazz funeral. Many venerable and respected jazz musicians are sent off to their reward in this fashion, in a procession that can seem inappropriately cheerful — to the unpracticed eye. Actually, the mourners are celebrating the deceased's liberation from this world (called *the return*). However, they also show their sorrow while marching in the procession, often signified by shuffling and clapping to a mournful beat while in the *second line*. (Hence, the term "second-line" as it applies to the popular shuffling beat employed by many brass bands and funk and R&B musicians.)

Named after one of the liveliest clubs in the early days of jazz (and for a tune made famous by legendary cornet player Buddy Bolden), the **Funky Butt** (714 N. Rampart St.; ☎ **504-558-0872;** www.funkybutt.com) performance space is on the second floor, topping a basic dive bar at the ground level. Expect a variety of performers whose styles range from eclectic modern and traditional jazz to rhythm and blues. Like Donna's, it's location is technically on the far edge of the Quarter, but it's worth the walk or taxi ride. If the walk works up your appetite, you can order from a menu featuring Creole and vegetarian cuisine. Shows begin nightly at 10 p.m. and midnight. No cover weekdays; the average cover on Friday or Saturday is between $5 and $10.

Keeping an Alternative Beat

Of course, New Orleans offers much more music than jazz, including the following premier music clubs. (Later in this chapter, you'll find listings for places that feature rock-and-roll, Cajun, and zydeco music; you'll also find more music venues mixed into the bar and club listings in Chapter 24.)

Uptown Music/Nightlife

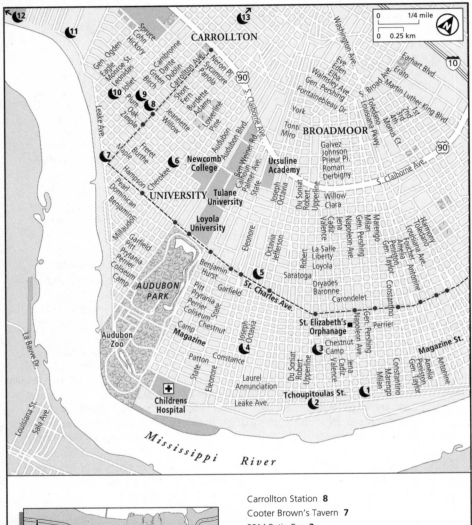

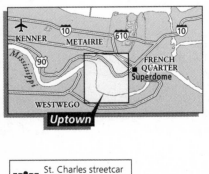

Carrollton Station **8**

Cooter Brown's Tavern **7**

F&M Patio Bar **2**

Jimmy's Music Club and Patio Bar **9**

Le Bon Temps Roule **3**

Live Bait Bar and Grill **11**

Maple Leaf **10**

Mid-City Lanes Rock 'N' Bowl **13**

Neutral Ground Coffeehouse **5**

Rivershack Tavern **12**

Snake & Jake's Xmas Club Lounge **6**

St. Joe's Bar **4**

Tipitina's **1**

✔ The **Maple Leaf** (8316 Oak St.; ☎ **504-866-9359**) is what a New Orleans club is all about. A small space, it features a hammered tin ceiling, a patio out back, and a pretty good bar. But its reputation is in inverse proportion to its size; the place is almost always packed, with crowds often spilling out into the street. The ReBirth Brass Band's regular Tuesday night gigs have become as much a local tradition as red beans and rice on Monday. If you're not already a fan of New Orleans music when you come, you will be when you leave. Shows usually begin around 10:30 p.m.; cover varies anywhere from $5 to $20.

✔ The **Old Point Bar** (545 Patterson St., just across the river in Algiers; ☎ **504-364-0950;** www.oldpointbar.com) is an agreeable hangout with a relaxed, neighborhood-bar feel and an eclectic menu of jazz, funk, blues, and rock. On any given night, you're likely to stumble across a chanteuse belting out jazz standards or adventurous jazz-funk from Stanton Moore of the popular New Orleans–based groove/jam-band Galactic. Shows usually begin around 10 p.m. (8 p.m. on Sunday nights), and covers generally run anywhere from $5 to $20.

✔ **Tipitina's** (501 Napoleon Ave.; ☎ **504-895-8477** or 504-897-3943; www.tipitinas.com) was, for a long time, *the* New Orleans music club. Posters advertising shows from the club's long history give the place a tangible sense of legacy and atmosphere. Local bands and touring national alternative rock acts play here, and during Jazz Fest the place is a thriving, visceral center of musical activity. If you can't make it out to Cajun Country, on Sunday afternoons this place holds a "Fais Do Do," complete with free food and dance lessons. The surrounding residential neighborhood isn't the greatest, so you may want to take a cab, though a decent parking lot is across the street. (Tipitina's also has a satellite French Quarter location at 233 N. Peters St., open only for private functions and special one-off events.) Shows begin at 10 p.m.; Fais Do Do begins at 5 p.m. Sunday. The cover varies from $5 to $20.

Pump That Accordion, Jack!
Cajun and Zydeco Music

Because Cajun and zydeco originated not in New Orleans, but in the swamps and bayous around Lafayette, you won't find true Cajun culture and music in New Orleans. The genuine article remains out in the country. Still, on any given night you can find a regional heavyweight playing somewhere.

AAIIEEE! Cajun and zydeco in two easy steps

While jazz was born in the Crescent City, Cajun and zydeco music originated in the country — the wetlands around Lafayette settled by the Acadians (see Chapter 22). Cajun music and zydeco both started out with Acadian folk music and French ballads, evolving into two distinctive new forms of music native to Louisiana and heavily influenced by the cultural diversity of the American Indian, Scotch-Irish, Spanish, Afro-Caribbean, and German folks who also lived in the bayous and swamps near Lafayette. While both of these native forms rely on the accordion as a core instrument, Cajun music today generally retains a rustic sound and feel, while zydeco has evolved into a more urbanized sound.

A lively style reminiscent of bluegrass and country music, Cajun dance music is traditionally played on button accordions, scratchy fiddles, triangles, and rub-boards (or *frottoir*). Expect to have a great time dancing to it, but don't try to sing along: Many Cajun songs are still sung in the Acadian dialect of French or with such thick accents that you probably won't understand many of the lyrics.

Zydeco began as Cajun dance music, but was flavored over 150 years by the African, blues, and R&B traditions also enjoyed by the rural Creole population. Zydeco has a faster beat than Cajun, especially because funkier rhythms have been mixed in recently. Old-school zydeco performers rely only on the accordion, drums, and trademark rub-board, but over the last few decades some innovative performers have introduced electric guitars and basses, saxophones, and trumpets as well. Some of the genre's elder statesmen good-naturedly compete for the title "King of Zydeco," which comes with a ceremonial crown.

Michaul's on St. Charles (840 St. Charles Ave.; ☎ 504-522-5517) and **Mulate's** (201 Julia St.; ☎ 504-522-1492) present the tourist version of the Cajun experience, with the requisite wood floors and walls, kitsch, and a whole lot of crawfish. However, both clubs offer Cajun dance lessons (Michaul's are free), and you may catch a really good band that's in town for the day. Shows begin at 7 p.m. in both spots; no covers.

Wednesdays and Thursdays are zydeco party time at the celebrity magnet **Mid-City Lanes Rock 'N' Bowl** (4133 S. Carrollton Ave.; ☎ 504-482-3133). Although the neighborhood is dicey, this is one of the most unique experiences in town, and well worth the trip. Show times vary: Tuesday through Thursday from 8:30 to 9:30 p.m.; Friday and Saturday at 10 p.m. Mid-City is closed both Sunday and Monday. Cover varies from $5 to $20.

Rock and Roll All Night

Although New Orleans R&B, as practiced by such legends as Fats Domino, laid the groundwork for what we today call rock and roll, the city isn't well known for its contributions to modern-day rock. Still, it *does* boast a good rock scene, including such well-traveled names as the Radiators and modern rockers Better Than Ezra. Following are some of the clubs where you may catch the Next Big Thing or a national touring act:

- **Checkpoint Charlie** (501 Esplanade Ave.; ☎ 504-947-0979) tends toward rock and R&B and feels like something between a biker bar and a college hangout. A part of the Frenchmen Street strip in the Faubourg Marigny, it doesn't really fit into the bohemian aesthetic of that hip enclave. This is a good place to check out young up-and-coming rock acts. Shows begin at 10:30 p.m.; no cover.

- From its humble beginnings as a suburban bar and venue for local alternative acts, **The Howlin' Wolf** (828 S. Peters St.; ☎ 504-522-WOLF [9653]; www.howlin-wolf.com) has grown into a Warehouse District landmark, and the main competitor with House of Blues (and, to a lesser extent, Tipitina's) for out-of-town acts. The Wolf's staff is among the friendliest in town, while the overall vibe is among the least pretentious and most agreeable in the city. Shows begin at 10 p.m.; cover varies from $5 to $20.

- **Jimmy's Music Club and Patio Bar** (8200 Willow St.; ☎ 504-861-8200) is right across the street from Carrollton Station, and on weekend nights you're likely to find a good crowd milling about in the street between the two. Jimmy's used to be a prime spot for local rock bands and touring acts, though its smaller capacity precludes it from competing with Tipitina's, the Howlin' Wolf, or House of Blues. Now, obscure local hard-rock acts are featured, plus some local and touring reggae, punk, and ska bands. Shows begin at 10 p.m.; cover varies from $5 to $15.

- The **Mermaid Lounge** (1100 Constance St. in the Central Business District; ☎ 504-524-4747; www.mermaidlounge.com) has, against all odds, carved a pretty nice niche for itself booking an eclectic mix of acts. The Brigadoon-like club can be hard to find, located on a cul-de-sac under an interstate ramp at the wrong end of a series of one-way streets. On any given night, the club books everything from a 70-year-old Cajun band to the most obscure college or indie-rock group. The mermaid motif, tiny stage, and dive-like atmosphere all contribute to one of the coolest vibes in town. Shows begin at 10 p.m.; cover varies from $5 to $20.

The name game

From Louis Armstrong (whose name graces Armstrong Park) to the ever-expanding Marsalis family, New Orleans is a city of musical names. Some of these can be found on the marquees of the city's most popular (and interesting) nightclubs. Following is the Who's Who of name clubs:

- Parrot heads abound at **Jimmy Buffett's Margaritaville Café** (1104 Decatur St.; ☎ 504-592-2565; www.margaritaville.com). This chain has contributed to the brand-name takeover of the Quarter. Some touring acts stop here and Buffett himself sometimes pops by when he's in town, but mostly it's a venue for journeyman local performers, from blues to R&B to reggae and New Orleans roots music. You'll find music all day long here, with shows generally beginning at 3, 6, and 9 p.m. No cover except for special shows on weekend nights, which start around 10:30 p.m.

- Pete Fountain is practically synonymous with New Orleans music. This local boy, once a member of Lawrence Welk's orchestra, plays sweet jazz clarinet Tuesday through Saturday at his club, **Pete Fountain's** (2 Poydras St., in the Hilton Hotel; ☎ 504-523-4374). The show's at 10 p.m. with a $20 cover charge that includes one drink. Children are not allowed, and you'll need reservations.

- The local **House of Blues** (225 Decatur St.; ☎ 504-529-BLUE [2583]; www.hob.com/venues/clubvenues/neworleans/) doesn't *really* fit here, unless you consider celebrity co-founder Dan Aykroyd's alter ego, Elwood Blues, a big name. Most major touring rock, reggae, and hip-hop acts play here. The restaurant is decent if pricey, with some inventive takes on local fare. This national chain has doggedly dedicated itself to the community, and even offers blues scholarships to children. Other chains should be this stylish. Shows usually begin at 9 p.m. Cover varies from $10 to $20.

- Remember the vintage R&B chestnut "Mother-In-Law"? Before his death in 2001, flamboyant singer Ernie K-Doe turned that song into a career — and later, a nightclub. **Ernie K-Doe's Mother-In-Law Lounge** (1500 N. Claiborne Ave. at Columbus; ☎ 504-947-1078), where K-Doe held court for years, remains open, but plans about the club's future have yet to emerge. If you're interested in New Orleans music history, it's worth a stop, but call first to make sure it's still open. And take a cab — the neighborhood is a bit rough.

- If you're in Mid-City, consider a foray into **The Lion's Den** (2655 Gravier St.; ☎ 504-822-4693). Owned by Irma Thomas, the "Soul Queen of New Orleans," it's especially worth a visit if she's playing, which has been known to happen. A great, sassy performer and a musical treasure, Ms. Thomas is still going strong. Shows begin at 9 p.m. Cover varies; call ahead for price.

- If you're looking for a little Vegas-style revue, the **Chris Owens Club** (500 Bourbon St.; ☎ 504-523-6400; www.chrisowens.com) may fit your bill. The energetic Ms. Owens (picture a Sin-City showgirl as played by a Botox-injected muppet) puts on a fun show filled with standards from the worlds of pop, jazz, blues, and country and western. Call for reservations and admission prices. Shows begin at 8:30 p.m. and 10 p.m.

Chapter 24

Hitting the Clubs and Bars

● ●

In This Chapter

▶ Checking out French Quarter nightlife

▶ Finding the best bars and clubs elsewhere in the city

▶ Discovering a spot to suit your style, from hip hangouts to piano bars

● ●

I don't want to lean on the horribly over-used cliché that New Orleans is the party capital of the United States, but you can't deny that things are definitely looser here. This is never as true as after dark, when the city marches to the beat of a decidedly different drummer than during the weekday 9-to-5 hours. And I don't just mean the slinky, greasy rhythms of funk and R&B or the stately clip of vintage jazz. I'm not just talking about music; I'm talking about mood. The city settles into a livelier, more offhand vibe as the night progresses. For proof, you need walk no farther than to the nearest bar.

What makes a good bar? Everyone's set of criteria is different. Some people want a nice, dark watering hole, while others want a high-energy dance workout and the chance to discreetly bump into an anonymous member of their preferred sex. This chapter explores all the nooks and crannies of New Orleans's bar scene. It stops in at some rowdy saloons, upscale bars, dance clubs, and your regular hole-in-the-wall dives. Because New Orleans has more than its fair share of bars offering live music, this chapter stops at a few of those, as well (for more music venues, see Chapter 23).

Keep in mind that the selections throughout this chapter are not all-inclusive. Because New Orleans boasts more bars and music clubs per capita than almost any other city in the United States, you will doubtless find a host of other happening places on your own.

Playing by the Rules

Some will be disappointed to learn that the legal drinking age in Louisiana is now 21 — for years, it was 18. If you are of drinking age, however, you'll be delighted to know that you can legally walk along any public street with a drink in your hand (though the drink must be in a

plastic cup, called a *go-* or *geaux-cup*). Drinking alcohol while in a vehicle is illegal, however, even if you're just a passenger. So if you feel the need to imbibe while getting somewhere, better to stick to the sidewalks.

Unless otherwise noted, most places listed in this chapter don't usually charge a cover (though all bets are off during Mardi Gras or Jazz Fest). For locations of nightlife spots outside the French Quarter, refer to the maps in Chapter 23; for spots inside the Quarter, check out the "French Quarter Nightlife" map later in this chapter.

Entering the Neon Party Zone: French Quarter Nightlife

Tourist nightlife centers around the French Quarter, as you may have guessed. Keep in mind, however, that the key word here is "tourist." Lots of clubs are concentrated here, many solely to cater to the constant influx of visitors (with *some* notable exceptions to this rule). Some are cheap, some are tacky; many are both. Of course, genuinely good haunts are here as well. Where the French Quarter is concerned, the epicenter of nightlife is Bourbon Street.

Drinking in Bourbon Street

Having just cautioned you against reading too much into the Quarter bar scene, I don't want to discourage you from checking out world-famous Bourbon Street at least once. But if you stroll down Bourbon and figure that you've experienced real New Orleans nightlife, you've missed the boat; in fact, you've missed the plane, too, and the train just left the station. Bourbon Street is a tourist attraction, first and foremost. Granted, like Beale Street in Memphis, it became an attraction because of something genuine and authentic; but almost all vestiges of that elusive something have been replaced by glitter, glitz, and spectacle (if glitter and glitz are terms that can be applied to some of the street's decidedly low-rent charms). Still, seedy as it can be, Bourbon Street can also be a fun barrage of sights, sounds, and, yes, smells. With every kind of music, from jazz, blues, and rock and roll to rhythm and blues, country, Celtic, and Cajun, it's not the quality so much as the sheer variety that's important here.

Many Bourbon Street establishments are open 24 hours. Others open late in the afternoon, when the area starts to come to life. After 8 p.m., the street is blocked off to traffic, and the streets and sidewalks are filled with people.

You may notice that St. Ann Street, about eight blocks from Canal, marks a division on Bourbon Street — it's the unofficial boundary between the straight and gay sections of the area. While not every bar or person east of St. Ann is gay, and not every bar or person west of it is straight, you'll likely notice a marked difference in the feel of the areas.

Be careful when exploring: The farther you get away from the river or the farther you go down Bourbon Street (away from Canal), the fewer people will be around and the less safe the area becomes. If you must explore more deserted sections, keep alert for trouble — remember the cliché about safety in numbers.

Hitting the quarter notes: Some prime French Quarter spots

The French Quarter is widely considered by locals to be one large tourist trap. You need a scorecard to distinguish the authentic, character-filled spots, which *do* exist, from the tourist magnets. Following is my subjective list:

✔ Check out the **Funky Pirate** (727 Bourbon St.; ☎ **504-523-1960**) for a true Bourbon Street blues experience. One of the area's biggest (literally and figuratively) blues musicians, Big Al Carson, deals out Chicago-style electric blues most nights. His schedule varies; call to find out when he's playing. No cover, but expect a one-drink minimum.

✔ **The Hideout** (1207 Decatur St.; ☎ **504-529-7119**) can best be described as a safe, friendly approximation of a hole-in-the-wall experience. The place used to house a pretty intimidating gay/biker bar, but these days most everyone, from punks to tourists, is made welcome.

✔ **Molly's at the Market** (1107 Decatur St.; ☎ **504-525-5169**) draws a strange cross-section of locals. Something of a hangout for local media types (especially on Thursday nights), the pub-crawling legions make this a frequent stop as well. That includes Goth-types as well as bohemians in tie-dyes who look like they haven't washed in weeks, and even just regular Joes out for a drink.

✔ **Ol'Toone's Saloon** (233 Decatur St.; ☎ **504-529-3422**) is a some-what nondescript bar next to House of Blues on Decatur. A good place to unwind after catching a show next door, it has a pretty good vibe when it fills up. It attracts its fair share of characters and is open 24 hours.

French Quarter Nightlife

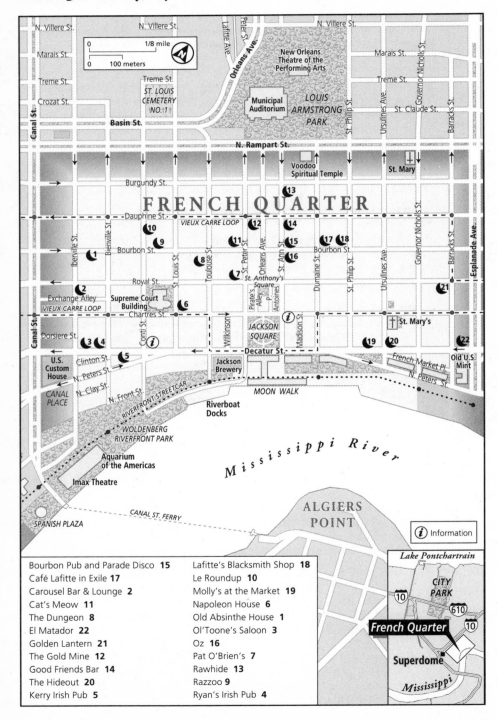

Bourbon Pub and Parade Disco **15**	Lafitte's Blacksmith Shop **18**
Café Lafitte in Exile **17**	Le Roundup **10**
Carousel Bar & Lounge **2**	Molly's at the Market **19**
Cat's Meow **11**	Napoleon House **6**
The Dungeon **8**	Old Absinthe House **1**
El Matador **22**	Ol'Toone's Saloon **3**
Golden Lantern **21**	Oz **16**
The Gold Mine **12**	Pat O'Brien's **7**
Good Friends Bar **14**	Rawhide **13**
The Hideout **20**	Razzoo **9**
Kerry Irish Pub **5**	Ryan's Irish Pub **4**

Seeking the See-and-Be-Seen Scene

These places, while wide-ranging, are some of the best spots if you're looking to socialize or just rub elbows with a roomful of strangers:

✔ **Ampersand** (1100 Tulane Ave.; ☎ 504-587-3737; www.ampersand nola.com) sits in the shell of the former Oil & Gas Building on the lip of the Central Business District, and serves as one of the city's premier are-you-cool-enough-to-get-in joints. The split-level club sports a European–nightspot vibe of the kind more frequently seen in bigger cities, and stylish dress and superior attitude are required. A charming space with a courtyard and sitting room nestled in a former bank vault, if aloof sophistication is your cup of Red Bull, this is your place.

✔ **d.b.a.** (618 Frenchmen St.; ☎ **504-942-3731;** www.drinkgoodstuff. com) is dedicated to the sale and consumption of quality beer and liquor, as its Web site address makes clear. An offshoot of a popular New York hangout, d.b.a. attracts a diverse mix of status-conscious drinkers to the burgeoning Frenchmen Street restaurant and bar scene. Its spacious, dark wooden interior and extensive beer list are both inviting and comforting. Although it's fairly open, crowds can become hard to navigate during prime weekend hours.

✔ **F&M Patio Bar** (4841 Tchoupitoulas St.; ☎ **504-895-6784**) is a venerable institution among the college and young-working-professional sets. Late night is prime time here, with service-industry types, sorority girls, and on-the-prowl yuppies commingling to chat each other up over a classic rock jukebox. Invariably, some sloshed individual will jump up on the pool table and start dancing, more because it's expected than because it's funny.

✔ As you may guess, red is the primary color of the **Red Room** (2040 St. Charles Ave.; ☎ **504-528-9759**), a modern-day jazz and supper club, which hosts touring swing bands, elegant jazz acts, and, of course, lounge singers. Be prepared to dress up if you're coming here, and if you have a red dress (or a red suit), so much the better. Buzz alert: The cast of *MTV's Real World New Orleans* hung out here a good bit, and Britney Spears has also been spotted a time or two.

✔ The **Sazerac Bar** (in the Fairmont Hotel, 123 Baronne St.; ☎ **504-529-4733**) is frequented by young professionals who come to mingle in the very posh atmosphere. This place was featured in the movie *The Pelican Brief.*

✔ The **Whiskey Bar** (201 St. Charles Ave. in the Central Business District/Warehouse District area; ☎ 504-566-7770) promises a New York–style lounge atmosphere, and the inhabitants delight in dressing up — lots of jackets and short black dresses. The decor is dark and stylish. The doormen really give you the New York experience; they look you over to make sure that you cut the mustard before deciding whether to admit you inside. The black marble bathrooms are neat.

Imbibing History

These special spots offer a little bit of history with your liquor; rumor has it that Andrew Jackson patronized one of them. (See Chapter 18 for more on the history of each of these joints.)

✔ Dating from 1772, **Lafitte's Blacksmith Shop** (941 Bourbon St.; ☎ 504-523-0066) is the oldest building in the Quarter and was reportedly the headquarters of the notorious pirate Jean Lafitte. It looks like it hasn't been touched since his heyday. Agreeably dark (barely candlelit at night), all types of characters frequent the popular hangout.

✔ Another dark and historic place that seems full of schemes — or maybe it's just the low-key lighting — is the **Napoleon House** (500 Chartres St.; ☎ 504-524-9752). If you're the imperial type, have a drink and muse over what the place would've been like if Napoleon had moved in here, as certain New Orleanians allegedly hoped he would.

✔ The **Old Absinthe House** (240 Bourbon St.; ☎ 504-523-3181; www.oldabsinthehouse.com) is supposed to be the place where Andrew Jackson and the Lafitte Brothers plotted their defense of the city in the Battle of New Orleans. William Makepeace Thackeray, Walt Whitman, and Oscar Wilde are also said to have knocked back a few inside these walls. This place is also said to have been a speakeasy during Prohibition, though when it was closed down in the 1940s, its antique fixtures — including the original marble-topped bar — were removed.

Keeping Cool: The Hip Spots

In different ways, the clientele of these spots gives off a certain aura of that indefinable, elusive quality known as "cool." As always, it can be a little difficult to separate the trendsetters from the fashion followers, but they're both here.

✔ **Café Brasil** (2100 Chartres St.; ☎ 504-949-0851) is the epicenter of the Frenchmen Street scene; no telling what you'll find on any given night, including R&B, funk, and even jazz. During Mardi Gras or Jazz Fest, it becomes a whirlwind of activity. The scene often spills out into the street (usually out of sheer necessity when the crowd becomes too large for the dance floor). Cover ranges from $5 to $15 when music is playing.

✔ **The Circle Bar** (1032 St. Charles Ave. at Lee Circle; ☎ 504-588-2616) is an enclave of hipness on the lip of the Warehouse District. It's a small, comfortable space, with easy bartenders and a clientele of musicians, workers, and just plain characters. Music runs toward singer-songwriters and local hard-to-define bands whose followings make getting around difficult — as I said, it's a tiny place.

✔ **The Dungeon** (738 Toulouse St.; ☎ **504-523-5530**) may seem a lot more imposing than it actually is, though it's still more of a habitat for fringe characters than college students or button-down tourists. It's a narrow, two-story hangout with an upstairs dance floor and all sorts of "spooky" decor. A real late-late-night spot, it doesn't open until midnight. Cover is around $3.

✔ **El Matador** (504 Esplanade Ave.; ☎ **504-569-8361**) sits right on Esplanade Avenue at Decatur Street on the site of a former gay/drag bar, whose tiny cabaret-style stage sometimes hosts rock bands. Part of almost every Quarter hipster's nightly itinerary, rock stars and local celebrities make their way here quite often. Cover is $5 to $15 when a live band plays.

✔ **The Shim Sham Club and Juke Joint Lounge** (615 Toulouse St.; ☎ **504-565-5400**) is named after an older French Quarter spot run by jazzman Louis Prima's brother back in the jazz/swing heyday. A smallish bar serves as a kind of anteroom to the performance area in the back, where wing tips, leather jackets, bowling shirts, and retro haircuts are among the fashion accessories. In keeping with its status as an embassy on the fringe, the Shim-Sham hosts bartender/stripper nights, '80s dance nights, and its own burlesque show, as well as occasional live music. Cover varies from $5 to $20.

Hanging Loose: More Casual Bars

Each in their own way, these places are fine for just milling around, talking, and taking in the scenery:

✔ **Le Bon Temps Roule** (4801 Magazine St.; ☎ **504-895-8117**) lets the good times roll by being all things to all people: a neighborhood joint, a college hangout, and (on weekends) a popular music destination (thanks in no small part to the lack of a cover charge).

✔ **Live Bait Bar and Grill** (501 River Rd. in Jefferson; ☎ **504-831-3070;** www.livebaitbarandgrill.com) is exactly what it says it is; a bait shop and neighborhood bar rolled into one. Bands (from locals to comeback-trail '80s hard-rock acts) regularly play in a large converted garage area just off to the side, and older regulars coexist peacefully with drunken college types at the bar. It's a loose, friendly place, even given the fleet of Harleys and other motorcycles often found parked in the vicinity.

✔ The **Rivershack Tavern** (3449 River Rd. in Jefferson; ☎ **504-834-4938**) is a popular drinking place for a pretty diverse cross-section of locals, from college students to bikers to medical professionals (Ochsner Hospital is just down the road), among others. Located on River Road along the Mississippi River, a very short drive from the Parish Line where the road becomes Oak Street, the Rivershack is renowned as "the home of the tacky ashtrays." You can listen to the jukebox and drink at this unpretentious hangout or enjoy occasional live music (mostly blues and rock). The food is a couple of notches above regular bar food; try the burgers, or anything made with alligator.

✔ **The R Bar** (1431 Royal St. in the Faubourg; ☎ 504-948-7499) attracts a mix of Marigny residents, bohemian types, local musicians, and Frenchmen scene stragglers. This place has one of the best vibes in town: slightly sophisticated, but in a low-key, grungy way. The atmosphere is an odd mish-mash of '50s-style decor and stylish neighborhood charm, with a pool table and a couch or two. An on-site inn (see Chapter 8) rents rooms.

✔ A very New Orleans kind of place, **St. Joe's Bar** (5535 Magazine St., Uptown; ☎ 504-899-3744) is a friendly, unpretentious, agreeably dark neighborhood corner bar with intentionally peeled walls and folk-art crosses. This long, narrow spot used to house Ms. Mae's, a popular Uptown hangout. Inside is a well-stocked jukebox and outside is a nice patio for relaxing in the soft Southern air.

✔ **Vic's Kangaroo Café** (636 Tchoupitoulas St.; ☎ 504-524-4329) is a friendly Warehouse District spot with an Australian theme (the phone number spells 524-GDAY) that caters to the after-work crowd; have a shepherd's pie and wash it down with something from an impressive beer selection. Regulars and visitors alike can have a good old time playing games of darts or pool. Vic's also offers some better-than-average local blues and R&B acts (not your French Quarter tourist-trap variety).

Drafting a Good Time: Prime Places for Beer Nuts

A beer-based bar has a special kind of feel, and one who seeks one out is a special kind of person. Here are some key spots with some killer brews:

✔ **Carrollton Station** (8140 Willow St.; ☎ 504-865-9190) is a small, folksy spot that's equal parts neighborhood joint, college hangout, and music venue (on the weekends). Order a draught beer (I recommend anything by Abita), strike up a conversation with the person next to you, and enjoy the gristly parade of New Orleans barflies. Occasional cover charge for music on weekends ranges from $5 to $10.

✔ **Cooter Brown's Tavern** (509 S. Carrollton Ave., Uptown at the Riverbend; ☎ 504-866-9104) features a staggering array of domestic and international beers. You can drink your way around the world, and if you follow a beer-a-night itinerary, you'll be in town for a long, long time. This is a popular hangout for college students, as well as older professionals, service-industry types, musicians — you name it, they're here. Pretty decent bar food is served until reasonably late.

✔ If you want to kick back in an Irish pub, you have some very good options, such as **Kerry Irish Pub** (331 Decatur St.; ☎ 504-527-5954). This establishment not only boasts a good variety of beers and other spirits, but can show you the proper way to pour pints of Guinness and hard cider. A great spot for throwing darts and shooting pool or for catching some live Irish and alternative folk music.

✔ Similarly, **O'Flaherty's Irish Channel Pub** (514 Toulouse St.; ☎ 504-529-1317) is a popular hangout for those with a palette for stout ale and other such spirits, as well as top-notch folk and Celtic music. Together, O'Flaherty's and the Kerry (along with **Ryan's Irish Pub** at 241 Decatur St.; ☎ 504-523-3500) make up what some jokingly refer to as the "Irish Quarter." Cover charge for music is around $5.

Digging for Gold: Hard to Find Gems

These bars are all located a good way off the beaten path, in distant sections of town or tucked away in residential neighborhoods.

✔ The **Hi-Ho Lounge** (2239 St. Claude Ave., between the Quarter and Bywater; ☎ 504-947-9344) is a particularly haphazard assortment of mismatched furniture that *Gambit Weekly* once called "grunge-dom's living room." The Hi-Ho is completely informal, and you'll occasionally hear live music from the fringes (including a group that plays on instruments made of old gas tanks). Legend has it that a friendly ghost hangs about the place. Occasional cover charge for music is $5 to $10.

✔ The **Neutral Ground Coffeehouse** (5110 Danneel St.; ☎ 504-891-3381; www.neutralground.org) is an amiable throwback to the coffeehouses of the 1960s. Volunteers run it, it has no cover charge, and it feels kind of like a college-dorm common room. Acoustic and folk performers are on hand most nights, and Sundays feature an open-mike night where anyone can join in.

✔ You've got to see this place to believe it. The **Saturn Bar** (3067 St. Claude Ave. in Bywater; ☎ 504-949-7532) offers a compelling down-and-dirty experience, populated by veteran barflies and slumming celebrities alike. The crumbling booths and utterly random decor (counters stacked with paper, a life-sized mummy, and so on) provide the backdrop for an assortment of characters who come for the renegade ambiance and the cheap drinks.

✔ **Snake & Jake's Xmas Club Lounge** (7612 Oak St.; ☎ 504-861-2802) is a petite, dimly lit dive, tucked into a residential neighborhood in a seedier part of Uptown's college area. The name comes from the Christmas wreath that hangs above the shack's front door year-round. The vibe is pretty laid-back (especially if you sink into one of the couches in front), and when I say dimly lit, what I really mean is dark. I've seen someone actually doze off here because of the dark, cozy environment (though imbibing lots of alcohol was probably a contributing factor, as well).

✔ **Vaughn's Lounge** (800 Lesseps St.; ☎ 504-947-5562) is a homey little place tucked into the residential Bywater neighborhood. The down-home atmosphere is charming, especially if you're lucky enough to be here when local trumpet player Kermit Ruffins (a modern-day Louis Armstrong) is playing (most Thursday nights, when he's in town); more than likely, he'll be cooking up some barbecue on a grill before the show. Be sure to take a cab; parts of this neighborhood can be rough going. Cover is $10 on Thursday nights.

Playing Your Song: Piano Bars

Piano bars are everywhere in New Orleans, popping up from hotel lobbies to tourist magnets such as Pat O'Brien's. Here are just a few of the choicest establishments:

✔ One of the most popular piano spots in town is the **Carousel Bar & Lounge** (214 Royal St., in the Hotel Montelone; ☎ 504-523-3341). The bar is literally a revolving carousel, so watch your step no matter how little you've had to drink. Catch some great piano music Tuesdays through Saturdays.

✔ The **Bombay Club** (830 Conti St., in the Prince Conti Hotel; ☎ 504-586-0972) offers not only live piano jazz Wednesdays through Saturdays but also world-famous martinis (often voted best in the city by the readers of *Gambit Weekly*).

✔ **Feelings** (2600 Chartres St. at Franklin Ave. in the Faubourg; ☎ 504-945-2222; www.feelingscafe.com) is a friendly, funky, low-key neighborhood restaurant in the Faubourg Marigny. People tend to gather in the classic New Orleans courtyard, unless they're inside singing along with the piano player.

✔ **Pat O'Brien's** (718 St. Peter St.; ☎ 504-525-4823; www.patobriens.com) is a popular tourist attraction in the heart of the French Quarter. Despite that (or maybe because of it), it can be a good place to get a look at the teeming masses of humanity. And quite a few members of the teeming masses will be drinking a *Hurricane*, the world-famous gigantic rum drink served in Hurricane lamp-style glasses. On weekends, tourists and college types often pack this place with more human flesh per square inch than you would imagine is possible, and sometimes the line outside stretches down the street, which is a bit of a mystery. The popularity of "Pat O's" has more to do with savvy marketing, I think, than anything else (though two indoor bars and an expansive patio/courtyard area with a nifty flaming fountain probably have something to do with it).

Dancing the Night Away

New Orleans features lots of places to go if you just want to shake your moneymaker.

- ✔ At the **Cat's Meow** (701 Bourbon St.; ☎ **504-523-2788**; www.catsmeow-neworleans.com), you can listen to popular rock songs all night long, or sing them yourself — karaoke is available if you've got the guts to make a fool out of yourself. Cover charge is $5 for those under 21; free for those over 21.

- ✔ **The Gold Mine** (701 Dauphine St.; ☎ **504-586-0745**) is a popular spot for college-age kids, who congregate here and dance all night long to the latest hits. If that's not your thing, you'd be more comfortable somewhere else. If you stay, try the flaming Dr. Pepper shot. Only open Friday and Saturday nights; $2 cover charge.

- ✔ **Razzoo** (511 Bourbon St.; ☎ **504-522-5100**) is another popular spot for the young dancing set; high-energy hits and dance mixes are the norm here. Mix it up on the dance floor, and then take a breather out on the patio, where you can watch everyone else dance and delude yourself into thinking that you don't look nearly as foolish on the floor as they do.

Frequenting the Best Gay Bars and Clubs

Word has it that the **Bourbon Pub and Parade Disco** (801 Bourbon St.; ☎ **504-529-2107**) is one of the largest gay nightclubs in the country. Downstairs is the Bourbon Pub, a 24-hour establishment with a video bar. The disco upstairs opens at 9 p.m.; a $5 to $10 cover is charged on weekends. Following are a few other spots worth exploring:

- ✔ A legendary spot in the gay community, **Café Lafitte in Exile** (901 Bourbon St.; ☎ **504-522-8397**; www.lafittes.com) was opened by Tom Caplinger, who used to run Lafitte's Blacksmith Shop. Reluctant to leave the original place behind, he brought friends and patrons (including Tennessee Williams) with him when he opened this place. Open 24 hours, this bar is usually crowded.

- ✔ **The Golden Lantern** (1239 Royal St.; ☎ **504-529-2860**) is a nice neighborhood spot where the bartender knows the patrons by name.

- ✔ **Good Friends Bar** (740 Dauphine St.; ☎ **504-566-7191;** www.good friendsbar.com) is a neighborhood type of place with a lot of atmosphere and a piano in the corner that invites karaoke-style misuse.

- ✔ The 24-hour **Le Roundup** (819 St. Louis St.; ☎ **504-561-8340**) has a friendly atmoshopere; so friendly, it attracts the most diverse crowd around. Occasional small covers for entertainment/revue-type shows.

- ✔ The hot dance spot **Oz** (800 Bourbon St.; ☎ **877-599-8200** or 504-592-8200; www.ozneworleans.com) is recognized both locally and nationally as a place to see and be seen. *Gambit Weekly* ranked it as the city's #1 dance club, and *Details* magazine ranked it as one of the top 50 clubs in the country. Cover is $3 on Wednesday and Sunday nights; $10, Friday and Saturday nights ($5 discount for gay males).

- ✔ Don't miss **The Rawhide** (740 Burgundy St.; ☎ **504-525-8106;** www.rawhide2010.com) if denim and leather make your scene. During Mardi Gras, this place hosts the best costume contest in town. Cover is $5 Thursday through Sunday nights.

Chapter 25

New Orleans's Cultural Scene

*H*istorically, New Orleans has enjoyed status as a small but thriving center for the performing arts; at one time, it boasted what may have been the continent's first opera house. Of course, the city hasn't seen the likes of that heady heyday in decades, due to its size and fluctuations in the local economy. That dry spell is over, but in truth, the theater and performing arts scene in New Orleans is still relatively small compared to similarly sized cities. Nonetheless, you can find most of the same options as in a larger city, though in smaller portions.

Finding Out What's Going On — and Getting Tickets for It

The *Times-Picayune* (in its weekly **Lagniappe** entertainment section) and *Gambit Weekly* are good places to look for listings, reviews, and previews of major arts events. If you're looking for information before you arrive, try their Web sites: www.nola.com and www.bestofnew orleans.com, respectively. Other sources are the local CitySearch site (http://neworleans.citysearch.com) and Inside New Orleans (www.insideneworleans.com).

A great spot to find out what's happening is www.culturefinder.com, a site with information on arts venues in a variety of cities. Select "New Orleans" from the menu of cities available; you'll be directed to a page with a search tool for arts events by date and a list of featured organizations and venues, with upcoming or ongoing events for that locale, along with contact information.

New Orleans doesn't have a ticket broker such as New York's TKTS, because it doesn't need one. Tickets to most local productions are easily available through the venue's box office, and most of the larger spaces (such as the Saenger, the Orpheum, and the Contemporary Arts Center) take credit cards; they'll also usually offer tickets via **Ticketmaster** (☎ 504-522-5555). Smaller theaters accept cash only (though Southern Rep and NORD accept local checks) at the door the night of the show. For a popular event, such as an opera production or a Broadway touring company, it's a good idea to call the box office or Ticketmaster as far in advance as possible. Even for smaller events, it wouldn't hurt to call in advance, or ask your hotel concierge (assuming your hotel has one) to find out about acquiring tickets for you.

Playing It Up: Theater

New Orleans actually boasts a very good theater scene, a small and vibrant community that makes up in passion, creativity, and (most importantly) quality what it lacks in size. Not only is it *possible* to spend practically every night of your visit taking in a play or a musical, but also the quality of the city's theater scene is such that you'd be well rewarded by such an undertaking. Though no heir apparent to Tennessee Williams is waiting in the wings to usher the city into a glorious new age of theater, theater in New Orleans is much more than touring companies of national productions and amateur dinner theater (though you'll find plenty of both).

Getting the inside scoop on theater

But what's hot right now? Well, as you can expect, national tours of big-name productions are always popular; whenever you come, the Saenger Theatre on Canal Street will, likely as not, have a company of *Rent, Fame,* or *The Lion King* (or whatever's currently popular) onstage for a small stay. Also, local classics, such as anything written by Williams, are a good bet.

But the most intriguing development in New Orleans theater lately is cabaret. Not the musical or the stage show, but the art form popularized by those entertainments. It's a natural fit for New Orleans, given the city's rich French background, but until very recently cabaret's presence has been pretty small and largely limited to the Quarter. Oddly enough, though the number of cabaret spots (one once-popular spot is now the **Shim-Sham Club,** a tattoos-and-piercings music club) seems to be dwindling, the goings-on at **le chat noir** are capturing the public's attention on a larger scale.

No matter what you're looking for, however, the odds are better than good that New Orleans will have it (or a close approximation). Without further ado, the following lists the more prominent theater spaces in the city:

- ✔ One of the city's major hubs for the arts, **Contemporary Arts Center** (900 Camp St. in the Warehouse District; ☎ **504-528-3800;** www.cacno.org) features exhibits of contemporary art (of course), and also hosts some small productions in its intimate performance spaces. You'll find experimental works by local playwrights, as well as the occasional comedy and musical (concerts, dance productions, and film screenings also take place here). The rooms are small enough that no seat is really bad. A cyber-cafe is also on the premises: Cybercafe @ the CAC. The CAC itself has no dress code, though the promoters/producers of specific shows or events may impose one.

- ✔ A relatively recent addition to the local scene, **le chat noir** (715 St. Charles Ave. in the Central Business District; ☎ **504-581-5812;** www.cabaretlechatnoir.com) is one of the hippest and hottest spots in the city. The intimate (135-seat) space lends itself to give-and-take exchanges between audience and performers. Typical fare may include a one-woman (or man) show of the life and songs of French chanteuse Edith Piaf, a performance art piece with audience participation, or a set by a singer or local jazz band. Stick around after the show; the piano bar on Saturday nights has been compared favorably to the edgy, unpredictable vibe of Parisian cabaret. Attire runs more to the semi-formal end of the spectrum.

- ✔ A long-running kid-friendly theater, **Le Petit Theatre du Vieux Carre** (616 St. Peter St. in the French Quarter; ☎ **504-522-2081**) produces three children's shows every season and is home to one of the oldest nonprofessional theater troupes in the country. The main performance stage, open from September to June, generally presents well-chosen plays and musicals. A smaller performance space sports edgier, experimental fare from local writers.

- ✔ **NORD Theater** (705 Lafayette St., in Gallier Hall, one block from Poydras Street in the Central Business District; ☎ **504-565-7860**), a long-running arm of the New Orleans Recreation Department, is primarily a vehicle for local children, though the productions and target audience aren't limited to children. The summer production is usually kid-oriented, while the fall one is a better bet for adults. The theater stages four productions a year, mostly musicals — Broadway, off-Broadway, or original. This comfortable, intimate theater (seating capacity is 120) has plenty of legroom, and no dress code.

- ✔ The venerable **Saenger Theatre** (143 N. Rampart St; ☎ **504-525-1052;** www.saengertheatre.com) opened in 1927, and restoration efforts managed to retain some of its original elegance. The decor is Florentine Renaissance, with Greek and Roman sculpture, fine marble statues, and cut-glass chandeliers. The ceiling looks like a night sky, with realistic clouds and stars. Against this backdrop, locals enjoy touring theater productions (some presented by the theater's Broadway Series) and popular music concerts, from Neil Young to "Weird" Al Yankovich.

- ✔ **Southern Rep Theatre** (Canal Place Shopping Center; ☎ 504-522-6545; www.southernrep.com) focuses on Southern playwrights and actors, and benefits from a convenient location on the lip of the Quarter at Canal Street; plenty of validated parking is in the shopping center's spacious, multilevel garage. The pace slows down in summer, but it does have children's programs. Performance space is intimate, but comfortable, as befits its high-rise digs; the atmosphere (and dress code) is casual.

- ✔ **True Brew Coffee House and Theater** (200 Julia St. in the Warehouse District; ☎ 504-524-8440) seats around 100 people in relative comfort, with the added benefit of coffees, teas, and pastries. Productions include one-act plays, some filled with local references and in-jokes that won't mean much to visitors. Comedy and live music are also regular offerings.

- ✔ **Zeitgeist Multi-Disciplinary Arts Center** (1724 Oretha Castle Haley Blvd.; ☎ 504-525-2767; www.zeitgeistinc.org) is sort of a complement to, and opposite of, the Contemporary Arts Center. The bill of fare is left-of-center all the way, from performance art to edgy original plays and independent films; everything from Andy Warhol to Leni Riefenstahl to original works on growing up homosexual in New Orleans.

Dressing for the theater

In keeping with its status as a casual, tourist-friendly city, New Orleans is pretty lax about dress codes. Exceptions exist, of course, but you can generally use the production or the venue as a guidepost. If you're attending part of the Saenger's Broadway series, for example, you can get by with a basic business-casual look. At le chat noir, which aspires to a hip atmosphere where dressing up is half the fun, a semi-formal approach is required. But after that, it's fair game. Obviously, attending a local production at True Brew isn't going to require that you be dressed to the nines, and local theaters such as Le Petit or Southern Rep don't pose strict requirements, either.

Dining before (and after) the show

The depth and breadth of the New Orleans dining scene (see Part IV) guarantees that you'll have no trouble making an evening of dining and theater in New Orleans. And if you're lucky, you can find a restaurant that matches the mood and feel of the play, musical, or piece you're going to see. A playbill for a touring show at the Saenger Theatre, for example, will likely include ads placed by the **Palace Café** (see Chapter 14), **Dominique's** (in the **Maison Dupuy** hotel, 1001 Toulouse St.,

☎ **504-522-8800**), or the **Veranda** restaurant (inside the **Hotel Inter-Continental,** 444 St. Charles Ave., ☎ **504-585-4383**). If you want to mingle, head to the **Sazerac** bar in the Fairmont Hotel (see Chapter 24) to see and be seen by some of the city's elite. All these spots are a fine start (or finish) to an evening at the elegant Saenger.

On your way to or from Southern Rep, a host of French Quarter choices are nearby, from the classic seafood fare of **Red Fish Grill** to the bistro elegance of **Mr. B's** (both Brennan family establishments; see Chapter 14). If you're looking for something earthier, but still retaining a Southern feel, try one of the handsomely overstuffed oyster po' boys at **Acme Oyster House** (see Chapter 15). Or if you still want the familiarity of the Brennan name, dig into a juicy ribeye at **Dickie Brennan's Steakhouse** (716 Iberville St., ☎ **504-522-2467;** reservations suggested). For a performance at Le Petit, the nearby **Bistro at Maison de Ville** is a favorite of theater patrons and performers; the elegant **Court of Two Sisters** is also a good spot (see Chapter 14 for both). To satisfy your post-theater munchies, head down St. Peter to Dumaine and plop yourself down at the **Clover Grill,** the "happiest grill on earth" (see Chapter 15).

In the Central Business District, the family-friendly **Bon Ton Café** (401 Magazine St.; ☎ **504-524-3386**) is the perfect complement to an evening at NORD Theater. Nothing nearby mirrors the unique Parisian cabaret experience at le chat noir, though **Mike Ditka's New Orleans** (just across the street) and **Mother's** both provide some amusing contrast (see Chapter 14 for both). Closer in spirit, the **Veranda** (see earlier in this chapter) and **Palace Café** (see Chapter 14) are a straight shot down St. Charles Avenue.

Supporting the Performing Arts

Despite its randy reputation, New Orleans's arts scene doesn't scrimp on the classics, offering fine symphony and opera companies, as well as stand-out ballet troupes. Most performances by these organizations take place at venues discussed in the "Performing arts venues" sidebar at the end of this chapter.

Hearing the symphony

The **Louisiana Philharmonic Orchestra** (☎ **504-523-6530;** www.lpo music.com) grew out of the ashes of the now defunct New Orleans Symphony. The most popular program is *Beethoven and Blue Jeans,* which relaxes the formal dress code in a successful attempt to introduce classical music to a wider audience. The season runs from September through May. Tickets range from $11 to $54; prices are higher for special events.

Eyeing the opera

The **New Orleans Opera Association** (☎ 800-881-4459 or 504-529-3000; www.neworleansopera.org) has been around since 1943, providing local opera buffs with a steady diet of classic performances each season. The company is talented and professional; this isn't the local amateur hour. Often, the association features a star performer from, say, the Metropolitan Opera Company, with local talents in supporting roles.

Keeping on your toes: Ballet

The **Delta Festival Ballet** is a local company comprised primarily of area talent that performs a seasonal schedule, including a popular annual production of **The Nutcracker** at Christmastime. Call ☎ 504-836-7166 for performance calendar, ticket prices, and other information. The **New Orleans Ballet Association,** despite its name, is not a local company. Instead, it presents a schedule of touring shows. The season generally runs from September to June. Tickets are available through Ticketmaster (☎ 504-522-5555) or through the Association box office (☎ 504-522-0996); tickets range from $15 to $70, and can increase for special events.

Performing arts venues

Unless otherwise noted, most of the events put on by the arts organizations in this chapter occur at one of the places listed here (all of which are wheelchair accessible). Tickets for these venues can generally be purchased at their box office or through Ticketmaster (☎ 504-522-5555). Keep in mind that unless you receive specific information to the contrary, appropriate dress for these venues is business dress or black-tie formal:

✔ **The Orpheum Theater** (129 University Pl. in the Central Business District; ☎ 504-524-3285) houses the Louisiana Philharmonic Orchestra. Other productions, and the occasional rock or pop concert, may also end up here.

✔ **The Mahalia Jackson Theatre of the Performing Arts** (801 N. Rampart St.; ☎ 504-565-8081) is the favored venue for touring musical shows, as well as the home of local opera and ballet performances. It sits inside the 32-acre New Orleans Cultural Center complex in Armstrong Park.

✔ **New Orleans Municipal Auditorium** (1201 St. Peter St.; ☎ 504-565-7490) was once the premier venue for concerts and events. It still hosts the occasional touring show, and often plays host to the Jazz and Heritage Festival's nighttime concert series. The auditorium is located inside the New Orleans Cultural Center in Armstrong Park, across a walkway from the Mahalia Jackson Theater of the Performing Arts.

Part VII
The Part of Tens

The 5th Wave   By Rich Tennant

IN THE ABSENCE OF ANY ALLIGATORS, GRIZZLED CAJUN "SWAMP RAT" LAFITTE WOULD OFTEN WRESTLE AN IBIS FOR CURIOUS TOURISTS

In this part . . .

As complex as its history and culture can be, New Orleans can also be a city of quick answers and easy solutions. At least, that's what these chapters attempt to provide. If you're looking for some authentically decadent New Orleans experiences or want the rundown on tourist spots worth your while, this part is your one-stop answer shop.

Chapter 26

Ten Sinful (But Legal) Experiences

Quick! Think "New Orleans" and "debauchery," and what's the first thing that comes to mind? Most likely your answer is Mardi Gras, or maybe Bourbon Street. Am I right? Well, sure, those two are the twin pinnacles of Crescent City decadence, and no travel guide would be complete without them. But they're far from the only things the Big Easy has to offer by way of a walk on the wild side. In this chapter, I run down ten experiences that engage one or more of the senses in one wicked way or another, from can't-miss music to scandalously rich gastronomic delights.

Gulping Gin from a "Go-Cup"

Barhopping in New Orleans is a marathon undertaking to begin with, but it'd be much longer and less fun without these handy timesaving measures. The city's permissive liquor laws allow bar patrons to leave the premises with their unfinished drink in hand — provided it's poured into a plastic cup, known as a *go-cup*. This lets drinkers leave at their leisure, without having to worry about finishing their drink in a hurry. You shouldn't be holding one in your hand if the car you're riding in gets pulled over — and I don't have to tell you to forget about driving with one, right? But if you're walking down Bourbon Street — or any street, for that matter — and want to savor your brew (hopefully one locally made; try a Dixie or an Abita) or just stand still for awhile to soak up the atmosphere, these cups are a godsend.

Delighting in Drive-Thru Daiquiris

It just makes a perverse kind of sense that the city that lets you walk around with liquor in your hand would let you drive around with it, too. Let's be clear: I'm certainly not advocating drinking and driving, and the city does have — and enforce — an "open container" law that prohibits imbibing while behind the wheel. But that said, ordering a daiquiri from the comfort of your car (as you can do at **New Orleans Original Daiquiris,** 3301 Veterans Blvd. in Metairie, ☎ **504-837-8474**) is a staple of suburban nightlife, and quite the "Am I really getting away with this?" experience for first-timers.

It may not be quite as much fun, but you can also grab daiquiris at walk-up windows throughout the city, including New Orleans Original Daiquiris locations in Mid-City (301 N. Carrollton Ave.) and on (where else?) Bourbon Street (633 Bourbon).

Succumbing to a Liuzza's Po' Boy

Sure, New Orleans has countless variations of this popular sandwich, most of them notable, at every po' boy shop in town. But this particular po' boy — served at **Liuzza's by the Track** (1518 N. Lopez St., ☎ **504-943-8667**), a neighborhood hangout within walking distance of the New Orleans Fair Grounds — is as rich a treat as you can legally consume. "Buttery" doesn't begin to describe its all-out assault on the taste buds, a pound-your-fist-on-the-table sensation if ever there was one. Try it and dare to prove me wrong.

Grooving at the Maple Leaf

Most Tuesday nights when it's not on the road, the ReBirth Brass Band makes the **Maple Leaf** (see Chapter 23) its home for a down-and-dirty whistle-stop tour of modern brass that's become an ingrained local tradition. College students (lots of them), tourists, and all-around music lovers stand shoulder to shoulder in this unassuming nightspot as the band conducts a raucous, sweaty, and propulsive dance workout. ReBirth is New Orleans's premier purveyor of "modern brass," mixing pop, funk, hip-hop, and gospel elements into the traditional brass band sound. The band's bawdy grooves and precision swagger are infectious, and a show at the Maple Leaf is a case study in jubilant musical abandon.

Trying Your Luck with a Lucky Dog

Popularized by John Kennedy Toole's classic novel, *A Confederacy of Dunces,* these high-cholesterol hot dogs are a junk-food staple in the

French Quarter. In fact, distinctive hot-dog-shaped Lucky Dog carts (each over 600 pounds!) are about as common a sight in the Quarter as drunken sailors, even late at night (when they're a godsend to stumbling drunks looking for a quick grease fix). Taste-wise, the mustard-heavy, calorie-laden Dog is a couple of steps above your normal hot dog. Though it also brings you a couple of steps closer to cardiac arrest, legions of French Quarter denizens swear that the taste is worth it.

Rolling the Bones

As seen in television and movies, the idea of a riverboat casino holds a certain Mark Twain kind of romance. The reality may not be quite as romantic, but it's an increasingly popular way for locals and tourists to willingly part with large amounts of their cash. Truth be told, not a lot of river can be seen on a riverboat casino, and not just because it doesn't have windows. Most riverboats are loathe to leave their berths (which is a sin in itself), for fear of driving away customers who want to be able to come and go at will rather than be stuck, you know, enjoying the sights, sounds, and spray of a riverboat cruise. Still, despite the lack of nautical atmosphere, riverboat casinos (see Chapter 18) combine modern-day avarice with the idyllic sheen of yesteryear, which is a hard combination to beat.

Drinking at Pat O'Brien's

Pat O'Brien's (see Chapter 24) is one of New Orleans's most popular bars, due in no small part to its signature drink, the Hurricane. Named for the glass it comes in (its shape resembles a hurricane lamp), this fruity concoction originated during World War II, when rum was so widely available that liquor distributors pushed it heavily and retailers had to find a way to use it all. The Hurricane is a potent little cocktail, but its true popularity likely derives as much from the souvenir glass it comes in — which, in case you're interested, has at least one use once you're finished with the drink: According to the bar's Web site, a Hurricane glass is said to hold exactly $10 in pennies.

Surrendering to Your Slothful Side

New Orleans's signature phrase is *"Let* the good times roll" (note the passive voice) for a reason: The city's atmosphere is perfectly suited for indolent lounging, whiling away the hours in as lazy a fashion as you can muster. From a leisurely breakfast of beignets and café au lait at **Café du Monde** (see Chapter 15) to a relaxed **carriage ride** around the Quarter (Chapter 19) to an unhurried afternoon sipping a Pimm's Cup at **Napoleon House** (Chapter 24), you can easily make a day out of doing next to nothing. And an evening, too: Idling at **Lafitte's Blacksmith Shop**

or nursing an anisette at **Old Absinthe House** (Chapter 24 again) is a perfect way to wind down after a hard day of, well, hardly moving. And if you're lucky enough to be staying at a swank hotel like **W French Quarter,** the **Ritz-Carlton,** or the **Windsor Court** (Chapter 8), all the better — it's possible (if not necessarily advisable) to spend a whole day lounging and being pampered without ever leaving the premises.

Meeting Creatures of the Night

New Orleans does enjoy a certain supernatural reputation, and some establishments (such as the **Hi-Ho Lounge** or **Hotel Provincial**) still claim to play host to spirits. But spending the night in a particular hotel or bar, waiting for a ghost to come to you, can be a frustrating endeavor, especially when you can be proactive and track down the specters yourself! Outfits such as **Haunted History Tours** and **Magic Walking Tours** (see Chapter 19) offer a variety of walking tours that are themed around ghosts, vampires, and cemeteries. The Cemetery/ Voodoo Tour offered by **Historic New Orleans Walking Tours** (again, Chapter 19) allows you to take in the tomb of famed voodoo priestess Marie Laveau and an actual voodoo temple, and **the New Orleans Historic Voodoo Museum** (Chapter 17) offers a voodoo tour as well.

Speaking of vampires, New Orleans's own Queen of the Damned, vampire novelist **Anne Rice,** used to allow tours of historical landmark **St. Elizabeth's** (at press time, Rice had put the former Napoleon Avenue orphanage up for sale). But fans can still get their fill of all things Rice (including, if they're lucky, autographed books, first editions, and other rarities) at the **Garden District Book Shop** (see Chapter 20). And if those options don't satisfy your need for spookiness, just wander into **The Dungeon** (see Chapter 24) or wander along reliable old **Bourbon Street** — you're sure to run into someone (or something) other-worldly before too long.

Suffering Through Saints Games

Yes, Saints games — the way New Orleans's long-suffering fans have to suffer through the team's tumultuous ups and downs is indeed a sin. Here's hoping that by the time you read this, the Saints saga is once again on the upswing of its never-ending roller-coaster ride.

Chapter 27

Ten (or so) Tourist Traps That Really Aren't

*O*ne of the most charming aspects of New Orleans is that even the parts that look contrived and maybe a little cheesy happen to be historic and authentic. If you think a museum dedicated to voodoo may seem a little touristy, well, certainly it is. But in New Orleans, it's also fun, informative, and based on historical fact. The following places and events may seem like tourist traps, but they are actually spots to soak up some authentic local history and character.

The French Quarter

What makes the French Quarter stand out is that it's a functioning neighborhood. Real people live, work, and play within its relatively small confines, acting out the historical dramas of their own lives among the museums, attractions, historic buildings, and walking tours. Legend and latter-day reality co-exist here — you may be sitting in a bar once patronized by a major historical figure, next to a self-exiled poet or a pierced and tattooed junior executive with a cellphone and laptop. What can be more real than that?

Bourbon Street

Some of the places you encounter in New Orleans will definitely reek of exploitation, lowest-common-denominator pandering, and commercial opportunism (some will also just reek, but that's another story). And Bourbon Street — the gaudy, tawdry, and tacky thoroughfare that most every visitor knows by name before arriving in New Orleans — is the prime example of this kind of commercialism. Filled with touristy establishments, flesh pots, fast food joints, and souvenir shops, not to mention street performers, hustlers, and scam artists all competing for your spare change, Bourbon Street is unquestionably a monument to the fine art of separating gullible visitors from their money.

Still, Bourbon Street offers more than just opportunism. As cheap, plastic, and gamy as Bourbon Street can be, it can also be oddly exhilarating. Walking along Bourbon Street at night definitely gets the adrenaline going, as you're caught in a current of exploring pedestrians, navigating throngs of tourists, locals, teens, drag queens, scam artists, and performers. Your actions happen in sync to a rich soundtrack of jazz, blues, Cajun, Celtic, and rock that blare out of every open doorway. The seedy spectacle — strip clubs, 24-hour bars, and alcohol in the streets — can be intoxicating.

Preservation Hall

Distinguishing the charms of this unassuming hideaway (see Chapter 23) may be difficult at first glance. This nondescript, bombed-out shell of a building is small, crowded, and not air-conditioned, with no seats, no drinks, and no good sight lines. Tourists are herded in, subjected to some traditional Dixieland jazz, and left to their own devices. But you'll likely be too busy enjoying the music to notice, or care about, the lack of creature comforts. Dixieland jazz is often derided as watered-down jazz for tourists, but in the talented hands of the **Preservation Hall Jazz Band,** it becomes so much more. It's a raucous, stately, elegant, and down-and-dirty musical celebration. So pay the cover, shuffle your way inside, and ignore the no-frills surroundings of this quintessential New Orleans experience.

New Orleans Historic Voodoo Museum

Surely, if a tourist trap exists in New Orleans, it must be a voodoo museum, right? Well, maybe. To be fair, the museum (now with two locations) *is* largely designed with tourists in mind, and some of the town's hard-core voodoo practitioners look down upon it with disdain — after all, would a *real* voodoo landmark have its own Web site (www.voodoo museum.com)? The museum is fun, in a campy sort of way. Best of all, despite a few stereotypical angles (after all, you can buy a voodoo doll), the museum strives to distinguish fact from fiction.

Mardi Gras

Why Mardi Gras, the greatest, largest free party on earth? Simple. To many people, Mardi Gras is just that: one very long excuse to act rowdy, cavort in the street, and generally make fools of themselves. In that way, it's no different from spring break at the beach. But if you take the trouble to learn the lore behind the show, you'll find a fascinating tradition, complete with pageantry, spectacle, and history galore, that has its roots in the city's large Catholic population. Definitely, the **Mardi Gras Indians** and the **Zulu** parade are two unique experiences, rich with their own histories and largely unknown to the outside world. Whereas spring break is nothing more than a giant excuse for a party, Mardi Gras is a party with a past and a purpose — a bacchanal with tradition.

Lafitte's Blacksmith Shop and Old Absinthe House

The story goes that **Lafitte's,** an actual blacksmith shop run by the legendary pirate Jean Lafitte and his brother, was a front for the duo's illegal enterprises (including, allegedly, the movement of slaves). This may or may not be true, as with the popular rumor that the Lafitte Brothers and Andrew Jackson plotted the defense of the city during the Battle of New Orleans at the **Old Absinthe House.** In any other city, such claims would be dubious at best. But in New Orleans, whether these stories are true is actually beside the point. The beautiful thing is that they very well *could* be true. And these places are legitimate local hangouts as well, independent of the stories attached to them.

Congo Square

If you drive by **Armstrong Park** today, you may not even see this historical area, where both voodoo and the early rhythms of jazz flourished and grew during the oppressive days of slavery. Congo Square was a meeting and gathering place for local slaves as a result of Napoleonic Law, which mandated that slave owners give their servants Sundays off and provide them with a place to socialize. An uncharacteristically humane impulse in the sordid history of slavery, the law had a completely unintended effect. The congregated slaves used the square for voodoo ceremonies (the religion flourished here as a result) and performed drumming rituals as well, keeping alive the rhythms of their lost homes. Over time, other regional forms, such as work songs, blues, and spirituals, were thrown into the mix. In short, both jazz and voodoo made inroads into the United States from this very parcel of land. And in how many other parks in major U.S. cities can you make such a claim?

Riverboat Cruises and Swamp Tours

Although these two popular draws *are* different, I've grouped them together because of their similarities: They both require water, and they both can seem really corny to the casual eye. Riverboat cruises, especially, come with a very high cheese factor. The very term conjures images of crews in period costumes, hamming up the Mark Twain angle and pointing out attractions on both riverbanks, which, of course, are too far away to make out clearly.

Cruises do consist of quickie jaunts on a brief section of the Mississippi River, but some riverboat cruises actually are worth taking. If you're at the **Aquarium of the Americas,** for example, a cruise on the stern-wheeler *John James Audubon* (see Chapter 17) can be a fun way to ride over to the aquarium's sister attraction, the **Audubon Zoo.** The paddle wheeler *Creole Queen* (see Chapters 19 and 21) is another fun ride, with a stop at **Chalmette Battlefield National Park** for extra educational value.

Swamp tours also come with a built-in eye-rolling factor — but only until you've actually gone on one. Swamp tours *are* fascinating. You can ride in a glass-bottomed boat, or a smaller, wooden affair, through breathtaking surroundings. You'll see lush tropical vegetation and maybe glimpse an alligator or two as you glide serenely through marshes and bayous.

Appendix

Quick Concierge

∙∙∙

Sometimes when you need information, you need it now, and you can't afford to spend valuable time flipping through chapter after chapter trying to find what you're looking for. That's where the Quick Concierge comes in: Whether you need help changing a flat, finding an Internet cafe, calling an airline, or figuring out Louisiana's minimum drinking age, the pertinent addresses, phone numbers, Web sites, and facts are listed below, from 911 emergency services to general business hours.

Fast Facts: New Orleans

AAA

For road service, call ☎ 800-222-4357 or 504-367-4095.

Ambulance

Call ☎ **911** for emergency ambulance service.

American Express

The American Express office (☎ 504-586-8201) is located at 201 St. Charles Ave. in the Central Business District. It's open Monday to Friday from 9 a.m. to 5 p.m. For cardholder services, call ☎ 800-528-4800; for lost or stolen traveler's checks, call ☎ 800-221-7282.

Area Codes

The area code for the greater New Orleans metropolitan area is 504, though a new area code (985) has recently been added to areas along the North Shore, the region north of the city, across Lake Pontchartrain, which includes Slidell, Covington, and Mandeville.

ATMs

Automatic teller machines are as ubiquitous in New Orleans as they likely are in your hometown. The 800 numbers for the major ATM networks are: ☎ 800-424-7787 (800-4CIRRUS) for Cirrus and ☎ 800-843-7587 for Plus.

Among the more convenient ATM locations in the French Quarter are the following: corner of Chartres and St. Ann; 400 block of Chartres near K-Paul's restaurant; corner of Chartres and Toulouse; corner of Royal and Iberville; and 240 Royal St.

Baby-sitters

Ask your hotel or call one of the following agencies for sitting services: Accents on Children's Arrangements, ☎ 504-524-1227 or Dependable Kid Care, ☎ 504-486-4001.

Business Hours

On the whole, most shops and stores are open from 10:00 a.m. to 6:00 p.m. Banks open at 9:00 a.m. and close between 3:00 p.m. and 5:00 p.m.

Camera Repair

Try AAA Camera Repair, 1631 St. Charles Ave. (☎ 504-561-5822).

Convention Center

Ernest M. Morial Convention Center, 900 Convention Center Blvd., New Orleans, LA 70130, ☎ 504-582-3000. Convention Center Blvd. sits at the end of the Warehouse District, on the river between Thalia and Water streets; the Vieux Carre bus drops you off right in front.

Credit Cards

Information numbers for American Express are listed earlier in this section (see "American Express"). MasterCard's general information number is ☎ 800-307-7309. For Visa, call ☎ 800-847-2911.

Customs

To reach the New Orleans office of the U.S. Customs Service, call ☎ 504-670-2206.

Dentists

Contact the New Orleans Dental Association (☎ 504-834-6449; www.nodc.org/noda.htm) to find a reliable dentist near you.

Doctors

If you're in need of a doctor, call one of the following: Orleans Parish Medical Society, ☎ 504-523-2474; Tulane Medical Clinic, ☎ 504-588-5800; Children's Hospital, ☎ 504-899-9511.

Emergencies

For fire, police, and ambulance call ☎ 911.

For the Poison Control Center, call ☎ 800-256-9822.

The Travelers Aid Society (846 Baronne St., ☎ 504-525-8726) also renders emergency aid to travelers in need. For help regarding a missing or lost child, call Child Find at ☎ 800-IAM-LOST (426-5678).

Hospitals

Should you become ill during your visit, most major hospitals have staff doctors on call 24 hours a day. If a doctor is not available in your hotel or guesthouse, call or go to the emergency room at Ochsner Medical Institutions, 1516 Jefferson Highway (☎ 504-842-3460), or the Tulane University Medical Center, 1415 Tulane Ave. (☎ 504-588-5800).

Hotlines

YWCA Rape Crisis is ☎ 504-483-8888; Travelers Aid Society is ☎ 504-525-8726; Gamblers Anonymous is ☎ 504-431-7867; Narcotics Anonymous is ☎ 504-899-6262; Alcoholics Anonymous is ☎ 504-779-1178.

Information

The local Tourist Information Center is at 529 St. Ann St., ☎ 504-568-5661 or 504-566-5031). Also see "Where to Get More Information" at the end of this appendix.

Internet Access

Three of the most convenient cyber cafes are: Cybercafe @ the CAC, inside the ground floor of the Contemporary Arts Center (900 Camp St.; ☎ 504-523-0990); Royal Access (621 Royal St.; ☎ 504-525-0401); and The Bastille Computer Cafe (605 Toulouse St.; ☎ 504-581-1150). For a comprehensive list of Internet cafes around the globe, visit www.netcafeguide.com.

Liquor Laws

The legal drinking age in New Orleans is 21. You can buy liquor most anywhere 24 hours a day, 7 days a week, 365 days a year. All drinks carried on the street must be in plastic cups; bars will often provide one of these plastic *go-cups* so that you can transfer your drink as you leave.

Mail

For U.S. Postal Service information and office hours, call ☎ 800-275-8777.

Maps

You can obtain maps at any of the information centers listed in Chapter 10 or at most hotels; www.mapquest.com is a good online resource for destination-specific U.S. maps, providing helpful driving information and hotel, restaurant, and attraction information.

Newspapers and Magazines

To find out what's going on around town, pick up a copy of the *Times-Picayune* (www.nola.com) or *Gambit Weekly* (www.bestofneworleans.com). *OffBeat* (www.offbeat.com) is an extensive monthly guide to the city's evening entertainment, art galleries, and special events; it's available in most hotels. Also refer to the "Where to Get More Information" section at the end of this appendix.

Pharmacies

The Walgreens Drug Store at 4400 S. Claiborne Ave. at Napoleon is the closest one to the French Quarter that offers 24-hour pharmacy service; call ☎ 504-891-0976. Take a cab here at night, or have the hotel send a taxi for your prescription.

Police

For non-emergency situations, call ☎ 504-821-2222. For emergencies, dial ☎ **911.**

Radio Stations

Some of the more helpful and/or popular radio stations in the city include WSMB, 1350 AM (sports talk); WWNO, 89.9 FM (National Public Radio, classical); WWOZ, 90.7 FM (New Orleans and Louisiana music; jazz, R&B, and blues); WQUE, 93.3 FM (urban/R&B); and KKND, 106.7 FM (modern rock)

Rest rooms

Public restrooms are located at Jax Brewery, Riverwalk Marketplace, Canal Place Shopping Center, Washington Artillery Park, and any of the major hotels.

Safety

Though many areas of New Orleans are perfectly safe, your best rule of thumb when visiting any city is to be on your guard all the time. Public transportation is relatively safe, though at night you'd be wise to take a cab if you're traveling to a dimly lit area. The St. Charles Avenue streetcar runs 24 hours, but it runs through a couple of iffy neighborhoods, which can change from nice to not-so-nice within a couple of blocks; again, take a cab at night. Always use caution when walking through an unlit area at night. Avoid the Iberville Housing Project located between Basin, N. Claiborne, Iberville, and St. Louis streets, just outside of the French Quarter; you should also avoid St. Louis Cemetery No. 2 near Claiborne on the lakeside of the Iberville Housing Project unless you're traveling with a large tour group. Also stay away from the area behind Armstrong Park. Remember: The city looks deceptively safe, and neighborhoods change very quickly.

Smoking

In this regard, New Orleans is like most major U.S. cities and more lenient than many. At most attractions and in most business buildings and shops, smokers should be prepared to stand around outside with all the other smokers. Most local restaurants cater to both smokers and non-smokers; a relative few (in relation to the rest of the country) prohibit smoking altogether. Ask before you sit down.

Taxes

Louisiana's sales tax is very confusing. In addition to the state and federal taxes, each parish may have additional taxes. To make things more confusing, some items such as unprepared food and some types of drugs are partially exempt, while prescriptions are totally exempt. In general, the total sales tax in New Orleans is 9 percent; it's 8.75 percent in Jefferson Parish.

Taxis

In most tourist areas, you can usually hail a taxi or get one at a taxi stand. If you can't find a taxi, call United Cab at ☎ 504-522-9771. If you have any complaints or left something in a taxi, call the Taxicab Bureau at ☎ 504-565-6272.

Time Zone

New Orleans is in the Central time zone. Daylight savings time is in effect from April through October.

Tipping

For most services — including restaurants and taxis — add 15 to 20 percent to your bill (before taxes). Many restaurants automatically add a 15-to-20 percent gratuity for parties of six or more. If you're just drinking at a bar, tipping 10 to 15 percent is typical. You should give bellhops $1 or $2 per bag, maids $1 per day, coat-check people $1 per garment, and automobile valets $1.

Transit Information

For information about streetcars and buses, call the Regional Transit Authority at ☎ 504-248-3900, or check out their Web site at www.regionaltransit.org.

Weather Updates

For the date, time, and temperature, as well as a prerecorded weather update, including a daily forecast and marine forecast, call ☎ 504-828-4000. On the Web, visit www.intellicast.com for weather updates on all 50 states and most major U.S. cities, including New Orleans. Another handy site is www.weather.com, the online home of The Weather Channel.

Toll-Free Numbers and Web Sites

Airlines

Air Canada
☎ 888-247-2262
www.aircanada.ca

AirTran Airways
☎ 800-247-8726
www.airtran.com

American Airlines
☎ 800-433-7300
www.aa.com

America West Airlines
☎ 800-235-9292
www.americawest.com

Continental Airlines
☎ 800-525-0280
www.continental.com

Delta Air Lines
☎ 800-221-1212
www.delta.com

Frontier Airlines
☎ 800-432-1359
www.frontierairlines.com

JetBlue Airways
☎ 800-538-2583
www.jetblue.com

Northwest Airlines
☎ 800-225-2525
www.nwa.com

Southwest Airlines
☎ 800-435-9792
www.iflyswa.com

United Airlines
☎ 800-241-6522
www.ual.com

US Airways
☎ 800-428-4322
www.usairways.com

Car-rental agencies

Alamo
☎ 800-GO-ALAMO
www.goalamo.com

Avis
☎ 800-230-4898
www.avis.com

Budget
☎ 800-527-0700
www.budgetrentacar.com

Dollar
☎ 877-253-9450
www.dollarcar.com

Enterprise
☎ 800-325-8007
www.enterprise.com

Hertz
☎ 800-654-3131
www.hertz.com

National
☎ 800-CAR-RENT
www.nationalcar.com

Thrifty
☎ 800-367-2277
www.thrifty.com

Major hotel and motel chains

Best Western International
☎ 800-780-7234
www.bestwestern.com

Clarion Hotels
☎ 800-CLARION
www.hotelchoice.com

Comfort Inns
☎ 800-228-5150
www.hotelchoice.com

Courtyard by Marriott
☎ 800-321-2211
www.courtyard.com

Days Inn
☎ 800-325-2525
www.daysinn.com

Doubletree Hotels
☎ 800-222-TREE
www.doubletree.com

Econo Lodges
☎ 800-55-ECONO
www.hotelchoice.com

Fairfield Inn by Marriott
☎ 800-228-2800
www.fairfieldinn.com

Hampton Inn
☎ 800-HAMPTON
www.hampton-inn.com

Hilton Hotels
☎ 800-HILTONS
www.hilton.com

Holiday Inn
☎ 800-HOLIDAY
www.sixcontinentshotels.com

Howard Johnson
☎ 800-406-1411
www.hojo.com

Hyatt Hotels & Resorts
☎ 800-228-9000
www.hyatt.com

ITT Sheraton
☎ 800-325-3535
www.starwood.com

La Quinta Motor Inns
☎ 800-531-5900
www.laquinta.com

Marriott Hotels
☎ 800-228-9290
www.marriott.com

Quality Inns
☎ 800-228-5151
www.hotelchoice.com

Radisson Hotels International
☎ 800-333-3333
www.radisson.com

Ramada Inns
☎ 800-2-RAMADA
www.ramada.com

Red Carpet Inns
☎ 800-874-7798
www.reservahost.com

Residence Inn by Marriott
☎ 800-331-3131
www.residenceinn.com

Super 8 Motels
☎ 800-800-8000
www.super8.com

Travelodge
☎ 800-255-3050
www.travelodge.com

Wyndham Hotels and Resorts
☎ 800-822-4200
www.wyndham.com

Where to Get More Information

An excellent source of information on New Orleans is the **New Orleans Metropolitan Convention and Visitors Bureau,** 1520 Sugar Bowl Dr., New Orleans, LA 70112 (☎ **800-672-6124** or 504-566-5011; www.new orleanscvb.com). The staff is extremely helpful and accessible, and they'll most likely be able to give you in-depth information on whatever you seek.

Another good resource is the **New Orleans Multicultural Tourism Network** (1520 Sugar Bowl Dr.; ☎ **800-725-5652** or 504-523-5652; www. soulofneworleans.com), which can point you to a number of local minority-owned businesses, from convention-related services (such as audio/visual services) to restaurants and hotels.

Tourist offices

The **Tourist Information Center** is located at 529 St. Ann St. (☎ **504-568-5661** or 504-566-5031). It's operated by the State of Louisiana, and is located in the French Quarter in the historic Pontalba Buildings next to Jackson Square. Following is a list of other centrally located information centers:

- ✔ **Canal Street and Convention Center Boulevard** (☎ **504-587-0739**), at the beginning of the 300 block of Canal Street on the downtown side of the street

- ✔ Close to the **World Trade Center** (☎ **504-587-0734**) at 2 Canal St.

- ✔ Near the **Hard Rock Cafe** (☎ **504-587-0740**) on the 400 block of N. Peters Street

- ✔ **Julia Street and Convention Center Boulevard** (walk-up booth)

✔ **Poydras Street and Convention Center Boulevard** (walk-up booth)

✔ **Vieux Carre Police Station** (☎ **504-565-7530**), located at 334 Royal St.

City guides

For a more comprehensive and detail-packed peek at New Orleans than you'll find in this book, check out *Frommer's New Orleans* (published by Wiley). Frommers.com (www.frommers.com) is an excellent resource, as well, full of travel tips, online booking options, and a daily e-mail newsletter offering bargains and travel advice.

Among other online city and entertainment guides, some of the most indispensable are the following:

✔ **Crescent City Connection** (www.satchmo.com) provides a roundup of musical events and resources for learning about local musicians. It's especially valuable during Jazz Fest.

✔ **Inside New Orleans** (www.insideneworleans.com) aims to be the site for locals looking for news, entertainment options, online ticket buying, and information on dining, shopping, and other activities. Although geared toward local residents, it does offer a wealth of information that visitors will find handy.

✔ **New Orleans CitySearch** (neworleans.citysearch.com), part of the extensive CitySearch network of city sites, offers staff picks and background information on food, music, entertainment, and the arts.

✔ **New Orleans Online** (www.neworleansonline.com) allows you to home in on exactly what you're looking for; click on "Cuisine" to search for a Cajun restaurant in the French Quarter, for example, and peruse a list of available options.

✔ **New Orleans Travel Guide** (www.neworleans.com) allows you to scan restaurant menus, look inside certain hotels, and order free coupon books online. It also has an extensive list of attractions, and links to dozens of useful, informative, and/or fun New Orleans pages.

Newspapers and magazines

The *Times-Picayune,* New Orleans's only daily newspaper, offers plenty of dining reviews, music, and entertainment news and information on its Web site, www.nola.com. Check out the BourboCAM, which offers a glimpse of Bourbon Street, or scroll the comments of locals in the 24-hour Yat Chat room.

Gambit Weekly, the city's free alternative weekly paper, offers news, commentary, and staff picks for the best in local dining, music, theater, special events, and more. Its Web site, www.bestofneworleans.com, offers all of the above, as well as a calendar of special events and weekly music club listings.

OffBeat is a local magazine dedicated to the music and musicians of New Orleans and Louisiana, from Cajun to folk to rock, R&B, jazz, and beyond. Its Web site, www.offbeat.com, reproduces many of the columns and features of the magazine, which boasts a dedicated readership of local music fans from all over the world.

Transit information

The **Regional Transit Authority** (☎ **504-248-3900;** www.regional transit.org) runs the city's public transportation; its Web site offers a comprehensive look at bus routes, the St. Charles and Riverfront streetcar routes, and information on **VisiTour** passes.

Making Dollars and Sense of It

Expense	Daily cost	x	Number of days	=	Total
Airfare					
Local transportation					
Car rental					
Lodging (with tax)					
Parking					
Breakfast					
Lunch					
Dinner					
Snacks					
Entertainment					
Babysitting					
Attractions					
Gifts & souvenirs					
Tips					
Other					
Grand Total					

Fare Game: Choosing an Airline

When looking for the best airfare, you should cover all your bases — 1) consult a trusted travel agent; 2) contact the airline directly, via the airline's toll-free number and/or Web site; 3) check out one of the travel-planning Web sites, such as www.frommers.com.

Travel Agency_____ Phone_____
    Agent's Name_____ Quoted fare_____

Airline 1_____ Quoted fare_____
    Toll-free number/Internet_____

Airline 2_____ Quoted fare_____
    Toll-free number/Internet_____

Web site 1_____ Quoted fare_____

Web site 2_____ Quoted fare_____

Departure Schedule & Flight Information

Airline_____ Flight #_____ Confirmation #_____

Departs_____ Date_____ Time _____ a.m./p.m.

Arrives_____ Date_____ Time _____ a.m./p.m.

Connecting Flight (if any)

Amount of time between flights_____ hours/mins

Airline_____ Flight #_____ Confirmation #_____

Departs_____ Date_____ Time _____ a.m./p.m.

Arrives_____ Date_____ Time _____ a.m./p.m.

Return Trip Schedule & Flight Information

Airline_____ Flight #_____ Confirmation #_____

Departs_____ Date_____ Time _____ a.m./p.m.

Arrives_____ Date_____ Time _____ a.m./p.m.

Connecting Flight (if any)

Amount of time between flights_____ hours/mins

Airline_____ Flight #_____ Confirmation #_____

Departs_____ Date_____ Time _____ a.m./p.m.

Arrives_____ Date_____ Time _____ a.m./p.m.

All Aboard: Booking Your Train Travel

Travel Agency_____ Phone_____

Agent's Name_____

Web Site_____

Departure Schedule & Train Information

Train #_____ Confirmation #_____ Seat reservation #_____

Departs_____ Date_____ Time_____ a.m./p.m.

Arrives_____ Date_____ Time_____ a.m./p.m.

Quoted fare_____ First class _____ Second class

Departure Schedule & Train Information

Train #_____ Confirmation #_____ Seat reservation #_____

Departs_____ Date_____ Time_____ a.m./p.m.

Arrives_____ Date_____ Time_____ a.m./p.m.

Quoted fare_____ First class _____ Second class

Departure Schedule & Train Information

Train #_____ Confirmation #_____ Seat reservation #_____

Departs_____ Date_____ Time_____ a.m./p.m.

Arrives_____ Date_____ Time_____ a.m./p.m.

Quoted fare_____ First class _____ Second class

Departure Schedule & Train Information

Train #_____ Confirmation #_____ Seat reservation #_____

Departs_____ Date_____ Time_____ a.m./p.m.

Arrives_____ Date_____ Time_____ a.m./p.m.

Quoted fare_____ First class _____ Second class

Sweet Dreams: Choosing Your Hotel

Make a list of all the hotels where you'd like to stay and then check online and call the local and toll-free numbers to get the best price. You should also check with a travel agent, who may be able to get you a better rate.

Hotel & page	Location	Internet	Tel. (local)	Tel. (Toll-free)	Quoted rate

Hotel Checklist

Here's a checklist of things to inquire about when booking your room, depending on your needs and preferences.

- ❏ Smoking/smoke-free room
- ❏ Noise (if you prefer a quiet room, ask about proximity to elevator, bar/restaurant, pool, meeting facilities, renovations, and street)
- ❏ View
- ❏ Facilities for children (crib, roll-away cot, babysitting services)
- ❏ Facilities for travelers with disabilities
- ❏ Number and size of bed(s) (king, queen, double/full-size)
- ❏ Is breakfast included? (buffet, continental, or sit-down?)
- ❏ In-room amenities (hair dryer, iron/board, minibar, etc.)
- ❏ Other _____

Places to Go, People to See, Things to Do

Enter the attractions you would most like to see and decide how they'll fit into your schedule. Next, use the "Going My Way" worksheets that follow to sketch out your itinerary.

Attraction/activity	Page	Amount of time you expect to spend there	Best day and time to go

Going "My" Way

Day 1

Hotel_____ Tel._____

Morning_____

_____

Lunch_____ Tel._____

Afternoon_____

_____

Dinner_____ Tel._____

Evening_____

_____

Day 2

Hotel_____ Tel._____

Morning_____

_____

Lunch_____ Tel._____

Afternoon_____

_____

Dinner_____ Tel._____

Evening_____

_____

Day 3

Hotel_____ Tel._____

Morning_____

_____

Lunch_____ Tel._____

Afternoon_____

_____

Dinner_____ Tel._____

Evening_____

_____

Going "My" Way

Day 4

Hotel _____ Tel. _____

Morning _____

_____

Lunch _____ Tel. _____

Afternoon _____

_____

Dinner _____ Tel. _____

Evening _____

_____

Day 5

Hotel _____ Tel. _____

Morning _____

_____

Lunch _____ Tel. _____

Afternoon _____

_____

Dinner _____ Tel. _____

Evening _____

_____

Day 6

Hotel _____ Tel. _____

Morning _____

_____

Lunch _____ Tel. _____

Afternoon _____

_____

Dinner _____ Tel. _____

Evening _____

_____

Going "My" Way

Day 7

Hotel _____ Tel. _____

Morning _____

_____

Lunch _____ Tel. _____

Afternoon _____

_____

Dinner _____ Tel. _____

Evening _____

_____

Day 8

Hotel _____ Tel. _____

Morning _____

_____

Lunch _____ Tel. _____

Afternoon _____

_____

Dinner _____ Tel. _____

Evening _____

_____

Day 9

Hotel _____ Tel. _____

Morning _____

_____

Lunch _____ Tel. _____

Afternoon _____

_____

Dinner _____ Tel. _____

Evening _____

_____

Index

See also separate Accommodations and Restaurant indexes at the end of this index.

General Index

• A •

from outside the area, 53
potholes, 118
road service, 309
in town, 93–94, 116–118
traffic, 105
Dryades Savings Bank, 120
Dungeon, The, 14, 248, 287, 304
Dyansen Gallery, 231

• *E* •

Econo Lodges, 313
Eddie Bauer, 223
1850 House, Lower Pontalba
    Building, 203
El Matador, 287
El Sid-O's, 256
emergency numbers, 310
Endymion krewe, parade route, 177
Enterprise Rent-A-Car, 94, 313
Ernest M. Morial Convention
    Center, 310
Ernie K-Doe's Mother-In-Law
    Lounge, 280
E-saver fares, 52
Escape Holidays, 47
escorted tours, 46–47
Essence Festival, 21
event listings, calendars, 19, 96, 293–294,
    311, 315–316
excursions
  day trips, 251–264
  riverboat cruises, 13, 218, 303, 308
Expedia Web site, 52, 95

• *F* •

Fair Ground Race Course, 209
Fairfield Inn by Marriott, 313
fall, visiting during, 17–18
F&M Patio Bar, 285
Farmer's Market, 227
fast food, "dives," 12
Fat Tuesday, 179
Fats Domino (musician), 11
Faubourg Marigny. *See also*
    Accommodations Index;
    Restaurant Index
  accommodations, 71, 88
  boundaries, 107, 109
  live music, nightclubs, 274
  pros and cons of lodging in, 60

restaurants, 145
sightseeing highlights, 187
snack foods, 161
Faulkner, William (author), 13
Faulkner House Books, 224, 237
Feelings, 290
Festival International de Louisiane, 23
Festival Tours International
    packages, 50
festivals, celebrations, 19–24
Festivals Acadiens, 23
Flea Market, 227
Flying Wheels Travel, 40
food and beverages. *See also* Restaurant
    Index; restaurants
average costs, 26, 27–28
  baked goods, 171–172
  candy stores, 172
  coffeehouses, 170, 171
  ice cream, 172
  late-night restaurants, 169–170
  neighborhood restaurants, 168
  po' boys, 162–164, 302
  snacks, light dining, 159–165
  street food, 166
  vegetarian restaurants, 165–166
football, 19, 22, 23
Fred Hatfield Cemetery tours, 216
Freeport McMoRan Daily Living Science
    Center, 201
French Market, 188–190, 227, 243, 248
French Quarter (Vieux Carre). *See also*
    Restaurant Index
  accommodations, 68, 88
  ATMs, cash machines, 120–121
  boundaries, 101, 106, 107
  driving and parking in, 116–117
  exploring, 111–112
  live music, nightlife, 271, 283, 285
  Mardi Gras parade route, 177
  pros and cons of lodging in, 58–59
  restaurants, 126, 135, 145
  shopping highlights, 221, 224–232,
    225, 230–232
  sightseeing highlights, 10, 14, 187,
    189, 305
  snack foods, 161, 163
French Quarter Bicycles, 117
French Quarter Festival, 20
French Quarter Reservation Service,
    42, 66
Frenchman Street, 239
Friends of the Cabildo walking tour, 213
Fritzel's European Jazz Pub, 14, 239, 273

Accommodations Index

Restaurant Index

FOR DUMMIES®

Helping you expand your horizons and realize your potential

PERSONAL FINANCE & BUSINESS

Investing FOR DUMMIES
0-7645-2431-3

Home Buying FOR DUMMIES
0-7645-5331-3

Grant Writing FOR DUMMIES
0-7645-5307-0

Also available:

Accounting For Dummies
(0-7645-5314-3)

Business Plans Kit For Dummies
(0-7645-5365-8)

Managing For Dummies
(1-5688-4858-7)

Mutual Funds For Dummies
(0-7645-5329-1)

QuickBooks All-in-One Desk Reference For Dummies
(0-7645-1963-8)

Resumes For Dummies
(0-7645-5471-9)

Small Business Kit For Dummies
(0-7645-5093-4)

Starting an eBay Business For Dummies
(0-7645-1547-0)

Taxes For Dummies 2003
(0-7645-5475-1)

HOME, GARDEN, FOOD & WINE

Feng Shui FOR DUMMIES
0-7645-5295-3

Gardening FOR DUMMIES
0-7645-5130-2

Cooking FOR DUMMIES
0-7645-5250-3

Also available:

Bartending For Dummies
(0-7645-5051-9)

Christmas Cooking For Dummies
(0-7645-5407-7)

Cookies For Dummies
(0-7645-5390-9)

Diabetes Cookbook For Dummies
(0-7645-5230-9)

Grilling For Dummies
(0-7645-5076-4)

Home Maintenance For Dummies
(0-7645-5215-5)

Slow Cookers For Dummies
(0-7645-5240-6)

Wine For Dummies
(0-7645-5114-0)

FITNESS, SPORTS, HOBBIES & PETS

Fitness FOR DUMMIES
0-7645-5167-1

Golf FOR DUMMIES
0-7645-5146-9

Guitar FOR DUMMIES
0-7645-5106-X

Also available:

Cats For Dummies
(0-7645-5275-9)

Chess For Dummies
(0-7645-5003-9)

Dog Training For Dummies
(0-7645-5286-4)

Labrador Retrievers For Dummies
(0-7645-5281-3)

Martial Arts For Dummies
(0-7645-5358-5)

Piano For Dummies
(0-7645-5105-1)

Pilates For Dummies
(0-7645-5397-6)

Power Yoga For Dummies
(0-7645-5342-9)

Puppies For Dummies
(0-7645-5255-4)

Quilting For Dummies
(0-7645-5118-3)

Rock Guitar For Dummies
(0-7645-5356-9)

Weight Training For Dummies
(0-7645-5168-X)

Available wherever books are sold.
Go to www.dummies.com or call 1-877-762-2974 to order direct

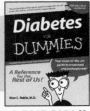

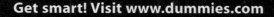